Logic in Asia: Studia Logica Library

Logic in Asia: Studia Logica Library

This book series promotes the advance of scientific research within the field of logic in Asian countries. It strengthens the collaboration between researchers based in Asia with researchers across the international scientific community and offers a platform for presenting the results of their collaborations. One of the most prominent features of contemporary logic is its interdisciplinary character, combining mathematics, philosophy, modern computer science, and even the cognitive and social sciences. The aim of this book series is to provide a forum for current logic research, reflecting this trend in the field's development.

The series accepts books on any topic concerning logic in the broadest sense, i.e., books on contemporary formal logic, its applications and its relations to other disciplines. It accepts monographs and thematically coherent volumes addressing important developments in logic and presenting significant contributions to logical research. In addition, research works on the history of logical ideas, especially on the traditions in China and India, are welcome contributions.

The scope of the book series includes but is not limited to the following:

- Monographs written by researchers in Asian countries.
- Proceedings of conferences held in Asia, or edited by Asian researchers.
- Anthologies edited by researchers in Asia.
- Research works by scholars from other regions of the world, which fit the goal of "Logic in Asia".

The series discourages the submission of manuscripts that contain reprints of previously published material and/or manuscripts that are less than 165 pages/ 90,000 words in length.

Please also visit our webpage: http://tsinghualogic.net/logic-in-asia/background/

Relation with Studia Logica Library

This series is part of the Studia Logica Library, and is also connected to the journal Studia Logica. This connection does not imply any dependence on the Editorial Office of Studia Logica in terms of editorial operations, though the series maintains cooperative ties to the journal.

This book series is also a sister series to Trends in Logic and Outstanding Contributions to Logic.

For inquiries and to submit proposals, authors can contact the editors-in-chief Fenrong Liu at fenrong@tsinghua.edu.cn or Hiroakira Ono at ono@jaist.ac.jp.

More information about this series at http://www.springer.com/series/13080

Shier Ju · Hu Liu · Hiroakira Ono
Editors

Modality, Semantics and Interpretations

The Second Asian Workshop on Philosophical Logic

Springer

Editors
Shier Ju
Institute of Logic and Cognition
Sun Yat-sen University
Guangzhou
China

Hiroakira Ono
Japan Advanced Institute of Science and Technology
Ishikawa
Japan

Hu Liu
Institute of Logic and Cognition
Sun Yat-sen University
Guangzhou
China

ISSN 2364-4613 ISSN 2364-4621 (electronic)
Logic in Asia: Studia Logica Library
ISBN 978-3-662-51717-8 ISBN 978-3-662-47197-5 (eBook)
DOI 10.1007/978-3-662-47197-5

Springer Heidelberg New York Dordrecht London

Softcover reprint of the hardcover 1st edition 2015

Printed on acid-free paper

Springer-Verlag GmbH Berlin Heidelberg is part of Springer Science+Business Media (www.springer.com)

Contents

1 Embedding Coalition Logic in the Minimal Normal Multimodal Logic with Intersection 1
Thomas Ågotnes and Natasha Alechina

2 Some Syntactic Interpretations in Different Systems of Full Lambek Calculus 23
Wojciech Buszkowski

3 Conditional Probability Logic over Conditional Probability Spaces 49
Mauricio S.C. Hernandes

4 Finite-Chain Graded Modal Logic 71
Minghui Ma and Shanxia Wang

5 Knowledge and Local Actions 87
R. Ramanujam

6 Avoiding Impossibility Theorems in Radical Inquisitive Semantics 107
Katsuhiko Sano

7 Epistemic Informativeness 121
Yanjing Wang and Jie Fan

8 Formalizing the IMA Language: Toward the Minimalist Program for Compositional Semantics 131
Xuefeng Wen

9 Similarity of States in Modal Logic 145
Fei Zha

10 An Explanation for the Ternary Relation R in the Relational Semantics of Relevance Logic 167
Beihai Zhou and Qing Jia

11 The Minimal System of Justification Logic with Names 179
Rui Zhu and Xinwen Liu

Chapter 1
Embedding Coalition Logic in the Minimal Normal Multimodal Logic with Intersection

Thomas Ågotnes and Natasha Alechina

Abstract We present a satisfiability-preserving embedding of coalition logic into a normal modal logic. An advantage of standard, normal, and modal logics is a well-understood theoretical foundation and the availability of tools for automated verification and reasoning. The target logic is multimodal K with intersection of modalities, interpreted over standard Kripke models corresponding to game structures. There is a restriction: we consider only game structures that are injective. We argue that this is a minor limitation, e.g., because coalition logic cannot discern between injective and non-injective game structures. We give a complete axiomatization of the corresponding models, as well as a characterization of key complexity problems. We also prove a representation theorem identifying the effectivity functions corresponding to injective games.

1.1 Introduction

Logics interpreted in *game structures* have received considerable interest in recent years. For several, including computational, reasons most such logics are modal logics [1]. One of the most popular approaches is reasoning about *coalitional ability*. Examples of logics in this category include *Coalition Logic* (CL) [2] and *Alternating-time Temporal Logic* (ATL) [3], and many extensions of these, which are interpreted in *game structures*. These logics have *coalition operators* of the form $[C]$ where C is a set of agents (a *coalition*), and $[C]\phi$ means that C can make ϕ true by choosing some joint action. On the other hand, it has been shown [4–7] that standard propositional

T. Ågotnes (✉)
Department of Information Science and Media Studies, University of Bergen, Bergen, Norway
e-mail: thomas.agotnes@infomedia.uib.no

T. Ågotnes
Center for the Study of Language and Cognition,
Zhejiang University, Hangzhou, China

N. Alechina
School of Computer Science, University of Nottingham, Nottingham, UK
e-mail: nza@cs.nott.ac.uk

S. Ju et al. (eds.), *Modality, Semantics and Interpretations*,
Logic in Asia: Studia Logica Library, DOI 10.1007/978-3-662-47197-5_1

dynamic logic (PDL) [8] is natural for reasoning about games. An advantage of using normal modal logics like PDL is that they are theoretically well understood, with a range of mathematical and computational tools available. Clearly, understanding the relationship between these two approaches are of interest. For example, van Benthem [9] states that "an explicit action/strategy version of coalition logic" is an interesting open problem.

In this paper, we take a clue from van Benthem [9]: that operators for *intersection* of strategies can be used to express coalitional ability. In particular, we observe that *standard* PDL *with intersection* can be used to express coalition operators. We study in detail a minimal variant, multimodal K with intersection of modalities ($K_n^{\cap}$), interpreted in game structures, and define a satisfiability-preserving embedding of CL into $K_n^{\cap}$. $K_n^{\cap}$ is a fragment of Boolean Modal Logic [10] which has been extensively studied (and implemented) as a variant of propositional dynamic logic with intersection and also by researchers in description logic (see for example [11]).

Although other logics that are normal modal, logics that can express coalition operators have been studied recently [12, 13], these logics are not standard PDL. The logic in [13] is *based* on PDL but also has non-PDL operators. The focus in the current paper is on reasoning about joint action in game structures using (a fragment of) *standard* PDL *with intersection*. Also, we study many types of research questions not considered in [13], and vice versa. See Sect. 1.7 for a further discussion about related work.

The main contributions of the paper are threefold. First, we give an interpretation of $K_n^{\cap}$ over models corresponding to game structures and give a sound and complete axiomatization as well as characterisations of key complexity problems. There is a limitation: this restricted model class does in fact not correspond to *all* game structures, only to *injective* game structures [14], i.e., game structures where two different strategy profiles never lead to the same outcome state. However, we argue that this is a minor limitation:

- Coalition Logic cannot discern between injective and non-injective game structures.
- Injectivity is a very common assumption in game theory. Indeed, the notion of outcome states is often (as in the standard textbook [15]) dispensed with altogether, and preferences defined directly over strategy profiles—implicitly defining an injective game.

Second, we show that coalition operators can be expressed in $K_n^{\cap}$, and that both the model checking and satisfiability problems for coalition logic can be reduced to the corresponding problems in $K_n^{\cap}$. In particular, we show that coalition logic is embedded in $K_n^{\cap}$, in the following sense: we present a satisfiability-preserving translation between coalition logic and $K_n^{\cap}$. Third, we prove a variant of Pauly's *representation theorem* [2, 16] for injective games: we characterize the class of effectivity functions that correspond to injective games.

We argue that the logic we study is interesting for several reasons. As a normal modal logic, it has a well-understood theoretical foundation, and it is well supported by tools for automated verification and reasoning as a fragment of standard computer science logics such as PDL. For example, model checking can be done using standard model checkers for PDL (with intersection). In contrast, CL is a non-normal modal logic, with only special purpose tool support (mainly tools developed for ATL) available. Our logic can also be seen as providing an additional set of model checking and theorem proving tools for CL. Last but not least, from a theoretical viewpoint, the logic establishes new connections between coalition logic and normal modal logics [17, 18].

The paper is based on [19]; the main additional contribution of the current paper is the sharpening of the embedding result. In [19], we defined a translation from CL into joint action logic *with a fixed number of actions*. In the current paper, we define a translation from CL which "reads off" the required number of actions from the CL formula.

The paper is organized as follows. We start with introducing CL and $K_n^{\cap}$. We then, in Sect. 1.3, discuss the restriction of CL to injective game structures and prove the representation theorem. In Sect. 1.4, we define the interpretation of $K_n^{\cap}$ in game structures, together with translations from CL and the embedding result, before axiomatization and complexity are discussed in Sects. 1.5 and 1.6. We discuss related work and conclude in Sect. 1.7.

An earlier version of this paper was presented at the CLIMA 2011 workshop [19].

1.2 Background

In this section, we provide some background on Coalition Logic (CL) [2] and multi-modal K with intersection of modalities.

1.2.1 Coalition Logic

Let $N = \{1, \ldots, g\}$ be a finite set of agents, and Θ a set of propositional variables. The language of $\mathcal{L}_{CL}(N, \Theta)$ of CL [2] is defined as follows:

$$\phi ::= p \mid \neg\phi \mid \phi \wedge \phi \mid [C]\phi$$

where $p \in \Theta$ and $C \subseteq N$. A set $C \subseteq N$ is called a *coalition*. Derived propositional connectives are defined as usual. We write $\overline{C}$ for $N \setminus C$ and sometimes abuse notation and write a singleton coalition $\{i\}$ as i. The language can be interpreted over *concurrent game structures* (CGSs) [3]. A CGS over N and Θ is a tuple $M = \langle S, V, Act, d, \delta\rangle$ where

- S is a set of *states*;
- V is a *valuation function*, assigning a set $V(s) \subseteq \Theta$ to each state $s \in S$;
- Act is a set of *actions*;

- For each $i \in N$ and $s \in S$, $d_i(s) \subseteq Act$ is a nonempty set of actions available to agent i in s. $D(s) = d_1(s) \times \cdots \times d_g(s)$ is the set of *full joint actions* in s. When $C \subseteq N$, $D_C(s) = \times_{i \in C} d_i(s)$ is the set of *C-actions* in s. If $\mathbf{a} \in D_C(s)$, a_i ($i \in C$) denotes the action taken from $d_i(s)$. When $C_1 \cap C_2 = \emptyset$ and $\mathbf{a} \in D_{C_1}(s)$ and $\mathbf{b} \in D_{C_2}(s)$, then $(\mathbf{a}, \mathbf{b})$ denotes the $C_1 \cup C_2$ action $\mathbf{c}$ with $c_i = a_i$ for $i \in C_1$ and $c_i = b_i$ for $i \in C_2$.
- δ is a *transition function*, mapping each state $s \in S$ and full joint action $\mathbf{a} \in D(s)$ to a state $\delta(s, \mathbf{a}) \in S$.

Let $\mathcal{M}_{cgs}(N, \Theta, Act)$ be the class of CGSs over N and Θ having Act as the set of actions.

A CGS can be seen as a state-transition system where the edges are labeled with full joint actions, but also, alternatively, as an assignment of a *strategic game form* to each state. A strategic game form is a tuple $G = \langle N, \{\Sigma_i : i \in N\}, S, o\rangle$ where for each $i \in N$, Σ_i is a set of *strategies* for i, and o: $\times_{j \in N} \Sigma_j \to S$ is an *outcome function*. For brevity, in the following, we will refer to a strategic game form as a *game form* or sometimes (abusing the terminology slightly) simply a *game*. When o is injective, we say that the game form G is injective. We write Σ_C for $\times_{i \in C} \Sigma_i$; the set of *strategy profiles* for coalition C. When $\sigma_C \in \Sigma_C$, we use $(\sigma_C)_i$ to denote the strategy for agent i. When $C_1 \cap C_2 = \emptyset$ and $\sigma_{C_1} \in \Sigma_{C_1}$ and $\sigma_{C_2} \in \Sigma_{C_2}$, then $(\sigma_{C_1}, \sigma_{C_2})$ denotes the strategy profile σ for group $C_1 \cup C_2$ such that $(\sigma)_i = (\sigma_{C_1})_i$ for $i \in C_1$ and $(\sigma)_i = (\sigma_{C_2})_i$ for $i \in C_2$. A CGS can be seen as an assignment of a game $G(s) = \langle N, \{\Sigma_i^s : i \in N\}, S, o^s\rangle$ to each state $s \in S$, where $\Sigma_i^s = d_i(s)$ and $o^s(\mathbf{a}) = \delta(s, \mathbf{a})$.

Intuitively, the CL expression $[C]\phi$ means that the coalition C is *effective* for formula ϕ, i.e., that they can ensure that ϕ holds in the next state no matter what the other agents do. Formally, a formula ϕ is interpreted in a state s of CGS M as follows:

$$M, s \models p \Leftrightarrow p \in V(s)$$
$$M, s \models \neg\phi \Leftrightarrow M, s \not\models \phi$$
$$M, s \models (\phi_1 \wedge \phi_2) \Leftrightarrow (M, s \models \phi_1 \text{ and } M, s \models \phi_2)$$
$$M, s \models [C]\psi \Leftrightarrow \exists \mathbf{a}_C \in D_C(s) \forall \mathbf{a}_{\overline{C}} \in D_{\overline{C}}(s),\ M, \delta(s, (\mathbf{a}_C, \mathbf{a}_{\overline{C}})) \models \psi$$

As effectivity is the only property of games relevant for the interpretation of coalition logic, we can in fact abstract away all other aspects of game structures. An *effectivity function* [2] over N and a set of states S is a function E that maps any coalition $C \subseteq N$ to a set of sets of states $E(C) \subseteq 2^S$. Given a strategic game form G, the (α-)*effectivity function* E_G of G is defined as follows:

$$X \in E_G(C) \text{ iff } \exists \sigma_C \in \Sigma_C \forall \sigma_{\overline{C}} \in \Sigma_{\overline{C}}, o(\sigma_C, \sigma_{\overline{C}}) \in X.$$

Which effectivity functions are the effectivity functions of strategic game forms? In [2], it is claimed that an effectivity function E is the α-effectivity function of a strategic game form iff E is *playable*:

1. ($X \in E(C)$ and $X \subseteq Y$ and $Y \subseteq S$) $\Rightarrow Y \in E(C)$ (*outcome monotonicity*);
2. $S \setminus X \notin E(\emptyset) \Rightarrow X \in E(N)$ (*N-maximality*);
3. $\emptyset \notin E(C)$ (*Liveness*);
4. $S \in E(C)$ (*Safety*);
5. ($C \cap D = \emptyset$ and $X \in E(C)$ and $Y \in E(D)$) $\Rightarrow X \cap Y \in E(C \cup D)$ (*superadditivity*).

However, it has recently been showed [16] that this claim is in fact not correct: there are playable effectivity functions over infinite sets, which are not α-effectivity functions of any strategic game forms. In [16], the result is also corrected: an effectivity function E is said to be *truly playable* iff it is playable and $E(\emptyset)$ has a *complete nonmonotonic core*. The *nonmonotonic core* $E^{nc}(C)$ of $E(C)$, for $C \subseteq N$, is defined as follows: $E^{nc}(C) = \{X \in E(C) : \neg\exists Y(Y \in E(C) \text{ and } Y \subset X)\}$. $E^{nc}(C)$ is *complete* if for every $X \in E(C)$ there exists $Y \in E^{nc}(C)$ such that $Y \subseteq X$. The corrected representation theorem [16] shows that E is the α-effectivity function of a strategic game form iff E is truly playable. A *coalition model* is a tuple $\mathcal{M} = \langle S, E, V\rangle$ where E gives a truly playable effectivity function $E(s)$ for each state $s \in S$, and V is a valuation function. The coalition logic language can alternatively and equivalently be interpreted in a coalition model, as follows:

$$\mathcal{M}, s \models [C]\phi iff \phi^{\mathcal{M}} \in E(s)(C)$$

where $\phi^{\mathcal{M}} = \{t \in S : \mathcal{M}, t \models \phi\}$. It is easy to see that the two semantics coincide: $M, s \models \phi$ iff $\mathcal{M}_\alpha, s \models \phi$ for all ϕ, where $M = (S, V, Act, d, \delta)$ and $\mathcal{M}_\alpha = (S, E_\alpha, V)$ and $E_\alpha(s) = E_{G(s)}$.

1.2.2 Multimodal K with Intersection of Modalities

Given a finite set of atomic modalities Π^0 of cardinality n and a countably infinite set of propositional variables Θ, the formulae $\phi \in \mathcal{L}_K^{\cap}(\Pi^0, \Theta)$ and modalities $\pi \in \Pi$ of multimodal K with intersection of modalities ($K_n^{\cap}$) are defined as follows:

$$\phi ::= p \mid \neg\phi \mid \phi \wedge \phi \mid [\pi]\phi \qquad \pi ::= a \mid \pi \cap \pi$$

where $p \in \Theta$ and $a \in \Pi^0$. As usual, $\langle\pi\rangle\phi$ is defined as $\neg[\pi]\neg\phi$, and derived propositional connectives are defined as usual. A (Kripke) model for the language $\mathcal{L}_K^{\cap}(\Pi^0, \Theta)$ is a tuple $M = \langle S, V, \{R_\pi : \pi \in \Pi\}\rangle$ where

- S is a set of *states*;
- $V : \Theta \to 2^S$ is a *valuation function*;
- For each $\pi \in \Pi$, $R_\pi \subseteq S \times S$
- $R_{\pi_1 \cap \pi_2} = R_{\pi_1} \cap R_{\pi_2}$ (INT)

The interpretation of a formula in a state of a model is defined as follows (other clauses as usual):

$$M, s \models [\pi]\phi \text{ iff } \forall s' \in S \text{ such that } (s, s') \in R_\pi, M, s' \models \phi$$

1.3 Injective Games

The idea of interpreting the $K_n^\cap$ language in game structures is very simple: view an action by a single agent as an atomic nondeterministic PDL action, where the nondeterminism is due to the actions chosen by the other agents. More formally: interpret a full joint action $\langle a_1, \ldots, a_g \rangle$ in a CGS as a set of g different ("atomic") transitions, one for each agent-action combination. This gives us a $K_n^\cap$ model, where the atomic modalities are agent-action pairs. Full joint actions can be recovered by taking the intersection between the relations for two or more atomic modalities for different agents.

For example, consider the CGS on the left in Fig. 1.1. The corresponding $K_n^\cap$ model is shown to the right. Coalition operators can now be captured approximately as follows. For example, If we want to say that there exists a joint action by agents 1 and 2, all executions of which result in the outcome p, in such a $K_n^\cap$ model, we can say something like $\bigvee_{a,b \in Act}[(1, a) \cap (2, b)]p$ (in addition, we must check that the actions a and b are actually available in the current state, but that is straightforward).

However, there is a problem with this approach. Consider the CGS to the left in Fig. 1.2. The approach above gives us the $K_n^\cap$ model to the right in the figure. This model has four atomic transitions from s to t: two labelled $(1, a_1)$ and $(2, b_1)$ which correspond to the full joint action (a_1, b_1), and two labeled $(1, a_2)$ and $(2, b_2)$ which

Fig. 1.1 CGS (*left*) and $K_n^\cap$ model (*right*)

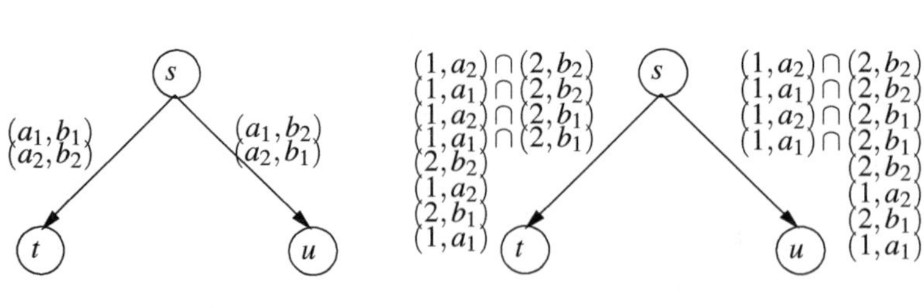

Fig. 1.2 CGS (*left*) and $K_n^\cap$ model (*right*). An *arrow* with more than one label represents a transition for each label

correspond to (a_2, b_2). The full joint actions can be recovered by intersection of the atomic transitions, but the problem is that too much is "recovered" in this way: we get the spurious transitions (a_1, b_2) and (a_2, b_1) which are not present between these states in the original model.

The problem is that by decomposing a full joint action into individual actions, we lose information about which *combinations* of actions relate the two states. That information is crucial, e.g., for the interpretation of coalition operators. We call a CGS without two or more different full joint actions between the same two states, i.e., with an injective δ, *injective* (following [14]). Injective CGSs do not suffer this problem.

It is relatively straightforward to see that any CGS is equivalent, in the sense of satisfying the same coalition logic formulae, to an injective CGS: take the *tree-unfolding* of the model (see [20] for relevant definitions of tree-unfoldings, bisimulations, and invariance under bisimulation, for the ATL language which contains the CL language). The tree-unfolding, however, is a model with infinitely many states, which may be a problem, e.g., if we want to do model checking. Fortunately it turns out that every finite CGS (finite state space) is CL-equivalent to a finite, and even "small," injective CGS. The following theorem follows immediately from a result by Goranko [14, Proposition12] (with some minor changes and amendments).

Theorem 1.1 *For every* CGS $M = \langle S, V, Act, d, \delta\rangle$ *there is an injective* CGS M' *with states* S' *such that* $S \subseteq S'$ *and for all* CL *formulae* ϕ *and states* $s \in S$, $M, s \models \phi$ *iff* $M', s \models \phi$. *Moreover, if* M *is finite, then* $|S'| \leq |S| + |\delta|$.

This makes it possible to translate a CGS into a $K_n^\cap$ model, such that we can recover a CGS that is CL-equivalent to the former from the latter. Before formally defining the translation in Sect. 1.4 we take a closer look at injective games; the reader mainly interested in the translation can skip directly to that section.

1.3.1 Effectivity Functions and Representation

Although coalition logic cannot discern between injective games and non-injective games, there is still another pertinent question if we want to restrict our attention to injective games: the question of representation using effectivity functions. Which truly playable effectivity functions correspond to injective games? The answer is not necessarily "all": this is similar to the relationship between playable and truly playable effectivity functions [16]; the latter is a proper subset of the former while coalition logic still cannot discern between the two. Indeed, not all truly playable effectivity functions are the α-effectivity functions of injective games:

Example 1.1 Let $N = \{1, 2\}$ and E be defined as follows:

$$E(\emptyset) = E(1) = E(2) = \{\{s, t\}\} \quad E(\{1, 2\}) = \{\{s\}, \{t\}, \{s, t\}\}$$

(where $s \neq t$). The reader can check that E is truly playable. However, it is not the α-effectivity function of an injective game. Assume that $E = E_G$ for some G. Because of Safety, the game has exactly two states s and t. Together with the fact that $\{s\}, \{t\} \in E(\{1,2\})$, that means that one of the agents must have exactly one strategy, and the other exactly two: all other combinations violate injectivity of a two-state game. Without loss of generality, assume that $\Sigma_1 = \{\sigma_1\}$ and $\Sigma_2 = \{\sigma'_1, \sigma'_2\}$. $\{s\} \in E_G(\{1,2\})$ implies that $o(\sigma_1, \sigma'_1) = s$ or $o(\sigma_1, \sigma'_2) = s$; without loss of generality assume the former. Then $\{t\} \in E_G(\{1,2\})$ implies that $o(\sigma_1, \sigma'_2) = t$. But that means that $\{s\}, \{t\} \in E_G(2)$, which is not the case.

We now state and prove a representation theorem (Theorem 1.2) for injective games. An effectivity function is *injectively playable* iff it is playable and (for all C, i, j, X, Y):

$$E(C) \text{ has a complete nonmonotonic core} \tag{1.1}$$

$$E^{nc}(C) = \{\bigcap_{i \in C} X_i : X_i \in E^{nc}(i)\} \quad C \neq \emptyset \tag{1.2}$$

$$X, Y \in E^{nc}(i) \text{ and } X \neq Y \Rightarrow X \cap Y = \emptyset \tag{1.3}$$

$$X \in E^{nc}(j) \text{ and } x \in X \Rightarrow \exists Y \in E^{nc}(i), x \in Y \tag{1.4}$$

Injective playability extends the true playability requirement of a complete nonmonotonic core [16] from the empty coalition to *all* coalitions. As a result, $E(C)$ is completely determined by its nonmonotonic core (stated formally in the following Lemma). In addition, there are some restrictions on the structure of the core. None of the additional properties of injective playability, (1.1)–(1.4), hold in general for truly playable effectivity functions (in particular, true playability does not imply complete nonmonotonic core for nonempty coalitions).

Lemma 1.1 *Let E be an outcome monotonic effectivity function.* $E(C)$ *has a complete nonmonotonic core iff* $E(C) = \{X : \exists Y \subseteq X, Y \in E^{nc}(C)\}$.

Proof For the implication to the right, assume that $E(C)$ has a complete nonmonotonic core. $E(C) \subseteq \{X : Y \subseteq X, Y \in E^{nc}(C)\}$ is immediate. If $Y \subseteq X$ and $Y \in E^{nc}(C)$, then $X \in E(C)$ by outcome monotonicity. The implication to the left is immediate. □

Two derived properties are the following.

Lemma 1.2 *If E is injectively playable, then*

$$(\forall_{i \in N} X_i \in E^{nc}(i)) \Rightarrow |\bigcap_{i \in N} X_i| = 1 \tag{1.5}$$

$$E^{nc}(\emptyset) = \{Z\} \text{ where } Z = \bigcup E^{nc}(N) \tag{1.6}$$

Proof (1.5) Let $X_i \in E^{nc}(i)$ for each $i \in N$. By (1.2), $\bigcap_{i \in N} X_i \in E^{nc}(N)$, and by true playability and [16, Proposition 5] there is an $x \in \bigcap_{i \in N} X_i$ such that $\{x\} \in E(N)$. That means that $\{x\} = \bigcap_{i \in N} X_i$; because $\bigcap_{i \in N} X_i \neq \{x\}$ contradicts the facts that $\bigcap_{i \in N} X_i \in E^{nc}(N)$, $\{x\} \in E(N)$ and $x \in \bigcap_{i \in N} X_i$.

(1.6) Let $Z = \bigcup E^{nc}(N)$. Since injective playability implies true playability, we know that $E^{nc}(\emptyset) = \{Z'\}$ for some Z' [16, Proposition 5]. We show that $Z' = Z$. We have that $S \backslash Z \notin E(N)$; otherwise there would be a $X \subseteq S \backslash Z$ such that $X \in E^{nc}(N)$ (by (1.1)) and thus $X \subseteq Z$ by definition of Z, which together with the fact that $X \neq \emptyset$ (Liveness) is a contradiction. By N-maximality, $S \backslash (S \backslash Z) = Z \in E(\emptyset)$. Thus, $Z' \subseteq Z$ by (1.1). Assume, toward a contradiction, that $Z \not\subseteq Z'$, i.e., that there is an $x \in Z$ such that $x \notin Z'$. That $x \in Z$ means that there is an $X \in E^{nc}(N)$ with $x \in X$. Let $X' = X \setminus \{x\}$. That $Z' \in E(\emptyset)$ and $X \in E(N)$ implies by superadditivity that $Z' \cap X \in E(N)$, and by the fact that $x \notin Z'$ we have that $Z' \cap X \subseteq X'$. By outcome monotonicity, $X' \in E(N)$. But that contradicts the fact that $X \in E^{nc}(N)$. Thus, $Z = Z'$. □

Before proving the main result (Theorem 1.2), we need the following lemma.

Lemma 1.3 *If E_G is the α-effectivity function of an injective game $G = (N, \{\Sigma_i : i \in N\}, o, S)$, then for all $C \subseteq N$:*

$$E_G^{nc}(C) = \{\ \{o(\sigma_C, \sigma_{\overline{C}}) : \sigma_{\overline{C}} \in \Sigma_{\overline{C}}\} : \sigma_C \in \Sigma_C\}$$

Proof $X \in E_G^{nc}(C)$ iff $\exists \sigma_C \forall \sigma_{\overline{C}} o(\sigma_C, \sigma_{\overline{C}}) \in X$ and there is no $Y \in E_G(C)$ such that $Y \subset X$. Let $P = \{\ \{o(\sigma_C, \sigma_{\overline{C}}) : \sigma_{\overline{C}} \in \Sigma_{\overline{C}}\} : \sigma_C \in \Sigma_C\}$.

First, let $X \in E_G^{nc}(C)$ and let σ_C be as above (a witness for X). Let $Y = \{o(\sigma_C, \sigma_{\overline{C}}) : \sigma_{\overline{C}} \in \Sigma_{\overline{C}}\}$. $Y \in P$. $Y \subseteq X$. We have that $Y \in E_G(C)$ (by definition of α-effectivity), so by the fact that $X \in E_G^{nc}(C)$ it follows that $Y \not\subset X$ and thus that $Y = X$.

Second, let $X = \{o(\sigma_C, \sigma_{\overline{C}}) : \sigma_{\overline{C}} \in \Sigma_{\overline{C}}\} \in P$ for some σ_C. $X \in E_G(C)$. Assume toward a contradiction that there is a $Y \in E_G(C)$ such that $Y \subset X$. Thus there is a $\sigma'_C \in \Sigma_C$ such that for all $\sigma'_{\overline{C}} \in \Sigma_{\overline{C}}$, $o(\sigma'_C, \sigma'_{\overline{C}}) \in Y$. $\sigma_C \neq \sigma'_C$; otherwise $X \subseteq Y$, a contradiction. $Y \neq \emptyset$, so there is a $y \in Y \cap X$. In other words, there are $\sigma_{\overline{C}}$ and $\sigma'_{\overline{C}}$ such that $o(\sigma_C, \sigma_{\overline{C}}) = o(\sigma'_C, \sigma'_{\overline{C}}) = y$. But this contradicts the fact that G is injective, since $\sigma_C \neq \sigma'_C$. Thus, there is no such Y, and $X \in E_G^{nc}(C)$. □

Theorem 1.2 *An effectivity function E is injectively playable iff it is the α-effectivity function of some injective game G.*

Proof First, let E_G be the α-effectivity function of some injective game G. We show that E_G is injectively playable. It is immediate from [2] that E_G is playable.

In order to show (1.1), let $X \in E_G(C)$, i.e., there is a σ_C such that for all $\sigma_{\overline{C}}$ $o(\sigma_C, \sigma_{\overline{C}}) \in X$. Let $Y = \{o(\sigma_C, \sigma_{\overline{C}}) : \sigma_{\overline{C}} \in \Sigma_{\overline{C}}\}$. $Y \subseteq X$, and $Y \in E_G^{nc}(C)$ by Lemma 1.3.

In order to show (1.2), assume that $|C| \geq 2$, since (1.2) holds trivially for $|C| = 1$. For one direction, let $X \in E_G^{nc}(C)$. By Lemma 1.3, $X = \{o(\sigma_C, \sigma_{\overline{C}}) : \sigma_{\overline{C}} \in \Sigma_{\overline{C}}\}$

for some σ_C. Let, for each $i \in C$, $\sigma_i = (\sigma_C)_i$ and $X_i = \{o(\sigma_i, \sigma_{\overline{i}}) : \sigma_{\overline{i}} \in \Sigma_{\overline{i}}\}$. $X_i \in E_G^{nc}(i)$ by Lemma 1.3. $X \subseteq \bigcap_{i \in C} X_i$. We must show that $\bigcap_{i \in C} X_i \subseteq X$. Let $x \in \bigcap_{i \in C} X_i$. For each $i \in C$, there exists some $\sigma_{\overline{i}}$ such that $x = o(\sigma_i, \sigma_{\overline{i}})$. For any arbitrary $i, j \in C$, $i \neq j$, from $o(\sigma_j, \sigma_{\overline{j}}) = x = o(\sigma_i, \sigma_{\overline{i}})$ we get that $(\sigma_{\overline{j}})_i = \sigma_i$ by injectivity. Thus, $o(\sigma_C, \sigma_{\overline{C}}) = o(\sigma_j, \sigma_{\overline{j}})$, for all $j \in C$ and some $\sigma_{\overline{C}}$, and thus $x \in X$.

For the other direction of (1.2), let $X = \bigcap_{i \in C} X_i$ with $X_i \in E_G^{nc}(i)$. Again, for each $i \in C$, $X_i = \{o(\sigma_i, \sigma_{\overline{i}}) : \sigma_{\overline{i}} \in \Sigma_{\overline{i}}\}$ for some σ_i. Let σ_C be defined by $(\sigma_C)_i = \sigma_i$. Let $Y = \{o(\sigma_C, \sigma_{\overline{C}}) : \sigma_{\overline{C}} \in \Sigma_{\overline{C}}\}$. $Y \in E_G^{nc}(C)$ by Lemma 1.3. We show that $Y = X$. First, let $\sigma_{\overline{C}} \in \Sigma_{\overline{C}}$ be arbitrary. Since $(\sigma_C)_i = \sigma_i$, $o(\sigma_C, \sigma_{\overline{C}}) \in X_i$ for all $i \in C$, and $o(\sigma_C, \sigma_{\overline{C}}) \in X$. Thus, $Y \subseteq X$. Let $x \in X$. For each $i \in C$, there is some $\sigma_{\overline{i}}$ such that $o(\sigma_i, \sigma_{\overline{i}}) = x$. We can now reason as above. Let $i, j \in C$, $i \neq j$. From $o(\sigma_j, \sigma_{\overline{j}}) = x = o(\sigma_i, \sigma_{\overline{i}})$, we get that $(\sigma_{\overline{j}})_i = \sigma_i$ by injectivity. Thus, $o(\sigma_j, \sigma_{\overline{j}}) = o(\sigma_C, \sigma_{\overline{C}})$, for some arbitrary $j \in C$ and some $\sigma_{\overline{C}}$, and thus $x \in Y$. Thus, $X \subseteq Y$.

In order to show that (1.3) holds, let $X \neq Y \in E_G^{nc}(i)$. By Lemma 1.3, there are σ_i, σ_i' such that $X = \{o(\sigma_i, \sigma_{\overline{i}}) : \sigma_{\overline{i}} \in \Sigma_{\overline{i}}\}$ and $Y = \{o(\sigma_i', \sigma_{\overline{i}}) : \sigma_{\overline{i}} \in \Sigma_{\overline{i}}\}$. Assume that $x \in X \cap Y$, i.e., that $o(\sigma_i, \sigma_{\overline{i}}) = o(\sigma_i', \sigma_{\overline{i}}')$ for some $\sigma_{\overline{i}}$ and $\sigma_{\overline{i}}'$. Since the game is injective that means that $\sigma_i = \sigma_i'$, but that contradicts the fact that $X \neq Y$. Thus, $X \cap Y = \emptyset$.

In order to show that (1.4) holds, let $X \in E_G^{nc}(j)$ and $x \in X$. By Lemma 1.3, there is a σ_j such that $X = \{o(\sigma_j, \sigma_{\overline{j}}) : \sigma_{\overline{j}} \in \Sigma_{\overline{j}}\}$. In particular, $x = o(\sigma_j, \sigma_{\overline{j}})$ for some $\sigma_{\overline{j}}$. Let $\sigma_i = (\sigma_{\overline{j}})_i$, and let $Y = \{o(\sigma_i, \sigma_{\overline{i}}) : \sigma_{\overline{i}} \in \Sigma_{\overline{i}}\}$. $x \in Y$, and $Y \in E_G^{nc}(i)$ by Lemma 1.3.

Second, let E be an injectively playable effectivity function over N and S. We construct a game $G = (N, \{\Sigma_i : i \in N\}, o, S)$ as follows:

$$\Sigma_i = E^{nc}(i) \qquad o(X_1, \ldots, X_g) = x \quad \text{where} \quad \{x\} = \bigcap_{i \in N} X_i$$

The property (1.5) (Lemma 1.2) ensures that the game is well defined. To see that G is injective, assume that $o(X_1, \ldots, X_g) = o(X_1', \ldots, X_g') = x$. That means that, for each i, $x \in X_i \cap X_i'$, and by (1.3) it follows that $X_i = X_i'$. Thus, G is injective.

We must show that $E_G = E$. By (1.1), outcome monotonicity and Lemma 1.1, it suffices to show that $E_G^{nc}(C) = E^{nc}(C)$ for all $C \subseteq N$.

First assume that $C \neq \emptyset$. For any X, $X \in E_G^{nc}(C)$ iff (by Lemma 1.3) $\exists \sigma_C$ such that $X = \{o(\sigma_C, \sigma_{\overline{C}}) : \sigma_{\overline{C}} \in \Sigma_{\overline{C}}\}$ iff $\exists \{X_i \in E^{nc}(i) : i \in C\}$ such that $X = \{x : \{x\} = \bigcap_{i \in N} X_i, X_j \in E^{nc}(j), j \in N \setminus C\}$. On the other hand, $X \in E^{nc}(C)$ iff $\exists \{X_i \in E^{nc}(i) : i \in C\}$ such that $X = \bigcap_{i \in C} X_i$, by (1.2). Thus, let, for each $i \in C$, $X_i \in E^{nc}(i)$. It suffices to show that $\{x : \{x\} = \bigcap_{i \in N} X_i, X_j \in E^{nc}(j), j \in N \setminus C\} = \bigcap_{i \in C} X_i$. For inclusion toward the left, assume that $x \in \bigcap_{i \in C} X_i$. If $C = N$ we are done. Otherwise, from (1.4) it follows that there is a $X_j \in E^{nc}(j)$ such that $x \in X_j$, for every $j \in N \setminus C$. Thus, $x \in \bigcap_{i \in N} X_i$. For inclusion toward the right, let $\{x\} = \bigcap_{i \in N} X_i$ for some $\{X_i \in E^{nc}(i) : i \in N \setminus C\}$. It immediately follows that $x \in \bigcap_{i \in C} X_i$.

Second, consider the case that $C = \emptyset$. $X \in E^{nc}_G(\emptyset)$ iff (by Lemma 1.3) $X = \{o(\sigma_N) : \sigma_N \in \Sigma_N\}$ iff $X = \{x : \{x\} = \bigcap_{i \in N} X_i, X_i \in E^{nc}(i)\}$ iff (by (1.2)) $X = \bigcup E^{nc}(N)$ iff (by Lemma 1.2) $X \in E^{nc}(\emptyset)$. □

1.4 Multimodal *K* with Intersection for Games

We now show how $K_n^{\cap}$ formulae can be interpreted in game structures, by identifying a class of $K_n^{\cap}$ models corresponding to (injective) game structures.

1.4.1 Joint Action Models

Let Act be a finite set of actions and N a set of g agents. Define a set of atomic modalities as follows:

$$\Pi^0_{ActN} = N \times Act$$

Intuitively, an atomic modality is a pair (i, a) intended to represent an action and the agent that executes that action. We will call an atomic modality in Π^0_{ActN} an *individual action*, and a composite modality $\pi = \pi_1 \cap \pi_2$ a *joint action*. Since the intersection operation is associative, we can write any joint action π as an intersection of a set of individual actions: $\pi = (i_1, a_1) \cap \cdots \cap (i_k, a_k)$. Joint actions of the form $(1, a_1) \cap \cdots \cap (g, a_g)$ with one individual action for *every* agent in N will be called *complete (joint) actions*.

The following are some properties of $K_n^{\cap}$ models over Π^0_{ActN} that will be of particular interest. We say that an action $a \in Act$ is *enabled* for agent i in a state s iff there is a state s' such that $(s, s') \in R_{(i,a)}$.

Seriality (SER) For any state s and agent i, at least one action is enabled in s for i.
Independent Choice (IC) For any state s, agents $C = \{i_1, \ldots, i_k\}$ and actions $a_1, \ldots, a_k \in Act$, if for every j a_j is enabled for i_j in s, then there is a state s' such that $(s, s') \in R_{(i_1,a_1)\cap\cdots\cap(i_k,a_k)}$.
Deterministic Joint Actions (DJA) For any complete joint action α and states s, s_1, s_2, $(s, s_1), (s, s_2) \in R_\alpha$ implies that $s_1 = s_2$.
Unique Joint Actions (UJA) For any complete joint actions α and β and states s, t, if $(s, t) \in R_\alpha \cap R_\beta$ then $\alpha = \beta$.

A $K_n^{\cap}$ model over Π^0_{ActN} (where Act is finite) is a *joint action model* if it satisfies the properties SER, IC, DJA, and UJA.

Given (finite) Act and N, we now translate any CGS over Act and N into a joint action model. We start with injective CGSs.

Definition 1.1 Given an injective CGS $M = \langle S, V, Act, d, \delta \rangle \in \mathcal{M}_{cgs}(N, \Theta, Act)$ where Act is finite, the corresponding joint action model $\hat{M} = \langle S, V, \{R_\pi : \pi \in \Pi\} \rangle$ over Θ and Π^0_{ActN} is defined as follows:

- $R_{(i,a)} = \{(s, s') : \exists \mathbf{a} \in D(s) \text{ such that } a_i = a \text{ and } s' = \delta(s, \mathbf{a})\}$, when $(i, a) \in \Pi^0_{ActN}$
- $R_{\pi_1 \cap \pi_2} = R_{\pi_1} \cap R_{\pi_2}$

As discussed in Sect. 1.3, this translation views an action by a single agent as a nondeterministic action where the nondeterminism is due to the possible choices by the other agents (the existential quantification over full joint actions in the definition above). Full joint actions are recovered by using intersection.

We use the following property to show that $\hat{M}$ is indeed a joint action model.

Lemma 1.4 *Let $M = \langle S, V, Act, d, \delta \rangle$ be injective and $\hat{M} = \langle S, V, \{R_\pi : \pi \in \Pi\} \rangle$ be the corresponding joint action model, and let $\pi = (i_1, a_1) \cap \cdots \cap (i_k, a_k)$. Then $(s, t) \in R_\pi$ iff there is an $\mathbf{a}' \in D(s)$ such that $a'_{i_j} = a_j$ for all $1 \le j \le k$ and $\delta(s, \mathbf{a}') = t$.*

Proof $(s, t) \in R_\pi$ iff there are $\mathbf{a}^1, \ldots, \mathbf{a}^k \in D(s)$ such that for all $1 \le j \le k$: $a^j_{i_j} = a_j$ and $t = \delta(s, \mathbf{a}^j)$. Since M is injective, it must be the case that $\mathbf{a}^1 = \cdots = \mathbf{a}^k$. □

Lemma 1.5 *$\hat{M}$ is a joint action model.*

Proof $\hat{M}$ is a proper $\mathcal{L}^{\cap}_K(\Pi^0_{ActN}, \Theta)$ model by definition. SER holds because $d_i(s)$ is always nonempty. IC holds because $D(s)$ is defined as the cross product of $d_i(s)$ for all i. For DJA, $(s, s_1), (s, s_2) \in R_\alpha$ implies that $\delta(s, \mathbf{a}) = s_1 = s_2$ by Lemma 1.4. For UJA, $(s, t) \in R_\alpha \cap R_\beta$ implies that $\delta(s, \mathbf{a}) = t$ and $\delta(s, \mathbf{b}) = t$ by Lemma 1.4, which by injectivity implies that $\mathbf{a} = \mathbf{b}$ which again implies that $\alpha = \beta$. □

Let us call a formula $\phi \in \mathcal{L}^{\cap}_K(\Pi^0_{ActN}, \Theta)$ a *complete action formula* if the modal operators in ϕ only contain complete actions. The following lemma shows that as far as complete action formulae are concerned, all joint action models correspond to CGSs, which is going to be useful in showing the embedding.

Lemma 1.6 *Given a finite set of actions Act, for every joint action model M' over Π^0_{ActN} with states S, there is an injective* CGS *$M \in \mathcal{M}_{cgs}(N, \Theta, Act)$ with corresponding joint action model $\hat{M}$ such that for all complete action formulas $\phi \in \mathcal{L}^{\cap}_K(\Pi^0_{ActN}, \Theta)$ and $s \in S$, $M', s \models \phi$ iff $\hat{M}, s \models \phi$.*

Proof Given a joint action model $M' = \langle S, V, \{R_\pi : \pi \in \Pi\} \rangle$ over Θ and Π^0_{ActN}, we construct $M = \langle S, V, Act, d, \delta \rangle$ as follows:

- $Act = \{(i, a) : (i, a) \in \Pi^0_{ActN}\}$
- $d_i(s) = \{(i, a) : \exists s' \; R_{(i,a)}(s, s')\}$
- $\delta(s, ((1, a_1), \ldots, (g, a_g))) = s'$ iff $R_{(1,a_1) \cap \ldots \cap (g,a_g)}(s, s')$.

Note that M is a well-defined CGS, in particular, $d_i(s) \neq \emptyset$ and δ is a function because of SER, IC, and DJA. M is injective because of UJA.

Now consider $\hat{M}$ which is the joint action model corresponding to M. $\hat{M}$ may be different from M' in that $R_{(i,a)}(s, s')$ holds in $\hat{M}$ only if s and s' are connected by a complete joint action. However, it is easy to show that for every complete joint action π, $R_\pi(s, s')$ holds in M' iff $R_\pi(s, s')$ holds in $\hat{M}$. Given this fact, it is easy to show by induction that for every complete action formula ϕ, and every state $s \in S$, $M', s \models \phi$ iff $\hat{M}, s \models \phi$. □

1.4.2 Embedding of CL

Given a coalition logic formula $\phi \in \mathcal{L}_{CL}(N, \Theta)$ and a finite set of actions Act, we define the translation $T^{Act}(\phi) \in \mathcal{L}_K^{\cap}(\Pi^0_{ActN}, \Theta)$ as follows:

$$
\begin{array}{ll}
T^{Act}(p) & \equiv p \\
T^{Act}(\neg\psi) & \equiv \neg T^{Act}(\psi) \\
T^{Act}(\psi_1 \wedge \psi_2) & \equiv T^{Act}(\psi_1) \wedge T^{Act}(\psi_2) \\
T^{Act}([\{i_1, \ldots, i_k\}]\psi) & \equiv \bigvee_{a_1,\ldots,a_k \in Act}(\\
\bigvee_{a_{k+1},\ldots,a_g \in Act} & \langle (i_1, a_1) \cap \cdots \cap (i_k, a_k) \cap (i_{k+1}, a_{k+1}) \cap \cdots \cap (i_g, a_g) \rangle \top \wedge \\
\bigwedge_{a_{k+1},\ldots,a_g \in Act} & [(i_1, a_1) \cap \cdots \cap (i_k, a_k) \cap (i_{k+1}, a_{k+1}) \cap \cdots \cap (i_g, a_g)] T^{Act}(\psi))
\end{array}
$$

The translation of the CL formula $[C]\psi$ says that there is an action for each agent in C, such that (i) the actions are enabled and (ii) for all possible states resulting from executing the actions at the same time together with any other actions by $N \backslash C$, the translation of ψ holds. The translation assumes that the set of possible actions Act is given and that it is finite.

The following theorem shows that the model and formula translations preserve satisfaction.

Theorem 1.3 *Let Θ, N and Act (finite) be given. For any $\phi \in \mathcal{L}_{CL}(N, \Theta)$ and any injective* CGS *$M \in \mathcal{M}_{cgs}(N, \Theta, Act)$ and any state s in M:*

$$M, s \models \phi \text{ iff } \hat{M}, s \models T^{Act}(\phi)$$

Proof Let Θ, N and Act (finite) be given, $\phi \in \mathcal{L}_{CL}(N, \Theta)$ and $M \in \mathcal{M}_{cgs}(N, \Theta, Act)$ be injective and s in M. The proof is by induction on the structure of ϕ. The only interesting case is when $\phi = [C]\psi$ where $C = \{1, \ldots, k\}$. $M, s \models [C]\psi$ iff there is a $\langle a_1, \ldots, a_k \rangle \in D_C(s)$ such that for all $\mathbf{a} \in D(s)$ with $\mathbf{a} = (a_1, \ldots, a_k, a_{k+1}, \ldots, a_g)$, $M, \delta(s, \mathbf{a}) \models \psi$ iff by the induction hypothesis and the construction of $\hat{M}$, there exists at least one t such that $R_{(1,a_1)\cap\ldots\cap(g,a_g)}(s, t)$ for some $a_{k+1}, \ldots, a_g$, and for all t with $R_{(1,a_1)\cap\ldots\cap(g,a_g)}(s, t)$, $\hat{M}, t \models T^{Act}(\psi)$ iff $\hat{M}, s \models T^{Act}([C]\psi)$. □

The following follows immediately from Theorems 1.1 and 1.3.

Corollary 1.1 *Let Θ, N and Act (finite) be fixed. For any $\phi \in \mathcal{L}_{CL}(N, \Theta)$ and any* CGS *$M \in \mathcal{M}_{cgs}(N, \Theta, Act)$ there is a joint action model $\overline{M}$ over Π^0_{ActN} such that for any state s in M:*

$$M, s \models \phi \text{ iff } \overline{M}, s \models T^{Act}(\phi)$$

The translation assumes that the (finite) set of actions Act is given. In model checking this can be obtained directly from the model. Thus, the model checking problem for CL can be reduced to the model checking problem for $K_n^{\cap}$.

But what about the satisfiability problem can that be translated? Here we are only given a CL formula, which does not mention actions explicitly. Here we can make use of a result from [21]: that every ATL-consistent formula ϕ has a model where the number of actions of each agent equals $1+|\{\theta \in ecl(\phi) : \theta = [C]\psi \text{ or } \theta = [C]\psi\}|$,[1] where $ecl(\phi)$ is the set of subformulas of ϕ closed under single negations and the condition that if $[C]\psi \in ecl(\phi)$, then $[C']\psi \in ecl(\phi)$ for all $C' \subseteq N$. The same result immediately applies to CL. For a CL formula ϕ, we will write Act^{ϕ} for the number of actions "required" to construct a satisfying model for ϕ. We use this fact ("bounded action property" of coalition logic) to provide a satisfiability-preserving embedding of CL into a normal modal logic.

Theorem 1.4 *For any $\phi \in \mathcal{L}_{CL}(N, \Theta)$: ϕ is satisfiable in some* CGS *(over an arbitrary set of actions Act) iff $T^{Act^{\phi}}(\phi)$ is satisfiable in some joint action model over $\Pi^0_{Act^{\phi}N}$.*

Proof Let $\phi \in \mathcal{L}_{CL}(N, \Theta)$. If ϕ is satisfiable in CL, it is satisfiable in a CGS over Act^{ϕ} [21]. By Corollary 1.1 $T^{Act^{\phi}}(\phi)$ is satisfiable in some joint action model over $\Pi^0_{Act^{\phi}N}$. The other way around follows from Corrollary 1.1 and Lemma 1.6, since $T^{Act^{\phi}}(\phi)$ is a complete action formula. □

Thus, the satisfiability problem for CL can be reduced to a satisfiability problem for $K_n^{\cap}$.

1.5 Axiomatization of Joint Action Models

We now give an axiomatization for the language $\mathcal{L}_K^{\cap}(\Pi^0_{ActN}, \Theta)$ and prove that it is sound and complete with respect to the class of all joint action models over Π^0_{ActN} and Θ. The axiom system $\mathcal{S}$ is defined as follows:

K $[\pi](\phi \to \psi) \to ([\pi]\phi \to [\pi]\psi)$
A1 $\bigvee_{a \in Act}\langle(i, a)\rangle\top$
A2 $\langle\pi\rangle\phi \to \bigvee_{a \in Act}\langle\pi \cap (i, a)\rangle\phi$

[1] We are using CL rather than ATL syntax here for clarity.

A3 $\bigwedge_{i \in N} \langle (i, a_i) \rangle \top \rightarrow \langle (1, a_1) \cap \ldots \cap (g, a_g) \rangle \top$
A4 $\langle (1, a_1) \cap \cdots \cap (g, a_g) \rangle \phi \rightarrow [(1, a_1) \cap \ldots \cap (g, a_g)] \phi$
A5 $[\pi]\phi \rightarrow [\pi \cap \pi']\phi$
A6 $[(i, a) \cap (i, b)]\bot$ when $a \neq b$
MP From $\phi \rightarrow \psi$ and ϕ infer ψ
G From ϕ infer $[\pi]\phi$

K, **MP** and **G** says that the $[\pi]$ modalities are normal. **A1** says that at least one action is enabled for each agent in every state, **A2** says that if there is a joint action for some agents that can ensure ϕ, then any agent can do some action at the same time such that ϕ is still ensured, **A3** says that all joint actions composed of enabled individual actions are enabled, **A4** says that complete joint actions are deterministic, **A5** is the standard axiom for intersection, and **A6** says that an agent cannot do two actions simultaneously.

Theorem 1.5 *The axiom system $\mathcal{S}$ is sound and complete wrt. all joint action models.*

Proof Soundness is straightforward. To prove completeness, we introduce some conventions and auxiliary concepts and show some intermediate properties. When $\pi = (i_1, a_1) \cap \cdots \cap (i_k, a_k)$ and $\pi' = (j_1, b_1) \cap \cdots \cap (j_l, b_l)$ are joint actions, we write $\pi \leq \pi'$ to denote that for every $1 \leq u \leq k$ there is a $1 \leq v \leq l$ such that $i_u = j_v$ and $a_u = b_v$. Recall that a complete joint action is an expression of the form $(1, a_1) \cap \cdots \cap (g, a_g)$ where $a_i \in Act$, giving one action for each agent in the system. Let JA denote the (finite) set of complete joint actions. We use $\alpha, \beta, \ldots$ to denote complete joint actions.

We will make use of a notion of *pseudomodels*, which only have transition relations for complete joint actions. Formally, a pseudomodel is a tuple $(S, \{R_\alpha : \alpha \in JA\}, V)$ where: S is a set of states, $R_\alpha \subseteq S \times S$ for each $\alpha \in JA$ and $V : \Theta \rightarrow 2^S$.

First, we construct the *canonical* pseudomodel $M^c = (S^c, \{R^c_\alpha : \alpha \in JA\}, V^c)$ as follows:

- S^c is the set of $\mathcal{L}^{\cap}_K(\Pi^0_{Act N}, \Theta)$-maximal $\mathcal{S}$-consistent sets Γ
- $V^c(p) = \{\Gamma : p \in \Gamma\}$
- $R^c_\alpha \Gamma\Gamma'$ iff for any ψ, if $\psi \in \Gamma'$ then $\langle \alpha \rangle \psi \in \Gamma$

Lemma 1.7 (Existence Lemma) *For any $s \in S^c$, if $\langle \alpha \rangle \gamma \in s$ for some $\alpha \in JA$, then there is an s' such that $(s, s') \in R^c_\alpha$ and $\gamma \in s'$.*

The proof of the existence lemma is as in standard normal modal logic.

Now let ϕ be a consistent formula; we show that it is satisfied in some joint action model. Let $x \in S^c$ be such that $\phi \in x$. We now take the *unraveling* of the canonical pseudomodel around x. The pseudomodel $M^x = (S^x, \{R^x_\alpha : \alpha \in JA\}, V^x)$ is defined as follows:

- S^x is the set of all finite sequences $(s_0, R^c_{\alpha_0}, s_1 \ldots, R^c_{\alpha_{k-1}}, s_k)$ such that $s_0, \ldots, s_k \in S^c$, $s_0 = x$, and $(s_i, s_{i+1}) \in R^c_{\alpha_i}$ for all $0 \leq i \leq k - 1$.

- $(s, u) \in R^x_\alpha$ iff $s = (x, R^c_{\alpha 0}, s_1 \ldots, R^c_{\alpha_{k-1}}, s_k)$ and $u = (x, R^c_{\alpha 0}, s_1 \ldots, R^c_{\alpha_{k-1}}, s_k, R^c_\alpha, s_{k+1})$ for some $s_{k+1} \in S^c$.
- $V^x(p) = \{(x, R^c_{\alpha 0}, s_1 \ldots, R^c_{\alpha_{k-1}}, s_k) : s_k \in V^c(p)\}$

We now transform the pseudomodel M^x into a (proper) model $M = (S^x, \{R_\pi : \pi \in \Pi\}, V^x)$ as follows:

- $R_{(i,a)} = \bigcup_{\alpha \in JA, (i,a) \leq \alpha} R^x_\alpha$
- $R_{\pi_1 \cap \pi_2} = R_{\pi_1} \cap R_{\pi_2}$

Lemma 1.8 $R_\alpha = R^x_\alpha$, *for any complete joint action* $\alpha \in JA$.

Proof Let $\alpha = (1, a_1) \cap \cdots \cap (g, a_g)$, and observe that

$$R_\alpha = (\bigcup_{(1,a_1) \leq \alpha'} R^x_{\alpha'}) \cap \cdots \cap (\bigcup_{(g,a_g) \leq \alpha'} R^x_{\alpha'}).$$

First, assume that $(s, t) \in R^x_\alpha$. It follows immediately that $(s, t) \in \bigcup_{(i,a_i) \subseteq \alpha'} R^x_{\alpha'}$ for all i by taking $\alpha' = \alpha$. Second, assume that $(s, t) \in R_\alpha$, i.e., that there are $\alpha_1, \ldots, \alpha_g$ such that $(i, a_i) \leq \alpha_i$ for all i and $(s, t) \in R^x_{\alpha_1} \cap \cdots \cap R^x_{\alpha_g}$. By construction of M^x, that implies that $\alpha_1 = \cdots = \alpha_g$. So $\alpha_1 = \cdots = \alpha_g = \alpha$. □

Let $last(s)$ denote the last element $s_k \in S^c$ in a sequence $s \in S^x$.

Lemma 1.9 (Truth Lemma) *For any* s *and* ψ, $M, s \models \psi$ *iff* $\psi \in last(s)$.

Proof The proof is by induction on the structure of ψ. The cases for propositional atoms and Boolean connectives are straightforward, so let $\psi = \langle\pi\rangle\gamma$. Let $\pi = (i_1, a_1) \cap \cdots \cap (i_k, a_k)$ for some $1 \leq k \leq n$.

First assume that $i_l = i_m = i$ and $a_l \neq a_m$ for some $l \neq m$. Observe that $R_\pi = (\bigcup_{(i_1,a_1) \leq \alpha'} R^x_{\alpha'}) \cap \cdots \cap (\bigcup_{(i_k,a_k) \leq \alpha'} R^x_{\alpha'})$. Let α_1 and α_2 be arbitrary complete joint actions such that $(i_l, a_l) \leq \alpha_1$ and $(i_m, a_m) \leq \alpha_2$. $\alpha_1 \neq \alpha_2$ since $i_l = i_m$ and $a_l \neq a_m$. By construction of M^x, $R^x_{\alpha_1} \cap R^x_{\alpha_2} = \emptyset$. Thus, $R_\pi = \emptyset$ (since α_1 and α_2 were arbitrary), and $M, s \not\models \langle\pi\rangle\gamma$ for any γ. On the other hand, by **A6** $\neg\langle(i, a_l) \cap (i, a_m)\rangle\gamma \in last(s)$ for any γ, and it follows by **A5** that $\neg\langle\pi\rangle\gamma \in last(s)$. Thus, the Lemma holds in this case and we henceforth assume that $a_l = a_m$ whenever $i_l = i_m$.

For the implication to the right, assume that $M, s \models \langle\pi\rangle\gamma$, i.e., that $M, t \models \gamma$ for some $(s, t) \in R_\pi = \bigcup_{(i_1,a_1) \leq \alpha'} R^x_{\alpha'} \cap \cdots \cap \bigcup_{(i_k,a_k) \leq \alpha'} R^x_{\alpha'}$. Thus, for each $1 \leq j \leq k$, there is an α_j such that $(s, t) \in R^x_{\alpha_j}$ and $(i_j, a_j) \in \alpha_j$. By construction of M^x, $\alpha_1 = \cdots = \alpha_k = \alpha$ (the state t has only one "incoming" transition). Thus, $(s, t) \in R^x_\alpha$ with $\pi \leq \alpha$. Assume that $s = (x, R^c_{\alpha 0}, s_1, \ldots, R^c_{\alpha_{k-1}}, s_k)$. Then $t = (x, R^c_{\alpha 0}, s_1, \ldots, R^c_{\alpha_{k-1}}, s_k, R^c_\alpha, s_{k+1})$ for some s_{k+1} such that $(s_k, s_{k+1}) \in R^c_\alpha$. By the induction hypothesis $\gamma \in last(t) = s_{k+1}$. By construction of R^c_α, $\langle\alpha\rangle\gamma \in s_k = last(s)$. By (repeated applications of) **A5**, $\langle\pi\rangle\gamma \in s_k = last(s)$.

For the implication to the left, let $s = (x, R^c_{\alpha_0}, s_1, \ldots, R^c_{\alpha_{k-1}}, s_k)$ and let $\langle \pi \rangle \gamma \in last(s) = s_k$. Let $X = \{l_0, \ldots, l_m\}$ be the agents not mentioned in π, i.e., $X = \{l \in N : l \neq i_j, 1 \leq j \leq n\}$. Let $\pi_0 = \pi$, and $\pi_{j+1} = \pi_j \cap (l_j, a_j)$ for each $0 \leq j \leq m$ where $a_j \in Act$ is such that $\langle \pi_j \cap (l_j, a_j) \rangle \gamma \in s_k$. The existence of such a_js is ensured by axiom **A2**. Finally, let $\alpha = \pi_{m+1}$. This construction together with the assumption that $a_l = a_m$ whenever $i_k = i_m$ ensures that α is a complete joint action. By the fact that $\langle \alpha \rangle \gamma \in s_k$ and the existence lemma, there is a state $s_{k+1} \in S^c$ such that $(s_k, s_{k+1}) \in R^c_\alpha$ and $\gamma \in s_{k+1}$. Let $t = (x, R^c_{\alpha_0}, s_1, \ldots, R^c_{\alpha_{k-1}}, s_k, R^c_\alpha, s_{k+1})$; $t \in S^x$ and $(s, t) \in R^x_\alpha$ by definition of M^x. By Lemma 1.8 $(s, t) \in R_\alpha$, and from the fact that $\pi \leq \alpha$ it is easy to see that $R_\alpha \subseteq R_\pi$ by definition of R_π, so $(s, t) \in R_\pi$. Since $\gamma \in last(t)$, by the induction hypothesis $M, t \models \gamma$, and thus $M, s \models \langle \pi \rangle \gamma$. □

Lemma 1.10 *M is a joint action model.*

Proof INT: Immediate from the definition.

SER: Let s be a state and i an agent. From **A1** and **A3** there is some $\alpha = (1, a_1) \cap \cdots \cap (g, a_g)$ such that $\langle \alpha \rangle \top \in s$. From the truth lemma and Lemma 1.8 there is s' such that $(s, s') \in R_\alpha = R^x_\alpha$. From the definition of $R_{(i,a_i)}$, $R^x_\alpha \subseteq R_{(i,a_i)}$, and thus $(s, s') \in R_{(i,a_i)}$.

IC: Let s be a state, $C = \{i_1, \ldots, i_k\}$ a coalition, and assume that for each j, (i_j, a_{i_j}) is enabled for i_j in s. Let $\pi = (i_1, a_{i_1}) \cap \cdots \cap (i_k, a_{i_k})$. By the truth lemma, $\bigwedge_{i_j \in C} \langle (i_j, a_{i_j}) \rangle \top \in last(s)$. For each $i_j \in N \setminus C$, let a_{i_j} be such that $\langle (i_j, a_{i_j}) \rangle \top \in last(s)$ – existing by **A1**. Let $\alpha = (1, a_1) \cap \cdots \cap (g, a_g)$. By **A3** $\langle \alpha \rangle \top \in last(s)$, and by **A5** $\langle \pi \rangle \top \in last(s)$. By the truth lemma, there is an s' such that $(s, s') \in R_\pi$.

DJA: Assume that $s = (x, R^c_{\alpha_0}, s_1, \ldots, R^c_{\alpha_{k-1}}, s_k)$. Let $(s, s_1), (s, s_2) \in R_\alpha$, where α is complete. By Lemma 1.8, there are $s^1_{k+1}, s^2_{k+1} \in S^c$ such that $s_1 = (x, R^c_{\alpha_0}, s_1, \ldots, R^c_{\alpha_{k-1}}, s_k, R^c_\alpha, s^1_{k+1})$, $s_2 = (x, R^c_{\alpha_0}, s_1, \ldots, R^c_{\alpha_{k-1}}, s_k, R^c_\alpha, s^2_{k+1})$, and $(s_k, s^1_{k+1}), (s_k, s^2_{k+1}) \in R^c_\alpha$. Assume that $s_1 \neq s_2$, i.e., since s_1 and s_2 are identical upto the last state, that $s^1_{k+1} \neq s^2_{k+1}$. By the definition of S^c, there must be a formula $\psi \in s^1_{k+1}$ such that $\neg\psi \in s^2_{k+1}$. By the truth lemma, $M, s_1 \models \psi$ and $M, s_2 \models \neg\psi$ and thus $M, s \models \langle \alpha \rangle \psi \wedge \langle \alpha \rangle \neg\psi$. By the truth lemma again, $\langle \alpha \rangle \psi, \langle \alpha \rangle \neg\psi \in last(s)$. By **A4**, $[\alpha]\psi, [\alpha]\neg\psi \in last(s)$. But $\langle \alpha \rangle \psi, [\alpha]\neg\psi \in last(s)$ contradicts, via standard modal reasoning, the fact that $last(s)$ is consistent. Thus, $s_1 = s_2$.

UJA: Immediate by Lemma 1.8 and construction of M^x. □

Since $\phi \in x = last(x)$, ϕ is satisfied in a joint action model by Lemmas 1.9 and 1.10. This concludes the completeness proof.

1.6 Complexity

We show that the complexity of deciding satisfiability in joint action models of $\mathcal{L}^{\cap}_K(\Pi^0_{ActN}, \Theta)$ formulae is in PSPACE. The proof uses ideas from [11].

In what follows, we assume without loss of generality that formulas do not contain diamond modalities and disjunctions. Given a set of formulas X, we use $Cl(X)$ to denote the smallest set containing all subformulas of formulas in X such that:

(a) for each agent i and action a, $[(i, a)]\bot \in Cl(X)$
(b) for every complete joint action $\alpha \in JA$, $[\alpha]\bot \in Cl(X)$
(c) if $\neg[(1, a_1)\cap\cdots\cap(g, a_g)]\psi \in Cl(X)$, then $[(1, a_1)\cap\cdots\cap(g, a_g)]{\sim}\psi \in Cl(X)$, where ${\sim}\psi = \neg\psi$ if ψ is not of the form $\neg\chi$, and ${\sim}\psi = \chi$ otherwise
(d) for each i and $a \neq b$, $[(i, a) \cap (i, b)]\bot \in Cl(X)$
(e) if $\psi \in Cl(X)$, then ${\sim}\psi \in Cl(X)$

The following procedure Tab is based on the $K_\omega^{\cap\cup}$-World procedure of [11]. For sets of formulas Δ and S where S is closed as above, $Tab(\Delta, S)$ returns true iff

(A) Δ is a maximally propositionally consistent subset of S, that is, for each $\neg\psi \in S$, $\psi \in \Delta$ iff $\neg\psi \notin \Delta$ and for each $\psi_1 \wedge \psi_2 \in S$, $\psi_1 \wedge \psi_2 \in \Delta$ iff $\psi_1 \in \Delta$ and $\psi_2 \in \Delta$.
(B) There is a partition of the set $\{\neg[\pi]\psi : \neg[\pi]\psi \in \Delta\}$ into sets W_α (at most one for each $\alpha \in JA$) such that if $\neg[\pi]\psi \in W_\alpha$ then $\pi \leq \alpha$ (where the definition of $\leq$ is as in the proof of Theorem 1.5) and

  (i) $\neg\psi \in \Delta_\alpha$
  (ii) for each π' and ψ', if $[\pi']\psi' \in \Delta$ and $\pi' \leq \alpha$, then $\psi' \in \Delta_\alpha$
  (iii) $Tab(\Delta_\alpha, S')$ returns true, where $S' = Cl(\{\psi' : [\pi']\psi' \in \Delta \text{ and } \pi' \leq \alpha\} \cup \{\neg\psi : \neg[\pi]\psi \in W_\alpha\})$

(C) for each $i \in N$, $\neg[(i, a)]\bot \in \Delta$ for some $a \in Act$
(D) if $\neg[(1, a_1)]\bot, \ldots, \neg[(g, a_g)]\bot \in \Delta$, then $\neg[(1, a_1)\cap\cdots\cap(g, a_g)]\bot \in \Delta$
(E) if $\neg[\alpha]\psi \in \Delta$, then $[\alpha]{\sim}\psi \in \Delta$
(F) for every $i \in N$ and $a, b \in Act$ such that $a \neq b$, $[(i, a) \cap (i, b)]\bot \in \Delta$

We require $Tab(\Delta, S)$ to terminate when the only modal formulas in S are those introduced by the clauses (a), (b), and (d) of the definition of $Cl(X)$. Note that otherwise formulas of the form $\neg[\alpha]\bot$ will continue triggering new calls to $Tab(\Delta, S)$.

Lemma 1.11 *A formula ϕ is satisfiable in a joint action model iff there exists $\Delta \subseteq Cl(\phi)$ with $\phi \in \Delta$ such that $Tab(\Delta, Cl(\phi))$ returns true.*

Proof One direction is easy. For the other direction, we will show how to construct a model for ϕ if there exists $\Delta \subseteq Cl(\phi)$ with $\phi \in \Delta$ such that $Tab(\Delta, Cl(\phi))$ returns true. Suppose for ϕ such Δ exists, and let us call it Δ_0. The model M and the state s_0 satisfying ϕ are constructed as follows. Each Δ in successive recursive calls of $Tab(\Delta, S)$ corresponds to a (partial specification of a) state. The existence of a propositional assignment satisfying formulas in Δ is ensured by clause (A). The initial state s_0 corresponds to Δ_0. In each Δ, each formula of the form $\neg[\pi]\psi$ by clause (B) belongs to a set W_α and has a "witness" Δ_α for $\neg\psi$ accessible by a complete joint action α such that $\pi \leq \alpha$ and $\neg\psi \in \Delta_\alpha$. In the model, we stipulate $R_\alpha(s_\Delta, s_{\Delta_\alpha})$ holds together with $R_{\pi'}(s_\Delta, s_{\Delta_\alpha})$ for every $\pi' \leq \alpha$. The rest of clause (B) makes sure that Δ_α contains all formulas ψ' such that $[\pi']\psi' \in \Delta$, which makes sure both that the truth definition for $[\pi]$ and the semantics of intersection work as expected. This part is almost identical to the proof for $K_\omega^\cap$ (apart from requiring a unique α-successor). All we need to prove is that, in addition, the resulting model satisfies the properties of seriality, independent choice, determinism for complete joint actions, and uniqueness of joint actions.

SER is trivial by clause (C). When we terminate the procedure, to ensure seriality we add one more successor state for each α with an α loop to itself. This modification will not affect the truth of ϕ in s_0 because it is at a modal distance from s_0 which is greater than the modal depth of ϕ. IC is ensured by clause (D). DJA is ensured by (B); the existence of partition is enabled by (E) which makes the set of formulas $\sim\psi$ for $\neg[\alpha]\psi \in \Delta$ consistent. UJA is ensured by (F); namely there is no Δ' accessible by $\alpha \cap \alpha'$ from Δ, where $\alpha, \alpha' \in JA$ and $\alpha \neq \alpha'$; otherwise by clause (F) for some agent i which performs a different action in α and α', $[(i, a) \cap (i, b)]\bot \in \Delta$ and hence $\bot \in \Delta'$, but by the definition of the procedure then it cannot return true for Δ'. □

Theorem 1.6 *The complexity of satisfiability problem of formulas in joint action models is PSPACE-complete.*

Proof Satisfiability is decided by $Tab(\Delta, Cl(\phi))$ by the previous lemma. To see that $Tab(\Delta, Cl(\phi))$ requires polynomial space, consider the size of $Cl(\phi)$. The set of subformulas of ϕ is clearly polynomial in $|\phi|$. The number of formulas added to $Cl(\phi)$ by clause (a) is gm, the number of formulas added by clause (b) is m^g, the number of formulas added by clause (d) is gm^2, and (c) and (e) at most double the number of formulas in $Cl(\phi)$. Note that g and m are constant factors, hence the size of $Cl(\phi)$ and Δ is polynomial in $|\phi|$. PSPACE-hardness follows from K being PSPACE-complete. □

The following is an immediate consequence of the result for model checking complexity of PDL with intersection [22]:

Theorem 1.7 *Model checking the $\mathcal{L}_K^\cap(\Pi^0_{ActN}, \Theta)$ language in joint action models is in PTIME.*

The complexity results above are encouraging from the point of view of using the logic of joint actions for verifying properties of game structures using standard theorem-proving and model checking tools for normal modal logic. However, verification of properties involving coalitional ability comes at the price of performing a translation from CL to the language of $K_n^\cap$. The size of the translation may grow exponentially in the size of the input formula (nested coalition modalities give rise to nested disjunctions and conjunctions over all possible complete actions).

1.7 Discussion

In this paper, we defined and studied a class of $K_n^\cap$ models corresponding to concurrent game structures that are (1) injective and (2) parameterized by a fixed and finite set of actions, and showed that on this model class coalition modalities can be expressed in the $K_n^\cap$ language. Along the way, we proved a representation theorem for injective games (this result holds also for games over infinite sets of actions). Given the fact that any satisfiable CL formula ϕ is satisfiable in an injective concurrent game structure with Act^ϕ actions, we also have a satisfiability-preserving embedding from CL into a normal modal logic based on $K_n^\cap$.

As mentioned in the introduction, the idea of interpreting PDL-like languages in games is not new, and the idea of using intersection of strategies to capture coalitional ability is also not entirely new (see below). However, we are not aware of existing completeness or complexity results for K_n with intersection interpreted in game structures.

van Benthem [4] uses propositional dynamic logic (PDL) interpreted directly in extensive-form games, and also suggests extending the language with a "forcing" operator $\{G, i\}\phi$, with the meaning that agent i has a strategy in game G which forces a set of outcomes that will satisfy ϕ. However, the forcing operator is not defined in terms of intersection, and the operator is only defined for singleton coalitions. van Benthem [9] briefly mentions that coalition operators can be captured by intersection, but does not work out the details of resulting logics or relate them to standard PDL. Broersen et al. [12] have already shown that coalition logic can be embedded in a normal modal logic, namely in a variant of STIT (*seeing-to-it-that*) logic [23]. While this is a valuable result for several reasons, we argue that embedding in $K_n^\cap$ is of additional interest because the latter is a more standard logic (see the introduction). A closely related work is [13], which sets out from a similar starting point as the current paper: defining a "minimalistic" logical framework based on PDL that is interpreted in models where agents perform joint actions. *Deterministic Dynamic Logic of Agency* ($\mathcal{DDLA}$) [13] has modalities of the form $\langle i : a \rangle$ where i is an agent and a is an action, very similar to the modalities in the current paper in other words, and is shown to embed coalition logic. The interpretation of the modalities is slightly different: $\langle i : a \rangle\phi$ informally means that "i performs action a and ϕ holds afterwards." The language is not standard PDL; it also includes a modality $\diamond$ that quantifies over actions. The language does not use intersection. In contrast, the current paper has focused on reasoning about joint action using only standard PDL modalities and operators, in particular intersection. Finally, the emphasis of [13] is somewhat different from the current paper, and does not contain most of the types of results (characterization of effectivity, translation of the model checking problem, complexity, etc.) found in the current paper. We leave the precise relationship between the two logics to future work.

In this paper we studied a "minimal" language with intersection, sufficient to capture the coalition operators. For future work, extensions of the language with other PDL operators would be of interest, building on existing results on PDL with intersection such as [24].

References

1. van der Hoek, W., Pauly, M.: Modal logic for games and information. In: J. van Benthem, P. Blackburn, F. Wolter (eds.) The Handbook of Modal Logic, pp. 1180–1152. Elsevier, Amsterdam, The Netherlands (2006)
2. Pauly, M.: A modal logic for coalitional power in games. Journal of Logic and Computation *12*(1), 149–166 (2002)
3. Alur, R.,Henzinger, T.A.,Kupferman,O.: Alternating-time temporal logic. Journal of the ACM **49**, 672–713 (2002)
4. van Benthem, J.: Games in dynamic-epistemic logic. Bulletin of Economic Research **53**(4), 219–248 (2001)
5. van Benthem, J.: Extensive games as process models. J. of Logic, Lang. and Inf. **11**, 289–313 (2002)
6. Parikh, R.: Propositional logics of programs: New directions. In: Foundations of Computation Theory, pp. 347–359. Springer (1983)
7. Parikh, R.: The logic of games and its applications. In: M. Karplnski, J. van Leeuwen (eds.) Topics in the Theory of Computation Selected Papers of the International Conference on Foundations of Computation Theory, FCT '83, *North-Holland Mathematics Studies*, vol. 102,pp. 111–139. North-Holland (1985)
8. Harel, D.: Dynamic logic. In: D. Gabbay, F. Guenthner (eds.) Handbook of Philosophical Logic, Volume II: Extensions of Classical Logic, *Synthese Library*, vol. 165, chap. II.10, pp. 497–604. D. Reidel Publishing Co., Dordrecht (1984)
9. van Benthem, J.: In praise of strategies. In: J. van Eijck, R. Verbrugge (eds.) Games, Actions and Social Software, *Lecture Notes in Computer Science*, vol. 7010, pp. 96–116. Springer, Berlin Heidelberg (2012)
10. Gargov, G., Passy, S.: A note on boolean modal logic. In: Mathematical Logic. Proc. of The Summer School and Conf. on Mathematical Logic "Heyting'88", pp. 311–321. Plenum Press, New York (1988)
11. Lutz, C., Sattler, U.: The complexity of reasoning with boolean modal logics. In: F. Wolter, H. Wansing, M. de Rijke, M. Zakharyaschev (eds.) Advances in Modal Logic, vol. 3, pp. 329–348. World Scientific (2002)
12. Broersen, J., Herzig, A., Troquard, N.: A normal simulation of coalition logic and an epistemic extension. In: D. Samet (ed.) Proceedings of the 11th Conference on Theoretical Aspects of Rationality and Knowledge (TARK-2007), Brussels, Belgium, June 25–27, 2007, pp. 92–101 (2007)
13. Lorini, E.: A dynamic logic of agency II: Deterministic DLA, coalition logic, and game theory. Journal of Logic, Language and Information **19**, 327–351 (2010)
14. Goranko, V.: Coalition games and alternating temporal logics. In: Proceeding of the Eighth Conference on Theoretical Aspects of Rationality and Knowledge (TARK VIII, pp. 259–272. Morgan Kaufmann (2001)
15. Osborne, M.J., Rubinstein, A.: A Course in Game Theory. The MIT Press: Cambridge, MA (1994)
16. Goranko, V., Jamroga, W., Turrini, P.: Strategic games and truly playable effectivity functions. In: Tumer, Yolum, Sonenberg, Stone (eds.) Proceedings of the 10th International Conference on Autonomous Agents and Multiagent Systems (AAMAS 2011), pp. 727–734. Taipei, Taiwan (2011)
17. Gasquet, O., Herzig, A.: Translating inaccessible worlds logic into bimodal logic. In: M. Clarke, R. Kruse, S. Moral (eds.) Symbolic and Quantitative Approaches to Reasoning and Uncertainty, *Lecture Notes in Computer Science*, vol. 747, pp. 145–150. Springer, Berlin Heidelberg (1993)
18. Kracht, M., Wolter, F.: Normal monomodal logics can simulate all others. The Journal of Symbolic Logic **64**(1), pp. 99–138 (1999). URL http://www.jstor.org/stable/2586754
19. Ågotnes, T., Alechina, N.: Reasoning about joint action and coalitional ability in K_n with intersection. In: J. Leite, P. Torroni, T. Ågotnes, G. Boella, L. van der Torre (eds.) Computational Logic in Multi-Agent Systems - 12th International Workshop (CLIMA XII, Proceedings, *Lecture Notes in Computer Science*, vol. 6814, pp. 139–156. Springer (2011)

20. Ågotnes, T., Goranko, V., Jamroga, W.: Alternating-time temporal logics with irrevocable strategies. In: D. Samet (ed.) Proceedings of the 11th Conference on Theoretical Aspects of Rationality and Knowledge (TARK XI), pp. 15–24. Presses Universitaires de Louvain, Brussels, Belgium (2007)
21. Goranko, V., van Drimmelen, G.: Complete axiomatization and decidability of alternating-time temporal logic. Theor. Comput. Sci. *353*(1–3), 93–117 (2006)
22. Lange, M.: Model checking propositional dynamic logic with all extras. J. Applied Logic *4*(1), 39–49 (2006)
23. Belnap, N., Perloff, M.: Seeing to it that: a canonical form for agentives. Theoria *54*, 175–199 (1988)
24. Danecki, S.: Nondeterministic propositional dynamic logic with intersection is decidable. In: A. Skowron (ed.) Proceedings of the 5th Symposium on Computation Theory, *LNCS*, vol. 208, pp. 34–53. Springer, Zaborów, Poland (1984)

Chapter 2
Some Syntactic Interpretations in Different Systems of Full Lambek Calculus

Wojciech Buszkowski

Abstract Buszkowski (Logical Aspects of Computational Linguistics, 2014 [8]) defines an interpretation of FL without 1 in its version without empty antecedents of sequents (employed in type grammars) and applies this interpretation to prove some general results on the complexity of substructural logics and the generative capacity of type grammars. Here this interpretation is extended for nonassociative logics (also with structural rules), logics with 1, logics with distributive laws for $\wedge$, $\vee$, logics with unary modalities, and multiplicative fragments.

2.1 Introduction and Preliminaries

Full Lambek Calculus is a basic substructural logic [12]. In the present paper Full Lambek Calculus is denoted by FL_1, its 1-free fragment by FL^*, and the subsystem of FL^* not allowing empty antecedents of sequents by FL. This notation differs from a standard one [12], where FL stands for our FL_1. The pure logicians, however, usually ignore logics like FL in our sense, and we need a notation discriminating these different systems.

Type grammars (or: categorial grammars) are formal grammars based on type-theoretic syntax and semantics. The language is described by an assignment of types to lexical items (words), and compound expressions are processed by means of a type logic. Type logics are certain basic substructural logics, usually presented as sequent systems: formulae of these logics are interpreted as types. Type grammars often employ logics not allowing empty antecedents of sequents, e.g., L, NL. NL$\Diamond$.

The present paper studies some relations between the versions allowing empty antecedents (more popular among logicians) and those not allowing them (more popular among linguists). We reduce the provability in the former systems to the provability in the latter, using two translations N and P of formulae in the language of FL (or its extension) into formulae of the same language. N (resp. P) acts on

W. Buszkowski (✉)
Faculty of Mathematics and Computer Science,
Adam Mickiewicz University in Poznań, Poznań, Poland
e-mail: buszko@amu.edu.pl

S. Ju et al. (eds.), *Modality, Semantics and Interpretations*,
Logic in Asia: Studia Logica Library, DOI 10.1007/978-3-662-47197-5_2

negative (resp. positive) occurrences of subformulae in sequents. More details are given at the end of this section.

FL_1 admits no structural rules except *associativity*. Type grammars also employ its nonassociative versions. The basic logics are Full Nonassociative Lambek Calculus (FNL_1), also named Groupoid Logic (GL) in [12, 13], and its subsystem FNL.

FNL_1 can be presented as a sequent system in language $(\cdot, \backslash, /, 1, \wedge, \vee)$. We refer to $\cdot$ as *product*, $\backslash$ as *right implication*, / as *left implication*, $\wedge$ as *and*, $\vee$ as *or*. We reserve metavariables p, q, r, s (possibly with subscripts, primes, etc.) for variables and $\alpha, \beta, \gamma, \delta$ for formulae. *Formula structures* are the elements of the free unital groupoid generated by the set of formulae. All formulae are (atomic) formula structures, λ is the unit (the empty structure), and the compound structures are of the form (Γ, Δ), where Γ and Δ are (nonempty) formula structures. We assume $(\Gamma, \lambda) = (\lambda, \Gamma) = \Gamma$, for any structure Γ. Sequents are of the form $\Gamma \Rightarrow \alpha$. One writes $\Rightarrow \alpha$ for $\lambda \Rightarrow \alpha$. *Contexts* are extended formula structures, containing one occurrence of a special atom x (a place for substitution). If Γ is a context, then $\Gamma[\Delta]$ denotes the substitution of Δ for x in Γ; see [13] for a more precise exposition.

FNL_1 is based on the following axioms and rules:

$$(\mathrm{Id})\ \alpha \Rightarrow \alpha$$

$$(\mathrm{L}\cdot)\frac{\Gamma[(\alpha, \beta)] \Rightarrow \gamma}{\Gamma[\alpha \cdot \beta] \Rightarrow \gamma} \quad (\mathrm{R}\cdot)\frac{\Gamma \Rightarrow \alpha;\ \Delta \Rightarrow \beta}{(\Gamma, \Delta) \Rightarrow \alpha \cdot \beta}$$

$$(\mathrm{L}\backslash)\frac{\Gamma[\beta] \Rightarrow \gamma;\ \Delta \Rightarrow \alpha}{\Gamma[(\Delta, \alpha\backslash\beta)] \Rightarrow \gamma} \quad (\mathrm{R}\backslash)\frac{(\alpha, \Gamma) \Rightarrow \beta}{\Gamma \Rightarrow \alpha\backslash\beta}$$

$$(\mathrm{L}/)\frac{\Gamma[\beta] \Rightarrow \gamma;\ \Delta \Rightarrow \alpha}{\Gamma[(\beta/\alpha, \Delta)] \Rightarrow \gamma} \quad (\mathrm{R}/)\frac{(\Gamma, \alpha) \Rightarrow \beta}{\Gamma \Rightarrow \beta/\alpha}$$

$$(\mathrm{L}\wedge)\frac{\Gamma[\alpha_i] \Rightarrow \gamma}{\Gamma[\alpha_1 \wedge \alpha_2] \Rightarrow \gamma} \quad (\mathrm{R}\wedge)\frac{\Gamma \Rightarrow \alpha;\ \Gamma \Rightarrow \beta}{\Gamma \Rightarrow \alpha \wedge \beta}$$

$$(\mathrm{L}\vee)\frac{\Gamma[\alpha] \Rightarrow \gamma;\ \Gamma[\beta] \Rightarrow \gamma}{\Gamma[\alpha \vee \beta] \Rightarrow \gamma} \quad (\mathrm{R}\vee)\frac{\Gamma \Rightarrow \alpha_i}{\Gamma \Rightarrow \alpha_1 \vee \alpha_2}$$

$$(\mathrm{L}1_l)\ \frac{\Gamma[\Delta] \Rightarrow \alpha}{\Gamma[(1, \Delta)] \Rightarrow \alpha} \quad (\mathrm{L}1_r)\ \frac{\Gamma[\Delta] \Rightarrow \alpha}{\Gamma[(\Delta, 1)] \Rightarrow \alpha} \quad (\mathrm{R}1)\ \Rightarrow 1$$

$$(\mathrm{CUT})\ \frac{\Gamma[\alpha] \Rightarrow \beta;\ \Delta \Rightarrow \alpha}{\Gamma[\Delta] \Rightarrow \beta}$$

FNL* denotes the subsystem of FNL_1, restricted to the formulae without 1; so $(L1_l)$, $(L1_r)$ and (R1) are omitted. FNL admits neither 1, nor λ; so the formula structures form the free groupoid generated by the set of 1-free formulae. One says that α is provable, if $\Rightarrow \alpha$ is provable.

We also consider structural rules: *associativity* (a), *exchange* (e), *integrality* (i) (also called: left weakening), and *contraction* (c).

$$(\mathrm{a})\ \frac{\Gamma[((\Delta_1, \Delta_2), \Delta_3)] \Rightarrow \gamma}{\Gamma[(\Delta_1, (\Delta_2, \Delta_3))] \Rightarrow \gamma} \quad (\mathrm{e})\ \frac{\Gamma[(\Delta_1, \Delta_2)] \Rightarrow \gamma}{\Gamma[(\Delta_2, \Delta_1)] \Rightarrow \gamma}$$

$$(\mathrm{i})\ \frac{\Gamma[\Delta_i] \Rightarrow \gamma}{\Gamma[(\Delta_1, \Delta_2)] \Rightarrow \gamma} \quad (\mathrm{c})\ \frac{\Gamma[(\Delta, \Delta)] \Rightarrow \gamma}{\Gamma[\Delta] \Rightarrow \gamma}$$

Since λ is the unit for the operation (,), rules (a), (e), (c) can be restricted to nonempty structures Δ_i, Δ, and similarly for (i) except the special case: from $\Rightarrow \alpha$ infer $\Delta \Rightarrow \alpha$.

Following [12], by FNL_e we denote FNL with (e), by FNL_{1ei} we denote FNL_1 with (e) and (i), and so on. Logics with (a) are *associative* substructural logics. FNL_{1a} is further denoted by FL_1 and called Full Lambek Calculus with 1 (this is precisely Full Lambek Calculus in the sense of [12]). We also define FL^* as FNL^*_a, FL as FNL_a, FL_e as FNL_{ae}, and so on. If S is a set of structural rules, then FNL^*_S (resp. FNL_S) denotes FNL^* (resp. FNL) enriched with all rules from S, and similarly for FL^*_S and FL_S.

In associative substructural logics the antecedents of sequents can be represented as finite sequences of formulae (then, (a) is implicit). The empty sequence is denoted by ϵ, and one writes $\Rightarrow \alpha$ for $\epsilon \Rightarrow \alpha$. We only recall rules (L $\cdot$) and (R $\cdot$) in this form (see [8] for the full list).

$$(\mathrm{L}\,\cdot)\ \frac{\Gamma, \alpha, \beta, \Gamma' \Rightarrow \gamma}{\Gamma, \alpha \cdot \beta, \Gamma' \Rightarrow \gamma}, \quad (\mathrm{R}\cdot)\ \frac{\Gamma \Rightarrow \alpha;\ \ \Delta \Rightarrow \beta}{\Gamma, \Delta \Rightarrow \alpha \cdot \beta}$$

One can also consider the constants $\bot$, $\top$ with the axioms:

$$(\mathrm{a}.\bot)\ \Gamma[\bot] \Rightarrow \alpha \ \ (\mathrm{a}.\top)\ \Gamma \Rightarrow \top\,.$$

In this paper 0 (used to define negations; see [12]) plays no essential role, like in type grammars. Nonetheless one might add it to all logics studied here, with no axioms, nor rules for 0. We do not consider sequents of the form $\Gamma \Rightarrow$; the rule of *right weakening* can be simulated by the definition $0 = \bot$.

In logics with (e) $\alpha\backslash\beta \Leftrightarrow \beta/\alpha$ is provable; this means: the sequents in both directions are provable. Therefore, one writes $\alpha \rightarrow \beta$ for $\alpha\backslash\beta$ and β/α (precisely, instead of two implications $\backslash$, $/$ one employs one implication $\rightarrow$).

All logics mentioned above satisfy *the cut-elimination theorem*: every provable sequent can be proved without (CUT). For the ($\cdot$, $\backslash$, $/$)-fragments of FL and FNL this theorem was proved by Lambek [20, 21] and for a version of FL_1 by Ono and Komori [32].

The ($\cdot$, $\backslash$, $/$)-fragment of FL was proposed by Lambek [20] as the calculus of syntactic types for type grammars. Lambek's name Syntactic Calculus was later replaced by Lambek Calculus. This logic is denoted by L and its nonassociative version by NL. The variants L*, L_1, L_e, NL*, NL_1, NL_e, etc., are defined as above.

In the terminology of linear logics, $\cdot, \backslash, /, 1, 0$ are the *multiplicative* connectives and constants, and $\wedge, \vee, \bot, \top$ are the *additive* ones. In this paper, we assume the higher priority of multiplicatives over additives. For instance, $p \vee q/r$ stands for $p \vee (q/r)$.

The cut-elimination theorem entails *the subformula property*: every provable sequent $\Gamma \Rightarrow \alpha$ has a proof in which all sequents consist of subformulae of the formulae appearing in $\Gamma \Rightarrow \alpha$. As a consequence, the logics allowing cut elimination are conservative extensions of their language-restricted fragments, e.g., FL_1 conservatively extends FL* and L*. On the other hand, NL* is not a conservative extension of NL; for instance, $p/(q/q) \Rightarrow p$ is provable in NL* but not in NL. Similarly, L* is not a conservative extension of L, FL* of FL, and so on. Another consequence is *the decidability* of all logics FNL_{1S}, FNL^*_S, and FNL_S such that S does not contain (c). By various methods it has been shown that all logics FL_{1S} but FL_{1c} are decidable; the undecidability of FL_{1c} and FL_c was announced by K. Chvalovsky and R. Horčik at *Logic, Algebra and Truth Degrees* 2014 (unpublished). Similarly, all logics FL_S are decidable except FL_c. For FNL_{1c}, FNL_{1ec}, FNL_c, FNL_{ec} the problem of (un)decidability is open; the remaining nonassociative logics FNL_{1S} and FNL_S are decidable.

A *type grammar*, based on the logic $\mathcal{L}$ (an $\mathcal{L}$-grammar) can be defined as a triple $G = (\Sigma_G, I_G, \delta_G)$ such that Σ_G is a nonempty finite set, I_G is a mapping which assigns a finite set of formulae of $\mathcal{L}$ to every element of Σ_G, and δ_G is a formula of $\mathcal{L}$. Σ_G is called *the lexicon* (or: alphabet) of G, I_G *the initial type assignment* of G, and δ_G *the designated type* of G. Most often δ_G is a fixed variable, and one denotes it by s_G (or: s).

Variables play the role of *atomic types*, corresponding to basic syntactic categories. Therefore, they are really understood as constants, but we treat them as variables in type logics (in particular, all provable sequents are closed under substitutions).

In mathematical linguistics, expressions of the language are often represented as *phrase structures*, i.e. (skeletal) trees whose leaves are labeled by words. To avoid drawing pictures we represent phrase structures as bracketed strings: (XY) represents the tree whose root has two daughters, being the roots of X and Y, respectively. The recursive definition is as follows: (i) all elements of Σ are phrase structures (on Σ), (ii) if X and Y are phrase structures, then (XY) is a phrase structure. Σ^P denotes the set of all phrase structures on Σ, and Σ^{P*} additionally contains the empty structure λ. This resembles the standard notation of the formal language theory: Σ^* (resp. Σ^+) for the set of all (resp. nonempty) finite strings on Σ. By *a language* (resp. *a phrase language*) on Σ one means an arbitrary set $L \subseteq \Sigma^*$ (resp. $L \subseteq \Sigma^{P*}$); it is said to be ϵ-free (resp. λ-free), if $\epsilon \notin L$ (resp. $\lambda \notin L$).

Clearly, the formula structures are precisely the phrase structures on the set of formulae. For better readability, the constituents of a formula structure are separated by a comma, but commas are omitted in phrase structures of language expressions. So we write (John works), but (n,n\s).

Let G be an $\mathcal{L}$-grammar. I_G is extended for phrase structures on Σ_G as follows: $I_G(\lambda) = \lambda$, $I_G((XY)) = \{(\Gamma, \Delta) : \Gamma \in I_G(X), \Delta \in I_G(Y)\}$. One defines: $X :_G \alpha$, for $X \in \Sigma_G^{P*}$, if there exists $\Gamma \in I_G(X)$ such that $\Gamma \Rightarrow \alpha$ is provable in $\mathcal{L}$. $L^P(G, \alpha)$ consists of all $X \in \Sigma_G^{P*}$ such that $X :_G \alpha$. $L^P(G, \delta_G)$ is called *the phrase language* of G and denoted by $L^P(G)$. *The language* of G consists of all yields of the trees from $L^P(G)$, i.e., the strings obtained by dropping all parentheses in the structures from $L^P(G)$.

For natural languages, the elements of Σ_G are interpreted as words (lexical items) and the elements of $L(G)$ as grammatically correct declarative sentences (statements). For formal languages, Σ_G consists of symbols of the language and $L(G)$ of all strings generated by G.

The size limits of this paper do not allow any serious discussion of type grammars applied to natural and formal languages. The reader is referred to the recent textbook [29] for linguistic applications. General overviews can also be found in [4, 27, 30].

We give a few examples. Let us fix the atomic types: s (sentence), n (proper noun), cn (common noun). $\alpha\backslash\beta$ (resp. β/α) is interpreted as the type of *functors* (or: functional expressions) which with any expression of type α on the left (resp. right) form a compound expression of type β. Thus, n\s is a type of (intransitive) verb phrase, e.g., 'works,' 'walks in the garden,' (n\s)/n of transitive verb phrase, e.g., 'likes,' 'desperately loves,' s/(n\s) of noun phrase as subject, e.g., 'he,' 'some student,' 'every teacher,' (s/n)\s of noun phrase as object, e.g., 'him,' 'her,' 'some student,' (s/(n\s))/cn of determiner, e.g. 'some,' 'every,' 'one,' cn/cn of adjective (as noun modifier), (cn/cn)/(cn/cn) of adverb (as adjective modifier), and so on.

This typing is by no way the only possible option. Different authors propose different types. For instance, np (noun phrase) is often counted to atomic types, verb phrases are typed np\s, and transitive verb phrases (np\s)/np. The particular choice is motivated by various reasons, e.g., semantics, analogies with logical formalisms, economy of typing, and others. Above we completely ignore tense, person, number, case. Lambek [22] employs 33 atomic types for a fragment of English, among them: s (statement), s_1 (statement in present tense), s_2 (statement in past tense), π (subject), π_k, for $k = 1, 2, 3$ (subject in kth person). Subtypes are linked with the main type by nonlogical assumptions, e.g., $\mathrm{s}_k \Rightarrow \mathrm{s}$, $\pi_k \Rightarrow \pi$.

Type logics like L and its extensions are more flexible than the classical type reduction procedure of [1] (going back to ideas of K. Ajdukiewicz (1935) and Y. Bar-Hillel (1953)), which is based on *the reduction laws*: $\alpha, \alpha\backslash\beta \Rightarrow \beta$ and $\beta/\alpha, \alpha \Rightarrow \beta$. The latter can be formalized as the subsystem of L (or NL), restricted to (\, /)-types and axiomatized by (Id), (L\), (L/) ((CUT) is admissible); one denotes this poor logic by AB. Since n,(n\s)/n,n $\Rightarrow$ s is provable in AB, then any AB-grammar with the types listed above accepts 'John likes Mary' as a sentence. Since s/(n\s),(n\s)/n,(s/n)\s$\Rightarrow$ s is provable in L, not in AB, then 'he likes her' is accepted by an L-grammar, but not an AB-grammar with these types. One can repair this failure by assigning new types, e.g. (s/n)/((n\s)/n) to 'he.' In general, AB-grammars require many initial types assigned to words, while L-grammars can reduce their number and explain logical relations between types. Here s/(n\s) can be expanded to the new type by the law $\alpha/\beta \Rightarrow (\alpha/\gamma)/(\beta/\gamma)$, provable in L. Proofs in L and its extensions determine semantic transformations, definable in typed lambda calculus. Due to size limits, we cannot discuss this topic here; again we refer to [4, 27, 29]. Logics of semantic types admit (a), (e) and, possibly, other structural rules.

In a sense, L is even too strong for linguistic purposes. By associativity, if G is an L-grammar, then $L^P(G)$ contains all possible phrase structures whose yields belong to $L(G)$. For instance, not only ((every student) (hates (some teacher))) and (((every student) hates) (some teacher)) are accepted, which well reflects the ∀∃ and ∃∀ readings of this sentence, but also (every ((student (hates some)) teacher)), which is linguistically weird (though admits a semantic reading). This and other reasons motivate some linguists to prefer NL as a basic type logic. NL does not accept all possible phrase structures, but it is certainly too weak for a satisfactory description of natural language. For instance, with the types listed above, NL accepts 'he likes Mary,' since (s/(n\s),((n\s)/n,n)) ⇒ s is provable, but not 'John likes her.'

The power of nonassociative logics can be strengthened in different ways. One possibility is to employ theories; for instance, we add to NL some assumptions, provable in L (assumptions are not closed under substitutions). Buszkowski [6] shows that the provability from assumptions in NL is decidable in polynomial time, so this approach leads to tractable parsing procedures. Another approach, elaborated by Morrill [30], Moortgat [26, 27] and others (see [29]), extends NL by new operators, e.g., unary modalities $\Diamond, \Box^{\downarrow}$, connected by the unary residuation law: $\Diamond a \leq b$ iff $a \leq \Box^{\downarrow} b$, also several pairs of modalities, new binary products, and other extras. Although associativity is not assumed in general, it is allowed for some modal formulae, and so like with other structural rules. This resembles the role of exponentials in linear logics [14]. Logics with $\Diamond, \Box^{\downarrow}$ will be considered in Sect. 2.4.

Although types with $\wedge, \vee$ were not frequently employed in type grammars, some authors considered them for different reasons. Lambek [21] used $\wedge$ to replace the multivalued type assignment $I_G(a) = \{\alpha_1, \ldots, \alpha_n\}$ by the one-valued type assignment $I_G(a) = \alpha_1 \wedge \cdots \wedge \alpha_n$. Kanazawa [17] considered a feature decomposition of types; for instance, singular (resp. plural) noun phrases are typed np $\wedge$ sing (resp. np $\wedge$ pl). Lambek's nonlogical assumptions can be replaced by definitions, e.g., $\pi = \pi_1 \vee \pi_2 \vee \pi_3$. Besides such concrete applications, type logics with $\wedge, \vee$ are interesting for theoretical reasons also from the viewpoint of type grammars. In particular, our translations N, P essentially employ additives.

The methods of this paper are proof-theoretic, not algebraic. Therefore we omit the definitions of algebras, corresponding to logics under consideration. We only note that NL is the strongly complete logic of residuated groupoids, NL_1 of unital residuated groupoids, L of residuated semigroups, L_1 of residuated monoids, FNL of lattice-ordered residuated groupoids, FL of residuated lattices, and so on; see [3, 12, 13]. In algebras, a formula structure Γ is interpreted as the formula $f(\Gamma)$, recursively defined as follows: $f(\lambda) = 1$, $f(\alpha) = \alpha$, $f((\Gamma, \Delta)) = f(\Gamma) \cdot f(\Delta)$. $\Gamma \Rightarrow \gamma$ is true in the algebra A for the valuation μ, if $\mu(f(\Gamma)) \leq \mu(\alpha)$.

In linguistics, the standard models of L are *language models*, i.e., the powerset algebras $\mathcal{P}(\Sigma^+)$. The operations are defined as follows: $L_1 \cdot L_2 = \{uv : u \in L_1, v \in$

$L_2\}$ and \, / are the residual operations. For L*, one replaces Σ^+ by Σ^*, for NL by Σ^P, and for NL* by Σ^{P*}.

In language models the connectives $\wedge$ and $\vee$ are naturally interpreted as intersection and union, respectively, of (phrase) languages. This yields distributive lattices. The distributive laws for $\wedge$, $\vee$ are not provable in logics considered above. One can add them as new axioms. It is sufficient to add:

$$\text{(D) } \alpha \wedge (\beta \vee \gamma) \Rightarrow (\alpha \wedge \beta) \vee (\alpha \wedge \gamma).$$

FNL with (D) is denoted by DFNL, and similarly for other systems, e.g. DFNL*, DFL, etc. The cut-elimination theorem does not hold for these axiomatizations, but can be proved for other, equivalent systems; see Sect. 2.4. DFL_1 is the complete logic of distributive residuated lattices.

Let us note that a linguistic interpretation can be found for logics like FL*, FL, FNL*, FNL, in terms of *syntactic concept lattices* of Clark [11]. Grammatical categories are defined by sets of contexts; the family of all categories is a complete residuated lattice (non-distributive, in general). This construction resembles models obtained by nuclear completion; see [2, 12, 13].

Now we briefly comment on some reasons for the usage of λ-free logics, like NL, FNL, L, FL, in type grammars. In these logics no single formula is provable, hence they cannot be formalized as Hilbert-style systems, nor easily related to other nonclassical logics. Therefore the pure logicians usually ignore them. In type grammars, however, they were extensively studied, starting from Lambek [20]. One reason is semantical: types are to be assigned to meaningful expressions only, and the 'empty expression' has no meaning. In linguistics, expressions are analyzed as syntactic structures, e.g., phrase structures, normally restricted to nonempty structures. Although the theory of production grammars and automata regards languages containing ϵ, type grammars are more natural and elegant, when they are restricted to ϵ-free languages. Since $\Rightarrow s$ is not provable in any consistent substructural logic, $L(G)$ is ϵ-free for any grammar G whose designated type is a variable. Moortgat and Oehrle [28] provide other arguments. Above we assigned type cn/cn to adjectives (noun modifiers) and (cn/cn)/(cn/cn) to adverbs (adjective modifiers). Since $\alpha/\alpha \Leftrightarrow (\alpha/\alpha)/(\alpha/\alpha)$ is provable in L*, then adjectives and adverbs are indistinguishable on the basis of L*, which is unacceptable for linguistics. This problem can be overcome by modifying the initial typing, e.g. assigning a new atomic type to adjectives, but this complicates the grammar and is less natural from the semantical viewpoint. Also the ϵ-free formal languages admit a simpler typing than their companions with ϵ; see [8].

This paper is organized as follows. In Sect. 2.2 we translate every formula of FNL into two formulae $N(\alpha)$ and $P(\alpha)$ of the same language (although N, P depend on the particular logic, their definition is uniform for all logics considered here). Theorem 2.1 states that $\Gamma \Rightarrow \gamma$ is provable in FNL^*_S if and only if $N(\Gamma) \Rightarrow P(\gamma)$ is provable in FNL_S, for any sequent $\Gamma \Rightarrow \gamma$ with $\Gamma \neq \lambda$ and any set of structural rules S. Theorem 2.2 provides an interpretation of FL_{1S} in FL^*_S, extending the interpretation of L_1 in L* from [19].

The functions N, P for FNL^*_S are computable if and only if FNL^*_S is decidable. We show that the decidability of FNL_S implies the decidability of FNL^*_S, and the decidability of FL_S implies the decidability of FL_{1S}.

In Sect. 2.3 the translation maps N, P are adapted for the multiplicative fragments; they obtain the form of multivalued maps which send each formula to a finite set of formulae. The method also works with arbitrary structural rules except (c). Section 2.4 extends the results of Sect. 2.2 for logics with the distributive laws for $\wedge$, $\vee$ and logics with unary modalities. Section 2.5 discusses some consequences of these results for the generative capacity of type grammars and the complexity of substructural logics (the theorem of [16] on the PSPACE-hardness of consistent substructural logics with the disjunction property is extended for logics not allowing empty antecedents and with restricted associativity).

The present paper continues [8], which focuses on FL* and FL. Some extensions, elaborated here, are announced in [8] without proof. No proof from [8] is rewritten here except some brief outlines in Sect. 2.5.

Since this paper is strongly motivated by linguistic applications of substructural logics, we refer to relatively many works in the tradition of type grammars. Not to overload the list of references we skip several references to relevant logical works. Much more can be found in [12, 13, 18].

2.2 An Interpretation of FNL^*_S in FNL_S

The *positive* and *negative* occurrences of subformulae in formulae are recursively defined as follows: (i) α is positive in α, (ii) γ is positive (resp. negative) in $\alpha \circ \beta$, where $\circ \in \{\cdot, \wedge, \vee\}$, if γ is positive (resp. negative) in α or β, (iii) γ is positive (resp. negative) in $\alpha\backslash\beta$, if either γ is positive (resp. negative) in β, or γ is negative (resp. positive) in α, (iv) the same for $\gamma = \beta/\alpha$. Further, γ is positive (resp. negative) in (Γ, Δ), if γ is positive (resp. negative) in Γ or Δ, and γ is positive (resp. negative) in $\Gamma \Rightarrow \alpha$, if γ is either negative (resp. positive) in Γ, or positive (resp. negative) in α.

We fix a set of structural rules S. To every formula γ in language $(\cdot, \backslash, /, \wedge, \vee)$ we assign two formulae $N(\gamma)$ (the negative translation of γ) and $P(\gamma)$ (the positive translation of γ) of the same language; see Table 2.1. By $\vdash^*$ and $\vdash$ we denote the provability in FNL^*_S and FNL_S, respectively. Since the side conditions depend on S, then, actually, the maps N and P also depend on S. It would be more precise to write P_S, N_S instead of P, N. We omit the subscript S, if it is clear from the context or inessential. For example, for FNL* we obtain $N(p/(q/q)) = p/(q/q) \wedge p$, $P(p\cdot(q/q)) = p\cdot(q/q) \vee p$. P (resp. N) acts on positive (resp. negative) occurrences of formulae in sequents.

N and P can also be defined for formulae containing $0, \bot, \top$. We set $N(\gamma) = P(\gamma) = \gamma$, for $\gamma \in \{0, \bot, \top\}$. We extend N for nonempty formula structures by the recursive clause: $N(\Gamma, \Delta) = (N(\Gamma), N(\Delta))$. The same definition works for contexts; we set $N(x) = x$. Clearly $N(\Gamma[\Delta]) = N(\Gamma)[N(\Delta)]$, for $\Delta \neq \lambda$.

Table 2.1 Translations N and P

γ	$N(\gamma)$	$P(\gamma)$	Condition
p	p	p	p is a variable
$\alpha \circ \beta$	$N(\alpha) \circ N(\beta)$	$P(\alpha) \circ P(\beta)$	$\circ \in \{\wedge, \vee\}$
$\alpha \cdot \beta$	$N(\alpha) \cdot N(\beta)$	$P(\alpha) \cdot P(\beta)$	$\nvdash^* \alpha$ and $\nvdash^* \beta$
$\alpha \cdot \beta$	As above	$P(\alpha) \cdot P(\beta) \vee P(\beta)$	$\vdash^* \alpha$ and $\nvdash^* \beta$
$\alpha \cdot \beta$	As above	$P(\alpha) \cdot P(\beta) \vee P(\alpha)$	$\nvdash^* \alpha$ and $\vdash^* \beta$
$\alpha \cdot \beta$	As above	$P(\alpha) \cdot P(\beta) \vee P(\alpha) \vee P(\beta)$	$\vdash^* \alpha$ and $\vdash^* \beta$
$\alpha\backslash\beta$	$P(\alpha)\backslash N(\beta)$	$N(\alpha)\backslash P(\beta)$	$\nvdash^* \alpha$
$\alpha\backslash\beta$	$P(\alpha)\backslash N(\beta) \wedge N(\beta)$	As above	$\vdash^* \alpha$
β/α	$N(\beta)/P(\alpha)$	$P(\beta)/N(\alpha)$	$\nvdash^* \alpha$
β/α	$N(\beta)/P(\alpha) \wedge N(\beta)$	As above	$\vdash^* \alpha$

Lemmas 2.1 and 2.2 below have been proved in [8] for FL and FL*; the same proofs work for FNL and FNL*. Here we outline different proofs of slightly stronger results.

Lemma 2.1 *For any set S and any formula γ, $N_S(\gamma) \Rightarrow \gamma$ and $\gamma \Rightarrow P_S(\gamma)$ are provable in FNL.*

Proof We prove both claims by simultaneous induction on γ. If γ is an atom, then they hold, by (Id) and the definition of N_S, P_S. For the inductive steps, one uses *the monotonicity rules*, derivable in FNL (in (MON) $\circ \in \{\cdot, \wedge, \vee\}$).

$$\text{(MON)}\ \frac{\alpha \Rightarrow \alpha' ;\ \beta \Rightarrow \beta'}{\alpha \circ \beta \Rightarrow \alpha' \circ \beta'}$$

$$\text{(MON}\backslash\text{)}\ \frac{\alpha \Rightarrow \alpha' ;\ \beta \Rightarrow \beta'}{\beta'\backslash\alpha \Rightarrow \beta\backslash\alpha'} \quad \text{(MON/)}\ \frac{\alpha \Rightarrow \alpha' ;\ \beta \Rightarrow \beta'}{\alpha/\beta' \Rightarrow \alpha'/\beta}$$

Furthermore, the following sequents are provable in FNL, for any formulae α, β and any set S.

$$P_S(\alpha) \cdot P_S(\beta) \Rightarrow P_S(\alpha \cdot \beta) \tag{2.1}$$

$$N_S(\alpha\backslash\beta) \Rightarrow P_S(\alpha)\backslash N_S(\beta),\ \ N_S(\beta/\alpha) \Rightarrow N_S(\beta)/P_S(\alpha). \tag{2.2}$$

Let $\gamma = \alpha\backslash\beta$. By the induction hypothesis, $N_S(\beta) \Rightarrow \beta$ and $\alpha \Rightarrow P_S(\alpha)$ are provable in FNL. Then, $P_S(\alpha)\backslash N_S(\beta) \Rightarrow \alpha\backslash\beta$ is provable, by (MON\), and consequently, $N_S(\gamma) \Rightarrow \gamma$ is provable, by (2.2) and (CUT). By the induction hypothesis, $N_S(\alpha) \Rightarrow \alpha$ and $\beta \Rightarrow P_S(\beta)$ are provable in FNL. Then, $\alpha\backslash\beta \Rightarrow N_S(\alpha)\backslash P_S(\beta)$ is provable, by (MON\), and we have $P_S(\alpha\backslash\beta) = N_S(\alpha)\backslash P_S(\beta)$.

The remaining cases are left to the reader.

In the proof of Lemma 2.2, $N = N_S$ and $P = P_S$.

Lemma 2.2 *Let S be fixed. For any formula γ, $N_S(\gamma) \Leftrightarrow \gamma$ and $P_S(\gamma) \Leftrightarrow \gamma$ are provable in FNL^*_S.*

Proof Although $N(\gamma) \Rightarrow \gamma$ and $\gamma \Rightarrow P(\gamma)$ are provable, by Lemma 2.1, it is convenient to prove both claims with $\Leftrightarrow$ by simultaneous induction on γ. For atoms, they are obvious. For the inductive steps, we use the fact that $\vdash^* \alpha \Leftrightarrow \beta$ is a congruence on the formula algebra. Furthermore, the following are provable in FNL^*_S, for any formulae α, β.

$$P(\alpha) \cdot P(\beta) \Leftrightarrow P(\alpha \cdot \beta) \tag{2.3}$$

$$P(\alpha)\backslash N(\beta) \Leftrightarrow N(\alpha\backslash\beta),\ N(\beta)/P(\alpha) \Leftrightarrow N(\beta/\alpha) \tag{2.4}$$

We show (2.3). $P(\alpha) \cdot P(\beta) \Rightarrow P(\alpha \cdot \beta)$ is provable, by (2.1), since FNL is a subsystem of FNL^*_S. We prove $\Leftarrow$. We consider four cases. (1°) $\nvdash^* \alpha$ and $\nvdash^* \beta$. The claim is obvious. (2°) $\vdash^* \alpha$ and $\nvdash^* \beta$. Then, $P(\alpha \cdot \beta) = P(\alpha) \cdot P(\beta) \vee P(\beta)$. By Lemma 2.1 and (CUT), $\vdash^* P(\alpha)$, hence $\vdash^* P(\beta) \Rightarrow P(\alpha) \cdot P(\beta)$, by (R $\cdot$), and $\vdash^* P(\alpha \cdot \beta) \Rightarrow P(\alpha) \cdot P(\beta)$, by (L$\vee$). For (3°) $\nvdash^* \alpha$, $\vdash^* \beta$, and (4°) $\vdash^* \alpha$, $\vdash^* \beta$, the arguments are similar. (2.4) is left to the reader.

Let $\gamma = \alpha \cdot \beta$. By the induction hypothesis, $N(\alpha) \Leftrightarrow \alpha$ and $N(\beta) \Leftrightarrow \beta$ are provable in FNL^*_S. Then, $N(\alpha) \cdot N(\beta) \Leftrightarrow \alpha \cdot \beta$ is provable. We have $N(\alpha \cdot \beta) = N(\alpha) \cdot N(\beta)$, which yields $N(\gamma) \Leftrightarrow \gamma$. By the induction hypothesis $P(\alpha) \Leftrightarrow \alpha$ and $P(\beta) \Leftrightarrow \beta$ are provable, hence $P(\alpha) \cdot P(\beta) \Leftrightarrow \alpha \cdot \beta$ is provable. Consequently, $P(\gamma) \Leftrightarrow \gamma$ is provable, by (2.3) and (CUT).

The remaining cases are left to the reader.

We are ready to prove the main result of this section.

Theorem 2.1 Let S be fixed. (I) For any sequent $\Gamma \Rightarrow \gamma$, where $\Gamma \neq \lambda$, $\Gamma \Rightarrow \gamma$ is provable in FNL^*_S if and only if $N_S(\Gamma) \Rightarrow P_S(\gamma)$ is provable in FNL_S. (II) Let (i) belong to S. For any formula γ, provable in FNL^*_S, and any $\Gamma \neq \lambda$, the sequent $\Gamma \Rightarrow P_S(\gamma)$ is provable in FNL_S.

Proof We prove the 'if' part of (I). Assume $\vdash N(\Gamma) \Rightarrow P(\gamma)$. Then, $\vdash^* N(\Gamma) \Rightarrow P(\gamma)$, hence $\vdash^* \Gamma \Rightarrow \gamma$, by Lemma 2.2 and (CUT).

The 'only if' part of (I), for S not containing (i), is proved by induction on cut-free proofs in FNL^*_S. For (Id), $\vdash N(\alpha) \Rightarrow P(\alpha)$ holds, by (Id), Lemma 2.1 and (CUT). If $\Gamma \Rightarrow \gamma$ is an axiom (a.$\bot$) or (a.$\top$), then $N(\Gamma) \Rightarrow P(\gamma)$ is also an axiom from this group.

The rules for $\wedge$, $\vee$ and (L $\cdot$), (R$\backslash$), (R/) are treated easily. Let us consider (L$\vee$). By the induction hypothesis, $\vdash N(\Gamma[\alpha]) \Rightarrow P(\gamma)$ and $\vdash N(\Gamma[\beta]) \Rightarrow P(\gamma)$. Then, $\vdash N(\Gamma)[N(\alpha)] \Rightarrow P(\gamma)$ and $\vdash N(\Gamma)[N(\beta)] \Rightarrow P(\gamma)$, and we apply (L$\vee$) in FNL_S.

Structural rules (a), (e), (c) cause no problem: the induction hypothesis applied to the premise directly yields our claim for the conclusion.

We consider (R $\cdot$). There are three subcases. (1°) $\Gamma \neq \lambda$ and $\Delta \neq \lambda$. By the induction hypothesis, $\vdash N(\Gamma) \Rightarrow P(\alpha)$ and $\vdash N(\Delta) \Rightarrow P(\beta)$. Then, $\vdash N((\Gamma, \Delta)) \Rightarrow P(\alpha) \cdot P(\beta)$, by (R $\cdot$). Using (R$\vee$), if necessary, we obtain $\vdash N((\Gamma, \Delta)) \Rightarrow P(\alpha \cdot \beta)$. (2°) $\Gamma = \lambda$ and $\Delta \neq \lambda$. Then, $\vdash^* \alpha$. Also $\vdash N(\Delta) \Rightarrow P(\beta)$, by the induction hypothesis. Consequently, $\vdash N(\Delta) \Rightarrow P(\alpha \cdot \beta)$, by (R$\vee$), possibly applied twice. (3°) $\Gamma \neq \lambda$ and $\Delta = \lambda$. One argues as for (2°).

We consider (L$\backslash$). There are two subcases. (1°) $\Delta \neq \lambda$. By the induction hypothesis, $\vdash N(\Gamma[\beta]) \Rightarrow P(\gamma)$ and $\vdash N(\Delta) \Rightarrow P(\alpha)$. By (L$\backslash$), we obtain $\vdash N(\Gamma)[(N(\Delta), P(\alpha)\backslash N(\beta))] \Rightarrow P(\gamma)$. Using (L$\wedge$), if necessary, we get $\vdash N(\Gamma)[(N(\Delta), N(\alpha\backslash\beta))] \Rightarrow P(\gamma)$, hence $\vdash N(\Gamma[(\Delta, \alpha\backslash\beta)]) \Rightarrow P(\gamma)$. (2°) $\Delta = \lambda$. Then, $\vdash^* \alpha$ and $N(\alpha\backslash\beta) = P(\alpha)\backslash N(\beta) \wedge N(\beta)$. As for (1°), we get $\vdash N(\Gamma[\beta]) \Rightarrow P(\gamma)$, hence $\vdash N(\Gamma[\alpha\backslash\beta]) \Rightarrow P(\gamma)$, by (L$\wedge$). The argument for (L/) is similar.

Let S contain (i). The 'only if' part of (I) and (II) are proved by simultaneous induction on cut-free proofs in FNL_S^* (precisely: on the number of sequents appearing in the cut-free proof). For (I), the argument copies the above, but we need one new case: rule (i).

(1°) $\Gamma[(\Delta_1, \Delta_2)] \Rightarrow \gamma$ results from $\Gamma[\Delta_2] \Rightarrow \gamma$, by (i), with $\Delta_1 \neq \lambda$, $\Delta_2 \neq \lambda$. By the induction hypothesis, $\vdash N(\Gamma[\Delta_2]) \Rightarrow P(\gamma)$, hence $\vdash N(\Gamma[(\Delta_1, \Delta_2)]) \Rightarrow P(\gamma)$, by (i) in FNL_S. (2°) As above with the premise $\Gamma[\Delta_1] \Rightarrow \gamma$. The argument is similar. (3°) $\Gamma \Rightarrow \gamma$ results from $\Rightarrow \gamma$, by (i). By the induction hypothesis for (II), $\vdash N(\Gamma) \Rightarrow P(\gamma)$.

We prove (II). Let γ be provable in FNL_S^*. Then, $\Rightarrow \gamma$ must be either an instance of (a.$\top$), or the conclusion of one of the rules: (R $\cdot$), (R$\backslash$), (R/), (R$\wedge$), (R$\vee$). We fix $\Gamma \neq \lambda$. For (a.$\top$), $\Gamma \Rightarrow P(\gamma)$ is also an instance of (a.$\top$). Let us consider the rules.

(R $\cdot$). Then $\gamma = \alpha \cdot \beta$, and the premises are $\Rightarrow \alpha$, $\Rightarrow \beta$. By the induction hypothesis, $\vdash \Gamma \Rightarrow P(\alpha)$, hence $\vdash \Gamma \Rightarrow P(\alpha \cdot \beta)$, by (R$\vee$) (applied twice).

(R$\backslash$). Then $\gamma = \alpha\backslash\beta$, and the premise is $\alpha \Rightarrow \beta$. By the induction hypothesis for (I), $\vdash N(\alpha) \Rightarrow P(\beta)$. Using (i) in FNL_S, we obtain $\vdash (N(\alpha), \Gamma) \Rightarrow P(\beta)$, hence $\vdash \Gamma \Rightarrow P(\gamma)$, by (R$\backslash$). For (R/), the argument is similar.

(R$\wedge$). Then, $\gamma = \alpha \wedge \beta$, and the premises are $\Rightarrow \alpha$, $\Rightarrow \beta$. By the induction hypothesis, $\vdash \Gamma \Rightarrow P(\alpha)$ and $\vdash \Gamma \Rightarrow P(\beta)$, hence $\vdash \Gamma \Rightarrow P(\gamma)$, by (R$\wedge$).

(R$\vee$). Then $\gamma = \alpha_1 \vee \alpha_2$, and the premise is $\Rightarrow \alpha_i$. By the induction hypothesis, $\vdash \Gamma \Rightarrow P(\alpha_i)$, hence $\vdash \Gamma \Rightarrow P(\gamma)$, by (R$\vee$).

Notice that the proof of Theorem 2.1 would not work, if (CUT) were not eliminated.

To better understand the relation between FNL_S^* and FNL_S we need an additional lemma. We define $\equiv$ as the smallest congruence in the formula algebra such that:

$$(\alpha \circ \beta) \circ \gamma \equiv \alpha \circ (\beta \circ \gamma), \;\; \alpha \circ \beta \equiv \beta \circ \alpha\,, \;\; \alpha \circ \alpha \equiv \alpha\,, \tag{2.5}$$

for all formulae α, β, γ and $\circ \in \{\wedge, \vee\}$. Clearly $\alpha \equiv \beta$ entails: $\alpha \Leftrightarrow \beta$ is provable in FNL.

Lemma 2.3 *Let S be fixed. For any formula* γ, $N_S(N_S(\gamma)) \equiv N_S(\gamma)$ *and* $P_S(P_S(\gamma)) \equiv P_S(\gamma)$.

Proof Again we proceed by induction on γ, using the fact: $\vdash^* \alpha$ iff $\vdash^* P(\alpha)$, which holds, by Lemma 2.2. Here we only consider the case $\gamma = \alpha \cdot \beta$. There are four subcases.

(1°) $\nvdash^* \alpha$, $\nvdash^* \beta$. We compute:

$$P(P(\gamma)) = P(P(\alpha) \cdot P(\beta)) = P(P(\alpha)) \cdot P(P(\beta)) \equiv P(\alpha) \cdot P(\beta) = P(\gamma).$$

(2°) $\vdash^* \alpha$, $\nvdash^* \beta$. We compute:

$$P(P(\gamma)) = P(P(\alpha) \cdot P(\beta) \vee P(\beta)) = P(P(\alpha) \cdot P(\beta)) \vee P(P(\beta)) =$$

$$P(P(\alpha)) \cdot P(P(\beta)) \vee P(P(\beta)) \vee P(P(\beta)) \equiv P(\alpha) \cdot P(\beta) \vee P(\beta) \equiv P(\gamma).$$

The remaining subcases are treated in a similar way. If $\vdash^* \alpha$, $\vdash^* \beta$, then all three patterns of (2.5) are needed.

A sequent of the form $N_S(\Gamma) \Rightarrow P_S(\gamma)$, where $\Gamma \neq \lambda$, is said to be *stable* in FNL_S. From Lemma 2.3 it follows that in FNL_S^* every sequent whose antecedent is nonempty is deductively equivalent to a stable sequent; $\Gamma \Rightarrow \gamma$ and $N(\Gamma) \Rightarrow P(\gamma)$ are derivable from each other (using (CUT)).

Corollary 2.1 *For any stable sequent in* FNL_S*, the sequent is provable in* FNL_S *if and only if it is provable in* FNL_S^*.

Proof Fix a sequent $N(\Gamma) \Rightarrow P(\gamma)$ with $\Gamma \neq \lambda$. The 'only if' part is obvious. For the 'if' part, assume that $N(\Gamma) \Rightarrow P(\gamma)$ is provable in FNL_S^*. By Theorem 1, $N(N(\Gamma)) \Rightarrow P(P(\gamma))$ is provable in FNL_S. Consequently, $N(\Gamma) \Rightarrow P(\gamma)$ is provable in FNL_S, by Lemma 2.3.

Notice that P, N are not extensional (hence not monotone) in FNL_S: $\vdash \alpha \Rightarrow \beta$ need not imply $\vdash P(\alpha) \Rightarrow P(\beta)$, nor $\vdash N(\alpha) \Rightarrow N(\beta)$, and similarly for $\Leftrightarrow$ instead of $\Rightarrow$. Let $\alpha = ((p/(q/q)) \cdot (q/q))/(q/q)$, $\beta = p/(q/q)$. Then, $\alpha \Leftrightarrow \beta$ in FNL, $P(\alpha) = ((p/(q/q)) \cdot (q/q) \vee p/(q/q))/(q/q)$, $P(\beta) = \beta$, and $\nvdash P(\alpha) \Rightarrow P(\beta)$.

Theorem 2.1 does not allow to interpret in FNL_S the provability of $\Rightarrow \gamma$ in FNL_S^*. An indirect reduction, however, is possible with the aid of the following properties of provability in FNL_S^*.

(Pr.1) $\nvdash^* p$, $\nvdash^* 0$, $\nvdash^* \bot$, $\vdash^* \top$,
(Pr.2) $\vdash^* \alpha \circ \beta$ iff $\vdash^* \alpha$ and $\vdash^* \beta$, for $\circ \in \{\cdot, \wedge\}$,
(Pr.3) $\vdash^* \alpha\backslash\beta$ iff $\vdash N(\alpha) \Rightarrow P(\beta)$, $\vdash^* \beta/\alpha$ iff $\vdash N(\alpha) \Rightarrow P(\beta)$,
(Pr.4) $\vdash^* \alpha \vee \beta$ iff $\vdash^* \alpha$ or $\vdash^* \beta$.

In (Pr.3) N, P are to be computed for the direct subformulae of $\alpha\backslash\beta$ and β/α, and this computation requires checking the provability of some proper subformulae of α or β. One easily obtains an algorithm which computes $N(\alpha)$, $P(\alpha)$ and checks $\vdash^* \alpha$, for any formula α; this algorithm is based on the algorithm for checking the provability in FNL_S. Accordingly, the decidability of FNL_S implies the decidability of FNL_S^*.

Theorem 2.1 remains true for some language-restricted fragments, e.g. the languages $(\cdot, \backslash, \wedge, \vee)$, $(\backslash, /, \wedge)$ and $(\backslash, /, \wedge, \vee)$ (also with $0, \bot, \top$), since these languages are closed under N, P.

The fragment $\mathrm{FL}_e^*[\rightarrow, \wedge, 0]$ is interesting, since it has the same expressive power as Multiplicative-Additive Linear Logic (MALL), denoted by InFL_e in [12]. On the one hand, FL_e^* is a conservative fragment of MALL. On the other hand, MALL can be faithfully interpreted in $\mathrm{FL}_e^*[\rightarrow, \wedge, 0]$; see [5]; also MALL with $\bot, \top$ can be interpreted in $\mathrm{FL}_e^*[\rightarrow, \wedge, 0, \top]$. By Theorem 2.1 and (Pr.1)–(Pr.4), one can reduce MALL to $\mathrm{FL}_e[\rightarrow, \wedge, 0]$. This also works for Cyclic MALL (CyInFL) and $\mathrm{FL}[\backslash, /, \wedge, 0]$ enriched with *the cyclic rule*:

$$(\mathrm{C})\ \frac{\Gamma, \Delta \Rightarrow 0}{\Delta, \Gamma \Rightarrow 0}.$$

For associative logics with 1, our interpretation can be composed with the one of Kuznetsov [19] who interprets L_1 in L^*; his interpretation remains correct for FL_{1S} and FL_S^*. Let us briefly describe this method for FL_1 and FL^* (structural rules cause no difficulty). Here the antecedents of sequents are finite sequences of formulae.

First, axioms (Id) of FL_1 are restricted to $p \Rightarrow p$, for any variable p. Then, all sequents $\alpha \Rightarrow \alpha$ are provable (without (CUT)).

Second, rule (L1) (of the form: from $\Gamma, \Gamma' \Rightarrow \alpha$ infer $\Gamma, 1, \Gamma' \Rightarrow \alpha$) is replaced by the new axioms: (a.1) $1^n \Rightarrow 1$, (a.2) $1^m, p, 1^n \Rightarrow p$, for $m, n \geq 0$ (here 1^n denotes the sequence of n copies of 1). Axiom (R1) equals (a.1) for $n = 0$, and $1 \Rightarrow 1$ is (a.1) for $n = 1$. It is obvious that every sequent provable in the new system is also provable in FL_1. The converse follows from the admissibility of (L1) in the new system (show it by induction on proofs). Let $\mathcal{L}$ denote the new system. One can show that $\mathcal{L}$ allows cut elimination, but it is not essential for this argument.

Third, define a substitution σ by: $\sigma(p) = (1 \cdot p) \cdot 1$, for any variable p. Let $\mathcal{L}^-$ denote $\mathcal{L}$ without (a.2). One shows: $\Gamma \Rightarrow \gamma$ is provable in FL_1 if and only if $\sigma(\Gamma \Rightarrow \gamma)$ is provable in $\mathcal{L}^-$. The 'if' part is obvious. The 'only if' part is proved by induction on proofs in $\mathcal{L}$.

Fourth, a pseudo-substitution η is defined by: $\eta(1) = q \backslash q$ (here q is a new variable, not occurring in sequents under consideration). One shows: $\Gamma \Rightarrow \gamma$ is provable in FL_1 if and only if $\eta(\sigma(\Gamma \Rightarrow \gamma))$ is provable in FL^*. The 'if' part is easy: substitute 1 for q in $\eta(\sigma(\Gamma \Rightarrow \gamma))$. The 'only if' part is a consequence of the following: if $\Gamma \Rightarrow \gamma$ is provable in $\mathcal{L}^-$, then $\eta(\Gamma \Rightarrow \gamma)$ is provable in FL^* (use induction on proofs in $\mathcal{L}^-$). Associativity is essential for proving $(q \backslash q)^n \Rightarrow q \backslash q$ in FL^*.

Theorem 2.2 Let S be a set of structural rules (e), (i), (c). For any sequent $\Gamma \Rightarrow \gamma$ with $\Gamma \neq \epsilon$, $\Gamma \Rightarrow \gamma$ is provable in FL_{1S} if and only if $N(\eta(\sigma(\Gamma))) \Rightarrow P(\eta(\sigma(\gamma)))$ is provable in FL_S.

Table 2.2 $P(\alpha \cdot \beta)$ for logics with (i)

γ	$P(\gamma)$	Condition
$\alpha \cdot \beta$	$P(\alpha) \cdot P(\beta)$	$\nvdash^* \alpha$ and $\nvdash^* \beta$
$\alpha \cdot \beta$	$P(\beta)$	$\vdash^* \alpha$
$\alpha \cdot \beta$	$P(\alpha)$	$\nvdash^* \alpha$ and $\vdash^* \beta$

Proof This theorem immediately follows from Theorem 2.1 and the equivalence proved above. Precisely, Theorem 2.1 should be rewritten in the form appropriate for antecedents represented as sequences of formulae.

For logics with (i), Kuznetsov's interpretation can be simplified. Since (L1) is an instance of (i), we omit (L1) in the axiomatization. Then, there is no need for auxiliary logics $\mathcal{L}$, $\mathcal{L}^-$. One directly proves: $\Gamma \Rightarrow \gamma$ is provable in FL_{1S} if and only if $\eta(\Gamma \Rightarrow \gamma)$ is provable in FL^*_S, and drops σ in Theorem 2.2. This also works for nonassociative logics with (i).

For S containing (i), $P(\alpha) \cdot P(\beta) \Rightarrow P(\alpha)$ and $P(\alpha) \cdot P(\beta) \Rightarrow P(\beta)$ are provable in FNL_S; also $P(\alpha) \Leftrightarrow P(\beta)$ is provable in FNL_S, if α and β are provable in FNL^*_S (use Theorem 2.1. (II)). Therefore, the clauses defining $P_S(\alpha \cdot \beta)$ can be simplified as in Table 2.2.

Notice that Kunetsov's interpretation is polynomial, while our is exponential: the size of $N(\alpha)$ and $P(\alpha)$ can be exponential in the size of α. We define $\alpha_0 = p$, $\alpha_{n+1} = (q\backslash q)\backslash\alpha_n$. The size of α_n is linear in n, but $N(\alpha_n)$ contains 2^n occurrences of p.

Since the provability in FL_{1S} is reducible to the provability in FL^*_S, and the latter to the provability in FL_S, then the decidability of FL_S implies the decidability of FL_{1S}. FL_{1c} is undecidable, hence FL^*_c and FL_c are undecidable (see Sect. 2.1).

2.3 Multiplicative Fragments

$N(\gamma)$ and $P(\gamma)$ may contain additives, if even γ is a multiplicative formula. Therefore, the results of Sect. 2.2 cannot directly be applied to multiplicative logics NL^* and NL, L^* and L, etc. We, however, show that N, P can be replaced by multivalued maps which send a formula to a finite set of formulae. Buszkowski [8] announces this solution for L^* and L (without proof). Here we also regard nonassociative logics, possibly with structural rules (a), (e), (i), and provide a proof, employing a multivalued interpretation of FNL_S in NL_S, working for sequents with limited occurrences of $\wedge$, $\vee$.

If U, V are sets of formulae and $\circ$ is a binary connective, then we define: $U \circ V = \{\alpha \circ \beta : \alpha \in U, \beta \in V\}$. Every formula γ in language $(\cdot, \backslash, /, \wedge, \vee)$ is translated into a set $I(\gamma)$, of formulae in language $(\cdot, \backslash, /)$. This also works with $1, 0, \bot, \top$ added to both languages.

(I.1) $I(\alpha) = \{\alpha\}$, for any atomic formula α,
(I.2) $I(\alpha \circ \beta) = I(\alpha) \circ I(\beta)$, for $\circ \in \{\cdot, \backslash, /\}$,
(I.3) $I(\alpha \circ \beta) = I(\alpha) \cup I(\beta)$, for $\circ \in \{\wedge, \vee\}$.

The occurrence of a connective $\circ$ in a formula (resp. sequent) is called *positive*, if $\circ$ is the main connective of a subformula which occurs positively in this formula (resp. sequent), and similarly for negative occurrences.

Lemma 2.4 *Let γ contain no positive (resp. negative) occurrence of $\wedge$ and no negative (resp. positive) occurrence of $\vee$. Then, for any $\delta \in I(\gamma)$, $\delta \Rightarrow \gamma$ (resp. $\gamma \Rightarrow \delta$) is provable in FNL.*

Proof Both claims are proved by simultaneous induction on γ. If γ is atomic, they are obvious.

$\gamma = \alpha \cdot \beta$. So $I(\gamma) = I(\alpha) \cdot I(\beta)$. Let $\delta \in I(\gamma)$. Then, $\delta = \delta_1 \cdot \delta_2$, for some $\delta_1 \in I(\alpha)$, $\delta_2 \in I(\beta)$. By the induction hypothesis, $\delta_1 \Rightarrow \alpha$ and $\delta_2 \Rightarrow \beta$ (resp. $\alpha \Rightarrow \delta_1$, $\beta \Rightarrow \delta_2$) are provable in FNL, hence $\delta \Rightarrow \gamma$ (resp. $\gamma \Rightarrow \delta$) is provable, by (MON).

$\gamma = \alpha\backslash\beta$. So $I(\gamma) = I(\alpha)\backslash I(\beta)$, α contains no negative (resp. positive) occurrence of $\wedge$ and no positive (resp. negative) occurrence of $\vee$, and β contains no positive (resp. negative) occurrence of $\wedge$ and no negative (resp. positive) occurrence of $\vee$. Let $\delta \in I(\gamma)$. So $\delta = \delta_1\backslash\delta_2$, for some $\delta_1 \in I(\alpha)$, $\delta_2 \in I(\beta)$. By the induction hypothesis, $\alpha \Rightarrow \delta_1$ and $\delta_2 \Rightarrow \beta$ (resp. $\delta_1 \Rightarrow \alpha$ and $\beta \Rightarrow \delta_2$) are provable, hence $\delta \Rightarrow \gamma$ (resp. $\gamma \Rightarrow \delta$) is provable, by (MON$\backslash$). For $\gamma = \beta/\alpha$, the reasoning is similar.

$\gamma = \alpha \wedge \beta$. Only the second claim is applicable. Let $\delta \in I(\gamma)$. Then, $\delta \in I(\alpha)$ or $\delta \in I(\beta)$. Assume $\delta \in I(\alpha)$. Clearly α satisfies the assumptions of the second claim. By the induction hypothesis, $\alpha \Rightarrow \delta$ is provable, hence $\gamma \Rightarrow \delta$ is provable, by (L$\wedge$). For $\delta \in I(\beta)$, the reasoning is similar.

$\gamma = \alpha \vee \beta$. Only the first claim is applicable. Let $\delta \in I(\gamma)$. Then, $\delta \in I(\alpha)$ or $\delta \in I(\beta)$. We only consider the first case. Again, α satisfies the assumptions of the first claim. By the induction hypothesis, $\delta \Rightarrow \alpha$ is provable, hence $\delta \Rightarrow \gamma$ is provable, by (R$\vee$).

We extend I to be defined for formula structures: $I(\lambda) = \{\lambda\}$, $I((\Gamma, \Delta)) = \{(\Gamma', \Delta') : \Gamma' \in I(\Gamma), \Delta' \in I(\Delta)\}$, and for sequents: $I(\Gamma \Rightarrow \gamma) = \{\Gamma' \Rightarrow \gamma' : \Gamma' \in I(\Gamma), \gamma' \in I(\gamma)\}$. In words, $I(\Gamma \Rightarrow \gamma)$ consists of all sequents which are obtained from $\Gamma \Rightarrow \gamma$ by replacing every formula α occurring in Γ (as an atomic structure) by some formula $\beta \in I(\alpha)$ and γ by some formula $\delta \in I(\gamma)$.

Lemma 2.5 *Let S be a set of structural rules (a), (e), (i). Let $\Gamma \Rightarrow \gamma$ be a sequent containing no positive occurrence of $\wedge$ and no negative occurrence of $\vee$. Then, $\Gamma \Rightarrow \gamma$ is provable FNL$_S$ (resp. FNL$^*_S$, FNL$_{1S}$) if and only if there exists a sequent $\Gamma' \Rightarrow \gamma' \in I(\Gamma \Rightarrow \gamma)$ such that $\Gamma' \Rightarrow \gamma'$ is provable in NL$_S$ (resp. NL$^*_S$, NL$_{1S}$). This remains true for logics with* $0, \bot, \top$.

Proof We only prove the lemma for FNL$_S$ and NL$_S$; for variants the argument is almost the same.

We prove the 'if' part. Let $\Gamma' \Rightarrow \gamma'$ be provable in NL_S and $\Gamma' \Rightarrow \gamma' \in I(\Gamma \Rightarrow \gamma)$. Every formula α occurring in Γ (as an atomic structure) contains no negative occurrence of $\wedge$ and no positive occurrence of $\vee$, and γ contains no positive occurrence of $\wedge$ and no negative occurrence of $\vee$. Each α in Γ is replaced in Γ' by some $\beta \in I(\alpha)$, but $\alpha \Rightarrow \beta$ is provable in FNL, by Lemma 2.4. Also $\gamma' \Rightarrow \gamma$ is provable in FNL, by Lemma 2.4. Consequently, $\Gamma \Rightarrow \gamma$ is provable in FNL_S, by (CUT).

The 'only if' part is proved by induction on cut-free proofs in FNL_S. For (Id) $\alpha \Rightarrow \alpha$, there exists $\beta \in I(\alpha)$, and $\beta \Rightarrow \beta$ is again (Id). For $\Gamma \Rightarrow \gamma$ being (a.$\top$) or (a.$\bot$), every sequent from $I(\Gamma \Rightarrow \gamma)$ is an axiom of the same kind.

Structural rules (a), (e), (i) cause no problem: we apply the induction hypothesis to the premise, then apply the same rule.

The remaining rules to be considered are all rules for multiplicative connectives and (L$\wedge$), (R$\vee$). For the former rules, the arguments are easy. We only consider (L$\backslash$). The premises are: $\Gamma[\beta] \Rightarrow \gamma$ and $\Delta \Rightarrow \alpha$, and the conclusion is: $\Gamma[(\Delta, \alpha\backslash\beta)] \Rightarrow \gamma$. By the induction hypothesis, there exist sequents $\Gamma'[\beta'] \Rightarrow \gamma' \in I(\Gamma[\beta] \Rightarrow \gamma)$ and $\Delta' \Rightarrow \alpha' \in I(\Delta \Rightarrow \alpha)$, provable in NL_S. By (L$\backslash$), $\Gamma'[(\Delta', \alpha'\backslash\beta')] \Rightarrow \gamma'$ is provable in NL_S, and the latter sequent belongs to $I(\Gamma[(\Delta, \alpha\backslash\beta)] \Rightarrow \gamma)$.

(L$\wedge$). The premise is $\Gamma[\alpha_i] \Rightarrow \gamma$, where $i = 1$ or $i = 2$, and the conclusion is $\Gamma[\alpha_1 \wedge \alpha_2] \Rightarrow \gamma$. By the induction hypothesis, there exists a sequent $\Gamma'[\alpha_i'] \Rightarrow \gamma' \in I(\Gamma[\alpha_i] \Rightarrow \gamma)$, provable in NL_S. Since $\alpha_i' \in I(\alpha_i)$, then $\alpha_i' \in I(\alpha_1 \wedge \alpha_2)$. Consequently, the latter sequent belongs to $I(\Gamma[\alpha_1 \wedge \alpha_2] \Rightarrow \gamma)$.

(R$\vee$). The premise is $\Gamma \Rightarrow \alpha_i$, where $i = 1$ or $i = 2$, and the conclusion is $\Gamma \Rightarrow \alpha_1 \vee \alpha_2$. By the induction hypothesis, there exists a sequent $\Gamma' \Rightarrow \alpha_i' \in I(\Gamma \Rightarrow \alpha_i)$, provable in NL_S. As above, this sequent also belongs to $I(\Gamma \Rightarrow \alpha_1 \vee \alpha_2)$.

Lemma 2.5 does not hold for logics with (c). For instance, $p \wedge q \Rightarrow p \cdot q$ is provable in FNL_c, but neither $p \Rightarrow p \cdot q$, nor $q \Rightarrow p \cdot q$ is provable. The limitation of occurrences of $\wedge$, $\vee$ is essential: $(p, r) \Rightarrow p \cdot r$ is provable, $(p \vee q, r) \Rightarrow p \cdot r$ is not provable, and $(p, r) \Rightarrow p \cdot r \in I((p \vee q, r) \Rightarrow p \cdot r)$, but the occurrence of $\vee$ is negative.

Using Lemma 2.4, one easily proves that for any sequent $\Gamma \Rightarrow \gamma$, containing no negative occurrence of $\wedge$ and no positive occurrence of $\vee$, if $\Gamma \Rightarrow \gamma$ is provable in FNL_S, then every sequent $\Gamma' \Rightarrow \gamma' \in I(\Gamma \Rightarrow \gamma)$ is provable in NL_S (similarly for variants). We leave it as an open problem whether the converse implication holds.

We define multivalued maps N_S' and P_S', which send each formula in language $(\cdot, \backslash, /)$ (possibly with $0, \bot, \top$) into a finite set of such formulae.

$$N_S'(\gamma) = I(N_S(\gamma)), \quad P_S'(\gamma) = I(P_S(\gamma))$$

$N_S'(\Gamma)$ is defined in a similar way as $I(\Gamma)$ above.

Theorem 2.3 Let S be a set of structural rules (a), (e), (i). Let $\Gamma \Rightarrow \gamma$ be a sequent in language $(\cdot, \backslash, /)$, possibly with $0, \bot, \top$, such that $\Gamma \neq \lambda$. Then, $\Gamma \Rightarrow \gamma$ is provable in NL_S^* if and only if there exist $\Gamma' \in N_S'(\Gamma)$, $\gamma' \in P_S'(\gamma)$, such that $\Gamma' \Rightarrow \gamma'$ is provable in NL_S.

Proof Since FNL^*_S is conservative over NL^*_S, then, by Theorem 1, $\Gamma \Rightarrow \gamma$ is provable in NL^*_S if and only if $N_S(\Gamma) \Rightarrow P_S(\gamma)$ is provable FNL_S. The latter sequent satisfies the assumptions of Lemma 2.5: $\wedge$ (resp. $\vee$) can only be introduced by N_S (resp. P_S), and N_S (resp. P_S) acts on negative (resp. positive) occurrences of subformulae in $\Gamma \Rightarrow \gamma$, hence all occurrences of $\wedge$ (resp. $\vee$) in $N_S(\Gamma) \Rightarrow P_S(\gamma)$ are negative (resp. positive). Therefore, $N_S(\Gamma) \Rightarrow P_S(\gamma)$ is provable in FNL_S if and only if there exists $\Gamma' \Rightarrow \gamma' \in I(N_S(\Gamma) \Rightarrow P_S(\gamma))$, provable in NL_S. Clearly $\Gamma' \in N'_S(\Gamma)$, $\gamma' \in P'_S(\gamma)$.

2.4 Distributive and Modal Logics

We extend the results of Sect. 2.2 for logics corresponding to algebras based on distributive lattices, i.e., DFNL^*_S and DFNL_S, and logics with unary modalities $\Diamond$, $\Box$.

As we have noted in Sect. 2.1, DFNL can be axiomatized as FNL with (D), but this system does not allow cut elimination. Another axiomatization (of DFL_1) was proposed by Kozak [18], following similar solutions for relevant logics, due to J.M. Dunn and G. Mints. We recall it (for DFNL and its variants) with minor modifications.

The new axiomatization admits two structural operators: besides $(,)$, corresponding to product, also $(,)_\wedge$, corresponding to $\wedge$. Precisely, the formula structures are recursively defined as follows: (i) all formulae are (atomic) formula structures, (ii) if Γ, Δ are formula structures, then (Γ, Δ) and $(\Gamma, \Delta)_\wedge$ are formula structures. In models, $(\Gamma, \Delta)_\wedge$ is interpreted as $f(\Gamma) \wedge f(\Delta)$ (see the definition of f in Sect. 2.1).

The axioms and rules of DFNL are those of FNL except that $(\mathrm{L}\wedge)$ is replaced by:

$$(\mathrm{L}\wedge\mathrm{D})\ \frac{\Gamma[(\alpha, \beta)_\wedge] \Rightarrow \gamma}{\Gamma[\alpha \wedge \beta] \Rightarrow \gamma},$$

and one adds structural rules (a), (e), (i), (c) for $(,)_\wedge$.

$$(\mathrm{a}\wedge)\ \frac{\Gamma[((\Delta_1, \Delta_2)_\wedge, \Delta_3)_\wedge] \Rightarrow \gamma}{\Gamma[(\Delta_1, (\Delta_2, \Delta_3)_\wedge)_\wedge] \Rightarrow \gamma} \quad (\mathrm{e}\wedge)\ \frac{\Gamma[(\Delta_1, \Delta_2)_\wedge] \Rightarrow \gamma}{\Gamma[(\Delta_2, \Delta_1)_\wedge] \Rightarrow \gamma}$$

$$(\mathrm{i}\wedge)\ \frac{\Gamma[\Delta_i] \Rightarrow \alpha}{\Gamma[(\Delta_1, \Delta_2)_\wedge] \Rightarrow \gamma},\quad (\mathrm{c}\wedge)\ \frac{\Gamma[(\Delta, \Delta)_\wedge] \Rightarrow \alpha}{\Gamma[\Delta] \Rightarrow \gamma}$$

DFNL^* admits the empty formula structure λ. Notice that λ is the unit for $(,)$ but not for $(,)_\wedge$. By adding the constant 1 and $(\mathrm{L}1_l)$, $(\mathrm{L}1_r)$, $(\mathrm{R}1)$, we obtain DFNL_1. As above, we can also add any set S, of structural rules (a), (e), (i), (c) (for $(,)$), which yields logics DFNL_S, DFNL^*_S and DFNL_{1S}. Again, logics with (a) are denoted by DFL_S, DFL^*_S and DFL_{1S}.

Formula structures $(\lambda, \Delta)_\wedge$ and $(\Delta, \lambda)_\wedge$ can be introduced by $(\mathrm{i}\wedge)$; in general, they are not equal to Δ. Nonetheless, one may ignore them in any system DFNL^*_S. If S does not contain (i), then these structures cannot appear in any proof tree (also involving (CUT)) of a sequent not containing them. If S contains (i), then they can appear in such proofs (λ can be eliminated, using (i)), but we assume that λ is the unit for both $(\,,\,)$ and $(\,,\,)_\wedge$; so $(\lambda, \Delta)_\wedge = (\Delta, \lambda)_\wedge = \Delta$.

Kozak [18] proves that DFL_1 without (CUT) is complete with respect to (finite) residuated distributive lattices, which yields an algebraic proof of the cut-elimination theorem ([18] employs quasi-embeddings, used earlier for other substructural logics in [2, 12, 31]). In a similar way (or by standard, syntactic arguments), one can prove the cut-elimination theorem for all systems DFNL_{1S}, DFNL^*_S, DFNL_S. All nonassociative logics DFNL_{1S}, DFNL^*_S, DFNL_S are decidable; each of them possesses the finite embeddability property, which yields the decidability of the corresponding consequence relation (with finitely many assumptions) [7, 9, 15]. Kozak [18] shows the finite model property of DFL_1, DFL_{1e}, DFL_{1i}, DFL_{1ei}, hence these logics are decidable. This yields the decidability of their 1-free fragments; similar methods bring the decidability of DFL, DFL_e, DFL_i, DFL_{ei}. With (i) all DFL_S are decidable; this problem is open for versions with (c) (but without (i)).

Theorem 2.1 remains true for DFNL^*_S versus DFNL_S with no essential changes in definitions and proofs (the new structural rules and (L$\wedge$D) cause no problems). N_S and P_S are defined by Table 2.1, and $N_S((\Gamma, \Delta)_\wedge) = (N_S(\Gamma), N_S(\Delta))_\wedge$. Warning: $\vdash^*$ and $\vdash$ denote here the provability in DFNL^*_S and DFNL_S, respectively. In the analogue of Theorem 2.1, we assume that no substructure of Γ is represented as $(\lambda, \Delta)_\wedge$ or $(\Delta, \lambda)_\wedge$.

Theorem 2.2 holds for associative systems. Since we do not represent formula structures as sequences, auxiliary axioms (a.1), (a.2), used in the proof, must be appropriately modified; the details are left to the reader.

The results of Sect. 2.3 remain true, but they bring nothing new, since the multiplicative fragment of DFNL^*_S (resp. DFNL_S) equals NL^*_S (resp. NL_S). This also holds for the fragments restricted to only negative occurrences of $\wedge$ and only positive occurrences of $\vee$.

Now we consider logics with unary modalities $\Diamond, \Box^\downarrow$, treated as multiplicative operators. The corresponding sequent systems admit one new unary structural operation, traditionally symbolized by $\langle\,\rangle$. The introduction rules for $\Diamond, \Box^\downarrow$ are as follows.

$$(\mathrm{L}\Diamond)\ \frac{\Gamma[\langle\alpha\rangle] \Rightarrow \beta}{\Gamma[\Diamond\alpha] \Rightarrow \beta}\quad (\mathrm{R}\Diamond)\ \frac{\Gamma \Rightarrow \alpha}{\langle\Gamma\rangle \Rightarrow \Diamond\alpha}$$

$$(\mathrm{L}\Box^\downarrow)\ \frac{\Gamma[\alpha] \Rightarrow \beta}{\Gamma[\langle\Box^\downarrow\alpha\rangle] \Rightarrow \beta}\quad (\mathrm{R}\Box^\downarrow)\ \frac{\langle\Gamma\rangle \Rightarrow \beta}{\Gamma \Rightarrow \Box^\downarrow\beta}$$

NL with $\Diamond, \Box^\downarrow$ and the above rules is denoted by $\mathrm{NL}\Diamond$, and a similar notation is used for other systems, e.g. $\mathrm{FNL}\Diamond^*$ is an analogous extension of FNL^*, $\mathrm{FNL}\Diamond_1$ of FNL_1, $\mathrm{FL}\Diamond_1$ of FL_1, and so on. These logics are special instances of systems of Full Generalized Lambek Calculus (FGL); see [7].

The cut-elimination theorem holds for systems of this kind, also with structural rules (a), (e), (i), (c); [26] provides some proofs. This remains true for these logics enriched with special modal rules:

$$(\text{r.K}_s)\ \frac{\Gamma[(\langle\Delta_1\rangle, \langle\Delta_2\rangle)] \Rightarrow \gamma}{\Gamma[\langle(\Delta_1, \Delta_2)\rangle] \Rightarrow \gamma},$$

$$(\text{r.T})\ \frac{\Gamma[\langle\Delta\rangle] \Rightarrow \gamma}{\Gamma[\Delta] \Rightarrow \gamma}\quad (\text{r.4})\ \frac{\Gamma[\langle\Delta\rangle] \Rightarrow \gamma}{\Gamma[\langle\langle\Delta\rangle\rangle] \Rightarrow \gamma}.$$

In systems with (CUT), these rules are equivalent to modal axioms:

$$(\text{K}_s)\ \Diamond(\alpha \cdot \beta) \Rightarrow (\Diamond\alpha) \cdot (\Diamond\beta),\ (\text{T.})\ \alpha \Rightarrow \Diamond\alpha,\ (4.)\ \Diamond\Diamond\alpha \Rightarrow \Diamond\alpha.$$

(K_s) is deductively equivalent to $\Box^{\downarrow}(\alpha\backslash\beta) \Rightarrow \Box^{\downarrow}\alpha\backslash\Box^{\downarrow}\beta$, the latter resembling the axiom (K) of classical modal logics. Without (c) all modal substructural logics of this kind are decidable. $\text{FL}\Diamond_{1c}$ and $\text{FL}\Diamond_c$ are undecidable, as conservative extensions of FL_{1c} and FL_c, respectively.

NL$\Diamond$ is complete with respect to residuated groupoids with unary operations $\Diamond, \Box^{\downarrow}$, satisfying *the unary residuation law*: $\Diamond a \leq b$ iff $a \leq \Box^{\downarrow}b$, for all elements a, b. Accordingly, $\Box^{\downarrow}$ is the right residual of $\Diamond$. Analogous completeness theorems hold for other logics of this kind with respect to the appropriate classes of algebras with $\Diamond, \Box^{\downarrow}$.

Substructural logics with $\Diamond, \Box^{\downarrow}$ are interesting for many reasons. Unary residuated pairs represent, in a sense, the basic species of residuation; up to the direction of order they amount to Galois connections. They were applied in type grammars in order to refine typing of natural language expressions; see [26, 29, 30]. Let us give one simple example. The initial types 'he': np, 'her': np, 'likes': (np\s)/np yield 'he likes her': s on the basis of NL. Proper nouns inhabit a subtype of np. Since $\Diamond\Box^{\downarrow}\alpha \Rightarrow \alpha$ is provable in NL$\Diamond$, one can define pn $= \Diamond\Box^{\downarrow}$np. Then, adjectives can be typed pn/pn, which yields 'he likes poor Jane': s, but 'he likes poor her': s cannot be derived, in accordance with the English grammar.

We extend the translations N_S, P_S for the language with $\Diamond, \Box^{\downarrow}$, by setting:

$$P_S(O\alpha) = OP_S(\alpha),\ N_S(O\alpha) = ON_S(\alpha),\ \text{for } O \in \{\Diamond, \Box^{\downarrow}\}.$$

Observe that sequents in $\text{FNL}\Diamond_S^*$ can contain substructures $\langle\lambda\rangle$. All explicit occurrences of λ in nonempty formula structures are of this form. In opposition to the situation for DFNL_S^*, these substructures can appear in proof trees of sequents not containing them. For instance, ($\text{R}\Box^{\downarrow}$) infers $\Rightarrow \Box^{\downarrow}\alpha$ from $\langle\lambda\rangle \Rightarrow \alpha$. $\langle\lambda\rangle$ can be introduced by ($\text{R}\Diamond$) and (i).

A formula structure Γ is said to be λ-*free*, if $\Gamma \neq \lambda$ and Γ contains no substructure $\langle\lambda\rangle$. For any structure Γ, $N_S(\Gamma)$ is obtained by replacing each formula α occurring in Γ (as an atomic substructure) by $N_S(\alpha)$.

The results of Sect. 2.2 can be extended for logics with $\Diamond, \Box^{\downarrow}$. In the proofs of Lemmas 2.1 and 2.2, we use the monotonicity (hence also extensionality) of $\Diamond$ and $\Box^{\downarrow}$ in these logics.

For S not containing (i), the claim (I) of Theorem 1 holds for all sequents $\Gamma \Rightarrow \gamma$ such that Γ is λ-free. It is essential that in proof trees of these sequents, only λ-free structures appear in antecedents except for the empty antecedents (handled as in Sect. 2.1) and the subproofs of sequents $\Rightarrow \alpha$ (not essential in the proof of (I)). The proof follows the one in Sect. 2.1; the 'only if' part involves new cases, corresponding to the introduction rules for $\Diamond, \Box^{\downarrow}$.

We consider (R$\Box^{\downarrow}$). The premise is $\langle\Gamma\rangle \Rightarrow \beta$, and the conclusion is $\Gamma \Rightarrow \Box^{\downarrow}\beta$. By the induction hypothesis, $\langle N(\Gamma)\rangle \Rightarrow P(\beta)$ is provable in FNL$\Diamond_S$, hence $N(\Gamma) \Rightarrow \Box^{\downarrow}P(\beta)$ is provable in FNL$\Diamond_S$ and $\Box^{\downarrow}P(\beta) = P(\Box^{\downarrow}\beta)$. The remaining rules are left to the reader.

For S containing (i), we need an auxiliary notion. A pseudo-substitution θ is defined as follows: $\theta(\Gamma)$ replaces each explicit occurrence of λ in Γ by $q\backslash q$, where q is a fixed variable (q may occur in the sequents under consideration). As above, Theorem 2.1 remains true for λ-free Γ (in both (I) and (II)). It is easier to prove the following, stronger version.

Theorem 2.4 Let S contain (i). (I) For any sequent $\Gamma \Rightarrow \gamma$ such that $\Gamma \neq \lambda$, $\Gamma \Rightarrow \gamma$ is provable in FNL$\Diamond^*_S$ if and only if $N_S(\theta(\Gamma)) \Rightarrow P_S(\gamma)$ is provable in FNL$\Diamond_S$. (II) For any formula γ, if γ is provable in FNL$\Diamond^*_S$, then for any λ-free Γ, $\Gamma \Rightarrow P_S(\gamma)$ is provable in FNL$\Diamond_S$.

Proof The proof is similar to that of Theorem 2.1. The 'if' part of (I) follows from the analogue of Lemma 2.2, the equality $N_S(q\backslash q) = q\backslash q$, and the provability of $\lambda \Rightarrow q\backslash q$ in FNL$\Diamond^*_S$. (II) and the 'only if' part of (I) are proved by simultaneous induction on cut-free proofs in FNL$\Diamond^*_S$ (precisely: on the number of sequents appearing in the proof tree). Most arguments are entirely similar, and we do not repeat them. We only consider two new cases.

The proof of (I): (R$\Diamond$) with the premise $\Rightarrow \alpha$ and the conclusion $\langle\lambda\rangle \Rightarrow \Diamond\alpha$. By the induction hypothesis, applied to (II), $q\backslash q \Rightarrow P(\alpha)$ is provable in FNL$\Diamond_S$, hence $\langle q\backslash q\rangle \Rightarrow \Diamond P(\alpha)$ is provable in FNL$\Diamond_S$. So $N(\theta(\langle\lambda\rangle)) \Rightarrow P(\Diamond\alpha)$ is provable in FNL$\Diamond_S$.

The proof of (II): (R$\Box^{\downarrow}$) with the premise $\langle\lambda\rangle \Rightarrow \beta$ and the conclusion $\Rightarrow \Box^{\downarrow}\beta$. By the induction hypothesis, applied to (I), $\langle q\backslash q\rangle \Rightarrow P(\beta)$ is provable in FNL$\Diamond_S$, hence $q\backslash q \Rightarrow P(\Box^{\downarrow}\beta)$ is provable in FNL$\Diamond_S$. Let Γ be λ-free. FNL$\Diamond_S$ proves $\Gamma \Rightarrow q\backslash q$, by (Id), (i), (L\), hence also $\Gamma \Rightarrow P(\Box^{\downarrow}\beta)$, by (CUT).

These results can also be proved for DFNL$\Diamond^*_S$ versus DFNL$\Diamond_S$; λ-free formula structures are required to contain neither $\langle\lambda\rangle$, nor structures of the form $(\lambda, \Delta)_\wedge$, $(\Delta, \lambda)_\wedge$. All nonassociative logics DFNL$\Diamond_{1S}$, DFNL$\Diamond^*_S$. DFNL$\Diamond_S$ are decidable [7]. We leave it for further research how to formulate and to prove them for logics with special modal rules (axioms). One faces new difficulties, especially for logics without (i). For instance, (r.K$_S$) and (r.T) can eliminate $\langle\lambda\rangle$, hence $\Gamma \Rightarrow \gamma$, where Γ is λ-free, can be inferred from sequents with $\langle\lambda\rangle$.

Without (i), the provability in FNL$\Diamond^*_S$ cannot be fully reduced to the provability in FNL$\Diamond_S$. $\Box^{\downarrow}\alpha$ is provable if and only if $\langle\lambda\rangle \Rightarrow \alpha$ is provable, but the latter is not expressible in FNL$\Diamond_S$. With (i), using Theorem 2.4.(I), we obtain the conditions:

(Pr.5) $\vdash^* \Box^{\downarrow}\alpha$ iff $\vdash \langle q\backslash q\rangle \Rightarrow P(\alpha)$,
(Pr.6) $\nvdash^* \Diamond\alpha$.

Kuznetsov's reduction does not work for $\mathrm{FL}\Diamond_{1S}$, if (i) is not in S. $(1, \langle p\rangle) \Rightarrow \Diamond p$ is provable, by (Id), (R$\Diamond$), (L1_l), but $(q\backslash q, \langle((q\backslash q)\cdot p)\cdot(q\backslash q)\rangle) \Rightarrow \Diamond(((q\backslash q)\cdot p)\cdot(q\backslash q))$ is not provable.

The results of Sect. 2.3 can be extended for multiplicative fragments of $\mathrm{FNL}\Diamond^*_S$, $\mathrm{FNL}\Diamond_S$, if S does not contain (c). For unary operators O, one defines $I(O\alpha) = O(I(\alpha))$, where $O(U) = \{O\alpha : \alpha \in U\}$.

2.5 Applications

We discuss two applications of the translations N, P. First, we show that, essentially, the (phrase) languages generated by type grammars based on the logic $\mathcal{L}^*$, allowing empty antecedents, are also generated by type grammars based on the subsystem $\mathcal{L}$, not allowing empty antecedents.

We assume that $\mathcal{L}^*$ and $\mathcal{L}$ are formalized in the same language and satisfy (N-P): for any sequent $\Gamma \Rightarrow \gamma$ such that $\Gamma \neq \lambda$ and all atomic substructures of Γ are formulae of the language, $\Gamma \Rightarrow \gamma$ is provable in $\mathcal{L}^*$ if and only if $N(\Gamma) \Rightarrow P(\gamma)$ is provable in $\mathcal{L}$. N, P are some fixed translations within this formal language. We assume $N(p) = p$, for any variable p.

Proposition 2.1 *For any $\mathcal{L}^*$-grammar G, there exists an $\mathcal{L}$-grammar G' such that $L^P(G') = L^P(G) - \{\lambda\}$ and $L(G') = L(G) - \{\epsilon\}$.*

Proof Let $G = (\Sigma_G, I_G, \delta_G)$. We define G' by: $\Sigma_{G'} = \Sigma_G$, $\delta_{G'} = P(\delta_G)$, $I_{G'}(a) = \{N(\alpha) : \alpha \in I_G(a)\}$. Since $\mathcal{L}$ does not admit λ, then $\lambda \notin L^P(G')$. By induction on the size of X, one proves: for any $X \in \Sigma^P_G$, $I_{G'}(X) = \{N(\Gamma) : \Gamma \in I_G(X)\}$. This yields: $X \in L^P(G')$ iff there exists $\Delta \in I_{G'}(X)$ such that $\Delta \Rightarrow \delta_{G'}$ is provable in $\mathcal{L}$ iff there exists $\Gamma \in I_G(X)$ such that $N(\Gamma) \Rightarrow P(\delta_G)$ is provable in $\mathcal{L}$ iff there exists $\Gamma \in I_G(X)$ such that $\Gamma \Rightarrow \delta_G$ is provable in $\mathcal{L}^*$ iff $X \in L^P(G)$. So $L^P(G') = L^P(G) - \{\lambda\}$, and consequently, $L(G') = L(G) - \{\epsilon\}$.

We additionally assume that no variable in provable in $\mathcal{L}^*$. For extensions of FNL*, this requirement is equivalent to the consistency of $\mathcal{L}^*$. Recall that a sequent system is *consistent*, if not all sequents are provable.

Corollary 2.2 *For any $\mathcal{L}^*$-grammar G such that δ_G is a variable, there exists an $\mathcal{L}$-grammar G' such that $L^P(G') = L^P(G)$ and $L(G') = L(G)$.*

Proof This follows from Proposition 2.1 and the unprovability of $\Rightarrow s_G$ (hence $\lambda \notin L^P(G)$).

These results (together with those from Sects. 2.2, 2.3 and 2.4) show that the generative capacity of type logics admitting λ is not essentially greater than that of type logics without λ, both for phrase languages and string languages.

Theorem 2.3 implies analogous consequences for type grammars without additives. Now $I_{G'}(a) = \bigcup\{N'(\alpha) : \alpha \in I_G(a)\}$. If δ_G is a variable, then $P'(\delta_G) = \{\delta_G\}$, which yields Corollary 2, for $\delta_{G'} = \delta_G$. If δ_G is compound, then $P'(\delta_G)$ may contain several types, say, $\delta_1, \ldots, \delta_n$. Let G'_i be defined as G' except that δ_i is the designated type. Clearly $L^P(G) - \{\lambda\}$ is the union of all $L^P(G'_i)$, for $i = 1, \ldots, n$, and similarly for string languages. All basic families of formal languages, e.g. regular languages, context-free languages, context-sensitive languages, r.e. languages, are closed under finite unions.

We omit a detailed discussion of the generative capacity of the particular classes of type grammars; the reader is referred to [4, 9, 29]. Let us only note that AB-grammars, L-grammars, NL-grammars generate the ϵ-free context-free languages, FL-grammars generate a proper superclass of ϵ-free context-free languages [17], but DFNL-grammars remain context-free [9]. Lin [23, 24] prove the context-freeness of type grammars based on some modal extensions of NL and DFNL.

The second application concerns the computational complexity of substructural logics. Horčik and Terui [16] prove the following, general theorem.

(HT) Every consistent substructural logic, possessing the disjunction property (DP), is PSPACE-hard.

By a substructural logic one means here an extension of FL_1 by additional axioms and rules (possibly in a richer language, e.g. with 0, $\bot$, $\top$; one can also add unary operators and others). (DP) means: if $\alpha \vee \beta$ is provable, then α is provable or β is provable.

Buszkowski [8] proves the following, stronger theorem: every logic $\mathcal{L}$ such that FL$\subseteq \mathcal{L} \subseteq \mathcal{L}'$, for some consistent substructural logic $\mathcal{L}'$, possessing (DP), is PSPACE-hard. Here $\subseteq$ denotes the inclusion between the sets of provable sequents of the form $\alpha \Rightarrow \beta$ or $\Rightarrow \alpha$. The reader is referred to [8, 16] for a discussion of the significance of these results. For some particular logics, the PSPACE-hardness (PSPACE-completeness) was proved earlier, e.g. IL (intuitionistic logic), FL_1, MALL ((DP) holds for each of them). By the theorem from [8], FL_S and DFL_S are PSPACE-hard: they extend FL and are contained in IL (IL can be identified with $FL_{1\bot eic}$ with $0 = \bot$). This cannot be inferred from (HT). See [8] for other examples.

Here we further generalize this theorem towards nonassociative logics. By $(a\downarrow)$ we denote the top-down direction of (a) (in algebras, this corresponds to right-associativity: $a \cdot (b \cdot c) \leq (a \cdot b) \cdot c$).

Proposition 2.2 *Every logic $\mathcal{L}$ such that $FNL_{(a\downarrow)} \subseteq \mathcal{L} \subseteq \mathcal{L}'$, for some consistent substructural logic $\mathcal{L}'$, possessing (DP), is PSPACE-hard.*

By symmetry, (a$\downarrow$) can be replaced by (a$\uparrow$), i.e., the bottom-up direction of (a). With (e) each of them yields (a).

To outline the proof we must recall some points of the proofs of (HT) and the version from [8].

Horčik and Terui [16] reduces the validity problem for closed quantified boolean formulae (QBFs) to the provability problem in the logic $\mathcal{L}$, fulfilling the assumptions of (HT). A closed QBF has the form $Q_n x_n \ldots Q_1 x_1 \varphi_0$, where $Q_i \in \{\forall, \exists\}$

and φ_0 is a boolean formula in DNF, whose variables are $x_1, \ldots, x_n$. Let $\varphi_k = Q_k x_k \ldots Q_1 x_1 \varphi_0$, for $k = 0, \ldots, n$. The formula φ_k is encoded by a formula α_k of $\mathcal{L}$.

We recall the encoding with minor changes of notation. One fixes different variables $p_k, \bar{p}_k, q_k$, for $k = 1, \ldots, n$. Let $\varphi_0 = \psi_1 \vee \cdots \vee \psi_m$, where each ψ_j is a finite conjunction of literals. One encodes ψ_j by $\beta_j = \delta_1 \cdot \delta_2 \cdots \delta_n$, where: (1) $\delta_i = p_i$ if ψ_j contains the literal x_i, (2) $\delta_i = \bar{p}_i$ if ψ_j contains the literal $\neg x_i$, (3) $\delta_i = p_i \vee \bar{p}_i$ otherwise. One defines $\alpha_0 = \beta_1 \vee \cdots \vee \beta_m$. For $k = 1, \ldots, n$, one defines: (1) $\alpha_k = (p_k \vee \bar{p}_k)\backslash\alpha_{k-1}$ if $Q_k = \forall$, (2) $\alpha_k = (p_k\backslash q_k \vee \bar{p}_k\backslash q_k)/(\alpha_{k-1}\backslash q_k)$ if $Q_k = \exists$.

For $k = 0, \ldots, n$, e_k denotes a partial valuation which assigns truth values to $x_{k+1}, \ldots, x_n$; so e_n is the empty valuation. One represents e_k by the sequence $\varepsilon_k = (r_{k+1}, \ldots, r_n)$, where: (1) $r_i = p_i$ if $e_k(x_i) = 1$, (2) $r_i = \bar{p}_i$ if $e_k(x_i) = 0$; so ε_n is the empty sequence. By set(ε_k) we denote the set of variables occurring in ε_k. Two crucial lemmas in [16] can be summarized as follows (in (iii) $\vdash$ denotes the provability from assumptions).

(T1) For any $k = 0, 1, \ldots, n$, the following conditions are equivalent: (i) e_k satisfies φ_k, (ii) $\varepsilon_k \Rightarrow \alpha_k$ is provable in $\mathcal{L}$, (iii) set(ε_k) $\vdash \alpha_k$ in $\mathcal{L}$.

As a consequence, φ is valid if and only if α_n is provable in $\mathcal{L}$, which yields the desired reduction. (T1) is proved by simultaneous induction on k. The implication (ii) $\Rightarrow$(iii) is obvious, so the nontrivial steps are (i) $\Rightarrow$(ii) and (iii) $\Rightarrow$(i). For $k = 0$, (iii) $\Rightarrow$(i) employs Lemma A: in any nontrivial residuated lattice, 1 is not a minimal element. (DP) is used to prove the inductive step (iii) $\Rightarrow$(i) for $Q_k = \exists$. In fact, one uses Lemma B: if U is a set of variables and $U \vdash \alpha \vee \beta$ in $\mathcal{L}$, then $U \vdash \alpha$ or $U \vdash \beta$ in $\mathcal{L}$ (this follows from (DP)).

We have no space to recall more details of the proof. Already from the above it can be seen that empty antecedents and models with 1 play an essential role. Also the proof of the inductive step (iii)$\Rightarrow$(i) employs the law $\beta/(\gamma\backslash\gamma) \Rightarrow \beta$, provable in FL*, not in FL. Furthermore, (DP) lacks sense for logics not allowing empty antecedents. This proof cannot directly be adapted for logics like FL, DFL, etc.

Buszkowski [8] observes that the proof from [16] yields a stronger result: every logic $\mathcal{L}$ such that $\mathrm{FL}_1 \subseteq \mathcal{L} \subseteq \mathcal{L}'$, for some consistent substructural logic $\mathcal{L}'$, possessing (DP), is PSPACE-hard. For, if φ is valid, then α_n is provable in FL_1, hence in $\mathcal{L}$; if α_n is provable in $\mathcal{L}$, then α_n is provable in $\mathcal{L}'$, hence φ is valid. Therefore, φ is valid if and only if α_n is provable in $\mathcal{L}$.

Buszkowski [8] replaces FL_1 by FL. We recall some main points. First, φ is replaced by χ, which is obtained from φ by adding the literal x_{n+1} to every ψ_j. All valuations e_k are supposed to assign 1 to x_{n+1}; so e_n is defined for x_{n+1} only and assigns 1 to it. Clearly φ is valid if and only if e_n satisfies χ. We encode χ_k by α_k, as above (but now we have one new variable p_{n+1}; we do not use $\bar{p}_{n+1}$).

(T1) entails (T2): φ is valid if and only if $p_{n+1} \Rightarrow \alpha_n$ is provable in $\mathcal{L}'$. In particular, (T2) holds for $\mathcal{L}' = \mathrm{FL}_1$, and FL_1 can be replaced by FL*, since α_n does not contain 1. One also shows: $P(\alpha_k) = \alpha_k$, for $k = 0, \ldots, n$; so $p_{n+1} \Rightarrow \alpha_n$ is stable in FL. The proof of this equality uses the unprovability of α_k, for any $k \leq n$.

By Corollary 2.1 and the above, φ is valid if and only if $p_{n+1} \Rightarrow \alpha_n$ is provable in FL. This equivalence holds for both FL and $\mathcal{L}'$, so it holds for $\mathcal{L}$ as well.

The proof does not work for nonassociative logics. A closer examination shows that (a) is essential precisely in the inductive step for (i)⇒(ii), with $Q_k = \exists$, in the proof of (T1). Let us recall the argument. Assume that e_k satisfies φ_k. Then, e_k can be extended to e_{k-1}, satisfying φ_{k-1}. Assume $e_{k-1}(x_k) = 1$. By the induction hypothesis, $p_k, \varepsilon_k \Rightarrow \alpha_{k-1}$ is provable. Hence $p_k, \varepsilon_k, \alpha_{k-1}\backslash q_k \Rightarrow q_k$ is provable, by (Id), (L\), which yields $\varepsilon_k, \alpha_{k-1}\backslash q_k \Rightarrow p_k\backslash q_k$, by (R\) (associativity). By (R∨), we get $\varepsilon_k, \alpha_{k-1}\backslash q_k \Rightarrow p_k\backslash q_k \vee \bar{p}_k\backslash q_k$, hence $\varepsilon_k \Rightarrow \alpha_k$, by (R/). For $e_{k-1}(x_k) = 0$, the argument is similar.

We can reconstruct the encoding and carry out all other steps of the proof in nonassociative logics: we replace sequences of formulae by formula structures with parentheses associated to the right, e.g. (p_1, p_2, p_3) by $(p_1, (p_2, p_3))$, and similarly for products of several formulae (in β_j). Lemma A holds for unital lattice-ordered residuated groupoids, and Lemma B for extensions of FNL_1. The argument in the preceding paragraph really employs (a↓). Indeed, from $((p_k, \varepsilon_k), \alpha_{k-1}\backslash q_k) \Rightarrow q_k$ we infer $(p_k, (\varepsilon_k, \alpha_{k-1}\backslash q_k)) \Rightarrow q_k$, then apply (R\), (R∨), (R/). This yields Proposition 2.2. As shown in [25], (a↓) is derivable in Residuated Basic Logic (RBL), being a conservative extension of Basic Propositional Logic, hence RBL is PSPACE-hard.

We can replace right-associativity by mixed associativity: $a \cdot (b \odot c) \leq (a \cdot b) \odot c$. Here $\cdot$ and $\odot$ are two products; \, / are the residual operations for the former, and $\backslash_\odot, /^\odot$ for the latter. FNL^2 denotes the variant of FNL admitting new connectives $\odot, \backslash_\odot, /^\odot$ and the new structural operator $(,)_\odot$. The rule of *mixed associativity* is the following:

$$\text{(ma)}\ \frac{\Gamma[((\Delta_1, \Delta_2), \Delta_3)_\odot] \Rightarrow \gamma}{\Gamma[(\Delta_1, (\Delta_2, \Delta_3)_\odot)] \Rightarrow \gamma}.$$

Algebraic models are lattice-ordered *double residuated groupoids*: the binary residuation law:

$$a \cdot b \leq c \text{ iff } b \leq a\backslash c \text{ iff } a \leq c/b$$

holds for both $\cdot, \backslash, /$ and $\odot, \backslash_\odot, /^\odot$. In unital algebras, 1 is the unit for $\cdot$ and $\odot$. The encoding is modified for $Q_k = \exists$: $\alpha_k = (p_k\backslash q_k \vee \bar{p}_k\backslash q_k)/^\odot(\alpha_{k-1}\backslash_\odot q_k)$. The proof, presented above, can be transformed into a proof of Proposition 2 with $\mathrm{FNL}^2_{(ma)}$ in the place of $\mathrm{FNL}_{(a\downarrow)}$.

Associativity can be entirely avoided in a different way. One may encode $Q_k = \exists$ by: $\alpha_k = p_k\backslash\alpha_{k-1} \vee \bar{p}_k\backslash\alpha_{k-1}$. Then, all arguments above remain correct for nonassociative logics. Unfortunately, the encoding is not polynomial. It becomes polynomial, if formulae are represented as directed acyclic graphs: each (free) subformula occupies only one node of the graph (like in circuits). Therefore, Proposition 2.2 is true for FNL in the place of $\mathrm{FNL}_{(a\downarrow)}$, with formulae represented as dags. With the standard representation, we can only prove the coNP-hardness (the validity of QBFs without $\exists$ can be reduced to the provability in FNL^*, hence in FNL, as above).

References

1. Y. Bar-Hillel, Ch. Gaifman, and E. Shamir. On categorial and phrase structure grammars. *Bulletin Res. Council Israel*, F(9):155–166, 1960.
2. F. Belardinelli, P. Jipsen, and H. Ono. Algebraic aspects of cut elimination. *Studia Logica*, 77(2):209–240.
3. W. Buszkowski. Completeness results for Lambek syntactic calculus. *Zeitschrift f. mathematische Logik und Grundlagen der Mathematik*, 32(1):13–28, 1986.
4. W. Buszkowski. Mathematical linguistics and proof theory. In van Benthem and ter Meulen [33], pages 683–736.
5. W. Buszkowski. Finite models of some substructural logics. *Mathematical Logic Quarterly*, 48(1):63–72, 2002.
6. W. Buszkowski. Lambek calculus with nonlogical axioms. In Casadio et al. [10], pages 77–93.
7. W. Buszkowski. Interpolation and FEP for logics of residuated algebras. *Logic Journal of the IGPL*, 19(3):437–454, 2011.
8. W. Buszkowski. An interpretation of Full Lambek Calculus in its variant without empty antecedents of sequents. In N. Asher and S.Soloviev, editors, *Logical Aspects of Computational Linguistics. LACL 2014*, volume 8535 of *LNCS*, pages 30–43. 2014.
9. W. Buszkowski and M. Farulewski. Nonassociative Lambek calculus with additives and context-free languages. In *Languages: From Formal to Natural*, volume 5533 of *LNCS*, pages 45–58. 2009.
10. C. Casadio, P. J. Scott, and R. A. Seely, editors. *Language and Grammar. Studies in Mathematical Linguistics and Natural Language*. CSLI Publications, 2005.
11. A. Clark. A learnable representation for syntax using residuated lattices. In P. de Groote, M. Egg, and L. Kallmeyer, editors, *Formal Grammar. FG 2009*, volume 5591 of *Lecture Notes in Artificial Intelligence*, pages 183–198. Springer, 2011.
12. N. Galatos, P. Jipsen, T. Kowalski, and H. Ono. *Residuated Lattices: An Algebraic Glimpse at Substructural Logics*. Studies in Logic and The Foundations of Mathematics. Elsevier, 2007.
13. N. Galatos and H. Ono. Cut elimination and strong separation for substructural logics: an algebraic approach. *Annals of Pure and Applied Logic*, 161(9):1097–1133, 2010.
14. J.-Y. Girard. Linear logic. *Theoretical Computer Science*, 50:1–102, 1987.
15. Z. Haniková and R. Horčik. The finite embeddability property for residuated groupoids. *Algebra Universalis*, 72(1):1–13, 2014.
16. R. Horčik and K. Terui. Disjunction property and complexity of substructural logics. *Theoretical Computer Science*, 412:3992–4006, 2011.
17. M. Kanazawa. The Lambek calculus enriched with additional connectives. *Journal of Logic, Language and Information*, 1(2), 1992.
18. M. Kozak. Distributive Full Lambek Calculus has the finite model property. *Studia Logica*, 91(2):201–216, 2009.
19. S. Kuznetsov. Lambek grammars with the unit. In P. de Groote and M.-J. Nederhof, editors, *Formal Grammar 2010/2011*, volume 7395 of *LNCS*, pages 262–266. Springer, 2012.
20. J. Lambek. The mathematics of sentence structure. *American Mathematical Monthly*, 65:154–170, 1958.
21. J. Lambek. On the calculus of syntactic types. In R. Jakobson, editor, *Structure of Language and Its Mathematical Aspects*, pages 166–178. American Mathematical Society, Providence, 1961.
22. J. Lambek. *From Word to Sentence: a computational algebraic approach to grammar*. Polimetrica, 2008.
23. Z. Lin. Modal nonassociative Lambek calculus with assumptions: complexity and context-freeness. In *Language and Automata Theory and Applications. LATA 2010*, volume 6031 of *LNCS*, pages 414–425. Springer, 2010.
24. Z. Lin. Distributive Full Nonassociative Lambek Calculus with S4-modalities is context-free. In *Logical Aspects of Computational Linguistics. LACL 2012*, volume 7351 of *LNCS*, pages 161–172. Springer, 2012.

25. M. Ma and Z. Lin. Residuated basic logic. Paper presented at AWPL 2, Guangzhou, 2014.
26. M. Moortgat. Multimodal linguistic inference. *Journal of Logic, Language and Information*, 5(3–4):349–385, 1996.
27. M. Moortgat. Categorial Type Logics. In van Benthem and ter Meulen [33], pages 93–177.
28. M. Moortgat and R.T. Oehrle. Pregroups and type-logical grammar: Searching for convergence. In Casadio et al. [10], pages 141–160.
29. R. Moot and C. Retoré. *The Logic of Categorial Grammars. A Deductive Account of Natural Language Syntax and Semantics*, volume 6850 of *LNCS*. Springer, 2012.
30. G. Morrill. *Type Logical Grammar*. Kluwer, Dordrecht, 1994.
31. M. Okada and K. Terui. The finite model property for various fragments of intuitionistic linear logic. *Journal of Symbolic Logic*, 64:790–802, 1999.
32. H. Ono and Y. Komori. Logics without the contraction rule. *Journal of Symbolic Logic*, 50:169–201, 1985.
33. J. van Benthem and A. ter Meulen, editors. *Handbook of Logic and Language*. Elsevier, 1997.

Chapter 3
Conditional Probability Logic over Conditional Probability Spaces

Mauricio S.C. Hernandes

Abstract We present a logical system sound and complete with respect to the class of conditional probability spaces. The universal modality has an important role in our language: conditional probabilities have a peculiar behavior when conditionalized over empty events, so we use the universal modality to express nonemptiness of events. We add public announcement to our language in a way that we are able to express sentences like: "the agent believes the probability of p is zero and after the announcement of p he/she believes the probability of p is greater than zero." Because of the Conditional Probability Language we are able to express reduction axioms for the probability Public Announcement Logic.

3.1 Introduction

Dynamics in epistemic logic is an important field of study for artificial intelligence, philosophy, and mathematics. While nonprobabilistic languages are well understood [19], the same is not true for languages which are able to express probabilistic beliefs; see for example [2]. We take the following problem as a motivation for the present work:

Problem 3.1 Let $[!p]$ stand for the announcement of a proposition p and let $L_r p$ stand for "agent believes in p with probability at least r." How to define a logical system (a set of axioms) where the formula $(L_1 \neg p) \wedge [!p]L_r p$ (with $r > 0$) is consistent? What should a model that satisfies such a formula be like?

This problem is traditionally treated within belief revision theories but the problem itself is interesting enough from the logical point of view. Kooi [11] defines public announcement logic for probabilistic epistemic logic but his update leaves the model

M.S.C. Hernandes (✉)
Informatics Department, SOKENDAI, Tokyo, Japan
e-mail: mauricio@nii.ac.jp

S. Ju et al. (eds.), *Modality, Semantics and Interpretations*,
Logic in Asia: Studia Logica Library, DOI 10.1007/978-3-662-47197-5_3

unchanged for formulas with probability zero,[1] so this approach means that an agent ignores an announcement which he/she believed to be false prior to the update. Kooi is aware of this issue and mentions that a standard solution for this problem in probability theory is to define the updated probability to be undefined under this situation (the announcement of an event of probability zero), but this is a problem for epistemic logic, since the truth valuation would become a partial function. Sack [14] also defines his own public announcement logic for probabilistic epistemic logic, but in this case the probabilistic function assigns zero to all events after the announcement of a formula that was believed to be false. This approach does not solve Problem 3.1 when $r > 0$; moreover, the new function is a subprobabilistic function.[2] Finally, Batlag and Smets [2] have a different approach to the problem, using discrete finite (Renyi-) conditional probabilistic spaces as models. However, Baltag and Smets' analysis is qualitative and solves Problem 3.1 only for the case $r = 1$.

In this paper we define a logical language able to express probabilistic beliefs to which we can add dynamic operators, like public announcements. Furthermore, unlike [2], our analysis uses a more general notion of conditional probabilistic spaces leading to a language that can express quantitative beliefs. Our system is strong enough to express sentences like "agent i believes that the probability of a formula ϕ given the formula ψ is at least r," which we denote by $L_r(\phi||\psi)$. This syntax is an extension of the logic presented in [10] and simplified in [21], where the set of axioms proposed was sound and complete for the class of type spaces introduced by [9].

The need for a language expressing conditional probability (rather than the standard probability) naturally arises when we try to find the reduction axioms for the probabilistic language with public announcement added to it. For example, the formula $[!\phi]L_r p$ is equivalent (in our system presented in Sect. 3.4) to the formula $\phi \rightarrow L_r([!\phi]p||\phi)$. The fact that such reduction axiom can be expressed is an advantage of the conditional probability language and is one of the most important reasons to expand the (standard probabilistic) language from [21].

Formal languages for conditional probabilities are relevant for the probability theory itself; Kooi [11] and Weatherson [20] analyze some popular puzzles in probability theory and the rigor of logical languages helps to understand the problem and solve it. Logical languages have been also useful in game theory; a good survey for logics for games using languages without probabilities can be found in [18]. For logics with probabilities [4] presents a logical system inspired on the idea of relative plausibility (the agent believes that event A is more plausible than event B) from [15]. Board also presents an example of how logic can simplify some results by proving in the logical framework the known result that common belief in rationality at the beginning of the game does not imply that the backward induction outcome will result. Inspired by the work of Board, Baltag and Smets [2] noticed that the same set of axioms was sound and complete with respect to the class of discrete finite

[1] Note that an agent believes with probability 1 that a formula is false is equivalent to the the agent beliefs in the proposition with probability zero.

[2] A probabilistic function that sums up at most to 1.

(Renyi-) conditional probability spaces (which we define formally later) and applied it to belief revision and actions. Briefly, a conditional probability space is a set with a two-place real-valued function from which the traditional probability measure is defined, which in some cases happens to be equal to the conditional probability in the traditional Kolmogorov probability theory.

Although the probability theory for conditional probability spaces was well described in [13] and game theorists adopted this approach some time later in [12] and more recently in [3], the logic community has not fully adopted this approach in its languages yet.

Currently, the logical community has two different approaches to logics that express probabilities. On one hand, Fagin and Halpern [6] proposed a language which could express sentences like "agent i believes that the probability of event A is greater than the probability of event B" ($P(A) > P(B)$), moreover, it allows linear combination of formulas (like $P(A) + P(B) > r$). In a previous work, Fagin et al. [7] discuss the possibility of expressing conditional probabilities extending their language to express product, e.g., they would express a formula of the form $P(A \mid B) \geq \frac{1}{2}$ by a formula of the form $2P(A \cap B) \geq P(B)$, however it would not make sense in the case of $P(B) = 0$, which shows that this syntax is still based on the traditional probability theory of Kolmogorov. More recently, van Benthem [16] added dynamics in this framework but the underlying probability theory was still the one defined by Kolmogorov.

On the other hand, Aumann [1] proposed a language less expressible than Halpern's in which only formulas of the form "agent believes that the probability of the event A is at least r" are allowed. Despite this difference of expressibility, Heifetz and Mongin [10] were able to propose a set of axioms sound and complete with the class of type spaces. One of the advantages of this system is its relatively simple syntax (there is no need for axioms relating inequalities and linear combinations); this point was strengthened in [21] where the system received a simpler set of axioms. Interestingly enough, the second perspective (Aummann's) has no conditional probability extensions so far. Although Aummann's system is included in Halpern's system, it seems interesting to study Aummann's approach and how it expands to express conditionals and dynamics.

One of the contributions of this paper is to extend the language of Zhou [21] to a system that is able to express conditional probability; furthermore, we propose another class of models as semantics (conditional probability spaces). Another contribution from our work is to solve two open problems proposed in [2]: 1. Axiomatize the corresponding logics for infinite conditional probability models and; 2. Study the logic obtained by adding quantitative modal operators.

A last comment about our language regards the use of the universal operator $\Box$—with the traditional intended meaning "$\Box\phi$ holds in a state if and only if ϕ is valid in the model." Our conditional probability function is not additive when conditionalizing over an empty event, and the way we express that an event A is not empty in the formal language is by $\Diamond A$.[3] Note that in a model where $\Box$ is interpreted as an universal modality, $\Diamond A$ holds in at least one state if and only if it holds in all states. So if $[\![A]\!]$ is the set of states of a model in which the formula A holds, then $[\![A]\!]$ is not empty if and only if $\Diamond A$ holds in a state of the model, or equivalently, if and only if $\Diamond A$ is valid in the model.

As noticed by one of the reviewers, the idea of having a combination of modal logic with probability logic is already present in [21–23]. However, in this paper we go a step further and propose a language for conditional probability logic.

In Sect. 3.2 of this paper we present some basic definitions in measure theory and our conditional probability space definition. In Sect. 3.3 we present our axiomatic system and prove its soundness and completeness. In Sect. 3.4 we define public announcement and give the reduction axioms for our extended language. In Sect. 3.5 we present our conclusions and further steps.

3.2 Conditional Probability Belief Logic

First, we state some basic definitions. For more details we suggest a look on [8]. The notion of conditional probability measure is a modified version from [13].

Fix a set X, recall that $\Sigma \subset \mathcal{P}(X)$ is a *σ-algebra* if $\varnothing, X \in \Sigma$, if $A, B \in \Sigma$, then $A \setminus B \in \Sigma$ and if N_0 is a countable set and $(A_n)_{n \in N_0} \in \Sigma$, then $\bigcup_{n \in N_0} A_n \in \Sigma$. Call (X, Σ) a *measurable space*.

Let (X, Σ) be a measurable space and denote by Σ^* the set $\Sigma \setminus \{\varnothing\}$, a function $\mu : \Sigma \times \Sigma \to [0, 1]$ is called a *conditional probabilistic measure* if the following is satisfied:

(1) $\mu(A \mid B) \geq 0$; further $\mu(B \mid B) = 1$;

(2) For any fixed $B \in \Sigma^*$, $\mu(\cdot|B)$ is σ-additive[4];

(3) $\mu(A \cap B \mid C) = \mu(A \mid B \cap C) \cdot \mu(B \mid C)$.

The traditional probability of an event A is defined as $\mu(A, X)$. It is useful to note that with $B = C = \varnothing$ in (3) we have $\mu(\varnothing|\varnothing) = \mu(A|\varnothing) \cdot \mu(\varnothing|\varnothing)$, hence $\mu(A|\varnothing)$ by (1). Also, letting $B = C$ in (3) we have

$$\mu(A \cap B|B) = \mu(A, B) \cdot \mu(B|B) = \mu(A|B).$$

A real-valued function $f : X \to [0, 1]$ is a *Σ-measurable function* if for all r between 0 and 1 we have $f^{-1}([0, r]) \in \Sigma$. A function $T : \Omega \times \Sigma \times \Sigma \to [0, 1]$ is a *conditional Markov kernel* if for any $x \in X$ the function $T(x, \cdot, \cdot)$ is a conditional probabilistic measure over Σ and for any $A, B \in \Sigma$ the function $T(\cdot, A, B)$ is a Σ-measurable function.

[3] We abbreviate $\neg\Box\neg A$ by $\Diamond A$.

[4] A function η is σ-additive if for a family of pairwise disjoint sets $(A_i)_{i \in \mathbb{N}}$ in Σ holds that $\eta(\bigcup_{i \in \mathbb{N}} A_i) = \sum_{i=0}^{\infty} \eta(A_i)$, for $i \neq j$.

Definition 3.2 A *conditional probability model* $\mathcal{M} = \langle \Omega, \Sigma, T, v \rangle$ is such that

- (Ω, Σ) is a measurable space;
- $T : \Omega \times \Sigma \times \Sigma \to [0, 1]$ is a conditional Markov kernel;
- v is a valuation, a function from the set of propositional letters to Σ.

The tuple $\langle \Omega, \Sigma, T \rangle$ is called a *conditional probability space* (CPS).

We define *conditional probability language* as follows. Let $P = \{p, q, \ldots\}$ be the set of propositional variables and consider the language obtained from the following BNF:

$$\phi \doteq \top | p | \neg\phi | \phi \wedge \phi | \Box\phi | L_r(\phi || \phi),$$

where $p \in P$ and $r \in [0, 1] \cap \mathbb{Q}$.[5]

We use the following abbreviations: $\bot \doteq \neg\top$, $M_r(\phi||\psi) \doteq L_{1-r}(\neg\phi||\psi)$, $L_r\phi \doteq L_r(\phi||\top)$, $\Diamond\phi \doteq \neg\Box\neg\phi$, $\phi \vee \psi \doteq \neg(\phi \wedge \psi)$ and $\phi \to \psi \doteq \neg\phi \vee \psi$.

The formula $M_r\phi$ has the intended meaning "the agent believes in ϕ with probability at most r." The connective $\Box$ is the universal operator.

Denote by $\mathcal{L}$ the set of all formulas in this language. Note that $\mathcal{L}$ is countable, assuming that the set of propositional variable $\mathcal{P}$ is countable.

Definition 3.3 Consider a conditional probability model $\mathcal{M} = \langle \Omega, \Sigma, T, v \rangle$ and define the relation $\vDash$ over $\mathcal{M}$ as follows:

$\mathcal{M}, w \vDash p$ iff $w \in V(p)$;
$\mathcal{M}, w \vDash \neg\phi$ iff $\mathcal{M}, w \nvDash \phi$;
$\mathcal{M}, w \vDash \phi \wedge \psi$ iff $\mathcal{M}, w \vDash \phi$ and $\mathcal{M}, w \vDash \psi$;
$\mathcal{M}, w \vDash \Box\phi$ iff $\mathcal{M}, w' \vDash \phi$, for all $w' \in W$;
$\mathcal{M}, w \vDash L_r(\phi||\psi)$ iff $T(w, [\![\phi]\!], [\![\psi]\!]) \geq r$;
where $[\![\phi]\!] = \{w \in \Omega : \mathcal{M}, w \vDash \phi\}$.

We say that a formula ϕ is satisfied in a state w of $\mathcal{M}$ if $\mathcal{M}, w \vDash \phi$ holds. We say that a formula ϕ is satisfied by $\mathcal{M}$ if it is satisfied by all w in $\mathcal{M}$. In this case we write $\mathcal{M} \vDash \phi$.

Lemma 3.4 *For any* $\phi \in \mathcal{L}$, $[\![\phi]\!] \in \Sigma$.

An important fact about the universal operator is that a formula of the form $\Diamond\phi$ is satisfied in a state if and only if $[\![\phi]\!] \neq \varnothing$.

Theorem 3.5 *For any state w of a model $\mathcal{M}$ the following conditions are equivalent:*

1. $[\![\phi]\!] \neq \varnothing$.
2. $\mathcal{M}, w \vDash \Diamond\phi$.

[5] $\mathbb{Q}$ is the set of rational numbers.

A note on multiagent: Technically, we should define a language with an epistemic operator L^i for each i an agent. However, this extra detail does not add any interesting feature in our goal in this paper, namely, the proof of soundness and completeness of the axiomatic system proposed. Of course a language designer when modeling some real situation within logical frameworks should consider this detail. For the rest of the paper, we will make nomention about the agent which the epistemic operator L_r refers to.

3.3 Axioms

Let System L_{cp} be the set of axioms below:

$(A0)$ propositional calculus
$(K_{\Box})$ $\Box(\phi \to \psi) \to (\Box\phi \to \Box\psi)$
$(T_{\Box})$ $\Box\phi \to \phi$
$(5_{\Box})$ $\Diamond\phi \to \Box\Diamond\phi$
$(A1)L_0(\phi||\psi)$
$(A2)L_r(\phi||\phi)$ for $0 \leq r \leq 1$
$(A3)L_r(\phi \wedge \psi||\chi) \wedge L_t(\phi \wedge \neg\psi||\chi) \to L_{r+t}(\phi||\chi)$, for $r + t \leq 1$
$(A4)\neg L_r(\phi \wedge \psi||\chi) \wedge \neg L_t(\phi \wedge \neg\psi||\chi) \to \neg L_{r+t}(\phi||\chi)$, for $r + t \leq 1$
$(A5)\Diamond\psi \to (L_r(\phi||\psi) \to \neg L_s(\neg\phi||\psi))$, for $r + s > 1$
$(C1)L_p(\phi||\psi \wedge \chi) \wedge L_q(\psi||\chi) \to L_{pq}(\phi \wedge \psi||\chi)$
$(C2)\neg L_p(\phi||\psi \wedge \chi) \wedge \neg L_q(\psi||\chi) \to \neg L_{pq}(\phi \wedge \psi||\chi)$
$(C_{\Box})$ $\Box(\phi \leftrightarrow \phi') \wedge \Box(\psi \leftrightarrow \psi') \to (L_r(\phi||\psi) \leftrightarrow L_r(\phi'||\psi'))$
$(N_{\Box})$ If $\vdash \phi$, then $\vdash \Box\phi$
$(ARCH)$ If $\vdash \gamma \to \neg M_s(\phi||\psi)$, for all $s < r$, then $\vdash \gamma \to L_r(\phi||\psi)$.

Axiom $(A0)$ contains all tautologies and the rule of *modus ponens*.

The axioms $(A1)$–$(A5)$ are essentially the axioms in the system presented in [21]. Let ψ be the *conditional part* of a formula of the form $L_p(\phi||\psi)$. Define the deduction rule (*DIS*) to be "if $\vdash (\phi \leftrightarrow \psi)$ then $\vdash L_r\phi \leftrightarrow L_r\psi$." Let the system L' be the axioms $(A1)$–$(A5)$ with their conditional part equivalent to $\top$ (changing $\Diamond\psi$ for $\top$ in $(A5)$). Let L' also contain the deduction rules (*DIS*) and (*ARCH*) with their conditional part equivalent to $\top$. Then L' is the same system from [21].

The restriction $\Diamond\phi$ in axiom $(A5)$ is important on the proof of additivity for the conditional probability function. For any A, B the following inequality holds $\mu(A|B) + \mu(X \setminus A|B) \geq \mu(A \cup (X \setminus A)|B)$. The other inequality $(\leq)$ holds only when B is nonempty. Axiom $(A5)$ is used for the proof of , e.g., Lemma 3.19 during the proof of completeness.

The axioms $(C1)$ and $(C2)$ were added to prove completeness in the conditional probability models and they are related to both inequalities that define the conditional probability of an event.[6] The axioms $(K_{\Box})$–$(5_{\Box})$ are the axioms of the standard $S5$

[6] $T(w, A \cap B|C) = T(w, A \mid B \cap C) \cdot T(w, B \mid C)$.

modal logic which is the correct and sound system for the universal operator (see [17]). Because of the universality of $\Box$ the deduction rule (*DIS*) from [21] is derivable from the axiom ($C_\Box$).

A set Γ of formulas is *inconsistent* in L_{cp} if there are $\gamma_1, \ldots, \gamma_n \in \Gamma$ such that $\neg(\gamma_1 \wedge \cdots \wedge \gamma_n)$ is provable in L_{cp}, and Γ is *consistent* if it is not inconsistent. A single formula ϕ is (in)consistent if $\{\phi\}$ is (in)consistent.

3.3.1 Soundness

The proof of soundness consists in showing that each axiom of $L_c p$ is valid in $\mathcal{M}$ for any $\mathcal{M}$ in the class of conditional probability model.

Theorem 3.6 *The system L_{cp} is sound.*

Proof We prove only axioms ($A3$) and ($C1$) since the others are routine verification.

Let $\mathcal{M} = \langle \Omega, \Sigma, T, v \rangle$ be a conditional probability model, and let $w \in \Omega$, $\phi, \psi \in \mathcal{L}, r \in [0, 1] \cap \mathbb{Q}$:

$\cdot (A3) L_r(\phi \wedge \psi || \chi) \wedge L_t(\phi \wedge \neg\psi || \chi) \rightarrow L_{r+t}(\phi || \chi)$, for $r + t \leq 1$

Suppose that $\mathcal{M}, w \vDash \Diamond\chi$, $\mathcal{M}, w \vDash L_r(\phi \wedge \psi || \chi)$, and $\mathcal{M}, w \vDash L_t(\phi \wedge \neg\psi || \chi)$. Then $T(w, [\![\phi \wedge \psi]\!], [\![\chi]\!]) \geq r$ and $T(w, [\![\phi \wedge \neg\psi]\!], [\![\chi]\!]) \geq t$. Since $[\![\phi \wedge \psi]\!] \cup [\![\phi \wedge \neg\psi]\!] = [\![\phi]\!]$, $[\![\phi \wedge \psi]\!] \cap [\![\phi \wedge \neg\psi]\!] = \varnothing$ and $[\![\chi]\!] \neq \varnothing$, adding each side of both inequalities we have:

$$T(w, [\![\phi]\!], [\![\chi]\!]) \geq r + t$$

Since $r + t \leq 1$ we have that $\mathcal{M}, w \vDash L_{r+t}(\phi || \chi)$.

Suppose that $\mathcal{M}, w \vDash \neg\Diamond\chi$. Then $[\![\chi]\!]$ is empty which implies that $\mathcal{M}, w \vDash L_{r+t}(\phi || \chi)$ always holds (because $T(w, A, \varnothing) = 1$ for every $A \in \Sigma$.)

$\cdot (C1) L_p(\phi || \psi \wedge \chi) \wedge L_q(\psi || \chi) \rightarrow L_{pq}(\phi \wedge \psi || \chi)$

Suppose $\mathcal{M}, w \vDash L_p(\phi || \psi \wedge \chi)$ and $\mathcal{M}, w \vDash L_q(\psi || \chi)$, which is equivalent to $T(w, [\![\phi]\!], [\![\psi \wedge \chi]\!]) \geq p$ and $T(w, [\![\psi]\!], [\![\chi]\!]) \geq q$. Multiplying both inequalities we have $T(w, [\![\phi \wedge \psi]\!], [\![\chi]\!]) = T(w, [\![\phi]\!], [\![\psi \wedge \chi]\!]) \cdot T(w, [\![\psi]\!], [\![\chi]\!]) \geq pq$. The first equality holds because $\mathcal{M}$ is a conditional probability space. The inequality implies that $\mathcal{M}, w \vDash L_{pq}(\phi \wedge \psi || \chi)$. $\Box$

The following theorems in this paragraph are technical results that we make use of a number of times for the proof of completeness. We state them as follows:

Theorem 3.7 *The following is provable in L_{cp}:*

(i) $\Box(\phi \rightarrow \psi) \rightarrow (L_r(\phi || \chi) \rightarrow L_r(\psi || \chi))$.

(ii) $\Box(\phi \rightarrow \psi) \rightarrow (\neg L_r(\psi || \chi) \rightarrow \neg L_r(\phi || \chi))$.

(iii) $\Box\neg(\phi \wedge \psi) \rightarrow (L_r(\psi || \chi) \wedge L_s(\phi || \chi) \rightarrow L_{r+s}(\phi \wedge \psi || \chi))$, *for* $r + s \leq 1$.

(iv) $\neg L_r(\phi || \chi) \wedge \neg L_s(\psi || \chi) \rightarrow \neg L_{r+s}(\phi \vee \psi || \chi)$, *for* $r + s \leq 1$.

1.	$(\phi \to \psi) \to (\phi \wedge \psi \leftrightarrow \phi)$	$(A0)$
2.	$\Box(\phi \to \psi) \to \Box(\phi \wedge \psi \leftrightarrow \phi)$	$1, (N_\Box)$
3.	$\Box(\phi \wedge \psi \leftrightarrow \phi) \to (\phi \wedge \psi \leftrightarrow \phi)$	$T_\Box$
4.	$\Box(\phi \to \psi) \to (\phi \wedge \psi \leftrightarrow \phi)$	$3, 2, (A0)$
5.	$\Box(\phi \to \psi) \to (L_r(\phi \wedge \psi \| \chi) \leftrightarrow L_r(\phi \| \chi))$	$4, (C_\Box), (N_\Box)$
6.	$L_r(\phi \wedge \psi \| \chi) \wedge L_0(\neg\phi \wedge \psi \| \chi) \to L_r(\psi \| \chi)$	$(A3)$
7.	$L_0(\neg\phi \wedge \psi \| \chi)$	$(A1)$
8.	$L_r(\phi \wedge \psi \| \chi) \to L_r(\psi \| \chi)$	$6, 7, (A0)$
9.	$\Box(\phi \to \psi) \to (L_r(\phi \| \chi) \to L_r(\psi \| \chi))$	$5, 8, (A0)$

Proof (i) $\Box(\phi \to \psi) \to (L_r(\phi||\chi) \to L_r(\psi||\chi))$:

(ii) Consequence of item (i).

(iii) $\Box\neg(\phi \wedge \psi) \to (L_r(\psi||\chi) \wedge L_s(\phi||\chi) \to L_{r+s}(\phi \wedge \psi||\chi))$:

1.	$\neg(\phi \wedge \psi) \to ((\phi \vee \psi) \wedge \psi \to (\phi \vee \psi) \wedge \neg\phi)$	$(A0)$
2.	$\Box\neg(\phi \wedge \psi) \to \Box((\phi \vee \psi) \wedge \psi \to (\phi \vee \psi) \wedge \neg\phi)$	$1, (N_\Box)$
3.	$\Box((\phi \vee \psi) \wedge \psi \to (\phi \vee \psi) \wedge \neg\phi) \to$ $(L_r((\phi \vee \psi) \wedge \psi \| \chi) \to L_r((\phi \vee \psi) \wedge \neg\phi \| \chi))$	(item (i))
4.	$\Box\neg(\phi \wedge \psi) \to (L_r((\phi \vee \psi) \wedge \psi \| \chi) \to L_r((\phi \vee \psi) \wedge \neg\phi \| \chi))$	$2, 3, (A0)$
5.	$L_r((\phi \vee \psi) \wedge \neg\phi \| \chi) \wedge L_s((\phi \vee \psi) \wedge \phi \| \chi) \to L_{r+s}(\phi \wedge \psi \| \chi)$	$(A3)$
6.	$\Box\neg(\phi \wedge \psi) \to$ $(L_r((\phi \vee \psi) \wedge \psi \| \chi) \wedge L_s((\phi \vee \psi) \wedge \phi \| \chi) \to L_{r+s}(\phi \wedge \psi \| \chi))$	$4, 5, (A0)$
7.	$(\phi \vee \psi) \wedge \phi \leftrightarrow \phi$	$(A0)$
8.	$(\phi \vee \psi) \wedge \psi \leftrightarrow \psi$	$(A0)$
9.	$L_r((\phi \vee \psi) \wedge \psi \| \chi) \leftrightarrow L_r(\phi \| \chi)$	$8, (N_\Box), (C_\Box)$
10.	$L_s((\phi \vee \psi) \wedge \phi \| \chi) \leftrightarrow L_s(\phi \| \chi)$	$7, (N_\Box), (C_\Box)$
11.	$\Box\neg(\phi \wedge \psi) \to (L_r(\psi \| \chi) \wedge L_s(\phi \| \chi) \to L_{r+s}(\phi \wedge \psi \| \chi))$	$9, 10, 6, (A0)$

(iv) $\neg L_r(\phi||\chi) \wedge \neg L_s(\psi||\chi) \to \neg L_{r+s}(\phi \vee \psi||\chi)$, for $r + s \leq 1$:

1.	$((\phi \vee \psi) \wedge \neg\psi) \to \phi$	$(A0)$
2.	$((\phi \vee \psi) \wedge \psi) \to \psi$	$(A0)$
3.	$\neg L_r(\phi \| \chi) \to \neg L_r((\phi \vee \psi) \wedge \neg\psi \| \chi)$	(item (ii)), 1
4.	$\neg L_t(\psi \| \chi) \to \neg L_t((\phi \vee \psi) \wedge \psi \| \chi)$	(item (ii)), 2
5.	$\neg L_r((\phi \vee \psi) \wedge \neg\psi \| \chi) \wedge \neg L_t((\phi \vee \psi) \wedge \psi \| \chi) \to \neg L_{r+t}(\phi \vee \psi \| \chi)$	$(A4)$
6.	$\neg L_r(\phi \| \chi) \wedge \neg L_t(\psi \| \chi) \to \neg L_{r+t}(\phi \vee \psi \| \chi)$	$3, 4, (A0)$

□

The following theorem presents some interesting and useful formulas that are theorems of L_{cp}.

Theorem 3.8 *The following is provable in* L_{cp}.

(i) $\Box(\psi \to \phi) \to L_r(\phi||\psi)$;

(ii) $\Box\phi \to L_1\phi$.

(iii) $L_r(\phi||\bot)$.

Proof (i) $\Box(\psi \to \phi) \to L_r(\phi||\psi)$:

1.	$\Box(\phi \to \psi) \to (L_r(\phi\|\|\phi) \to L_r(\psi\|\|\phi))$	(Theorem 3.7-item (i))
2.	$L_r(\phi\|\|\phi)$	$(A2)$
3.	$\Box(\psi \to \phi) \to L_r(\phi\|\|\psi)$	1, 2, $(A0)$

(ii) $\Box\phi \to L_1\phi$.

1.	$\phi \to (\phi \leftrightarrow \top)$	$(A0)$
2.	$\Box(\phi \to (\phi \leftrightarrow \top))$	$(N_\Box)$, 1
3.	$\Box\phi \to \Box(\phi \leftrightarrow \top)$	$(K_\Box)$, 2, $(A0)$
4.	$\Box(\top \leftrightarrow \top)$	$(A0)$, $(N_\Box)$
5.	$\Box(\phi \leftrightarrow \top) \to (L_1\phi \leftrightarrow L_1\top)$	$(C_\Box)$, 4, $(A0)$
6.	$\Box\phi \to (L_1\phi \leftrightarrow L_1\top)$	3, 5, $(A0)$
7.	$L_1\top$	(A2)
8.	$\Box\phi \to L_1\phi$	6, 7, $(A0)$

(iii) $L_r(\phi||\bot)$. □

1.	$\Box(\bot \to \phi) \to L_r(\phi\|\|\bot)$	(item (i))
2.	$\Box(\bot \to \phi)$	$(A0)$, $(N_\Box)$
3.	$L_r(\phi\|\|\bot)$	1, 2, $(A0)$

Finally, we state two other theorems which we use for the proof of completeness on next section.

Theorem 3.9 *The following is provable in* L_{cp}.
(i) $\neg L_r(\phi||\psi) \to M_r(\phi||\psi)$.
(ii) $L_r(\phi||\psi) \to L_s(\phi||\psi)$ *if* $r \geq s$.

Proof (i) $\neg L_r(\phi||\psi) \to M_r(\phi||\psi)$:

1.	$\neg L_r(\top \wedge \phi\|\|\psi) \wedge \neg L_{1-r}(\top \wedge \neg\phi\|\|\psi) \to \neg L_1(\top\|\|\psi)$	$(A4)$
2.	$\neg L_r(\phi\|\|\psi) \wedge \neg L_{1-r}(\neg\phi\|\|\psi) \to \neg L_1(\top\|\|\psi)$	$(C_\Box)$, $(A0)$
3.	$L_1(\top\|\|\psi)$	(*Theorem* 3.8-item (i)), $(K_\Box)$, $(A0)$
4.	$\neg L_r(\phi\|\|\psi) \to M_r(\phi\|\|\psi)$	2, 3, $(A0)$

(ii) $L_r(\phi||\psi) \to L_s(\phi||\psi)$ if $r \geq s$:
If $r = s$, there is nothing to do. Suppose $r > s$, □

1.	$\neg L_s(\phi \wedge \phi\|\|\psi) \wedge \neg L_{r-s}(\phi \wedge \neg\phi\|\|\psi) \to \neg L_r(\phi\|\|\psi)$	$(A4)$
2.	$\Diamond\psi \to (L_r(\top\|\|\psi) \to \neg L_{r-s}(\bot\|\|\psi))$	$(A5)$
3.	$\Diamond\psi \to (L_r(\phi\|\|\psi) \to L_s(\phi\|\|\psi))$	2, (Theorem 3.8-item (i)), 1, $(A0)$
4.	$\Box(\psi \to \bot) \to (L_r(\phi\|\|\bot) \leftrightarrow L_r(\phi\|\|\psi))$	$(C_\Box)$, $(A0)$
5.	$\Box\neg\psi \to L_r(\phi\|\|\psi)$	4, (Theorem 3.8-item (iii)), $(A0)$
6.	$\Box\neg\psi \to L_s(\phi\|\|\psi)$	$(C_\Box)$, (Theorem 3.8-item (iii)), $(A0)$
7.	$\Box\neg\psi \to (L_r(\phi\|\|\psi) \to L_s(\phi\|\|\psi))$	5, 6, $(A0)$
8.	$(\Box\neg\psi) \vee (\Diamond\psi) \to (L_r(\phi\|\|\psi) \to L_s(\phi\|\|\psi))$	3, 7, $(A0)$
9.	$L_r(\phi\|\|\psi) \to L_s(\phi\|\|\psi)$	8, $(A0)$

3.3.2 Completeness

The strategy for the proof of completeness is to build a canonical model (the set of states are maximal consistent sets of formulas).

In our case the set of states is finite, to bound its size we allow only formulas up to a fixed depth. The depth of a formula is the maximum of L operators nested in a row. We define depth formally as follows:

Definition 3.10 *(Local Language)* The *depth* $dp(\phi)$ of a formula ϕ is defined inductively:

- $dp(p) = 0$, for propositional letters p;
- $dp(\neg\phi) = dp(\phi)$;
- $dp(\phi_1 \wedge \phi_2) = \max\{dp(\phi_1), dp(\phi_2)\}$;
- $dp(\Box\phi) = dp(\phi)$;
- $dp(L_r(\phi||\psi)) = 1 + \max\{dp(\phi), dp(\psi)\}$.

Let the *index* of a formula of the form $L_r(\phi||\psi)$ be the rational number r. Let $Q \subset P, q > 0$ and $d \geq 0$. We define a *local language* $\mathcal{L}(Q, q, d)$ to be the set of all formulas ϕ satisfying the following:

- Every propositional letter occurring in ϕ is in Q;
- Every index in ϕ is a multiple of $\frac{1}{q}$; and
- $dp(\phi) \leq d$.

The integer q is called *accuracy* of the language $\mathcal{L}(Q, q, d)$.

We regard the elements of $\mathcal{L}(Q, q, d)$ as equivalence classes of formulas that are logically equivalent. Under this equivalence the local language is finite. We spell out the details as follows:

For $\phi \in \mathcal{L}(Q, q, d)$, we write $\bar{\phi}$ for the equivalence class

$$\{\, \psi \in \mathcal{L}(Q, q, d) \mid \psi \leftrightarrow \phi \text{is a theorem of} L_{cp} \,\}.$$

Lemma 3.11 *If Q is finite, then $\{\, \bar{\phi} \mid \phi \in \mathcal{L}(Q, q, d) \,\}$ is finite.*

Proof This is proved by induction on d. Suppose $|Q| = n$. Note that formulas of $\mathcal{L}(Q, q, 0)$ are simply formulas of propositional modal logic over n propositional variables. From [5] we know that every modal formula is provably equivalent in S5 to a finite conjunction of formulas of the form

$$\beta \vee \Box\gamma_1 \vee \cdots \vee \Box\gamma_n \vee \Diamond\delta, \tag{†}$$

where $\beta, \gamma_1, \ldots, \gamma_n, \delta$ are propositional formulas. Over n propositional variables, there are at most

$$f(n) = 2^{2^n} \cdot 2^{2^{2^n}} \cdot 2^{2^n}$$

non-S5-equivalent disjunctions of the form (†), and at most

$$g(n) = 2^{f(n)}$$

non-S5-equivalent finite conjunctions of such disjunctions. Since L_{cp} contains S5, this takes care of the induction basis. Let $h(n, q, 0) = g(n)$.

Now assume that every formula in $\mathcal{L}(Q, q, d)$ is provably equivalent in L_{cp} to one of the finite number $h(n, q, d)$ of formulas. Call a formula in $\mathcal{L}(Q, q, d+1)$ a *modal atom* if it is a propositional variable in Q or a formula of the form $L_{i/q}(\psi||\chi)$, where $0 \leq i \leq q$ and $\psi, \chi \in \mathcal{L}(Q, q, d)$. Evidently, every formula ϕ in $\mathcal{L}(Q, q, d+1)$ is constructed from modal atoms using $\Box$, $\neg$, and $\wedge$ only. By the modal conjunctive normal form theorem, ϕ is provably equivalent to a finite conjunction of formulas of the form (†), where $\beta, \gamma_1, \ldots, \gamma_n, \delta$ are Boolean combinations of modal atoms. Since there are at most $(q+1) \cdot h(n, q, d)^2$ nonequivalent formulas of the form $L_{i/q}(\psi||\chi)$ with $\psi, \chi \in \mathcal{L}(Q, q, d)$, the number of nonequivalent modal atoms in $\mathcal{L}(Q, q, d)$ is at most $n + (q+1) \cdot h(n, q, d)^2$. So the number of nonequivalent formulas in $\mathcal{L}(Q, q, d+1)$ is bounded by

$$h(n, q, d+1) = g(n + (q+1) \cdot h(n, q, d)^2). \qquad \Box$$

By Lemma 3.11, if $\Gamma \subseteq \mathcal{L}(Q, q, d)$ for some finite Q, there is a finite subset $\{\psi_1, \ldots, \psi_k\}$ of Γ such that every formula in Γ is provably equivalent to one of $\psi_1, \ldots, \psi_k$. We denote by $\bigwedge \Gamma$ the conjunction $\psi_1 \wedge \cdots \wedge \psi_k$. Note that $\bigwedge \Gamma \in \mathcal{L}(Q, q, d)$, and up to provable equivalence, $\bigwedge \Gamma$ is independent of the choice of $\psi_1, \ldots, \psi_k$.

A set $\Gamma \subseteq \mathcal{L}(Q, q, d)$ is said to be a *maximal consistent* subset of $\mathcal{L}(Q, q, d)$ if Γ is consistent and there exists no consistent Γ' such that $\Gamma \subset \Gamma' \subseteq \mathcal{L}(Q, q, d)$. If Γ is a maximal consistent subset of $\mathcal{L}(Q, q, d)$, then for every $\Delta \subseteq \Gamma$, $\bigwedge \Delta$ belongs to Γ.

Lemma 3.12 *Let Γ, Γ' be maximal consistent subsets of $\mathcal{L}(Q, q, d)$. If $\bigwedge \Gamma \in \Gamma'$, then $\Gamma = \Gamma'$.*

Proof If $\bigwedge \Gamma \in \Gamma'$, then $\Gamma \subseteq \Gamma'$. Since Γ is maximal consistent and Γ' is consistent, $\Gamma = \Gamma'$. $\Box$

If $\chi \in \mathcal{L}$, then $\mathcal{L}(\chi)$ is defined as $\mathcal{L}(P_\chi, q_\chi, d_\chi)$, where P_χ is the set of all propositional letters in ψ, the index q_χ is the least common multiple of all the denominators of the indices in χ and d_χ is the depth of χ .

Fix χ in $\mathcal{L}$ and suppose it is consistent in L_{cp}. Let Ω be the set of all maximal consistent sets of formulas in $\mathcal{L}(\chi)$.

Given a maximal consistent set of formulas Γ in Ω, define $U(\Gamma) = \{\phi \in \Gamma : \phi$ is of the form $\neg\Box\psi$ or $\Box\psi\}$ and for any $\Gamma, \Delta \in \Omega$ we say that $\Gamma \sim \Delta$ iff $U(\Gamma) = U(\Delta)$. Let Γ_χ be a maximal consistent set of formulas that contain χ, define $\Omega_\chi = \{\Delta \in \Omega : \Delta \sim \Gamma_\chi\}$. Let $[\phi]_\chi = \{\Delta \in \Omega_\chi : \phi \in \Delta\}$ and $\Sigma_\chi = \{[\phi]_\chi : \phi \in \mathcal{L}(\chi)\}$ ($\Sigma^*_\chi = \Sigma_\chi \setminus \{\varnothing\}$). Denote by $\gamma_\Box$ the conjunction $\bigwedge U(\Gamma_\chi)$.

Lemma 3.13 $\Omega_\chi = \{\Delta \in \Omega : \gamma_\Box \in \Delta\}(\doteq [\gamma_\Box])$.

Proof Let $\Delta \in \Omega_\chi$, then $U(\Delta) = U(\Gamma_\chi)$, and clearly $\bigwedge U(\Delta) \in \Delta$, hence $\gamma_\Box \in \Delta$, i.e., $\Delta \in [\gamma_\Box]$.

For the other inclusion let $\Delta \in [\gamma_\Box]$ and let us show that $U(\Delta) = U(\Gamma_\chi)$. Consider $\phi \in U(\Gamma_\chi)$. Clearly, $\vdash \gamma_\Box \to \phi$, so $\phi \in \Delta$. Since ϕ is of the form $\neg\Box\psi$ or $\Box\psi$, we have $\phi \in U(\Delta)$. Now let $\phi \in U(\Delta)$ and suppose it is not in $U(\Gamma_\chi)$. By maximality, $\Gamma_\chi \vdash \neg\phi$. Then $\neg\phi \in U(\Gamma_\chi)$ and $\vdash \gamma_\Box \to \neg\phi$. It follows that $\neg\phi \in \Delta$, which is a contradiction. □

Lemma 3.14 $\Sigma_\chi = \mathcal{P}(\Omega_\chi)$.

Proof It is easy to see that if $\phi \in \mathcal{L}(\chi)$, then $[\phi]_\chi \in \mathcal{P}(\Omega_\chi)$.

Let $X = \{\Gamma_1, \ldots, \Gamma_n\} \subseteq \Omega_\chi$. Let γ_i be $\bigwedge \Gamma_i$ and let ϕ be $\bigvee_{i=1}^n \gamma_i$. Clearly, $\phi \in \Gamma_i$, for all $i = 1, \ldots, n$. If $\phi \in \Delta$ for some $\Delta \in \Omega_\chi$, then some $\gamma_i \in \Delta$. By Lemma 3.12, $\Gamma_i = \Delta$. It follows that $X = [\phi]_\chi$. □

The pair $(\Omega_\chi, \Sigma_\chi)$ is the measurable space for our canonical model. For the conditional Markov kernel we need some steps that we prove first.

Let Δ be a maximal consistent set of formulas in $\mathcal{L}(Q, q, d+1)$ and let ϕ and ψ be formulas in $\mathcal{L}(Q, q, d)$. Define

$$\alpha^\Delta_{\phi,\psi} = \max\{\alpha : L_\alpha(\phi||\psi) \in \Delta\},$$

$$\beta^\Delta_{\phi,\psi} = \min\{\beta : M_\beta(\phi||\psi) \in \Delta\}.$$

Let $\mathcal{L}^+$ be the language $\mathcal{L}(P_\chi, q_\chi, d_\chi + 1)$. For each Γ in Ω let Γ^+ be a maximal consistent extension of Γ in $\mathcal{L}^+$. Note that this choice is not unique; fix one extension for each $\Gamma \in \Omega$. Note that $L_{\alpha^{\Gamma^+}_{\phi,\psi}}(\phi||\psi) \in \Gamma^+$ and $M_{\beta^{\Gamma^+}_{\phi,\psi}}(\phi||\psi) \in \Gamma^+$.

Lemma 3.15 *For any* $\Gamma \in \Omega_\chi$ *and* $\phi, \psi \in \mathcal{L}(\chi)$:

(a) If $\Diamond\psi \in \Gamma$, *then either* $\beta^{\Gamma^+}_{\phi,\psi} = \alpha^{\Gamma^+}_{\phi,\psi}$ *or* $\beta^{\Gamma^+}_{\phi,\psi} = \alpha^{\Gamma^+}_{\phi,\psi} + \frac{1}{q_\chi}$;

(b) If $\Diamond\psi \notin \Gamma$, *then* $\alpha^{\Gamma^+}_{\phi,\psi} = 1$ *and* $\beta^{\Gamma^+}_{\phi,\psi} = 0$.

Proof (a) ($\alpha^{\Gamma^+}_{\phi,\psi} \leq \beta^{\Gamma^+}_{\phi,\psi}$) Suppose $\alpha^{\Gamma^+}_{\phi,\psi} > \beta^{\Gamma^+}_{\phi,\psi}$. It follows that $(1 - \beta^{\Gamma^+}_{\phi,\psi}) + \alpha^{\Gamma^+}_{\phi,\psi} > 1$.

We have that $L_{\alpha^{\Gamma^+}_{\phi,\psi}}(\phi||\psi) \in \Gamma^+$ and by (A5), $\neg L_{1-\beta^{\Gamma^+}_{\phi,\psi}}(\neg\phi||\psi) = \neg M_{\beta^{\Gamma^+}_{\phi,\psi}}(\phi||\psi) \in \Gamma^+$, but this contradicts the fact that $M_{\beta^{\Gamma^+}_{\phi,\psi}}(\phi||\psi) \in \Gamma^+$.

($\alpha^{\Gamma^+}_{\phi,\psi} \geq \beta^{\Gamma^+}_{\phi,\psi} - \frac{1}{q_\chi}$) Let $s = \alpha^{\Gamma^+}_{\phi,\psi} + \frac{1}{q_\chi}$. Then s is a multiple of $\frac{1}{q_\chi}$ and $\alpha^{\Gamma^+}_{\phi,\psi} < s$, so $L_s(\phi||\psi) \notin \Gamma^+$. Since Γ^+ is a maximal consistent subset of $\mathcal{L}(P_\chi, q_\chi, d+1)$, we must have $\neg L_s(\phi||\psi) \in \Gamma^+$. By Theorem 3.9, $M_s(\phi||\psi) \in \Gamma^+$, so $s \geq \beta^{\Gamma^+}_{\phi,\psi}$, i.e., $\alpha^{\Gamma^+}_{\phi,\psi} \geq \beta^{\Gamma^+}_{\phi,\psi} - \frac{1}{q_\chi}$.

(b) If $\Diamond\psi \notin \Gamma$, then $\Box\neg\psi \in \Gamma$. Since $\neg\psi \to (\psi \leftrightarrow \bot)$ is a tautology, $\Box(\psi \leftrightarrow \bot) \in \Gamma$ by $(N_\Box)$ and $(K_\Box)$. Since for any γ, $L_1(\gamma||\bot)$ is a theorem of L_{cp}, we get $L_1(\phi||\psi) \in \Gamma$ and $M_0(\phi||\psi) \in \Gamma$ by $(C_\Box)$. So $\alpha^{\Gamma^+}_{\phi,\psi} = 1$ and $\beta^{\Gamma^+}_{\phi,\psi} = 0$. □

Definition 3.16 Let Γ^∞ be a maximal consistent extension of Γ^+ in $\mathcal{L}$ and ϕ, ψ in $\mathcal{L}(\chi)$. Define

$$\alpha^{\Gamma^\infty}_{\phi,\psi} = \sup\{\alpha : L_\alpha(\phi||\psi) \in \Gamma^\infty\},$$

$$\beta^{\Gamma^\infty}_{\phi,\psi} = \inf\{\beta : M_\beta(\phi||\psi) \in \Gamma^\infty\}.$$

Lemma 3.17 *If r is a rational number and $r < \alpha^{\Gamma^\infty}_{\phi,\psi}$, then $L_r(\phi||\psi) \in \Gamma^\infty$.*

Proof Let s be a rational number such that $r \leq s < \alpha^{\Gamma^\infty}_{\phi,\psi}$ and $L_s(\phi||\psi) \in \Gamma^\infty$. Note that if $L_s(\phi||\psi) \notin \Gamma^\infty$ for all such s, then we can derive a contradiction with the fact that $\alpha^{\Gamma^\infty}_{\phi,\psi}$ is the supremum.

By Theorem 3.9.(ii), $L_s(\phi||\psi) \to L_r(\phi||\psi)$ is a theorem, hence also in Γ^∞. By the maximality of Γ^∞, it holds that $L_r(\phi||\psi) \in \Gamma^\infty$. □

Lemma 3.18 *Let $\Diamond\psi \in \Gamma$ and $\phi, \psi \in \mathcal{L}(\chi)$. Then $\alpha^{\Gamma^\infty}_{\phi,\psi} = \beta^{\Gamma^\infty}_{\phi,\psi}$*

Proof Suppose $\alpha^{\Gamma^\infty}_{\phi,\psi} < \beta^{\Gamma^\infty}_{\phi,\psi}$. Then there is a rational r such that $\alpha^{\Gamma^\infty}_{\phi,\psi} < r < \beta^{\Gamma^\infty}_{\phi,\psi}$, which implies $L_r(\phi||\psi) \notin \Gamma^\infty$, i.e., $\neg L_r(\phi||\psi) \in \Gamma^\infty$. Hence $M_r(\phi||\psi) \in \Gamma^\infty$, contradicting $r < \beta^{\Gamma^\infty}_{\phi,\psi}$.

If $\alpha^{\Gamma^\infty}_{\phi,\psi} > \beta^{\Gamma^\infty}_{\phi,\psi}$, let r_1 and r_2 be rationals such that $\alpha^{\Gamma^\infty}_{\phi,\psi} > r_1 > r_2 > \beta^{\Gamma^\infty}_{\phi,\psi}$. Then $L_{r_1}(\phi||\psi) \in \Gamma^\infty$ and by $(A5)$[7] we have $\neg M_{r_2}(\phi||\psi) \in \Gamma^\infty$, contradicting $r_2 > \beta^{\Gamma^\infty}_{\phi,\psi}$. □

Lemma 3.19 *Let $\phi_1, \phi_2, \psi \in \mathcal{L}(\chi)$ and $\Gamma \in \Omega_\chi$. If $\neg\Diamond(\phi_1 \wedge \phi_2) \in \Gamma$ and $\Diamond\psi \in \Gamma$, then*

$$\alpha^{\Gamma^\infty}_{\phi_1\vee\phi_2,\psi} = \alpha^{\Gamma^\infty}_{\phi_1,\psi} + \alpha^{\Gamma^\infty}_{\phi_2,\psi}. \quad (3.1)$$

[7]Since $r_1 > r_2$ implies $(1 - r_2) + r_1 > 1$, an instance of $(A5)$ is $L_{r_1}(\phi||\psi) \to \neg L_{1-r_2}(\neg\phi||\psi)$.

Proof Let α_1, α_2 and α_+ denote $\alpha^{\Gamma^\infty}_{\phi_1,\psi}, \alpha^{\Gamma^\infty}_{\phi_2,\psi}$ and $\alpha^{\Gamma^\infty}_{\phi_1\vee\phi_2,\psi}$, respectively. So we only need to show that $\alpha_1 + \alpha_2 = \alpha_+$.

Suppose $\alpha_1 + \alpha_2 < \alpha_+$. Then there are rationals $\alpha_1' > \alpha_1$ and $\alpha_2' > \alpha_2$ such that $\alpha_1' + \alpha_2' < \alpha_+$. It follows that $L_{\alpha_1'}(\phi_1||\psi) \notin \Gamma^\infty$ and hence $\neg L_{\alpha_1'}(\phi_1||\psi) \in \Gamma^\infty$. Similarly, $\neg L_{\alpha_2'}(\phi||\psi) \in \Gamma^\infty$; by Theorem 3.7 it holds that $\neg L_{\alpha_1'+\alpha_2'}(\phi_1 \vee \phi_2||\psi) \in \Gamma^\infty$. That is a contradiction because $\alpha_1 + \alpha_2 < \alpha_+$ and α_+ is the greatest lower bound such that $L_r(\phi_1 \vee \phi_2||\psi) \in \Gamma^\infty$.

Suppose that $\alpha_1 + \alpha_2 > \alpha_+$. Then there are rationals $\alpha_1'' < \alpha_1$ and $\alpha_2'' < \alpha_2$ such that $\alpha_1'' + \alpha_2'' > \alpha_+$. It follows that $L_{\alpha_1''}(\phi_1||\psi), L_{\alpha_2''}(\phi_2||\psi) \in \Gamma^\infty$. We want to prove that $\alpha_1'' + \alpha_2'' \leq 1$. Suppose that $\alpha_1'' + \alpha_2'' > 1$; since $\Diamond(\phi_1 \to \neg\phi_2) \in \Gamma$, by Theorem 3.7 we have $L_{\alpha_1''}(\phi_1||\psi) \to L_{\alpha_1''}(\neg\phi_2||\psi) \in \Gamma$ and clearly $L_{\alpha_1''}(\neg\phi_2||\psi) \in \Gamma^\infty$. By axiom $(A5)$,

$$\vdash \Diamond\psi \to (L_{\alpha_1''}(\neg\phi_2||\psi) \to \neg L_{\alpha_2''}(\phi_2||\psi));$$

we know that $\Diamond\psi, L_{\alpha_1''}(\phi_2||\psi) \in \Gamma^\infty$, hence we have $\neg L_{\alpha_2''}(\phi_2||\psi) \in \Gamma^\infty$ which is a contradiction. Therefore, we have $\alpha_1'' + \alpha_2'' \leq 1$. By Theorem 3.7, $L_{\alpha_1''+\alpha_2''}(\phi_1 \vee \phi_2||\psi) \in \Gamma^\infty$. But this is impossible because $\alpha_1'' + \alpha_2'' > \alpha_+$ and α_+ is the greatest lower bound such that $L_r(\phi_1 \vee \phi_2||\psi) \in \Gamma^\infty$. □

Lemma 3.20 *For any $\phi, \psi \in \mathcal{L}(\chi)$ and for any $\Gamma \in \Omega_\chi$ the following equation holds:*

$$\alpha^{\Gamma^\infty}_{\phi_1\wedge\phi_2,\psi} = \alpha^{\Gamma^\infty}_{\phi_1,\phi_2\wedge\psi} \cdot \alpha^{\Gamma^\infty}_{\phi_2,\psi}$$

Proof Suppose $\alpha^{\Gamma^\infty}_{\phi_1\wedge\phi_2,\psi} < \alpha^{\Gamma^\infty}_{\phi_1,\phi_2\wedge\psi} \cdot \alpha^{\Gamma^\infty}_{\phi_2,\psi}$.

Let x, y be rationals such that $x \leq \alpha^{\Gamma^\infty}_{\phi_1,\phi_2\wedge\psi}, y \leq \alpha^{\Gamma^\infty}_{\phi_2,\psi}$ and $\alpha^{\Gamma^\infty}_{\phi_1\wedge\phi_2,\psi} < xy$. Then $L_x(\phi_1||\phi_2 \wedge \psi) \in \Gamma^\infty$, $L_y(\phi_2||\psi) \in \Gamma^\infty$ and $L_{xy}(\phi_1 \wedge \phi_2||\psi) \notin \Gamma^\infty$. Since Γ^∞ is a maximal consistent subset of $\mathcal{L}$, by axiom $(C1)$ we have $L_{xy}(\phi_1 \wedge \phi_2||\psi) \in \Gamma^\infty$, a contradiction with the consistency of Γ^∞.

Suppose $\alpha^{\Gamma^\infty}_{\phi_1\wedge\phi_2,\psi} > \alpha^{\Gamma^\infty}_{\phi_1,\phi_2\wedge\psi} \cdot \alpha^{\Gamma^\infty}_{\phi_2,\psi}$.

Let x, y be rationals such that $x > \alpha^{\Gamma^\infty}_{\phi_1,\phi_2\wedge\psi}$, $y > \alpha^{\Gamma^\infty}_{\phi_2,\psi}$, and $\alpha^{\Gamma^\infty}_{\phi_1\wedge\phi_2,\psi} > xy$. Then $L_x(\phi_1||\phi_2 \wedge \psi) \notin \Gamma^\infty$, $L_y(\phi_2||\psi) \notin \Gamma^\infty$, and $L_{xy}(\phi_1 \wedge \phi_2||\psi) \in \Gamma^\infty$. Since Γ^∞ is a maximal consistent subset of $\mathcal{L}$, we have $\neg L_x(\phi_1||\phi_2 \wedge \psi) \in \Gamma^\infty$ and $\neg L_y(\phi_2||\psi) \in \Gamma^\infty$. By $(C2)$, we get $\neg L_{xy}(\phi_1 \wedge \phi_2||\psi) \in \Gamma^\infty$, contradicting the consistency of Γ^∞. □

For each $\Gamma \in \Omega_\chi$ and each $\phi, \psi \in \mathcal{L}(\chi)$ we want to define the conditional Markov kernel $T(\Gamma, [\phi]_\chi, [\psi]_\chi)$ to be $\alpha^{\Gamma^\infty}_{\phi,\psi}$ (Definition 3.23). Lemmas 3.22 and 3.25 below shows that T as proposed makes sense.

Lemma 3.21 *The following is a theorem in L_{cp}*

$$\gamma_\Box \to \Box\gamma_\Box.$$

Proof Recall that $\gamma_\Box$ is a finite conjunction of formulas of the form $\Box\delta$ or $\neg\Box\delta$. Since $\Box\delta \to \Box\Box\delta$, $\neg\Box\delta \to \Box\neg\Box\delta$, and $(\Box\delta_1 \wedge \Box\delta_2) \to \Box(\delta_1 \wedge \delta_2)$ are theorems of modal logic S5, $\gamma_\Box \to \Box\gamma_\Box$ is a theorem of L_{cp}. □

Lemma 3.22 *For any* $\Gamma \in \Omega_\chi$, $\alpha^{\Gamma^\infty}_{\phi\wedge\gamma_\Box,\psi\wedge\gamma_\Box} = \alpha^{\Gamma^\infty}_{\phi,\psi}$.

Proof Since $\gamma_\Box \to (\phi \leftrightarrow (\phi \wedge \gamma_\Box))$ is an instance of a propositional tautology, we get $\Box\gamma_\Box \to \Box(\phi \leftrightarrow (\phi \wedge \gamma_\Box))$ by $(N_\Box)$ and $(K_\Box)$. For any $\Gamma \in \Omega_\chi$, by Lemma 3.21, $\Box\gamma_\Box \in \Gamma$. Hence it holds that $\Box(\phi \leftrightarrow (\phi \wedge \gamma_\Box)) \in \Gamma$.

Analogously, $\Box(\psi \leftrightarrow (\psi \wedge \gamma_\Box)) \in \Gamma$.

By axiom $(C_\Box)$ we have $L_r(\phi||\psi) \leftrightarrow L_r(\phi \wedge \gamma_\Box||\psi \wedge \gamma_\Box) \in \Gamma^\infty$. Therefore, $\alpha^{\Gamma^\infty}_{\phi,\psi} = \alpha^{\Gamma^\infty}_{\phi\wedge\gamma_\Box,\psi\wedge\gamma_\Box}$. □

Definition 3.23 Let $\Gamma \in \Omega_\chi$ and $\phi, \psi \in \mathcal{L}(\chi)$. Define $T_\chi(\Gamma, [\phi]_\chi, [\psi]_\chi) = \alpha^{\Gamma^\infty}_{\phi,\psi}$.

Note that the definition of T_χ depends on the choice of Γ^∞ for each Γ. We will later select a particular choice with a certain desirable property (Lemma 3.28), but we will first prove some facts about T_χ that do not depend on any particular choice.

The proof for the next lemma is straightforward.

Lemma 3.24 *For any* $\phi, \psi \in \mathcal{L}(\chi)$, $\vdash \phi \wedge \gamma_\Box \to \psi \wedge \gamma_\Box$ *iff* $[\phi]_\chi \subseteq [\psi]_\chi$.

Lemma 3.25 T_χ *as defined above is well defined.*

Proof If $[\phi]_\chi = [\phi']_\chi$ and $[\psi]_\chi = [\psi']_\chi$, then by Lemma 3.24 we have $\vdash \phi \wedge \gamma_\Box \leftrightarrow \phi' \wedge \gamma_\Box$ and $\vdash \psi \wedge \gamma_\Box \leftrightarrow \phi' \wedge \gamma_\Box$. By $(N_\Box)$ and axiom $(C_\Box)$ we have $\vdash (L_r(\phi_1 \wedge \gamma_\Box||\psi \wedge \gamma_\Box) \leftrightarrow L_r(\phi' \wedge \gamma_\Box||\psi' \wedge \gamma_\Box)) \wedge (M_s(\phi \wedge \gamma_\Box||\psi \wedge \gamma_\Box) \leftrightarrow M_s(\phi' \wedge \gamma_\Box||\psi' \wedge \gamma_\Box))$, and hence $\alpha^{\Gamma^\infty}_{\phi\wedge\gamma_\Box,\psi\wedge\gamma_\Box} = \alpha^{\Gamma^\infty}_{\phi'\wedge\gamma_\Box,\psi'\wedge\gamma_\Box}$. By Lemma 3.22 we get $T_\chi(\Gamma, [\phi]_\chi, [\psi]_\chi) = T_\chi(\Gamma, [\phi']_\chi, [\psi']_\chi)$. □

To see that $T_\chi(\cdot, [\phi]_\chi, [\psi]_\chi)$ is a Σ_χ-measurable function it is enough to note that by Lemma 3.14 every subset of Ω_χ is measurable.

To show that for any Γ, $T_\chi(\Gamma)$ is a conditional probabilistic measure we first should note that the model is finite. Therefore, σ-additivity is equivalent to finite additivity.

To prove that $T_\chi(\Gamma)$ is additive we should prove that if $B \in \Sigma^*_\chi$ and $A_1, A_2 \in \Sigma_\chi$ are such that $A_1 \cap A_2 = \varnothing$, then $T_\chi(\Gamma, A_1 \cup A_2, B) = T_\chi(\Gamma, A_1, B) + T_\chi(\Gamma, A_2, B)$.

We finish proving that T_χ is a conditional Markov Kernel with the next lemma.

Lemma 3.26 *For any* $\Gamma \in \Omega_\chi$*:*

(*a*) *if* $A, B \in \Sigma_\chi$, *then* $T_\chi(\Gamma, A, B) \geq 0$ *and* $T_\chi(\Gamma, B, B) = 1$*;*

(*b*) *if* $B \in \Sigma^*_\chi$ *and* $A_1, A_2 \in \Sigma_\chi$ *are such that* $A_1 \cap A_2 = \varnothing$, *then* $T_\chi(\Gamma, A_1 \cup A_2, B) = T_\chi(\Gamma, A_1, B) + T_\chi(\Gamma, A_2, B)$*;*

(*c*) *if* $A, B, C \in \Sigma_\chi$, *then*

$$T_\chi(\Gamma, A \cap B, C) = T_\chi(\Gamma, A, B \cap C) \cdot T_\chi(\Gamma, B, C).$$

Proof a. Since $L_1(\psi||\psi) \in \Gamma_i^+$, it is easy to see that $T_\chi(\Gamma_i, B, B) = 1$.

b. If $B \in \Sigma_\chi^*$, then there is a $\psi \in \mathcal{L}(\chi)$ such that $B = [\psi]_\chi$. Since $B \neq \varnothing$, there is a $\Delta \in \Omega_\chi$ such that $\psi \in \Delta$. Suppose that $\neg\Diamond\psi \in \Gamma_i$, then $\Box\neg\psi \in \Gamma_i$. Clearly, $\Box\neg\psi \in U(\Gamma_i) = U(\Delta)$; and by axiom $(T_\Box)$ we have $\neg\psi \in \Delta$, which is a contradiction. Therefore, $\Diamond\psi \in \Gamma_i$.

If $\phi_1, \phi_2 \in \mathcal{L}(\chi)$ are such that $A_1 = [\phi_1]_\chi$ and $A_2 = [\phi_2]_\chi$, then we have that $\vdash \neg((\phi_1 \wedge \gamma_\Box) \wedge (\phi_2 \wedge \gamma_\Box))$. We have to prove that

$$T_\chi(\Gamma, [\phi_1 \wedge \gamma_\Box]_\chi \cup [\phi_2 \wedge \gamma_\Box]_\chi, [\psi]_\chi) = T_\chi(\Gamma, [\phi_1 \wedge \gamma_\Box]_\chi, [\psi]_\chi) + T_\chi(\Gamma, [\phi_2 \wedge \gamma_\Box]_\chi, [\psi]_\chi).$$

That is the same as $\alpha^{\Gamma\infty}_{\phi_1\wedge\gamma_\Box \vee \phi_2\wedge\gamma_\Box, \psi} = \alpha^{\Gamma\infty}_{\phi_1\wedge\gamma_\Box, \psi} + \alpha^{\Gamma\infty}_{\phi_2\wedge\gamma_\Box, \psi}$, which is true by Lemma 3.19. By Lemma 3.22 we have the desired equality:

$$\alpha^{\Gamma\infty}_{\phi_1\vee\phi_2, \psi} = \alpha^{\Gamma\infty}_{\phi_1, \psi} + \alpha^{\Gamma\infty}_{\phi_2, \psi}.$$

c. If $\phi_1, \phi_2, \psi \in \mathcal{L}(\chi)$ are such that $A = [\phi_1]_\chi$, $B = [\phi_2]_\chi$ and $C = [\psi]_\chi$, then we have to prove

$$T_\chi(\Gamma, [\phi_1 \wedge \phi_2]_\chi, [\psi]_\chi) = T_\chi(\Gamma, [\phi_1]_\chi, [\phi_2 \wedge \psi]_\chi) \cdot T_\chi(\Gamma, [\phi_2]_\chi, [\psi]_\chi).$$

It is enough to notice that the following equality holds by Lemma 3.20:

$$\alpha^{\Gamma\infty}_{\phi_1\wedge\phi_2, \psi} = \alpha^{\Gamma\infty}_{\phi_1, \phi_2\wedge\psi} \cdot \alpha^{\Gamma\infty}_{\phi_2, \psi}.$$

□

Lemma 3.27 *Let Γ be in Ω_χ, let Φ be a finite set of formulas in $\mathcal{L}$ such that $\Delta = \Gamma^+ \cup \Phi$ is consistent. For any $\phi, \psi \in \mathcal{L}(\chi)$, if $\alpha^{\Gamma+}_{\phi,\psi} < \beta^{\Gamma+}_{\phi,\psi}$, then there is a rational r such that $\Delta \cup \{M_r(\phi||\psi)\}$ is consistent.*

Proof Let Δ be as in the hypothesis and suppose that ϕ and ψ are such that $\alpha^{\Gamma+}_{\phi,\psi} < \beta^{\Gamma+}_{\phi,\psi}$.

Suppose that for all $r < \beta^{\Gamma+}_{\phi,\psi}$, $\vdash \bigwedge\Delta \rightarrow \neg M_r(\phi||\chi)$. Then by the (ARCH) rule we have $\vdash \bigwedge\Delta \rightarrow L_{\beta^{\Gamma+}_{\phi,\psi}}(\neg\phi||\psi)$. By maximality we know that $L_{\beta^{\Gamma+}_{\phi,\psi}}(\neg\phi||\psi) \vee \neg L_{\beta^{\Gamma+}_{\phi,\psi}}(\neg\phi||\psi) \in \Gamma^+$ and by consistency we have that $L_{\beta^{\Gamma+}_{\phi,\psi}}(\neg\phi||\psi) \in \Gamma^+$. This contradicts the fact that $\alpha^{\Gamma+}_{\phi,\psi}$ is the greatest number among the indices such that $L_s(\phi||\psi) \in \Gamma^+$ holds. Therefore, there is an r_0 such that $\Delta \cup \{M_{r_0}(\phi||\psi)\}$ is consistent. □

The following property is a modified version of property (E) from [21].

Lemma 3.28 *For each Γ in Ω_χ there is a maximal consistent Θ^∞ extension of Γ^+ in $\mathcal{L}$ such that the following property is satisfied:*

(F): for any $\phi, \psi \in \mathcal{L}(\chi)$, if $\alpha^{\Gamma+}_{\phi,\psi} < \beta^{\Gamma+}_{\phi,\psi}$, then $\alpha^{\Gamma+}_{\phi,\psi} \leq \alpha^{\Theta\infty}_{\phi,\psi} = \beta^{\Theta\infty}_{\phi,\psi} < \beta^{\Gamma+}_{\phi,\psi}$.

Proof Fix $\Gamma \in \Omega_\chi$, and enumerate all the pairs of formulas (ϕ_i, ψ_i) in $\mathcal{L}(\chi)$ $\{(\phi_1, \psi_1), \dots (\phi_k, \psi_k)\}$ such that $\alpha^{\Gamma^+}_{\phi_i,\psi_i} < \beta^{\Gamma^+}_{\phi_i,\psi_i}$. Define the following sequence of sets of formulas,

$$\Theta_0 = \Gamma^+;$$
$$\Theta_{n+1} = \Theta_n \cup \{M_{s_{n+1}}(\phi_{n+1}||\psi_{n+1})\}.$$

The consistency of each Θ_i and the existence of each r_i is given in Lemma 3.27. Fix Θ^∞ to be an extension of Θ_k in the language $\mathcal{L}$.

Now we prove that $\alpha^{\Theta^\infty}_{\phi_i,\psi_i} = \beta^{\Theta^\infty}_{\phi_i,\psi_i}$. If $\Diamond\psi_i \notin \Gamma$, then by Lemma 3.15 $\alpha^{\Gamma^+}_{\phi_i,\psi_i} = 1$ and $\beta^{\Gamma^+}_{\phi_i,\psi_i} = 0$, contradicting the hypothesis. Hence, $\Diamond\psi_i \in \Gamma \subset \Theta^\infty$ and by Lemma 3.18, $\alpha^{\Theta^\infty}_{\phi_i,\psi_i} = \beta^{\Theta^\infty}_{\phi_i,\psi_i}$. □

Enumerate all maximal consistent sets in Ω_χ, $\Gamma_1, \Gamma_2, \dots, \Gamma_n$. From the above lemma it follows that for each Γ_i there is a Θ_i^∞ satisfying property (F). Redefine T_χ as follows: $T_\chi(\Gamma_i, [\phi]_\chi, [\psi]_\chi) = \alpha^{\Theta_i^\infty}_{\phi,\psi}$.

Define the canonical model

$$\mathcal{M}_\chi = \langle \Omega_\chi, \Sigma_\chi, T_\chi, v_\chi \rangle,$$

where $v_\chi(p) = [p]_\chi$.

Lemma 3.29 (Truth Lemma)
Let $\phi \in \mathcal{L}(\chi)$, then

$$\mathcal{M}_\chi, \Gamma_i \models \phi \textit{ iff } \phi \in \Gamma_i.$$

Proof The proof is by the complexity of ϕ, we prove the cases $\phi = L_r(\psi_1||\psi_2)$ and $\phi = \Box\psi$.

(Case $\phi = L_r(\psi_1||\psi_2)$)

Assume $\mathcal{M}_\chi, \Gamma_i \models L_r(\psi_1||\psi_2)$, i.e., $T_\chi(\Gamma_i, [\psi_1]_\chi, [\psi_2]_\chi) \geq r$.

If $\Diamond\chi \in \Gamma_i$ we have two cases to consider:

(Case $\alpha^{\Gamma_i^+}_{\psi_1,\psi_2} = \beta^{\Gamma_i^+}_{\psi_1,\psi_2}$) In this case $T_\chi(\Gamma_i, [\psi_1]_\chi, [\psi_2]_\chi) = \alpha^{\Gamma_i^+}_{\psi_1,\psi_2}$. Therefore, $r \leq \alpha^{\Gamma_i^+}_{\psi_1,\psi_2}$ and clearly $L_r(\psi_1||\psi_2) \in \Gamma_i$.

(Case $\alpha^{\Gamma_i^+}_{\psi_1,\psi_2} < \beta^{\Gamma_i^+}_{\psi_1,\psi_2}$) In this case $T_\chi(\Gamma_i, [\psi_1]_\chi, [\psi_2]_\chi) \geq r$. Then $r \leq \alpha^{\Theta_i^\infty}_{\psi_1,\psi_2} < \beta^{\Gamma_i^+}_{\psi_1,\psi_2} = \alpha^{\Gamma_i^+}_{\psi_1,\psi_2} + \frac{1}{q_\chi}$. The last equality holds because of Lemma 3.15, but since $L_r(\psi_1||\psi_2) \in \mathcal{L}(\chi)$ we have $r \leq \alpha^{\Gamma_i^+}_{\psi_1,\psi_2}$. Hence, $L_r(\psi_1||\psi_2) \in \Gamma_i$.

If $\Diamond\chi \notin \Gamma_i$, then by Lemma 3.15, $L_1(\psi_1||\psi_2) \in \Gamma_i$, and by Theorem 3.9 it holds that $L_r(\psi_1||\psi_2) \in \Gamma_i$.

For the other direction, assume $\mathcal{M}_\chi, \Gamma_i \not\models L_r(\psi_1||\psi_2)$. Then

$$\alpha^{\Theta_i^\infty}_{\psi_1,\psi_2} = T_\chi(\Gamma_i, [\psi_1]_\chi, [\psi_2]_\chi) < r.$$

Therefore, $L_r(\psi_1||\psi_2) \notin \Gamma_i$.

(Case $\phi = \Box\psi$) Suppose $\mathcal{M}_\chi, \Gamma \models \Box\psi$.

Fact: If $\Box\psi \notin \Gamma$ then $U(\Gamma) \cup \{\neg\psi\}$ is consistent.

(Proof of the fact) If $U(\Gamma) \cup \{\neg\psi\}$ is inconsistent, then $\vdash \bigwedge U(\Gamma) \rightarrow \psi$, and by ($N_\Box$) and ($K_\Box$) we have that $\vdash \Box \bigwedge U(\Gamma) \rightarrow \Box\psi$. By Lemma 3.21 we also have that $\vdash \bigwedge U(\Gamma) \rightarrow \Box \bigwedge U(\Gamma)$. With both implications $\vdash \bigwedge U(\Gamma) \rightarrow \Box\psi$ holds. Since $\Box\psi \in \mathcal{L}(\chi)$, it holds that $\Box\psi \in \Gamma$. This contradicts the hypothesis. Therefore, $U(\Gamma) \cup \{\neg\psi\}$ is consistent.

Suppose $\Box\psi \notin \Gamma$. By the fact above we know that $U(\Gamma) \cup \{\neg\psi\}$ is consistent, so there is a maximal consistent set of formulas Γ' such that $U(\Gamma) \cup \{\neg\psi\} \subseteq \Gamma'$. We know that Γ' is in Ω_χ because $U(\Gamma) \subset \Gamma'$.

In this way, Γ' is such that $\Gamma \sim \Gamma'$ and $\psi \notin \Gamma'$. By the induction hypothesis $\mathcal{M}_\chi, \Gamma' \not\models \psi$. Then $\mathcal{M}_\chi, \Gamma \not\models \Box\psi$, which contradicts our assumption. Therefore, $\Box\psi \in \Gamma$.

Now for the other direction assume $\Box\psi \in \Gamma$. To prove $\mathcal{M}_\chi, \Gamma \models \Box\psi$, take any $\Gamma' \in \Omega_\chi$. It suffices to show $\mathcal{M}_\chi, \Gamma' \models \psi$. Since $\Box\psi \in U(\Gamma)$ and $U(\Gamma) = U(\Gamma')$, we have $\Box\psi \in U(\Gamma') \subseteq \Gamma'$. Since $\vdash \Box\psi \rightarrow \psi$, it follows that $\psi \in \Gamma'$. By the induction hypothesis, $\mathcal{M}_\chi, \Gamma' \models \psi$. □

Theorem 3.30 (Completeness) *For any formula χ of $\mathcal{L}$, if χ is consistent, then there is a model $\mathcal{M} = \langle \Omega, \Sigma, T, v \rangle$, such that $\mathcal{M}, w \models \chi$ for some $w \in \Omega$.*

An immediate consequence of this Theorem is the *finite model property*, which we state as follows:

Corollary 3.31 (Finite Model Property) *A formula ϕ of $\mathcal{L}$ is valid in all conditional probability models if and only if it is valid in all finite conditional probability models.*

The last corollary does not imply decidability[8] because the canonical model is not finitely constructed (the valuer of T_χ may be irrational).

For the proof of completeness on the multiagent case one has to build the canonical model considering a different conditional Markov kernel T_i for each agent i. Then, one applies Lemma 3.28 for each i guarantying that the truth lemma holds for each formula of the form $L_r^i(\phi||\psi)$.

3.4 Public Announcement Logic

One strength of conditional probability lies on the property that the agent is able to conditionalize over events of probability zero. An application of that for logic is the possibility of expressing: "agent 1 believes in ϕ to be false when it is true, and when faced with the facts his/her belief on ϕ is greater than zero" (Problem 3.1). We spell out this argument formally with the help of Public Announcement Logic (PAL).

[8] A logic is decidable if there is an algorithm that given any formula of the language decides whether it is a theorem.

The goal of this section is to define a sound and complete language for probabilistic PAL.

Let $P = \{p, q, \ldots\}$ be the set of propositional variables. The language of probabilistic PAL is given by the following BNF:

$$\phi = p|\neg\phi|\phi \wedge \phi|L_r(\phi||\psi)|\Box\phi|[!\phi]\phi$$

The intended reading of $[!\phi]\psi$ is "after the public announcement of ϕ the formula ψ is the case."

Given a conditional probability model $\mathcal{M} = \langle \Omega, \Sigma, T, v\rangle$ the definition of truth of formulas of probabilistic PAL is like before, with the added clause:

$$\mathcal{M}, w \vDash [!\phi] \text{ iff } \mathcal{M}, w \vDash \text{ implies } \mathcal{M}_\phi, w \vDash \psi;$$

where $\mathcal{M}_\phi = \langle \Omega_\phi, \Sigma_\phi, T_\phi, v_\phi\rangle$ is defined as follows:
$\Omega_\phi = [\![\phi]\!]$;
$\Sigma_\phi = \{B \cap \Omega_\phi : B \in \Sigma\}$;
$T_\phi(w, A, B) = T(w, A, B)$;
$v_\phi(\cdot) = v(\cdot) \cap \Omega_\phi$
Define $[\![\psi]\!]_\phi \doteq \{w \in \Omega_\phi : \mathcal{M}_\phi, w \vDash \psi\}$.

Lemma 3.32 *Let ϕ and ψ be formulas and $\mathcal{M}$ a model for probabilistic PAL, then:*

$$[\![\psi]\!]_\phi = [\![\phi \wedge [!\phi]\psi]\!]$$

Proof Suppose $x \in [\![\phi \wedge [!\phi]\psi]\!]$. Then $\mathcal{M}, x \vDash \phi$ and ($\mathcal{M}, x \vDash \phi$ implies $\mathcal{M}_\phi, x \vDash \psi$). Therefore $\mathcal{M}_\phi, x \vDash \psi$, which is the same as $x \in [\![\psi]\!]_\phi$.

Suppose $x \in [\![\psi]\!]_\phi$, i.e., $x \in [\![\phi]\!]$ and $\mathcal{M}_\phi, x \vDash \psi$. This is the same as to say that $\mathcal{M}, x \vDash \phi$ and ($\mathcal{M}, x \vDash \phi$ implies $\mathcal{M}_\phi, x \vDash \psi$), which is exactly $x \in [\![\phi \wedge [!\phi]\psi]\!]$. □

We prove the completeness of probabilistic PAL by giving a set of reduction axioms. Reduction axioms are a schema of formulas which describes how to replace a formula with the connective $[!\phi]$ by an equivalent formula without the connective.

Theorem 3.33 *The reduction axioms for probabilistic PAL, given by the schemata of formulas below, are valid.*
$\cdot[!\phi]p \leftrightarrow \phi \rightarrow p$
$\cdot[!\phi]\neg\psi \leftrightarrow \phi \rightarrow \neg[!\phi]\psi$
$\cdot[!\phi]\Box\psi \leftrightarrow (\phi \rightarrow \Box[!\phi]\psi)$
$\cdot[!\phi][!\psi]\chi \leftrightarrow [!\phi \wedge [!\phi]\psi]\chi$
$\cdot[!\phi](\psi \wedge \chi) \leftrightarrow ([!\phi]\psi \wedge [!\phi]\chi)$
$\cdot[!\phi]L_r(\psi||\chi) \leftrightarrow \phi \rightarrow L_r([!\phi]\psi||\phi \wedge [!\phi]\chi)$

Proof We prove only the probabilistic formula. The others are routine.

Let $\mathcal{M}$ be a probabilistic PAL and let w be a state in the model.

$\mathcal{M}, w \vDash [!\phi]L_r(\psi||\chi)$ iff $\mathcal{M}, w \vDash \phi$ implies $T_\phi(w, [\![\psi]\!]_\phi, [\![\chi]\!]_\phi) \geq r$, which is equivalent, by the previous lemma, to:

$$\mathcal{M}, w \vDash \phi \text{ implies } T(w, [\![\phi \wedge [!\phi]\psi]\!], [\![\phi \wedge [!\phi]\chi]\!]) \geq r.$$

Since $T(w, A, B) = T(w, A \cap B, B)$ always holds,

$$T(w, [\![[!\phi]\psi]\!], [\![\phi \wedge [!\phi]\chi) = T(w, [\![\phi \wedge [!\phi]\psi]\!], [\![\phi \wedge [!\phi]\chi).$$

So the above condition is equivalent to $\mathcal{M}, w \models \phi \rightarrow L_r([!\phi]\psi||\phi \wedge [!\phi]\chi)$. □

The last reduction axiom cannot be expressed in probabilistic logic. We can see that the conditional probability operator appears in the reduction schema for the nonconditional probability operator if we take $\chi = \top$ in the last reduction axiom:

$$[!\phi]L_r(\psi) \leftrightarrow \phi \rightarrow L_r([!\phi]\psi||\phi).$$

The ability to express this equivalence is one of the advantages of conditional probability logic over the standard probability logic of [21].

Theorem 3.34 *The System L_{cp} together with the reduction axioms in Theorem 3.33 is a complete system for probabilistic PAL.*

Proof Let ϕ be a formula in the probability PAL such that it is valid in all models in the class of conditional probability models.

If ϕ is a formula in the conditional probability logic (a formula without the operator $[!\cdot]$), by the proof of completeness of conditional probability logic (Theorem 3.30) we know that there is a proof of ϕ using the axioms in L_{cb}.

If ϕ have the operator $[!\cdot]$, by Theorem 3.33 we know that ϕ is equivalent to a formula in the conditional probability logic, which again by the proof of completeness we know have a proof. □

With this language we can express interesting formulas. The following theorem solves Problem 3.1.

Theorem 3.35 *The formula $L_1 \neg p \wedge [!p]L_r p$ is satisfiable for any $r > 0$.*

We finish this section with an example of a model that satisfies this formula.

Suppose that today He and She are in a room without windows and that it is raining outside but He does not know. In fact, He believes (with probability 1) that it is not raining. He believes that when it is raining She has an umbrella 70 % of the time. And He believes that when it is not raining She carries the umbrella 40 % of the time.

It is very clear that without anything else He believes with probability 40 % that She has an umbrella today (but in fact the probability is 70 % as it is raining but He does not know).

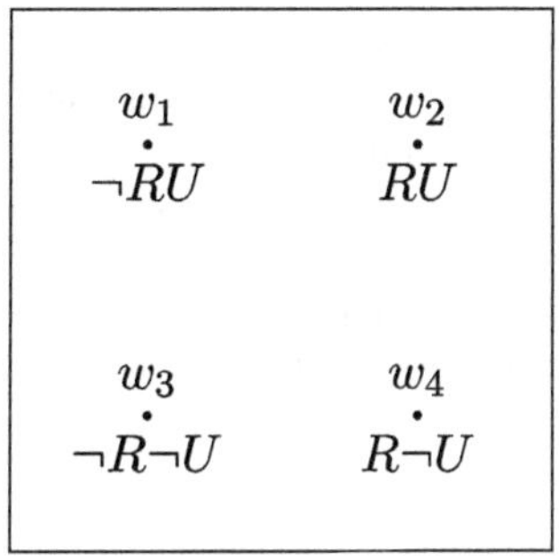

Fig. 3.1 Model. R stands for the states where it is raining. U stands for the states where you have an umbrella

It should also be clear that after She tells Him that it is raining He should believe with probability 70 % that She has an umbrella today.

Let $\mathcal{M} = \langle \Omega, \Sigma, T, v \rangle$ be the following conditional probability model with any conditional Markov kernel T satisfying the equalities below:

$\Omega = \{w_1, w_2, w_3, w_4\}$

$\Sigma = \mathcal{P}(\Omega)$

$T(w, U, R) = 0.7, T([\![U]\!], [\![\neg R]\!]) = 0.4$ and $T(w, [\![\neg R]\!], \Omega) = 1$, for all $w \in \Omega$.

$v(R) = \{w_2, w_4\}$ and $v(U) = \{w_1, w_2\}$,

where R reads as "it is raining" and U as "She has an umbrella." See Fig. 3.1 for a picture of the model. For simplicity we write RU for $R \wedge U$, $R\neg U$ for $R \wedge \neg U$, $\neg RU$ for $\neg R \wedge U$, etc.

Note that $\mathcal{M} \models L_1\neg R \wedge [!R]L_1 R$ holds. It is also interesting to note that $\mathcal{M} \models L_1\neg(RU) \wedge [!R]L_{0.7}RU$.

3.5 Conclusion

We have proposed a language for conditional probability beliefs. With that language we extended standard probabilistic languages (like [21]). Moreover, our language has characteristics that solve two problems described in [2]. First, the language proposed in the present work is complete with respect to the class of infinite conditional probability spaces, more general than discrete finite models.

Second, the conditional probability logic allowed us to express quantitative levels of beliefs. The language containing a formula of the form $L_{0.5}(p||q)$ has more expressive power than a language restricted to the connective for conditional belief $B^q p$ meaning "given q, the agent believes in p."

It is also important to note that conditional probability logic played a central role in expressing the reduction axioms for probability PAL, which was one of the main reasons for the departure from probability languages.

The logic proposed here has the finite model property, but it did not imply decidability. It is worth mentioning that in [21] this problem is solved by proposing an alternative axiomatization (an alternative (*ARCH*) rule) which was proved to be decidable. It is an open question if a similar technique can be applied in our system.

As future directions we aim to express a wider variety of dynamic languages and use conditional probability logic to express real-world situations, like games.

Acknowledgments I am grateful to my Ph.D. advisor Makoto Kanazawa for his helpful comments and ideas to simplify some of the proofs in many ways.

References

1. R. J. Aumann, 'Interactive Epistemology II: Probability', International Journal of Game Theory 28, 301–314, 1999.
2. A. Baltag and S. Smets, 'Probabilistic Dynamic Belief Revision', TARK 2007.
3. P. Battigalli and M. Siniscalchi, 'Hierarchies of conditional beliefs and interactive epistemology in dynamic games', Journal of Economic Theory 88:188–230, 1999.
4. O. Board, 'Dynamic interactive epistemology', Games and Economic Behavior 49–80, 2004.
5. M.J. Cresswell and G.E. Hughes, 'A New Introduction to Modal Logic', Routledge, 1996.
6. R. Fagin and J.Y. Halpern, 'Reasoning about knowledge and probability', Journal of the Association for computing machinery vol 41 N 2, 340–367, 1994.
7. R. Fagin, J.Y. Halpern and R. Megiddo, 'A Logic for Reasoning about Probabilities', Information and Computation, 87 78–128, 1990.
8. P.R. Halmos, 'Measure theory', Springer-Verlag New York-Heidelberg-Berlin, 1950.
9. J.C. Harsanyi, 'Games with incomplete information played by Bayesian players', parts I–III, Management Sci. 14, 159–182, 320–334, 486–502, 1967–1968.
10. A. Heifetz and P. Mongin, 'Probability Logic for Type Spaces', Games and Economic Behaviour 35, 31–53, 2001.
11. B. P. Kooi, 'Probabilistic Epistemic Logic', Journal of Logic, Language and Information 12: 381–408, 2003.
12. R.B. Myerson, 'Multistage games with communication', Econometrica 54:323–358, 1985.
13. A. Renyi, 'On a new axiomatic theory of probability', 1955.
14. J. Sack, 'Extending Probability Dynamic Epistemic Logic', Synthese 169, 241–257, 2009.
15. R. Stalnaker, 'Extensive and strategic forms: Games and models for games', Research in Economics 53, 293–319, 1999.
16. J. van Benthem, 'Conditional Probability meets Update Logic', Journal of Logic, Language and Information 12, 409–421, 2003.
17. J. van Benthem, 'Modal Logic for Open Minds', CSLI, 2010.
18. W. van der Hoek and M. Pauly, 'Modal logic for games and information', in Handbook of Modal Logic, 2006.
19. H. van Ditmarsch, W. van der Hoek and B. Kooi, 'Dynamic Epistemic Logic', Synthese Library, vol. 337, 2007.
20. Weatherson, B, 'Stalnaker on sleeping beauty', Philosophical studies. 155 issue 3, 445–456, 2011.
21. C. Zhou, 'A complete deductive System for probability logic', Journal of Logic and Computation, 19 issue 6, 1427–1454, 2009.
22. C. Zhou, 'Complete Deductive Systems for Probability Logic with Application in Harsanyi Type Spaces'. PhD. Thesis, 2007.
23. C. Zhou, 'Probability for Harsanyi Type Space,' Logical Methods in Computer Science, 2014.

Chapter 4
Finite-Chain Graded Modal Logic

Minghui Ma and Shanxia Wang

Abstract Kripke frames are generalized to finite-chain graded frames. The minimal finite-chain graded modal logic is shown to be sound and complete with respect to the class of all finite-chain graded frames. Finite-chain algebras are defined for giving algebraic semantics for this modal logic. A Jónsson-Tarski style representation theorem for finite-chain algebras is proved. This new kind of multimodal logic differs from both classical normal modal logic and graded modal logic. Some results for extensions of the minimal finite-chain graded modal logic are also obtained.

4.1 Introduction

Algebras for classical modal logic are Boolean algebras with operators (BAOs) [14, 15]. It is well-known that the minimal normal modal logic K is sound and complete with respect to the class of all BAOs [7], just like that the classical propositional logic is determined by Boolean algebras, and that intuitionistic logic is determined by Heyting algebras [7]. The model-theoretic semantics for classical modal logic was introduced around 1950s by logicians from different perspectives, for example, by Kripke [17]. The duality theory between BAOs and Kripke frames was developed since 1970s [3, 13]. A Kripke frame is a relational structure $\mathscr{F} = (W, R)$ where W is a nonempty set, and $R \subseteq W \times W$ is a binary relation over W. From categorical point of view, the category of Kripke frames with bounded morphisms, and the category of BAOs with homomorphisms are dually equivalent.

Both authors are supported by the China National Fund for Social Sciences (No. 12CZX054), and Chongqing Funding of Social Sciences (No. 2013YBZX008).

M. Ma (✉)
Institute for Logic and Intelligence, Southwest University,
Tiansheng Road No.2, Beibei, Chongqing, China
e-mail: mmh.thu@gmail.com

S. Wang
School of Computer Science, Southwest University, Tiansheng Road No.2, Beibei, Chongqing, China
e-mail: wangxia@swu.edu.cn

S. Ju et al. (eds.), *Modality, Semantics and Interpretations*,
Logic in Asia: Studia Logica Library, DOI 10.1007/978-3-662-47197-5_4

We develop a new sort of structures obtained by generalizing Kripke frames, and hence BAOs on the algebraic side are expanded. The idea behind our work can be described as follows. A binary relation R over W can be written as a function $R : W \times W \to \{0, 1\}$. The range of R is the lattice or Boolean algebra of two elements. Thus we may generalize the binary relation R in the way that the range of R is replaced by a lattice A. Thus we obtain a function $\sigma : W \times W \to A$. A structure obtained in this way is said to be a *lattice graded frame*. There is a similar kind of structure called *multiset* [4], which is often used in mathematics, computer science, and philosophy when the repetition of objects is involved. A multiset is a pair (W, m) where $m : W \to \mathbb{N}$ is a function from W to the set of all natural numbers. It is not hard to see that Kripke frames are multisets, and multisets are lattice graded frames.

Other closely related structures are transition systems used in computer science [2, 18] as models for describing the behavior of various systems. They are typical directed graphs consisting of states and edges. Actions in a system are executed among states via edges. Usually, there are no assumptions on the structure of actions in a transition system. However, we may introduce protocols on actions, and hence introduce a kind of protocol transition system. In lattice graded frames, actions between states form a lattice structure. Thus, the logic we develop can be applied to reasoning in protocol transition systems where relations between actions are needed.

The logic we are going to develop is also contrasted with graded modal logic (GML) which was first presented by Kit Fine [12] as the modal logic of numerical or counting first-order quantifiers. The language of GML is obtained by adding counting modalities $\Diamond_n$ ($n \in \omega$) to classical propositional logic. Each counting modality $\Diamond_n \varphi$ is true at a state w in a Kripke model iff w has at least n successors where φ is true. The minimal graded modal logic was shown to be complete with respect to the class of all Kripke frames [9, 11, 12]. The completeness of extensions of the minimal GML was studied in [6, 10]. The application of GML into epistemic logic was first studied in [21], where the natural numbers are used in GML to compare 'grades' of formulae. The addition of numbers is used for calculating grades of compound formulae in a Kripke model. However, in our new structure with a lattice, we use only the lattice order without the addition to calculate grades of formulae.

Graded modal logic is also applied to epistemic logics in different ways. In [21], the graded modal operator $\Box_n \varphi$ (the dual of $\Diamond_n$) is interpreted as that at most n states refute φ. In epistemic terms, the agent reckons with at most n exceptions for φ. However, in our lattice graded structures, we can model uncertainties of agent's knowledge and compare the grades of knowledge in a more natural way by treating natural numbers as restrictions on uncertainty (accessibility) relations between epistemic states. An example of a system combining knowledge and plausibility degrees of belief is given by Aucher [1]. Aucher introduced the operator $B_j^n \varphi$ which means that 'in world w, the agent j believes with plausibility (a degree of) at most n that φ is true.' Aucher's epistemic model contains a function assigning a natural number (with a bound) to each state, and so the plausibility degree of a belief can be calculated. It is not hard to observe that Aucher's model can be generalized using our lattice graded structures in a more natural way technically.

For technical reasons, we fix a lattice A which is a finite chain in this paper, and define the modal language $\mathscr{L}_A$ which is the extension of propositional logic by adding modal operators $\Diamond_a$ ($a \neq 1$ and $a \in A$). Then we define the semantics for $\mathscr{L}_A$ over models based on lattice graded frames. Then we give a sound and complete Hilbert-style axiomatization of the minimal finite-chain graded modal logic. The result is that those modal operators $\Diamond_a$ are normal, and so they differ from graded modalities in GML. The logic we obtain differs also from normal modal logics since we have new axioms corresponding to the lattice order.

In [5], Bou, Esteva, and Godo developed a many-valued modal logic over finite residuated lattice, where Kripke frames are generalized to **A**-valued Kripke frames where **A** is a given residuated lattice. The modal language for this logic is the classical one, i.e., the modal language in which only two unary modalities $\Box$ and $\Diamond$ are introduced. The lattice-valued model consists of a frame, and a valuation which assigns a value in **A** to each propositional variable. Thus each formula gets a value in **A**. The modal operators are defined in terms of product and lattice operations, and they are not monotonic. Our finite-chain graded modal logic differs from the many-valued modal logic in [5], both in the modal language and semantics.

4.2 Language and Semantics

We assume basic knowledge on lattices and ordered sets (cf. [8]). Here we recall some basic concepts. Given a lattice $\mathbb{A} = (A, \wedge, \vee)$, define the partial order $\leq$ over A by: $a \leq b$ iff $a \wedge b = a$ iff $a \vee b = b$. We write $a < b$, if $a \leq b$ and $a \neq b$. A lattice A is *bounded*, if there exist a bottom $0 \in A$ and a top $1 \in A$. We say that A is *linear* or a *chain*, if the order $\leq$ is linear, i.e., every two elements are comparable with respect to the order $\leq$. For any $a, b \in A$, we say that a is a *lower cover* of b (or b is a *upper cover* of a) (notation: $a \prec b$), if $a < b$ and $a < c \leq b$ implies $c = b$. For a bounded lattice $\mathbb{A} = (A, \wedge, \vee, 0, 1)$, let $A^* = A \setminus \{1\}$.

Fact 4.1 *Every finite chain satisfies the following conditions:*

(U) For all $a \in A^*$, there exists $b \in A$ such that $a \prec b$.
(L) For all $0 \neq a \in A^*$, there exists $b \in A$ such that $b \prec a$.
(D) Any nonempty $X \subseteq A$ has a minimal element.

The condition (U) says that any non-top element has a (unique) upper cover, and the condition (L) says that any element except 0, 1 has a lower cover. The condition (D) means that the lattice order $\leq$ is well-ordering.

Definition 4.1 Given a finite-chain lattice $\mathbb{A} = (A, \wedge, \vee, 0, 1)$, the modal language $\mathscr{L}_A$ is the extension of classical propositional logic by adding the set $\{\Diamond_a : a \in A^*\}$ of modal operators. The set of all $\mathscr{L}_A$-formulae is defined by the following rule:

$$\varphi = p \mid \bot \mid \varphi \to \varphi \mid \Diamond_a \varphi$$

where $p \in \mathsf{Prop}$, a fixed set of propositional variables. Define $\top := \bot \to \bot$, $\neg\varphi := \varphi \to \bot$ and $\Box_a\varphi := \neg\Diamond_a\neg\varphi$. Other connectives $\wedge$, $\vee$ and $\leftrightarrow$ are defined as usual. We define $\Diamond!_a\varphi := \Diamond_a\varphi \wedge \neg\Diamond_b\varphi$ where $a \prec b$ (b is unique since $\mathbb{A}$ is a finite chain).

Definition 4.2 A $\mathscr{L}_A$-frame (or finite-chain graded frame) is a pair $\mathscr{F} = (W, \sigma)$ where W is a nonempty set of states, and $\sigma : W \times W \to A$ is a function.

A $\mathscr{L}_A$-model is a triple $\mathscr{M} = (W, \sigma, V)$ where (W, σ) is a $\mathscr{L}_A$-frame and $V : \mathsf{Prop} \to \wp(W)$ is a valuation in (W, σ).

Let Frm_A be the class of all $\mathscr{L}_A$-frames. The function σ in a $\mathscr{L}_A$-frame can be written as a function $\sigma : W \to (W \to A)$ from W to the set of all functions from W to A. Thus we write $\sigma(w)(u)$ instead of $\sigma(w, u)$ for any pair $(w, u) \in W \times W$.

Definition 4.3 (*Semantics*) The truth of a $\mathscr{L}_A$-formula φ at a state w in a $\mathscr{L}_A$-model $\mathscr{M} = (W, \sigma, V)$ (notation: $\mathscr{M}, w \models \varphi$) is defined recursively as follows:

$\mathscr{M}, w \models p$ iff $w \in V(p)$, for each $p \in \mathsf{Prop}$.
$\mathscr{M}, w \not\models \bot$.
$\mathscr{M}, w \models \varphi \to \psi$ iff $\mathscr{M}, w \not\models \varphi$ or $\mathscr{M}, w \models \psi$.
$\mathscr{M}, w \models \Diamond_a\varphi$ iff $\exists u \in W(\sigma(w)(u) \geq a \;\&\; \mathscr{M}, u \models \varphi)$.

By definition, we have the following:

$$\mathscr{M}, w \models \Box_a\varphi \text{ iff } \forall u \in W(\sigma(w)(u) \geq a \Rightarrow \mathscr{M}, u \models \varphi).$$

A formula φ is *true* in a $\mathscr{L}_A$-model $\mathscr{M}$ (notation: $\mathscr{M} \models \varphi$), if $\mathscr{M}, w \models \varphi$ for all $w \in W$. A formula φ is *valid* in a $\mathscr{L}_A$-frame $\mathscr{F}$ (notation: $\mathscr{F} \models \varphi$), if $\mathscr{F}, V \models \varphi$ for all valuations V in $\mathscr{F}$. Given any class $\mathscr{C}$ of $\mathscr{L}_A$-frames, a formula φ is *valid* in $\mathscr{C}$ (notation: $\mathscr{C} \models \varphi$), if $\mathscr{F} \models \varphi$ for all $\mathscr{F} \in \mathscr{C}$.

By the definition of semantics, if we regard $\sigma(w)(u) \geq a$ as a binary relation between w and u, it is clear that the interpretation of modal operators is quite similar to that in classical modal logic.

Definition 4.4 The *minimal finite-chain graded modal logic* is defined as the set K_A of all formulae valid in all $\mathscr{L}_A$-frames:

$$\mathsf{K}_A = \{\varphi \mid \mathscr{F} \models \varphi \text{ for all } \mathscr{F} \in \mathsf{Frm}_A\}$$

More generally, given any class $\mathscr{C}$ of $\mathscr{L}_A$-frames, we define the logic of $\mathscr{C}$ as the set $\mathsf{Log}(\mathscr{C}) = \{\varphi \mid \mathscr{C} \models \varphi\}$.

4.3 Hilbert-Style Axiomatization

We show in this section that the minimal finite-chain graded modal logic K_A is axiomatizable. Let us introduce a Hilbert-style axiomatization for K_A, and show the completeness theorem.

Definition 4.5 The Hilbert-style axiomatic system $\mathbf{H}_A$ for K_A consists of the following axioms and inference rules:

(A1) All instances of propositional tautologies.
(A2) $\Diamond_0 p \leftrightarrow \top$.
(A3) $\Diamond_a \bot \leftrightarrow \bot$, for $a \neq 0$.
(A4) $\Diamond_a(p \vee q) \leftrightarrow \Diamond_a p \vee \Diamond_a q$.
(A5) $\Diamond_b p \to \Diamond_a p$, for $a \leq b$.
(MP) from φ and $\varphi \to \psi$ infer ψ.
(Sub) from φ infer any uniform substitution instance of φ.

A formula φ is a *theorem* of $\mathbf{H}_A$ (notation: $\vdash_{\mathbf{H}_A} \varphi$), if there is a proof of φ in $\mathbf{H}_A$. Let $\mathsf{Thm}(\mathbf{H}_A)$ be the set of all theorems in $\mathbf{H}_A$.

Proposition 4.1 *The following conditions hold in* $\mathbf{H}_A$*:*

(i) $\vdash_{\mathbf{H}_A} \Box_0\varphi \leftrightarrow \bot$.
(ii) if $a \neq 0$, *then* $\vdash_{\mathbf{H}_A} \Box_a \top \leftrightarrow \top$.
(iii) $\vdash_{\mathbf{H}_A} \Box_a(\varphi \to \psi) \to (\Box_a\varphi \to \Box_a\psi)$.
(iv) if $a \neq 0$ *and* $\vdash_{\mathbf{H}_A} \varphi$, *then* $\vdash_{\mathbf{H}_A} \Box_a\varphi$.
(v) if $\vdash_{\mathbf{H}_A} \varphi \to \phi$, *then* $\vdash_{\mathbf{H}_A} \Diamond_a\varphi \to \Diamond_a\psi$ *and* $\vdash_{\mathbf{H}_A} \Box_a\varphi \to \Box_a\psi$.

Proof Exercise. □

In the Proposition 4.1, the condition (iv) is often taken as the rule of generalization for $\Box_a$ $(a \neq 0)$, and we use the notation (Gen) for this rule. The rule (v) is often called monotonicity of modal operators.

Definition 4.6 A *normal finite-chain graded modal logic* is a set Λ of $\mathscr{L}_A$-formulae such that $\mathsf{Thm}(\mathbf{H}_A) \subseteq \Lambda$, and Λ is closed under rules (MP) and (Sub), and (Gen), i.e., for $a \neq 0$, if $\varphi \in \Lambda$, then $\Box_a\varphi \in \Lambda$.

Remark 4.1 Normal finite-chain graded modal logics defined as in the Definition 4.6 differ from multimodal logics in, for example, [3, 16]. In general, there is no interaction between modalities in multimodal logics, while the chain order between indexes of modalities in normal finite-chain graded modal logics is assumed and the axiom (A5) is contained to the minimal logic $\mathbf{H}_A$. A generalization of our logic to arbitrary chain or lattice setting could show a big difference between our logics and multimodal logics. See the discussion in Sect. 4.7.

For any normal finite-chain graded modal logic Λ, a $\mathscr{L}_A$-formula φ is *derivable* from a set Γ in Λ (notation: $\Gamma \vdash_\Lambda \varphi$), if $\varphi \in \Lambda$ or there is a finite subset Δ of Γ such that $\vdash_\Lambda \bigwedge \Delta \to \varphi$. We say that a set Γ of $\mathscr{L}_A$-formulae is Λ-*consistent*, if $\Gamma \nvdash_\Lambda \bot$. We say that Γ is *maximal* Λ-*consistent*, if Γ is Λ-consistent and has no consistent proper extension. The following facts can be shown regularly.

Fact 4.2 *Let* Γ *be any maximal* Λ-*consistent set of formulae,* φ *and* ψ *be formulae. Then the following hold:*

(i) $\varphi \notin \Gamma$ *iff* $\neg\varphi \in \Gamma$.
(ii) $\varphi \wedge \psi \in \Gamma$ *iff* $\varphi \in \Gamma$ *and* $\psi \in \Gamma$.
(iii) $\varphi \vee \psi \in \Gamma$ *iff* $\varphi \in \Gamma$ *or* $\psi \in \Gamma$.
(iv) *If* $\varphi \in \Gamma$ *and* $\varphi \to \psi \in \Gamma$, *then* $\psi \in \Gamma$.
(v) *If* $\vdash_\Lambda \varphi$, *then* $\varphi \in \Gamma$.
(vi) *If* $\varphi \in \Gamma$ *and* $\vdash_\Lambda \varphi \to \psi$. *Then* $\psi \in \Gamma$.

Fact 4.3 *Every* Λ*-consistent set of formulae can be extended to a maximal* Λ*-consistent set of formulae.*

Lemma 4.1 *Assume that* Γ *is a maximal* Λ*-consistent set. Then for any formulae* φ, ψ *and* $a, b \in A^*$, *the following hold:*

(i) $\Diamond!_a\varphi \in \Gamma$ *iff* $\Diamond_a\varphi \in \Gamma$ *and* $\Diamond_b\varphi \notin \Gamma$, *where* $a \prec b$.
(ii) *If* $\Diamond!_a\varphi \in \Gamma$, *then* a *is unique.*
(iii) *Either* $\forall a \in A^*(\Diamond_a\varphi \in \Gamma)$, *or* $\exists b \in A(\Diamond!_b\varphi \in \Gamma)$.
(iv) *If* $\vdash_\Lambda \varphi \to \psi$ *and* $\Diamond!_a\psi \in \Gamma$, *then there exists unique* $b \leq a$ *with* $\Diamond!_b\varphi \in \Gamma$.

Proof (i) is easy by Fact 4.2 and the definition of $\Diamond!_a\varphi$. For (ii), assume that $\Diamond!_a\varphi \in \Gamma$ but a is not unique. Then there is $b \in A$ such that $a \neq b$ and $\Diamond!_b\varphi \in \Gamma$. Assume $a \leq b$ without loss of generality. Then there are $c \in A$ such that $a \prec c \leq b$. Since $\Diamond!_a\varphi \in \Gamma$, by (i), we have $\Diamond_c\varphi \notin \Gamma$. Since $c \leq b$, we have $\vdash_\Lambda \Diamond_b\varphi \to \Diamond_c\varphi$. Hence $\Diamond_b\varphi \notin \Gamma$, a contradiction to $\Diamond!_b\varphi \in \Gamma$.

For (iii), assume that there is $a \in A \setminus \{1\}$ with $\Diamond_a\varphi \notin \Gamma$. Obviously $a \neq 0$, since $\vdash_\Lambda \Diamond_0\varphi \leftrightarrow \top$. Let $c = min\{x \in A \mid \Diamond_x\varphi \notin \Gamma\} \neq 0$. Thus by the (LC) condition in the lattice A, let $b \prec c$, and so $\Diamond_b\varphi \in \Gamma$. By (i), we get $\Diamond!_b\varphi \in \Gamma$.

For (iv), assume that $\vdash_{\mathbf{H}_A} \varphi \to \psi$ and $\Diamond!_a\psi \in \Gamma$. By (i), $\Diamond_c\psi \notin \Gamma$ where $a \prec c$. Then $\vdash_\Lambda \Diamond_c\varphi \to \Diamond_c\psi$. So $\Diamond_c\varphi \notin \Gamma$. By (ii) and (iii), there exists a unique $b \in A$ with $\Diamond!_b\varphi \in \Gamma$. Assume $a < b$. There exists $c \in A$ such that $a \prec c \leq b$. Since $\Diamond!_a\psi \in \Gamma$, by (i), we have $\Diamond_c\psi \notin \Gamma$. Since $\vdash_\Lambda \Diamond_b\psi \to \Diamond_c\psi$ and $\Diamond_c\psi \notin \Gamma$, we have $\Diamond_b\psi \notin \Gamma$. By $\vdash_\Lambda \varphi \to \psi$, $\Diamond_b\varphi \notin \Gamma$, a contradiction to $\Diamond!_b\varphi \in \Gamma$. Then $a \not< b$ and so $b \leq a$. □

Definition 4.7 For any normal finite-chain graded modal logic Λ, define the canonical model $\mathscr{M}^\Lambda = (W^\Lambda, \sigma^\Lambda, V^\Lambda)$ for Λ as follows:

(i) $W^\Lambda = \{w \mid w \text{ is a maximal } \Lambda\text{-consistent set of formulae}\}$
(ii)

$$\sigma^\Lambda(u)(v) = \begin{cases} 1, & \text{if } \forall a \in A^* \forall \varphi \in v(\Diamond_a\varphi \in u). \\ min\{a \in A \mid \Diamond!_a\varphi \in u \ \&\ \varphi \in v\}, & \text{otherwise.} \end{cases}$$

(iii) $V^\Lambda(p) = \{u \in W^\Lambda \mid p \in u\}$, for all $p \in \mathsf{Prop}$.

We say that the frame $\mathscr{F}^\Lambda = (W^\Lambda, \sigma^\Lambda)$ is the canonical frame for Λ.

In the definition of canonical model, the definition of the function σ^Λ is sound. If there exist $a \in A$ and $\varphi \in v$ such that $\Diamond_a\varphi \notin u$, then by Lemma 4.1, there exists unique $b \in A$ such that $\Diamond_b!\varphi \in u$. Note that this definition differs from the definition of canonical model in classical modal logic (cf. [3]).

Lemma 4.2 *For all $a \neq 1$ and formula φ, the following hold in canonical model $\mathscr{M}^\Lambda$ for any normal finite-chain graded modal logic Λ:*

(i) $\sigma^\Lambda(u)(v) \geq a$ iff $\{\Diamond_a\varphi \mid \varphi \in v\} \subseteq u$ iff $\{\varphi \mid \Box_a\varphi \in u\} \subseteq v$.
(ii) if $\Diamond_a\varphi \in u$, then there exists $v \in W^\Lambda$ such that $\sigma^\Lambda(u)(v) \geq a$ and $\varphi \in v$.

Proof (i) The second biconditional is easy. For the first biconditional, first, we assume $\sigma^\Lambda(u)(v) = b \geq a$. If $b = 1$, by definition of σ^Λ, we have $\{\Diamond_a\varphi \mid \varphi \in v\} \subseteq u$. Suppose $b \neq 1$. Let $\varphi \in v$. We show $\Diamond_a\varphi \in u$. Suppose $\Diamond_a\varphi \notin u$. Let $m = min\{t \in A \mid \Diamond_t\varphi \notin u\}$. Obviously $m \neq 0$. Hence there is $n \in A$ such that $\Diamond_n\varphi \in u$ and $n \prec m$. So $\Diamond!_n\varphi \in u$. Since $\sigma^\Lambda(u)(v) = b$, we have $b \leq n$. But $b \geq a \geq m > n$, a contradiction.

Conversely, assume $\sigma^\Lambda(u)(v) = b < a$. Obviously $b \neq 1$. Thus there exists $\varphi \in v$ such that $\Diamond!_b\varphi \in u$. Then $\Diamond_c\varphi \notin u$ where $b \prec c$. By $b < a$ and $b \prec c$, we have $c \leq a$. Since $\Diamond_c\varphi \notin u$ and $\vdash \Diamond_a\varphi \to \Diamond_c\varphi$, we have $\Diamond_a\varphi \notin u$.

(ii) Assume $\Diamond_a\varphi \in u$. Let $Y = \{\psi \mid \Box_a\psi \in u\} \cup \{\varphi\}$. Now we show that Y is Λ-consistent. Suppose not. Then there are $\psi_1, \ldots, \psi_n \in \{\psi \mid \Box_a\psi \in u\}$ such that $\vdash_\Lambda (\psi_1 \wedge \cdots \wedge \psi_n \wedge \phi) \to \bot$. So $\vdash_\Lambda (\psi_1 \wedge \cdots \wedge \psi_n) \to \neg\varphi$. Then by the monotonicity of modal operators, we have $\vdash_\Lambda \Box_a(\psi_1 \wedge \cdots \wedge \psi_n) \to \Box_a\neg\varphi$. By (A3), we have $\vdash_\Lambda \Box_a(\psi_1 \wedge \cdots \wedge \psi_n) \leftrightarrow (\Box_a\psi_1 \wedge \cdots \wedge \Box_a\psi_n)$. So $\vdash_\Lambda \Box_a\psi_1 \wedge \cdots \wedge \Box_a\psi_n \to \neg\Diamond_a\varphi$. Since $\Box_a\psi_1, \ldots, \Box_a\psi_n \in u$, we have $\neg\Diamond_a\varphi \in u$, and so $\Diamond_a\varphi \notin u$, a contradiction. It follows that Y is Λ-consistent. Then Y can be extended to a maximal Λ-consistent set v of formulae. Hence $\varphi \in v$ and $\{\psi \mid \Box_a\psi \in u\} \subseteq v$. By (i), $\sigma^\Lambda(u)(v) \geq a$. □

Theorem 4.4 *For any formula φ and $u \in W^\Lambda$, $\mathscr{M}^\Lambda, u \models \varphi$ iff $\varphi \in u$.*

Proof By induction on the length of φ. The atomic and boolean cases are easy. We prove only the modal case. Let $\varphi = \Diamond_a\psi$. Assume $\mathscr{M}^\Lambda, u \models \Diamond_a\psi$. Then there exists $\mathscr{M}^\Lambda, v \in W^\Lambda$ such that $v \models \psi$ and $\sigma^\Lambda(u)(v) \geq a$. By the inductive hypothesis, $\psi \in v$. By Lemma 4.3(i), $\Diamond_a\psi \in u$. Conversely, assume $\Diamond_a\psi \in u$. By Lemma 4.2, there exists $v \in W^\Lambda$ such that $\sigma^\Lambda(u)(v) \geq a$ and $\psi \in v$. By the inductive hypothesis, $\mathscr{M}^\Lambda, v \models \psi$. Hence $\mathscr{M}^\Lambda, u \models \Diamond_a\psi$. □

Corollary 4.1 $\mathsf{K}_A = \mathsf{Thm}(\mathbf{H}_A)$.

The Proof of the Theorem 4.4 is rather similar to that in classical modal logic [3, 7]. The minimal logic K_A is a conservative extension of the classical minimal normal modal logic K in the sense that the 'normal' part of K_A is just the same as multimodal K. The only difference is that we add axioms (A2) and (A5).

4.4 Normal Finite-Chain Graded Modal Logics

Given a family $\{\Lambda_i : i \in I\}$ of normal finite-chain graded modal logics, it is easy to show that the intersection $\bigcap_{i \in I} \Lambda_i$ is also a normal finite-chain graded modal logic. Given a normal finite-chain graded modal logic Λ and a set Γ of $\mathscr{L}_A$-formulae, define the normal extension of Λ generated by Γ as the set $\Lambda \oplus \Gamma = \bigcap\{\Lambda' : \Lambda \cup \Gamma \subseteq \Lambda'$ and Λ' is a normal finite-chain graded modal logic$\}$.

For any normal finite-chain graded modal logic Λ, let $\mathsf{NExt}(\Lambda)$ be the class of all normal finite-chain graded modal logics extending Λ. Then it is easy to see that $(\mathsf{NExt}(\Lambda), \cap, \oplus)$ is a lattice of logics.

Let us consider some normal finite-chain graded modal logics corresponding to those classical normal modal logics usually studied in the literature. Consider the following sets of axioms:

$$(T_A)\ \{p \to \Diamond_a p : a \in A^*\} \qquad (B_A)\ \{p \to \Box_a \Diamond_b p : a, b \in A^*\}$$
$$(4_A)\ \{\Diamond_a \Diamond_b p \to \Diamond_c p : a, b, c \in A^*\} \qquad (5_A)\ \{\Diamond_a p \to \Box_b \Diamond_c p : a, b, c \in A^*\}$$

These formulae have their correspondents in classical modal logic.

The immediate observation is that these formulae describe first-order properties of $\mathscr{L}_A$-frames. We may consider the first-order language $\mathscr{L}_A$ the nonlogical relational symbols of which are binary relations $\{R_a : a \in A^*\}$. For any $\mathscr{L}_A$-frame $\mathscr{F} = (W, \sigma)$, the interpretation of R_a is $\sigma(x)(y) \geq a$. Then we may prove the following correspondence result between our modal formulae and the first-order formulae.

Lemma 4.3 *Let $\mathscr{F}$ be a $\mathscr{L}_A$-frame. Then the following hold:*

(i) $\mathscr{F} \models p \to \Diamond_a p$ *iff* $\mathscr{F} \models \forall x R_a xx$.
(ii) $\mathscr{F} \models p \to \Box_a \Diamond_a p$ *iff* $\mathscr{F} \models \forall xy(R_a xy \to R_b yx)$.
(iii) $\mathscr{F} \models \Diamond_a \Diamond_b p \to \Diamond_c p$ *iff* $\mathscr{F} \models \forall xyz(R_a xy \wedge R_b yz \to R_c xz)$.
(iv) $\mathscr{F} \models \Diamond_a p \to \Box_b \Diamond_c p$ *iff* $\mathscr{F} \models \forall xyz(R_a xy \wedge R_b xz \to R_c zy)$.

Proof We show only (i) and (iii). Other items are similar. For (i), the right-to-left direction is easy. For the other direction, let x be a point in $\mathscr{F}$. Define the valuation V in $\mathfrak{F}$ by putting $V(p) = \{x\}$ for each propositional letter p. Then $x \models p$, and so $x \models \Diamond_a p$. Then there is a point z such that $z \models p$ and $\sigma(x)(z) \geq a$. Hence $t = x$, and so $\sigma(x)(x) \geq a$. For (iii), we check only again the left-to-right direction. Let x, y, z be any points in $\mathscr{F}$. Suppose that $\sigma(x)(y) \geq a$ and $\sigma(y)(z) \geq b$. Define the valuation V by putting $V(p) = \{z\}$ for all propositional letters p. So $y \models \Diamond_b p$. Then $x \models \Diamond_a \Diamond_b p$. Hence we have $x \models \Diamond_c p$. Then there exits a point u such that $u \models p$ and $\sigma(x)(u) \geq c$. Since $V(p) = \{z\}$, we have $u = z$, and so $\sigma(x)(z) \geq c$. □

We say that a $\mathscr{L}_A$-frame $\mathscr{F}$ satisfies the conditions $\forall x R_a xx$, $\forall xy(R_a xy \to R_b yx)$, $\forall xyz(R_a xy \wedge R_b yz \to R_c xz)$, and $\forall xyz(R_a xy \wedge R_b xz \to R_c zy)$ respectively, are *reflexive*, *symmetry*, *transitive* and *Euclidean* respectively.

Consider the following normal finite-chain graded modal logics: (i) $\mathsf{T}_A = \mathsf{K}_A \oplus T_A$, (ii) $\mathsf{B}_A = \mathsf{K}_A \oplus B_A$, (iii) $\mathsf{K4}_A = \mathsf{K}_A \oplus 4_A$, (iv) $\mathsf{S4}_A = \mathsf{K4}_A \oplus T_A$; (v) $\mathsf{S5}_A = \mathsf{S4}_A \oplus B_A = \mathsf{T}_A \oplus 5_A$. Using canonical models, we may show that above normal finite-chain graded modal logics are complete with respect to their corresponding frame classes.

Theorem 4.5 *The normal finite-chain graded modal logics* T_A, B_A, $\mathsf{K4}_A$, $\mathsf{S4}_A$ *and* $\mathsf{S5}_A$ *are complete with respect to the classes of reflexive, symmetry, transitive, reflexive transitive, and reflexive Euclidean* $\mathscr{L}_A$*-frames respectively.*

Proof We check only the completeness of $\mathsf{K4}_A$. It suffices to show the canonical model $\mathscr{M}$ for $\mathsf{K4}_A$ is transitive. Let x, y, z be points in the canonical model $\mathscr{M}$. Suppose $\sigma(x)(y) \geq a$ and $\sigma(y)(z) \geq b$. It suffices to show $\sigma(x)(z) \geq c$. Assume $\varphi \in z$. Then $\Diamond_b\varphi \in y$. So $\Diamond_a\Diamond_b\varphi \in x$. By $\vdash_{\mathsf{K4}_A} \Diamond_a\Diamond_b p \to \Diamond_c p$, we have $\Diamond_c\varphi \in x$. □

We say that a normal finite-chain graded modal logic Λ is *canonical*, if the canonical frame $\mathscr{F}^\Lambda$ for it is a frame for the logic Λ. Logics T_A, B_A, $\mathsf{K4}_A$, $\mathsf{S4}_A$ are canonical. It is clear that every canonical normal finite-chain graded modal logic is complete. Which normal finite-chain graded modal logics are canonical? Sahlqvist [19] proved that all classical normal modal logics generated by Sahlqvist formulae are canonical. This theorem can be extended to normal finite-chain graded modal logics.

Definition 4.8 A $\mathscr{L}_A$-formula φ is *positive* (*negative*), if each propositional letter p in φ occurs only in a even (odd) number of occurrences of $\neg$. A *boxed atom* is a formula of the form $\Box_{a_1} \ldots \Box_{a_n} p$ $(n > 0)$.

A Sahlqvist antecedent is a formula built from $\top$, $\bot$, boxed atoms and negative formulae using $\wedge$, $\vee$ and $\Diamond_a$ $(a \neq 1)$. A Sahlqvist implication is a formula of the form $\varphi \to \psi$ where φ is a Sahlqvist antecedent, and ψ a positive formula.

A Sahlqvist $\mathscr{L}_A$-formula is built from Sahlqvist implications using $\wedge$ and $\Box_a$ $(a \neq 1)$ freely, and using disjunction only between formulae without common propositional letters.

Theorem 4.6 *Every Sahlqvist formula* $\mathscr{L}_A$*-formula is equivalent to a first-order formula in* $\mathscr{L}_A$ *over* $\mathscr{L}_A$*-frames. Moreover, every normal finite-chain graded modal logic generated by Sahlqvist* $\mathscr{L}_A$*-formulae is canonical.*

Proof For each Sahlqvist $\mathscr{L}_A$-formula φ, there exists an equivalent formula φ^* which may contains only modalities $\Diamond_a$ and $\Box_a$ for $a \neq 0$, since $\Diamond_0\varphi \leftrightarrow \top \in \Lambda$ and $\Box_0\varphi \leftrightarrow \bot \in \Lambda$. Then by using the Sahlqvist–van Benthem algorithm, we get the first-order correspondent. Moreover, the canonicity of Sahlqvist normal finite-chain graded modal logics is shown in the same way as that for classical Sahlqvist normal modal logics. See [3, 16] for a proof. □

4.5 Algebraic Completeness

In this section, we show that the minimal logic K_A is also determined by a variety of algebras. First, we define the notion of finite-chain algebras as follows.

Definition 4.9 A finite-chain algebra ('FCA' for short) is an algebra $\mathfrak{B} = (B, \vee, \neg, \bot, \{\Diamond_a\}_{a\in A^*})$ where $(B, \vee, \neg, \bot)$ is a Boolean algebra and each $\Diamond_a$ satisfies the following conditions for all $x, y \in B$:

(1) $\Diamond_0 x = \top$.
(2) $\Diamond_a \bot = \bot$, for $a \neq 0$.
(3) $\Diamond_a (x \vee y) = \Diamond_a x \vee \Diamond_a y$.
(4) $\Diamond_b x \leq \Diamond_a x$, for $a \leq b$.

where $\top := \neg\bot$, and $\leq$ is defined as: $a \leq b$ iff $a \vee b = b$. We denote the class of all finite-chain algebras by $\mathbb{FCA}$.

It is clear that every finite-chain algebra is a Boolean algebra with normal modal operators with additional axioms (1) and (4).

Given a finite-chain algebra $\mathfrak{B}$, an *assignment* in $\mathfrak{B}$ is a function $\theta : \mathsf{Prop} \to B$. Then θ can be extended to all formulae homomorphically. Let $\widehat{\theta}(\varphi)$ be the denotation of φ under θ. A formula φ is true under an assignment θ in $\mathfrak{B}$ (notation: $\mathfrak{B}, \theta \models \varphi$), if $\widehat{\theta}(\varphi) = \top$. We say that φ is *valid* in $\mathfrak{B}$, if $\mathfrak{B}, \theta \models \varphi$ for all assignments θ in $\mathfrak{B}$. By $\mathbb{FCA} \models \varphi$ we mean that $\mathfrak{B} \models \varphi$ for all $\mathfrak{B} \in \mathbb{FCA}$.

For any normal finite-chain graded modal logic Λ, let $\mathbb{V}_\Lambda$ be the variety for Λ, i.e., the class of all finite-chain algebras validating all theorems in Λ.

For showing the algebraic completeness of normal finite-chain graded modal logics, we need the Lindenbaum–Tarski construction. Let $\mathfrak{Fml}(A)$ be the set of all $\mathscr{L}_A$-formulae. For any normal finite-chain graded modal logic Λ, define the binary relation $\sim_\Lambda$ over $\mathfrak{Fml}(A)$ by:

$$\varphi \sim_\Lambda \psi \text{ iff } \vdash_\Lambda \varphi \leftrightarrow \psi.$$

Then it is easy to show that $\sim_\Lambda$ is a congruence relation. For any formula φ, let $|\varphi| = \{\psi \mid \varphi \sim_\Lambda \psi\}$ be the equivalent class of φ. Let $\mathfrak{Fml}(A)/_{\sim_\Lambda} = \{|\varphi| : \varphi \in \mathfrak{Fml}(A)\}$ be the quotient set. Define the Lindenbaum–Tarski algebra for Λ as the algebra $\mathfrak{B}^\Lambda = (\mathfrak{Fml}(A)/_{\sim_\Lambda}, \vee, \neg, \bot, \{\Diamond_a\}_{a \in A^*})$ where

$$|\varphi| \vee |\psi| = |\varphi \vee \psi|, \neg|\varphi| = |\neg\varphi|, \bot := |\bot|, \text{ and } \Diamond_a|\varphi| := |\Diamond_a \varphi|.$$

Proposition 4.2 *For any normal finite-chain graded modal logic Λ, $\mathfrak{B}^\Lambda \in \mathbb{V}_\Lambda$.*

Proof We only verify the condition (4) in the definition of finite-chain algebras. Others conditions can be shown easily. Let $a \leq b$ and φ be any formula. Then $\vdash_\Lambda \Diamond_b \varphi \to \Diamond_a \varphi$. Thus $\vdash_\Lambda \Diamond_b \varphi \vee \Diamond_a \varphi \leftrightarrow \Diamond_a \varphi$. Then $|\Diamond_b \varphi| \vee |\Diamond_a \varphi|_\Lambda = |\Diamond_a \varphi|_\Lambda$. Then $|\Diamond_b \varphi| \leq |\Diamond_a \varphi|$. Therefore $\Diamond_b |\varphi| \leq \Diamond_a |\varphi|$. □

Theorem 4.7 (Algebraic Completeness) *For any formula φ and normal finite-chain graded modal logic Λ, $\vdash_\Lambda \varphi$ iff $\mathfrak{B}^\Lambda \models \varphi$*

Proof The left-to-right direction is shown by induction on the proof of φ in Λ. Conversely, assume that $\nvdash_\Lambda \varphi$. Then $\varphi \leftrightarrow \top \notin \Lambda$, i.e., $|\varphi| \neq |\top|$. Define an assignment θ by: $\theta(p) = |p|$ for every variable p. Then by induction on the complexity of ψ we may show that $\widehat{\theta}(\psi) = |\psi|$. Hence φ is refuted by θ in $\mathfrak{B}^\Lambda$. Therefore $\mathfrak{B}^\Lambda \not\models \varphi$. □

Corollary 4.2 *For any formula φ, $\vdash_{\mathbf{H}_A} \varphi$ iff $\mathbb{FCA} \models \varphi$.*

Some weak completeness results for classical modal logics can be obtained via Jónsson-Tarski representation theorem for modal algebras: every normal modal algebra is embeddable into a complex modal algebra. Here we extend this result to our finite-chain algebras. Let us give some basic notions first.

Definition 4.10 For any $\mathscr{L}_A$-frame $\mathfrak{F} = (W, \sigma)$, define the *complex algebra* of $\mathfrak{F}$ as the power set algebra $\mathfrak{F}^+ = (\wp(W), \cup, -, \varnothing, \{\Diamond_a\}_{a \in A^*})$ where $\cup$ is the union, and $-$ is the complement operation in $\wp(W)$, and each $\Diamond_a$ is defined by:

$$\Diamond_a X = \{w \in W \mid \sigma(w)(u) \geq a \text{ for some } u \in X\}.$$

Then define the dual $\Box_a$ of $\Diamond_a$ by: $\Box_a X = -\Diamond_a - X = \{w \in W \mid \sigma(w)(u) \geq a \text{ implies } u \in X\}$. It is easy to check that each complex algebra $\mathfrak{F}^+$ is a FCA.

Definition 4.11 For any FCA $\mathfrak{B} = (B, \vee, \neg, \bot, \{\Diamond_a\}_{a \in A^*})$, define the dual frame of $\mathfrak{B}$ as the $\mathscr{L}_A$-frame $\mathfrak{B}_+ = (Uf(B), \sigma)$ as follows:

(i) $Uf(B)$ is the set of all ultrafilters in $\mathfrak{B}$.
(ii) Define a binary relation R_a over $Uf(B)$ for each $a \in A^*$ by

$$uR_a v \text{ iff } \Diamond_a X \in u \text{ for all } X \in v.$$

(iii)

$$\sigma(u)(v) = \begin{cases} 1, & \text{if } uR_a v \text{ for all } a \in A^*. \\ max\{b : uR_b v\}, & \text{otherwise.} \end{cases}$$

Now let us show that the definition of σ is sound.[1] Assume that not $uR_a v$ for some $a \in A^*$. By definition of R_a, there exists $X \in v$ such that $\Diamond_a X \notin u$. For any $c \geq a$, since $\Diamond_a X \leq \Diamond_c X$, we have $\Diamond_c X \notin u$. Hence $max\{b : uR_b v\}$ exists.

Proposition 4.3 *Given any FCA $\mathfrak{B} = (B, \vee, \neg, \bot, \{\Diamond_a\}_{a \in A^*})$ and its dual frame $\mathfrak{B}_+ = (Uf(B), \sigma)$, for any $u, v \in Uf(B)$ and $a \in A^*$, the following hold:*

(i) $\sigma(u)(v) \geq a$ iff $uR_a v$ iff $\{\Diamond_a X : X \in v\} \subseteq u$.
(ii) If $\Diamond_a X \in u$ and $X \neq \bot$, there exists $v \in Uf(B)$ with $X \in v$ and $\sigma(u)(v) \geq a$.

Proof It is easy to show (i) by the definition of σ. For (ii), assume $\Diamond_a X \in u$ and $X \neq \emptyset$. If $a = 0$, $\sigma(u)(v) \geq 0$ where v is an ultrafilter extending $\{X\}$. Note that $\{X\}$ has finite intersection property. Assume that $a \neq 0$. Then $\Box_a(X \cap Y) = \Box_a X \cap \Box_a Y$. Thus $\{Y : \Box_a Y \in u\}$ is closed under conjunction. Consider the set $T = \{X\} \cap \{Y : \Box_a Y \in u\}$. Suppose that $X \cap Y = \emptyset$ for some Y with $\Box_a Y \in u$. Then $X \leq \neg Y$. Hence $\Diamond_a X \leq \Diamond_a \neg Y$. Then $\Diamond_a X \leq \neg \Box_a Y$. Since $\Diamond_a X \in u$, we get $\neg \Box_a Y \in u$, a contradiction. Hence T has the finite intersection property. Then T can be extended to a ultrafilter v such that $X \in v$ and $\sigma(u)(v) \geq a$. □

[1] This definition of σ was first suggested by Katsuhiko Sano (Japan Advanced Institute of Science and Technology).

Theorem 4.8 (Representation) *Every finite-chain algebra $\mathfrak{B}$ is embeddable into the complex algebra* $(\mathfrak{B}_+)^+$.

Proof Let $\mathfrak{B} = (B, \vee, \neg, \bot, \{\Diamond_a\}_{a\in A^*})$ and $\mathfrak{B}_+ = (Uf(B), \sigma)$. Define the map $r : B \to Uf(B)$ by putting: $r(x) = \{u \in Uf(B) \mid x \in u\}$. We show that r is injective. Assume $x \neq y$. Then there exists an ultrafilter u such that $x \in u$ but $y \notin u$. Hene $r(x) \neq r(y)$. It suffices to show that r preserves all Boolean and modal operations. The Boolean cases are easy. For each $\Diamond_a$, we show that $r(\Diamond_a x) = \Diamond_a r(x)$. First, suppose $u \in \Diamond_a r(x)$. Then there exists $v \in r(x)$ such that $x \in v$ and $\sigma(u)(v) \geq a$. By Proposition 4.3 (i), we have $\Diamond_a x \in u$. Hence $u \in r(\Diamond_a x)$. Conversely, let $u \in r(\Diamond_a x)$. Then $\Diamond_a x \in u$. Suppose $x = \bot$. Then $a = 0$, otherwise $\Diamond_a \bot = \bot \in u$, a contradiction. Hence $u \in \Diamond_0 r(x) = Uf(B)$. Suppose that $x \neq \bot$. By Proposition 4.3 (ii), there exists $v \in Uf(B)$ such that $x \in v$ and $\sigma(u)(v) \geq a$. Hence $u \in \Diamond_a r(x)$. □

By the representation theorem, the weak completeness of $\mathbf{H}_A$ with respect to the class of all $\mathscr{L}_A$-frames can be shown as follows: First the Hilbert-style system $\mathbf{H}_A$ can be characterized by the variety $\mathbb{FCA}$. Then the set K_A of all validities can be characterized by the class of all complex FCAs. Since every FCA is embeddable in a complex FCA, a formula is valid in $\mathbb{FCA}$ iff it is valid in Frm_A. Therefore, the weak completeness of $\mathbf{H}_A$ follows.

4.6 Applications

In this section, we show how finite-chain graded modal logic can be applied to model checking in computer science, and to epistemic logic of belief. For model checking, we concentrate on transition systems. For epistemic logic, we analyze the notion of plausibility of belief.

Transition Systems. Model checking prerequisite a model of the system under consideration. Usually transition systems are used to model the system behavior. we recall some basic notions of transition system from [2]. A *transition system* is a tuple $\mathfrak{T} = (S, Act, \Rightarrow, I, AP, L)$ where S is a set of sates, Act is a set of actions, $\rightarrow \subseteq S \times Act \times S$ is a transition relation, $I \subseteq S$ is a set of initial states, AP is a set of atomic propositions, and $L : S \to 2^{AP}$ is a labeling function. Here action names are used for describing communication mechanisms between processes.

We see immediately from mathematical point of view that each transition system is a multiset with initial states and valuations. Given a transition system $\mathfrak{T} = (S, Act, \Rightarrow\ , I, AP, L)$, the transition relation $\rightarrow$ can be rewrite into a function $\Rightarrow: S \times S \to Act$. Here Act is a pure set of actions without any structure. We can find many examples of such transition systems, for example, in [2], where we find no any restrictions on actions.

Restrictions or conditions on actions in some transition systems may play the role of protocols for action. It is plausible to add some structure to the set of actions in transition systems. Let us give an simple example of transition system with ordered action sets. Let $S = \{A, B\}$ be the set of states in which A and B stand for two places. Let $Act = \{a, b, c\}$ be action set where a, b, c stand for the channels from A to B:

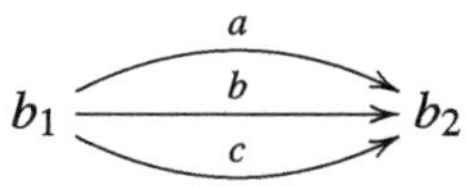

This is a nondeterministic transition system. Now consider the following situation: the channels a, b, c are closed at times $1:00, 2:00, 3:00$ respectively. This is a protocol over the action set. Hence the order $a \leq b \leq c$ is induced. This kind of structures can be analyzed in transition systems with protocol actions. Finite-chain graded models introduced in this paper are exactly a sort of transition system with the lattice under consideration as the protocol.

Epistemic Doxastic Logic of Belief. One approach in [20] for the epistemic doxastic logic is to introduce plausibility order over states in epistemic model. An epistemic–doxastic model is a structure $M = (W, \{\sim_i\}_{i\in I}, \{\leq_{i,s}\}_{i\in I\ \&\ s\in W}, V)$ where W is a set of states, I is a set of agents, $\sim_i$ stands for the epistemic accessibility relation for agent i, and $\leq_{i,s}$ stands for the plausibility order for agent i at state s read as follows:

$x \leq_{i,s} y$ if in state s agent i reckons that state y is at least plausible as x.

Let $B_i\varphi$ mean that agent i believes that φ is the case. Then for any epistemic doxastic model M and state s, the formula $B_i\varphi$ is true at s in M iff φ is true at the most plausible world t, i.e., the maximal world in the order $\leq_{i,s}$.

Using our finite-chain graded models, it is easy to capture the plausibility reading of belief. Fix a set I of agents. Consider a finite-chain graded model $\mathfrak{M} = (W, \{\sigma_i\}_{i\in I})$ where $\sigma_i : W \times W \to A$ stands for the doxastic function for agent i. The plausibility order for agent i is determined by the function σ and the lattice order in A. The semantics of $B_i\varphi$ can be given as follows:

$B_i\varphi$ is true at a state s iff φ is true at the most plausible world t, i.e., the state t such that $\sigma_i(s, t)$ is the least upper bound of the set $\{\sigma(s, x) \mid x \in W\}$.

In such simplified models, the plausibility order determines belief directly.

4.7 Conclusion and Future Directions

The minimal finite-chain modal logic K_A presented in this paper is different from other related logics. First, it differs from classical modal logic. From the algebraic point of view, this logic extends BAOs by adding special axioms. The axioms (A3) and (A4) show that those operators $\Diamond_a$ for $a \neq 0, 1$ are normal modal operators. Second, K_A is different from the minimal graded modal logic developed in [12]. Graded modal operators $\Diamond_n$ are not normal for $n \geq 2$. Thus our finite-chain modal logic is incomparable with graded modal logic. Third, K_A is a conservative extension of the classical minimal modal logic K. It is a new modal logic different from existing multimodal logics. From technical point of view, the relationship between modalities is introduced by the finite chain. This kind of generalization can be applied to many practical scenarios. For further study on this kind of modal logics, we may consider the following further directions:

Lattice-based graded modal logic. As we comment on the semantics for modal operators, if we change the finite chain to other lattices, we may get rather different modal logics. Graded modal logic is an example, where the infinite chain of natural numbers is used. More generally, consider any lattice $(A, \wedge, \vee)$, we get a modal language $\mathscr{L}_A$ as the language for finite-chain graded modal logic. A more general semantics can be defined for it.

For any nonempty set $X \subseteq W$, we mean by $X \subseteq_\omega W$ that X is a finite subset of W. Given a subset $X \subseteq_\omega W$ and a state $w \in W$, we define

$$\sigma(w)(X) = \bigvee\{\sigma(w)(u) \mid u \in X\},$$

i.e., the least upper bound of $\{\sigma(w)(u) \mid u \in X\}$. The element $\sigma(w)(X)$ exists in A since X is finite. In particular, for $X = \varnothing$, we have $\sigma(w)(\varnothing) = \bigvee \varnothing = 0$. In this case, $\sigma(w)(X) \geq a$ is not equivalent to $\sigma(w)(u) \geq a$ for some $u \in X$.

Then we may define the satisfaction relation $\mathscr{M}, w \models \varphi$ as follows:

$$\mathscr{M}, w \models \Diamond_a\varphi \text{ iff } \exists X \subseteq_\omega W(\sigma(w)(X) \geq a \;\&\; \forall u \in X. \mathscr{M}, u \models \varphi).$$

Dually, we have $\mathscr{M}, w \models \Box_a\varphi$ iff $\forall X \subseteq_\omega W(\sigma(w)(X) \geq a \Rightarrow \exists u \in X. \mathscr{M}, u \models \varphi)$. In such a semantic, $\Diamond_a$ is not additive, i.e., not distributive over disjunction. Similarly, $\Box_a$ is not distributive over conjunction. Thus we get a logic which is different from finite-chain graded modal logic. Here the open problem is to axiomatize it.

Residuated lattice graded modal logic. As we mentioned in the introduction, Bou et al. [5] generalizes Kripke structures to residuated lattice-valued ones, and gives a new semantics for classical modal language. A new modal logic with canonical truth-constants based on a finite residuated lattice is shown to be complete. One direction for applying our approach to residuated lattice setting is to define a graded modal logic based on the semantics given in Bou et al. [5].

Let $(A, \wedge, \vee, \odot, \rightarrow, 0, 1)$ be a residuated lattice, where $\rightarrow$ is the right residual of $\odot$. As we do for finite-chain graded modal logic, we also introduce a modal language where modalities are $\Diamond_a$ and $\Box_a$ for $a \in A^*$. An A-valued model is a structure $\mathscr{M} = (W, R, V)$ where W is a nonempty set of states, $R : W \times W \rightarrow A$ is the accessibility relation, and $V : \mathsf{Prop} \times W \rightarrow A$ is a valuation. Then we may define the satisfaction relation as usual. In particular, we have the following clauses:

$\mathscr{M}, w \models p$ iff $V(p, w) = 1$.
$\mathscr{M}, w \models \Diamond_a\varphi$ iff $\bigvee\{R(w, w') \odot V(\varphi, w') : w' \in W\} \geq a$.

Moreover, for $\Box_a$, we may define it as the dual operation of $\Diamond_a$, or define it, using the clause in [5], as follows:

$$\mathcal{M}, w \models \Box_a \varphi \text{ iff } \bigwedge \{R(w, w') \to V(\varphi, w') : w' \in W\} \leq a.$$

Then the problem is to develop calculi for this logic.

Acknowledgments We would like to give our thanks to the anonymous review for very insightful comments which led us to improve the paper. We also thank for the comments from Prof. Wojciech Buszkowski (Poland), Prof. Hiroakira Ono (Japan), and other audience on the occasion of the Second Asian Workshop on Philosophical Logic.

References

1. G. Aucher. A combined system for update logic and belief revision. Master's thesis, Unviersiteit van Amsterdam, 2003.
2. C. Baier and J. P. Katoen. *Principles of Model Checking*. Cambridge MA: MIT Press, 2008.
3. P. Blackburn, M. de Rijke, and Y. Venema. *Modal Logic*. Cambridge University Press, 2001.
4. W. D. Blizard. Multiset theory. *Notre Dame Journal of Formal Logic*, 30(1):36–66, 1988.
5. F. Bou, F. Esreva, L. Godo, and Rodríguez. On the minumum many-valued modal logic over a finite residuated lattice. *Journal of Logic and Computation*, 21(5):739–790, 2011.
6. C. Cerrato. General canonical models for graded normal logics (graded modalities iv). *Studia Logica*, 49(2):241–252, 1990.
7. A. Chagrov and M. Zakharyaschev. *Modal Logic*. Oxford: Clarendon Press, 1997.
8. B. A. Davey and H. A. Priestley. *Introduction to Lattices and Order*. Cambridge University Press, 2nd edition, 2002.
9. F. De Caro. Graded modalities, ii (canonical models). *Studia Logica*, 47(1):1–10, 1988.
10. M. Fattorosi-Barnaba and C. Cerrato. Graded modalities. iii (the completeness and compactness of s4^0). *Studia Logica*, 47(2):99–110, 1988.
11. M. Fattorosi-Barnaba and F. De Caro. Graded modalities i. *Studia Logica*, 44(2):197–221, 1985.
12. K. Fine. In so many possible worlds. *Notre Dame Journal of formal logic*, 13(4):516–520, 1972.
13. R. Goldblatt. Varieties of complex algebras. *Annals of Pure and Applied Logic*, 44(3):173–242, 1989.
14. B. Jónnson and A. Tarski. Boolean algebras with operators. part ii. *American Journal of Mathematics*, 74(1):127–162, 1952.
15. B. Jónsson and A. Tarski. Boolean algebras with operators. part i. *American Journal of Mathematic*, 73(4):891–939, 1951.
16. M. Kracht. *Tools and Techniques in Modal Logic*. Amsterdam: North-Holland Publishing Co., 1999.
17. S. Kripke. A completeness theorem in modal logic. *The Journal of Symbolic Logic*, 24(1):1–14, 1959.
18. R. Milner. *Communicating and Mobile Systems: the pi Calculus*. Cambridge University Press, 1999.
19. H. Sahlqvist. Correspondence and completeness in the first and second-order semantics for modal logic. In *Proceedings of the 3rd Scandinavial Logic Symposium*, pages 110–143. Uppsala, 1975.
20. J. van Benthem. *Logical Dynamics of Information and Interaction*. Cambridge University Press, 2011.
21. W. Van der Hoek and J. J. C. Meyer. Graded modalities in epistemic logic. In *Logical Foundations of Computer Science-Tver '92*, volume LNCS 620, pages 503–514. Springer, Berlin Heidelberg, 1992.

Chapter 5
Knowledge and Local Actions

R. Ramanujam

Abstract The study of epistemic dynamics has largely concentrated on how knowledge of an agent changes due to communication and other 'global' actions that involve engagement of several agents. Local actions under the control of agents are treated as a special case. We point out that there are some specific issues of both technical and philosophical interest when we focus on local actions. For instance, when two agents can perform such actions concurrently, their knowledge changes independently as well. This has crucial implications for any dynamic logic of knowledge leading to high undecidability, suggesting that more subtlety is called for.

Keywords Epistemic logic · Dynamics · Local action

5.1 Overview

[1]Since the 1980s, propositional modal logics of knowledge and action have been investigated extensively, see [3, 5, 23]. There are principally two schools of thought: one that uses model change [3, 24] as its main tool, whereby epistemic structures are altered by actions, and the other [5, 17, 18] calculates knowledge change by watching the temporal flow of events. These views can be reconciled [26, 28] leading to many new technical insights [29].

What is the notion of action in such a study? We refer to the books cited for the notion (and papers such as [2, 7, 27]) as various authors articulate it, but attempt a basic outline here, with a view towards focussing on a specific aspect. Our aim is not to offer either a summary or critique of the extant models, but to train the light on a small nook in them. If this corner is typically overlooked, it is because the studies march on grand vistas where this issue is often not relevant. And yet, we suggest that there is meaningful education to be found in this corner.

[1] I wish to thank Fenrong Liu and Hiraokira Ono for their encouragement; I am indebted to Kamal Lodaya and Rohit Parikh for many discussions on this theme.

R. Ramanujam (✉)
Institute of Mathematical Sciences, Chennai, India
e-mail: jam@imsc.res.in

S. Ju et al. (eds.), *Modality, Semantics and Interpretations*,
Logic in Asia: Studia Logica Library, DOI 10.1007/978-3-662-47197-5_5

5.1.1 In Praise of Local Action

Central to the study of epistemic dynamics is the notion of agency, and the models begin with a (typically finite fixed) set of actors or reasoners who have partial access to information and perform informative (or other) acts with intention which leads to epistemic change. Moreover, their acts influence others in some way, and the very act may be in expectation of this influence. They observe event occurrences (which may or not be acts of others) and learn, which in turn causes them to act. This interplay of information and action, as well as mutual intersubjectivity in agent beliefs or knowledge that leads to the richness of epistemic dynamics.

Viewed thus, the most interesting actions are information gathering and information dissemination, typically involving more than one agent in a communication, public or private (between agents), or observation. Local action by an agent out of sight of other agents is hardly interesting, except perhaps to observe (disdainfully) that the knowledge of other agents does not change by such an act. This is precisely the point of departure for the study we undertake, and leads to several questions.

1. Can we conceive of situations where local action by agents do cause change in epistemic states of other agents, even their knowledge?
2. If not, does the remark above (that the knowledge of other agents does not change by a local action of one agent) amount to the sum total of *all* that we can say about locally controlled actions?
3. Does this property characterise local action? That is, whenever an action causes the knowledge of exactly one agent to change, it must be local in some sense?
4. Given a state of knowledge, we expect to precisely compute the new state of knowledge that results by the performance of some local action. Does this ability have any consequence in terms of computational power?
5. Can we characterize local actions that cause only a *finite* change in an agent's knowledge?

To see that these questions are interesting, we can consider many examples of rather mundane local acts. First, background knowledge can make a difference. It may well be the case that I typically have a cup of tea at 9:00 a.m., but if this is known to be a part of my routine, a colleague may well drop by at that hour hoping to join me in drinking tea. In stronger versions, the striking of the hour would induce knowledge rather than hopeful expectation. Second, suppose that I am looking for the precise statement of a theorem; I consider doing a Google search, or alternatively look up a treatise on the subject from the library. Both are informative local acts of mine that would cause no significant change in others' knowledge of anything at all, but are distinct in terms of my own learning and possibly, my subsequent behaviour. Third, consider I am sending a message to you saying, 'If you get this, for sure wear blue tomorrow', and see you wearing red the next day. Under certain conditions, I can well conclude that you did not get the message and are indeed unaware of my inference.

The last two questions listed above are technical, and relate to what kind of algorithms can be employed on models embodying such assumptions, and whether the reasoning can be restricted to finite means.

Note that actions can cause factual change as well as information change, and this holds for local actions as well. For instance, the act of my attempting to lift a bag may cause a factual change: the bag being no longer on the floor, or it may cause an information change without factual change, that it is too heavy for me to lift.

Two important aspects of actions in the context of agency are worth noting: one is the agent's *capability* to carry out the action, and the other is the action being enabled. The latter relates to background behaviour or protocol: I can easily walk out when you are talking to me, but it is 'not the done thing' and in that sense, the action is not enabled. Capability is of course dependent on my epistemic state (though perhaps not determined).

An important question then is whether the enabling of one action can disable another. Suppose that I perform one local action a in a state s in which you can perform an action b. Surely if I consider the state s' resulting when only I have performed a, your action b should still be enabled. Moreover, the state after both a and b are performed should be the same whichever be the order in which the two actions were performed. Such *causal independence* of local actions is often assumed as a matter of course, but then such assumptions need to be explicated in epistemic models, since I know that your b continues to be enabled after my a, whether I (can) observe its occurrence or not.

While the foregoing discussion has largely been philosophical, it must be pointed out that these considerations apply in concrete situations involving computational agents. In programs, local actions causing factual change correspond to updating local memory or file system, whereas local informative actions are typically *tests* on conditions. The element of controllability of actions is reflected by rigorous scope rules [1], and one may see this as the definition of locality in these systems. However, updates of local variables can leave traces elsewhere that become visible remotely; or indeed, an observer of routine periodic usage of a resource may infer something of the activity being carried out, in a manner akin to the examples discussed above. *Information flow analysis* of programs is an area [22] where such considerations are very relevant.

Another area where similar considerations apply is that of *distributed games* [15, 21]. These are games of imperfect information where each player moves on her own game board, and signalling is used to convey information. Local moves can carry a great deal of indirect information in such games.

5.1.2 This Study

Rather than situating the study of locally controlled action in dynamic epistemic logics or epistemic temporal logics, we concentrate on a transition system model underlying both (to reflect the fact that we assume very little structure) and instead, explore assumptions of the kind listed above. This allows us to formally pose some of these questions and answer them. Moreover, we study a simple propositional modal logic of knowledge with minimal dynamics interpreted on these transition systems. We show that for multiagent systems encapsulating some of the natural assumptions discussed above, there is no finite axiomatization of the valid formulas of the logic. For the one agent case, we can indeed get a complete axiomatization and a decision procedure for satisfiability.

Admittedly, the results are not technically hard to obtain, and the kind of undecidability we refer to is endemic in such systems. What we hope for is that this study contributes in a small way towards epistemic dynamics in which action structure is spelt out explicitly, and the interaction between locality, concurrency and communication is clarified in detail. The paper concludes with a discussion of this nature.

A technical point: in [8], lower bounds are derived for the complexity of reasoning about knowledge and time in a variety of logics. The logics which are highly undecidable in [8] are interpreted over frames which do not allow agents to forget or learn (calling for unbounded memory), and insist on unique initial states. Our negative result does not need such assumptions, but arises from the essential use of asynchronous local actions, often called "true concurrency;" this is closer in spirit to the work in [12], rather than [8].

5.2 Single Agent Systems

We begin with the simplest case, that of a single agent, and discuss the interaction between knowledge and action. Note that the agent is not even conscious of other agents' existence here. Even in this context, we ignore many important considerations. For instance, action can have complex structure, which is important for planning and strategizing, and we only consider 'atomic' actions without further structure.

Let Σ_0 be a fixed finite set of actions, and P a countable set of propositional symbols or conditions. We define $\Sigma = \Sigma_0 \cup \{p? \mid p \in P\}$. We call the latter *test actions*.

A **local control system** over Σ is a tuple $TS = (S, \rightarrow, \sim, V)$, where S is a set of states, $\rightarrow \subseteq (S \times \Sigma \times S)$ is a transition relation on states, and $\sim \subseteq S \times S$ is an equivalence relation (called the indistinguishability relation) satisfying the following conditions:

- For every $s_1, s_2 \in S, a \in \Sigma$, if $s_1 \sim s_2$ then (there exists $s_1' : s_1 \stackrel{a}{\rightarrow} s_1'$ if and only if there exists $s_2' : s_2 \stackrel{a}{\rightarrow} s_2'$).
- if $s \stackrel{p?}{\rightarrow} s'$ then $(V(s) = V(s'))$ and (for every $s'' \sim s'$, $p \in V(s'')$ iff $p \in V(s')$).

The first condition ensures that the action capabilities of the agent are the same in two states which look indistinguishable to the agent. The second condition ensures that test actions do not cause truth values of propositions to change, and also that the result of the test is to give the agent firm knowledge about the truth value of the proposition being tested.

Note that the conditions are very weak. We only speak of the enabling of a locally controlled action in all indistinguishable states, but do not identify their effects, since the performance of the action can result in learning. Further, we consider only basic informative tests and not complex ones. Such minimality is mainly to show that there is some interest in studying even such weakly structured systems.

In the rest of this section, we refer to local control systems simply as models. We can understand these models as follows: each state implicitly contains an $S5$ Kripke structure and actions coarsen or refine the equivalence relation represented in these Kripke structures. Being transition systems admitting cycles, we have the possibility of the agent returning to the same state of knowledge ("forgetting," in the terminology of [8]), and the set of possible *runs* can change at each state of knowledge ("learning," in the terminology of [8]). This gives us a considerably general model of knowledge revision. Of specific interest are finite state models, which correspond to a (realistic) bounded memory restriction on the agent.

An important notion in transition systems is that of reachability. Given the transition system TS, we define the **reachability set** of $s_0 \in S$, denoted $\mathcal{R}_{TS}(s_0)$, as the least subset of S containing s_0 satisfying:

$$\text{If } s \in \mathcal{R}_{TS}(s_0), \text{ and } s \xrightarrow{a} s', a \in \Sigma, \text{ then } s' \in \mathcal{R}_{TS}(s_0).$$

We write $\mathcal{R}(s_0)$ if the underlying transition system is clear from the context.

The logic for specifying properties of these systems is the standard propositional dynamic logic of knowledge with minimal action structure. The formulas of $\mathcal{L}_1$ are specified inductively as

- Every member of P is a formula.
- If α and β are formulas then so are $\neg\alpha$, $\alpha \vee \beta$, $\langle a \rangle\alpha$, $\Diamond\alpha$ and $\mathbf{K}\alpha$, where $a \in \Sigma$.

Let $M = ((S, \rightarrow, \sim), V)$ be a model, $s \in S$. Then the notion of α holding at the state s in the model is denoted by $M, s \models \alpha$ and is defined inductively as follows:

- $M, s \models p$ iff $p \in V(s)$.
- $M, s \models \neg\alpha$ iff $M, s \not\models \alpha$.
- $M, s \models \alpha \vee \beta$ iff $M, s \models \alpha$ or $M, s \models \beta$.
- $M, s \models \mathbf{K}\alpha$ iff for every s' such that $s \sim s'$, $M, s' \models \alpha$.
- $M, s \models \Diamond\alpha$ iff there exists $s' \in \mathcal{R}(s)$ such that $M, s' \models \alpha$.
- $M, s \models \langle a \rangle\alpha$ iff there exists s' such that $s \xrightarrow{a} s'$ and $M, s' \models \alpha$, $a \in \Sigma$.

The derived connectives of propositional calculus such as $\wedge$, $\implies$ and $\equiv$ are defined in terms of $\neg$ and $\vee$ in the usual way. Let *True* abbreviate the formula $p_0 \vee \neg p_0$ and let *False* stand for $\neg$*True*.

The derived modalities $\Box$, $[a]$ and $\mathbf{L}$ are given by:
$\Box\alpha \stackrel{\text{def}}{=} \neg\Diamond\neg\alpha$; $[a]\alpha \stackrel{\text{def}}{=} \neg\langle a \rangle\neg\alpha$; $\mathbf{L}\alpha \stackrel{\text{def}}{=} \neg\mathbf{K}\neg\alpha$. $\mathbf{L}\alpha$ is usually read as "the agent allows for α."

We will also use the derived connective $\bigcirc\alpha \stackrel{def}{=} \bigvee_{a\in\Sigma} \langle a\rangle\alpha$ and its dual $\odot\alpha \stackrel{def}{=} \neg\bigcirc\neg\alpha$. $\bigcirc\alpha$ asserts that α holds in some successor state while its dual asserts α at every successor state.

The formula α is **satisfiable** if $M, s \models \alpha$ in some model $M = ((S, \rightarrow, \sim), V)$ with $s \in S$. α is valid in the model M if $M, s \models \alpha$ for every $s \in S$. α is **valid** (denoted $\models \alpha$) if α is valid in every model M.

This logic can be used to express a variety of interesting properties. $\Box\Diamond\langle a\rangle True$ expresses the fact that one can always reach a state where it is possible to make an a-move. $\Box\Diamond\mathbf{K}\alpha$ asserts that α is eventually known no matter what sequence of actions are performed. Note that $\Box\mathbf{L}\alpha$ and $\mathbf{L}\Box\alpha$ assert very different situations. We can now speak of an agent knowing that α will be reached eventually.

Consider the following axiom system:

Axiom System A
Axiom schemes

(A0) All the substitutional instances of the tautologies of PC
(A1) $[a](\alpha \Longrightarrow \beta) \Longrightarrow ([a]\alpha \Longrightarrow [a]\beta)$
(A2) $\Box(\alpha \Longrightarrow \beta) \Longrightarrow (\Box\alpha \Longrightarrow \Box\beta)$
(A3) $\mathbf{K}(\alpha \Longrightarrow \beta) \Longrightarrow (\mathbf{K}\alpha \Longrightarrow \mathbf{K}\beta)$
(A4) $\Box\alpha \Longrightarrow \alpha \wedge [a]\alpha \wedge \Box\Box\alpha$
(A5) $\mathbf{K}\alpha \Longrightarrow \alpha \wedge \mathbf{K}\mathbf{K}\alpha$
(A6) $\neg\mathbf{K}\alpha \Longrightarrow \mathbf{K}\neg\mathbf{K}\alpha$
(A7) $\Box(\alpha \Longrightarrow \odot\alpha) \Longrightarrow (\alpha \Longrightarrow \Box\alpha)$
(A8) $\langle a\rangle True \Longrightarrow \mathbf{K}\langle a\rangle True$
(A9) $[p?](\mathbf{K}p \vee \mathbf{K}\neg p)$
(A10) $(p \Longrightarrow [q?]p) \wedge (\neg p \Longrightarrow [q?]\neg p)$

Inference rules

$$(MP)\ \frac{\alpha,\ \alpha \Longrightarrow \beta}{\beta} \qquad (TG)\ \frac{\alpha}{\Box\alpha} \qquad (KG)\ \frac{\alpha}{\mathbf{K}\alpha}$$

Axioms (A1), (A2) and (A3) are deductive closure axioms for each of the three different modalities in the logic. (A4) and (A5) refer to the fact both $\Box$ and $\mathbf{K}$ modalities are reflexive and transitive. In addition, (A6) asserts symmetry of $\sim$. (A7) is an induction axiom: it says that any assertion left invariant by every single action must in fact hold henceforth. (A8) says that $\sim$ preserves action capabilities. (A9) asserts that test actions result in knowledge of the truth value being tested, while (A10) ensures that tests leave the truth values of propositions unchanged. Note that the schemes (A9) and (A10) refer only to propositions, and not arbitrary formulas.

Theorem 5.2.1 *The axiom system A yields a sound and complete axiomatization of the valid formulas of $\mathcal{L}_1$ and satisfiability for the logic is deterministic exponential time complete.*

The proof of this theorem is omitted here; a completeness cum decidability argument can be given on the lines of [10, 12]. Such logics have been extensively studied in modal logics of concurrency [25]. Our motivation for discussing this logic here is philosophical, rather than technical.

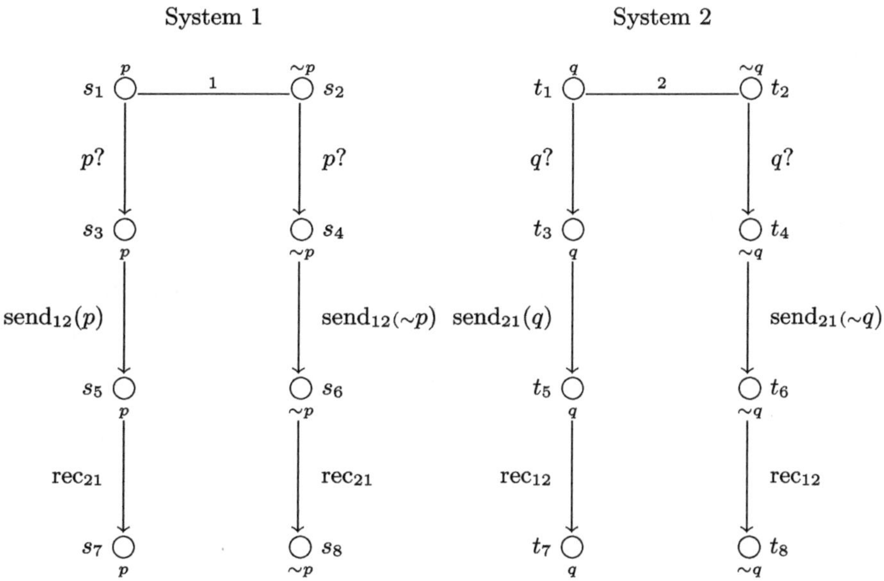

Fig. 5.1 Two agents that test p, q respectively, and inform each other

5.3 Systems with Many Agents

Locality is obviously more interesting in the multiagent context. Consider a system of two agents, and propositions p and q. Below we use $\mathbf{K}_1$ and $\mathbf{K}_2$ to refer to the knowledge modality for agents 1 and 2, respectively.

- Initially neither agent knows anything about p, q, so $\neg\mathbf{K}_i\alpha \wedge \neg\mathbf{K}_i\neg\alpha$ holds, for $i \in \{1, 2\}$ and $\alpha \in \{p, q\}$.
- The agent 1 performs a test action to check if p is true; if not, she takes corrective action ensuring that p becomes true, and in any case, informs agent 2 that p is true now.
- The agent 2 performs a test action to check if q is true; if not, he takes corrective action ensuring that q becomes true, and in any case, informs agent 1 that q is true now.

The obvious way of modelling this situation is to have two local control systems. In Fig. 5.1, we have such a pair of transition systems. Note that we have assumed communication to be message passing of the send/receive type.

What can we say about the knowledge of each agent at any state? To make sense of agents' knowledge, we must consider the global states of the system. This is easily done: simply consider the product transition system, and set two global states to be i-equivalent, if and only if they have the same ith component. As the product system for example in Fig. 5.1 becomes quite big, we have given a portion of it in Fig. 5.2.

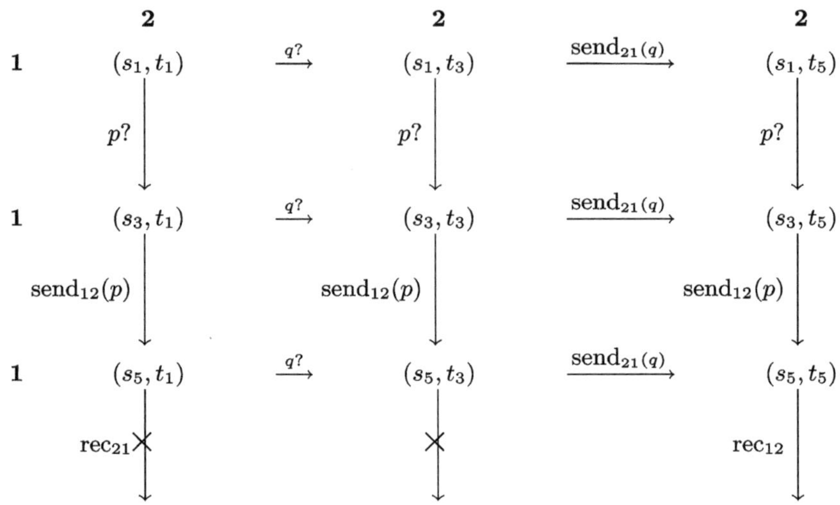

Fig. 5.2 A part of the product of the system in Fig. 5.1

The horizontal lines represent equivalence classes for agent 1, and the vertical ones for agent 2.

There are some important points to note here:

- The action capabilities are no longer the same for an agent i in two i -indistinguishable states! For example, the global states (s_5, t_3) and (s_5, t_5) look the same for agent 1, but the action rec_{21} is enabled in the latter but not in the former. Clearly, this is because a message can be received only after it is sent. Thus the global states include information on states of channels as well as local states of agents.
- Every *internal* action of one agent leaves the knowledge of the other agent unchanged. This, of course, is entirely reasonable.
- Whenever an action a_1 of agent 1 as well as an action a_2 of agent 2 are both enabled at a global state, there is a "square" by which the sequence a_1a_2 leads to the same state as the sequence a_2a_1. This is simply a property of the product construction [13].

We have used propositions p and q as those local to agents 1 and 2, respectively. However, since knowledge is asserted at global states, it is convenient to assume that propositions come from a single global language. We will return to this point again in the concluding section.

With this motivation, we define knowledge transition systems. They were first defined in [11] with more detailed concurrency theoretic motivations and an automata theory was developed based on them in [14]. Here we use them to illustrate the interaction between knowledge and locality of action. First, we need the notion of a distributed alphabet of actions.

5.3.1 Distributed Alphabets

Fix $n \in \mathbf{N}$, the number of agents for the rest of the discussion. We will assume $n > 1$ for non-triviality. Let $Loc = \{1, \ldots, n\}, n > 1$. We model locality of actions among the agents by a *distributed alphabet* $\widetilde{\Sigma}$, which is a tuple $(\Sigma_1, \ldots, \Sigma_n)$, where each Σ_i is a finite non-empty set of actions and is called an *agent alphabet*. These alphabets are not required to be disjoint. In fact, when $a \in \Sigma_i \cap \Sigma_j, i \neq j$, we think of it as a potential synchronisation action between i and j.

Given a distributed alphabet $\widetilde{\Sigma}$, we call the set $\Sigma \stackrel{\text{def}}{=} \Sigma_1 \cup \cdots \cup \Sigma_n$ as the alphabet of the system. For any action in Σ, we have the notion of agents participating in this action. Let $loc : \Sigma \to 2^{\{1,\ldots,n\}}$ be defined by $loc(a) \stackrel{\text{def}}{=} \{i \mid a \in \Sigma_i\}$. So $loc(a)$(called "locations of a") gives the set of agents that participate in (or, synchronise on) the action a. By definition, for all $a \in \Sigma$, $loc(a) \neq \emptyset$. Once again we extend Σ_i with test actions of the form $p?$ for $p \in P$, but leave the definition implicit now.

Consider a distributed alphabet $\widetilde{\Sigma}$ and let $a \in \Sigma$. We call a an i-local action if $loc(a) = \{i\}$. We say that $\widetilde{\Sigma}$ has non-trivial locality if $\widetilde{\Sigma}$ contains at least one i-local action a and one j-local action b, $i \neq j$.

5.3.2 Knowledge Transition Systems

We extend systems of local control to the multiagent context in a natural way, with additional constraints induced by partial observability of actions by agents due to locality.

Definition 5.3.1 A **knowledge transition system (KTS)** over a distributed alphabet $\widetilde{\Sigma}$ is a tuple $KTS = (S, \to, \sim_1, \ldots, \sim_n, V)$, where

1. S is a set of *states*,
2. $\to \ \subseteq (S \times \Sigma \times S)$ is the *transition relation*,
3. $\sim_i \ \subseteq S \times S, i \in \{1, \ldots, n\}$ are equivalence relations, and
4. $V : S \to 2^P$ is a valuation function, and the following conditions are satisfied in a KTS:
   (a) if $s \xrightarrow{a} s'$ then $s \not\sim_i s'$ for all $i \in loc(a)$ and $s \sim_j s'$, for all $j \notin loc(a)$.
   (b) if $s \xrightarrow{a} s_1$, $s \xrightarrow{b} s_2$ and $loc(a) \cap loc(b) = \emptyset$, then there exists s_3 such that $s_1 \xrightarrow{b} s_3$ and $s_2 \xrightarrow{a} s_3$.
   (c) if $s_1 \sim_i s_2$ for all $i \in loc(a)$, then there exists s_1' such that $s_1 \xrightarrow{a} s_1'$ iff there exists s_2' such that $s_2 \xrightarrow{a} s_2'$.
   (d) if $s \xrightarrow{p?} s'$ and $p \in P$ then $(V(s) = V(s'))$ and (for every $s'' \sim_i s'$, $p \in V(s'')$ iff $p \in V(s')$.

The first condition says that every action has a *local* epistemic effect. It can be understood this way: if the knowledge of an agent changes due to a state transition, then the agent must have actively participated in that transition. Thus the effect of a local action is invisible to other agents. This is an essential characteristic of *asynchrony*; the effect of even a 'send message' action becomes visible to another agent only if the latter performs a 'receive message' action. On the other hand, local control also means that an agent participating in an action knows that the action has occurred and thus can distinguish the precondition and the postcondition.

The second condition asserts that the changes in the knowledge of agents 1 and 2 are independent of each other, and 'summing up the changes in any order' yields the same result. This again ties up with the idea of local actions discussed above. In essence, such a property says that the global state can be decomposed into local states of agents.

Reachability in KTSs is as before; we use $\mathcal{R}(s)$ to denote the set of reachable states from s.

The logic $\mathcal{L}_n$ is the obvious generalisation of $\mathcal{L}_1$:

- Every member of P is a formula.
- If α and β are formulas then so are $\neg\alpha$, $\alpha \vee \beta$, $\langle a\rangle\alpha$, $\Diamond\alpha$ and $\mathbf{K}_i\alpha$, $i \in \{1, \ldots, n\}$.

The semantics of formulas is defined as before. The meaning of the $\mathbf{K}_i$ modality is given by

$$M, s \models \mathbf{K}_i\alpha \text{ iff for every } s' \sim_i s,\ M, s' \models \alpha$$

When $\widetilde{\Sigma}$ contains i-local actions, we use the notation $\bigcirc_i\alpha = \bigvee_{a:loc(a)=\{i\}} \langle a\rangle\alpha$. As before $\odot_i\alpha = \neg\bigcirc_i\neg\alpha$.

Note that when we now speak of satisfiability of formulas, we mean satisfiability over the class of models based on knowledge transition systems.

We can now seek to extend the axiom system in the previous section to the multiagent case. Certain valid formulas suggest themselves as axioms.

- $\langle a\rangle True \implies \mathbf{K}_i\langle a\rangle True$, $i \in loc(a)$.
- $\mathbf{K}_j\alpha \implies [a]\alpha$, $j \notin loc(a)$.
- $([a]\alpha \wedge [b]\beta) \implies ([a]\langle b\rangle(\alpha \wedge \beta) \wedge [b]\langle a\rangle(\alpha \wedge \beta))$, where $loc(a) \cap loc(b) = \emptyset$.
- $[p?](\mathbf{K}_i p \vee \mathbf{K}\neg p)$, $p \in P_i$.

The obvious question to ask is: are these axioms strong enough to give completeness? It turns out that they are not. Indeed, in the next section, we show that there is no finite axiomatization of the valid formulas. In fact, for the negative result we only need to have non-trivial locality in KTSs. Note that the formula:

$$K_1\alpha \equiv \odot_2 K_1\alpha$$

is valid, and this is important for what follows.

5.4 Undecidability

Fix $n > 1$ and let $\mathcal{K}_n$ denote the class of *KTS*s with n agents over the distributed alphabet $\widetilde{\Sigma}$ having non-trivial locality. Let SAT_n denote the set of all $\mathcal{L}_n$ formulas satisfiable over $\mathcal{K}_n$. In this section, we show that the membership problem for SAT_n is Σ_1^1-hard and hence not decidable. We will often omit the subscript n leaving it implicit. We will see that we only need $n = 2$.

The *Recurring Colouring Problem* [16] will be used to establish our negative result. Colouring problems correspond to *tiling problems* (see [9]) and in this section the colouring problem that we consider (called simply RCP) corresponds to the so-called origin constrained recurring tiling problem (RTP) in [9]. RTP was proved to be Σ_1^1-complete by [9, 16] showed the recursive equivalence of RCP and RTP. In this section, we show that every instance of RCP can be reduced to the membership of a formula in SAT, thus showing that satisfiability is as hard as RCP.

An *instance* of RCP is a tuple $\Delta = (C, R, U, c_r)$ where $C = \{c_0, c_1, \ldots, c_k\}$ is a finite non-empty set of colours, $c_r \in C$ and $R, U : C \rightarrow (\wp(C) - \emptyset)$ are called "right" and "up" functions.

A *solution* to Δ is a colouring function $Col : \mathbf{N} \times \mathbf{N} \rightarrow C$ which satisfies

1. $Col(0, 0) = c_0$.
2. $\forall (i, j) \in \mathbf{N} \times \mathbf{N}$, $Col(i + 1, j) \in R(Col(i, j))$ and $Col(i, j + 1) \in U(Col(i, j))$.
3. $\forall m \in \mathbf{N} : \exists k > m : Col(0, k) = c_r$.

It is easily seen that the second condition above simply asks for a colouring of the $\mathbf{N} \times \mathbf{N}$ "grid" which is coherent with respect to the "right" and "up" functions. The first specifies a start condition. The third condition can be restated as follows: along the Y-axis, an infinite number of grid points are to be coloured with the recurring colour c_r.

We now reduce each instance of RCP to a membership problem for *SAT*. In other words, we shall uniformly encode each instance Δ of RCP into a formula α_Δ such that Δ has a solution iff $\alpha_\Delta \in SAT$. In order to capture the effect of functions R and U, we reserve two propositions p and q, respectively. We reserve $k+1$ atomic propositions in P to denote the colours in $C = \{c_0, c_1, \ldots, c_k\}$. For notational convenience, these atomic propositions will also be written as $c_0, c_1, \ldots, c_k$. We will also use a special proposition Y to code the Y-axis; note that $\{p, q, Y\}$ is assumed to be disjoint from C.

Definition 5.4.1 Let $\Delta = (C, R, U, c_r)$ be an instance of RCP, where C is a non-empty finite set $\{c_0, \ldots, c_k\}$. Then $\alpha_\Delta \stackrel{\text{def}}{=} \bigwedge_{i=1}^{7} \alpha_i$, where

- $\alpha_1 \stackrel{\text{def}}{=} c_0 \wedge Y \wedge \mathbf{K}_1 p \wedge \mathbf{K}_2 q$.
- $\alpha_2 \stackrel{\text{def}}{=} \Box \bigwedge_{i=0}^{k} (c_i \equiv \bigwedge_{j \neq i} \neg c_j)$.

- $\beta_1 \stackrel{\text{def}}{=} (\mathbf{K}_1 p \implies \bigcirc_1 \mathbf{L}_1 \neg p) \wedge (\mathbf{L}_1 \neg p \implies \bigcirc_1 \mathbf{K}_1 p)$.
- $\beta_2 \stackrel{\text{def}}{=} (\mathbf{K}_2 q \implies \bigcirc_2 \mathbf{L}_2 \neg q) \wedge (\mathbf{L}_2 \neg q \implies \bigcirc_2 \mathbf{K}_2 q))$.
- $\alpha_3 \stackrel{\text{def}}{=} \Box(\beta_1 \wedge \beta_2)$.
- $\gamma_1(c_i) \stackrel{\text{def}}{=} (\mathbf{K}_1 p \implies \odot_1(\mathbf{L}_1 \neg p \implies \bigvee_{c \in R(c_i)} c))$.
- $\gamma_1^{-1}(c_i) \stackrel{\text{def}}{=} (\mathbf{L}_1 \neg p \implies \odot_1(\mathbf{K}_1 p \implies \bigvee_{c \in R(c_i)} c))$.
- $\alpha_4 \stackrel{\text{def}}{=} \Box(\bigwedge_{i=0}^{k}(c_i \implies (\gamma_1(c_i) \wedge \gamma_1^{-1}(c_i)))$.
- $\gamma_2(c_i) \stackrel{\text{def}}{=} (\mathbf{K}_2 q \implies \odot_2(\mathbf{L}_2 \neg q \implies \bigvee_{c \in U(c_i)} c))$.
- $\gamma_2^{-1}(c_i) \stackrel{\text{def}}{=} (\mathbf{L}_2 \neg q \implies \odot_2(\mathbf{K}_2 q \implies \bigvee_{c \in U(c_i)} c))$.
- $\alpha_5 \stackrel{\text{def}}{=} \Box(\bigwedge_{i=0}^{k}(c_i \implies (\gamma_2(c_i) \wedge \gamma_2^{-1}(c_i))))$.
- $\delta \stackrel{\text{def}}{=} ((Y \wedge \mathbf{K}_2 q) \implies \odot_2(\mathbf{L}_2 \neg q \equiv Y))$.
- $\delta^{-1} \stackrel{\text{def}}{=} ((Y \wedge \mathbf{L}_2 \neg q) \implies \odot_2(\mathbf{K}_2 q \equiv Y))$.
- $\alpha_6 \stackrel{\text{def}}{=} \Box(\delta \wedge \delta^{-1})$.
- $\alpha_7 \stackrel{\text{def}}{=} \Box(Y \implies \Diamond(Y \wedge c_r)) \wedge \Box(\neg Y \implies \Box \neg Y)$.

The formula α asserts two different things: one, the existence of a grid, and two, the fact that the colour c_r occurs infinitely often on the Y-axis.

The recurring colour property is coded in α_6 and α_7. The former states that (since initially Y holds at the origin, by α_1) every move of agent 2 simply propagates Y. This ensures that Y does hold on the Y-axis. α_7 says that there are infinitely many points where both Y and c_r hold. This means that c_r holds infinitely often on the Y-axis. α_6 and α_7 ensure that any move which leaves the knowledge of agent 2 unchanged (say, a move by 1, or an external transition) cannot lead to Y and thus Y holds only on the Y-axis.

How α asserts the grid will become clear in the proof of Lemma 5.4.3 below. Let us first see how it forces each agent to make an independent move: α_3 asserts that from any reachable state, there is a way of making a move whereby the knowledge of agent 1 (with respect to proposition p) changes. But then, by assumption of asynchrony, the knowledge of agent 2 cannot change due to such an action by agent 1. α_3 also asserts that *at the same state* (by similar logic), a move of agent 2 is also enabled. These two must commute, thus forcing a 'square'.

Lemma 5.4.2 *Let $\Delta = (C, R, U, c_r)$ be an instance of RCP. If Δ has a solution, then $\alpha_\Delta \in SAT$.*

Proof Let $Col : \mathbf{N} \times \mathbf{N} \to C$ be a solution to RCP. Consider the simple distributed alphabet $\widetilde{\Sigma} = (\{a\}, \{b\})$. Define now $KTS = (S, \to, \sim_1, \sim_2, V)$ as follows:

$$
\begin{aligned}
S &\stackrel{\text{def}}{=} \mathbf{N} \times \mathbf{N}.\\
\to &\stackrel{\text{def}}{=} \{((i, j), a, (i+1, j)) \mid (i, j) \in \mathbf{N} \times \mathbf{N}\}\\
&\quad \cup \{((i, j), b, (i, j+1)) \mid (i, j) \in \mathbf{N} \times \mathbf{N}\}\\
\sim_1 &\stackrel{\text{def}}{=} \{((i, j), (i, k)) \mid i, j, k \in \mathbf{N}\}\\
\sim_2 &\stackrel{\text{def}}{=} \{((i, j), (k, j)) \mid i, j, k \in \mathbf{N}\}
\end{aligned}
$$

Further define $V : S \to \wp(P)$ as: $V(i, j) \stackrel{\text{def}}{=} \{Col(i, j)\} \cup \chi(i, j)$.

Then it is clear that *KTS* is a knowledge transition system. Now let χ be any function $\chi : \mathbf{N} \times \mathbf{N} \to \wp\{p, q, Y\}$ which satisfies the following conditions:

1. $Y \in \chi(i, j)$ iff $i = 0$.
2. $p \in \chi(i, j)$ iff i is even.
3. $q \in \chi(i, j)$ iff j is even.

That such a function χ exists is trivial.

Let $M \stackrel{\text{def}}{=} (KTS, V)$. In Fig. 5.3, the model is depicted. It is straightforward to show that $M, (0, 0) \models \alpha_\Delta$.

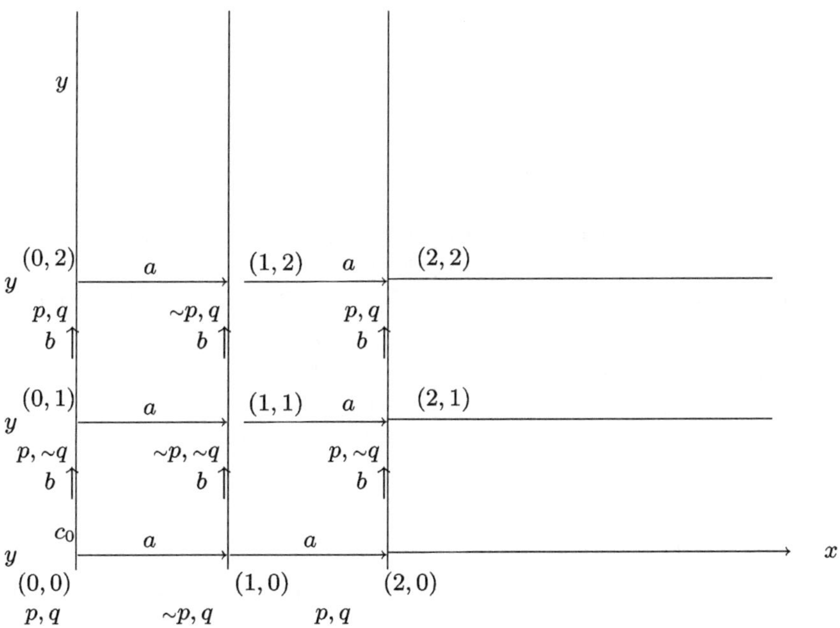

Fig. 5.3 The constructed model

Note that M is much more generous than it needs to be: we could have kept p and q invariant throughout the grid, and had separate points outside which have differing truth values which are equivalent for 1 and 2 suitably, to force the formulas $\mathbf{K}_1 p$ etc. That way, the actions of the agents would only change knowledge without disturbing truth values (as in test actions).

Lemma 5.4.3 *Let $\Delta = (C, R, U, c_r)$ be an instance of RCP such that $\alpha_\Delta \in SAT$. Then Δ has a solution.*

Proof Let $M, s_0 \models \alpha_\Delta$, where $M = (KTS, V)$, $KTS = (S, \rightarrow, \sim_1, \ldots, \sim_n)$ is a knowledge transition system and $s_0 \in S$.

For constructing a colouring function for Δ, we adapt the following strategy: we first decide the colours on the Y-axis in $\mathbf{N} \times \mathbf{N}$ and then inductively fill out column after column. For each point on the grid, we associate a state in $\mathcal{R}(s_0)$; this is sufficient since the formula $\alpha_2 \wedge \alpha_4 \wedge \alpha_5$ is satisfied at that state and hence the colouring function can be easily "pulled out."

The function $Yax : \mathbf{N} \rightarrow \mathcal{R}(s_0)$ is defined as follows. Let $Yax(0) \stackrel{\text{def}}{=} s_0$. Note that $M, s_0 \models Y$. By α_7, we also have that $M, s_0 \models \Diamond(Y \wedge c_r)$. Hence there exists a sequence of states $s_0 = t_0 \rightarrow t_1 \rightarrow \cdots \rightarrow t_k$, $M, t_k \models (Y \wedge c_r)$. Note that for all $l : 0 \leq l \leq k$, we have $M, t_l \models Y$. (Otherwise, such a t_l would satisfy $\neg Y$ and by α_7 it would also satisfy $\Box\neg Y$; but then t_k is reachable from t_l and $M, t_k \models Y$, giving a contradicition.)

Thus for all $l : 0 \leq l < k$: we have $M, t_l \models (Y \wedge (\mathbf{K}_2 q \vee \mathbf{L}_2 \neg q))$. Suppose $M, t_l \models (Y \wedge \mathbf{K}_2 q)$. Since $t_l \rightarrow t_{l+1}$ and $M, t_{l+1} \models Y$, by α_6, we get $M, t_{l+1} \models \mathbf{L}_2 \neg q$. Thus we have $t_l \not\sim_2 t_{l+1}$; that is, $t_l \stackrel{2}{\rightarrow} t_{l+1}$. For the other case, when $M, t_l \models (Y \wedge \mathbf{L}_2 \neg q)$, we can show by a similar reasoning that $t_l \stackrel{2}{\rightarrow} t_{l+1}$.

We thus have $s_0 = t_0 \stackrel{2}{\rightarrow} \cdots \stackrel{2}{\rightarrow} t_k$ and $M, t_k \models (Y \wedge c_r)$. Set $Yax(l) \stackrel{\text{def}}{=} t_l, 0 \leq l \leq k$. By α_3, there exists s such that $t_k \stackrel{2}{\rightarrow} s$. Define $Yax(k+1) \stackrel{\text{def}}{=} s$. Now, by α_7, we again have $M, Yax(k) \models \Diamond(Y \wedge c_r)$ and we can repeat the construction above to find a new sequence of states where each transition is a move of agent 2. Repeating thus, we get Yax, where every move is made by 2.

We now construct a series of functions, $C_k : \mathbf{N} \rightarrow S, k \geq 0$, such that for all $j \geq 0$, $C_k(j) \stackrel{2}{\rightarrow} C_k(j+1)$. C_k stands for the kth column. For $k = 0$, $C_0(l) \stackrel{\text{def}}{=} Yax(l), l \in \mathbf{N}$. Note that there are infinitely many j such that $M, C_0(j) \models c_r$.

Now assume C_m is defined, for $m \geq 0$. Let $C_m(0) = s$. Now, either $M, s \models \mathbf{K}_1 p$ or $M, s \models \mathbf{L}_1 \neg p$. In either case, by α_3, we have s' such that $s \rightarrow s'$ and $s \not\sim_1 s'$. We thus have $s \stackrel{1}{\rightarrow} s'$. Fix $C_{m+1}(0) \stackrel{\text{def}}{=} s'$.

Now inductively assume that we already have $C_{m+1}(i), i \geq 0$ and that for all $l \leq i$, $C_m(l) \stackrel{1}{\rightarrow} C_{m+1}(l)$, and for all $l < i$, $C_{m+1}(l) \stackrel{2}{\rightarrow} C_{m+1}(l+1)$. Let $C_m(i) = s \stackrel{1}{\rightarrow} s_1 = C_{m+1}(i)$. We already know that $s \stackrel{2}{\rightarrow} s_2 = C_m(i+1)$. (See Fig. 5.4). By definition of KTSs, there exists s_3 such that $s_2 \stackrel{1}{\rightarrow} s_3$ and $s_1 \stackrel{2}{\rightarrow} s_3$. Set $C_{m+1}(i+1) \stackrel{\text{def}}{=} s_3$. This completes the construction of C_{m+1}.

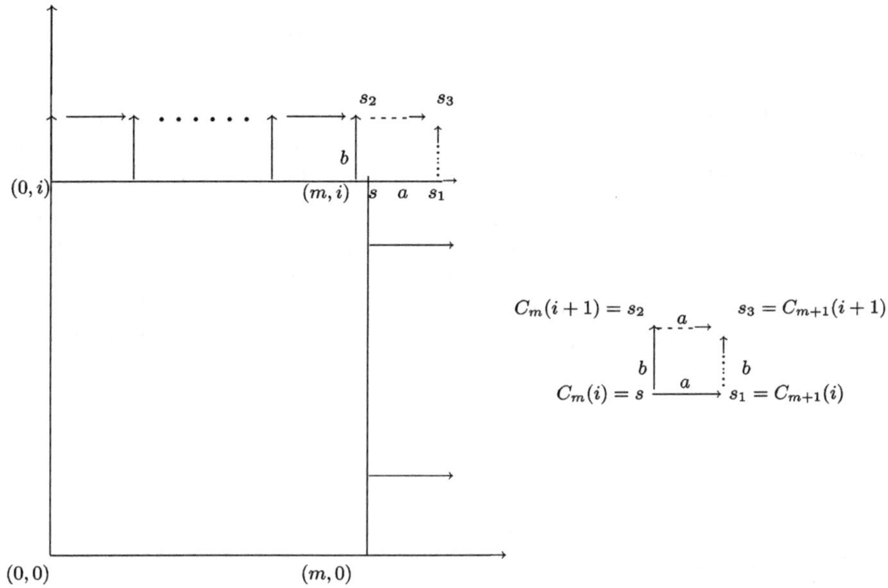

Fig. 5.4 The inductive step

We now have C_k for all k. Define $Col : \mathbf{N} \times \mathbf{N} \rightarrow C$ by $Col(i, j) \stackrel{\text{def}}{=} V(C_j(i)) \cap C$. The formula α_2 ensures that Col is well-defined. α_4 and α_5 together ensure coherence of Col with respect to the Right and Up functions of Δ. Thus the given instance of RCP has a solution.

We thus have the following theorem:

Theorem 5.4.4 *The membership problem for SAT_n is Σ_1^1-hard. Hence the validity problem for formulas in $\mathcal{L}_n$ over knowledge transition systems with n agents is Π_1^1-hard and hence validity is not axiomatizable.*

Proof By Lemmas 5.4.2 and 5.4.3, we find that for any instance Δ of RCP there is a formula of $\mathcal{L}_2$ such that Δ has a solution if and only if that formula is in SAT_2. This gives us a procedure for solving RCP. Thus, satisfiability is at least as hard as RCP, which is shown to be Σ_1^1-complete by [16]. This certainly means that the set of valid formulas cannot be recursively enumerable.

Given this (strong) negative result, one may suggest: why not restrict attention to *finite* knowledge transition systems? After all, these are the only kind that arise in computation. Moreover, the set of finite transition systems is recursively enumerable.

We say that a formula α is **finitely satisfiable** if there is a model $M = ((S, \rightarrow, \sim_1, \ldots, \sim_n), V)$ and $s \in S$ such that $M, s \models \alpha$, where S is finite. Let $FSAT_n$ denote the set of all finitely satisfiable formulas.

Clearly, $FSAT_n$ is at most recursively enumerable. Is it also recursive? The following theorem asserts that it is not.

Theorem 5.4.5 *The membership problem for $FSAT_n$ is not recursive. Hence the set of formulas of $\mathcal{L}_n$ valid over* finite *KTSs with n agents is not axiomatizable.*

Proof If both satisfiability and validity are recursively enumerable, then both must be recursive. Hence, if satisfiability is not recursive, then validity cannot be recursively enumerable, and hence is not axiomatizable. To show that $FSAT_n$ is not a recursive set, we can code the Finite Colouring Problem into our logic on the lines of [12]. This problem asks whether there is a finite $m \times k$ grid which can be coloured using the colours in C, maintaining coherence with respect to the functions R and U, and such that the colour at the origin is c_0 and the colour at (m, k) is c_1. The coding is similar to the one given above, but considerably more complicated technically.

5.5 Discussion

We have argued that local actions are worthy of technical study. The main points made are as follows:

- When there are many knowers, local (test) actions being performed by one agent cannot change the knowledge of another agent and hence are independent, so that the resulting state of knowledge is the same independent of the order of performing them.
- This (reasonable) assumption leads to (high) undecidability.

Note that the negative results here apply to fully asynchronous systems where for all $i \neq j$, $\Sigma_i \cap \Sigma_j = \emptyset$. This is because in such systems, any knowledge change of agent 1 must mean a local action of agent 1, which will leave the knowledge of other agents invariant. Note that this is exactly the form in which formulas in the coding are structured. Message passing systems are examples of this kind: in such system, *every* communication is split into send–receive pairs, which cannot be synchronized into common actions, even if there is a guarantee that every message is delivered. This also means that most models of epistemic change have some built in synchrony assumptions on underlying communication among agents.

The logic $\mathcal{L}_1$ requires a much deeper study than attempted here. For example, consider the following issue: consider a model $M = ((S, \rightarrow), V)$, where for some $s \sim s'$, $V(s) = V(s')$. Now let $a \in \Sigma$ be an action performed by the agent. Then, we have assumed that the action a is enabled at s if and only if it is enabled at s'. However, the effect of performing a at s can be very different from that at s'. In itself this is reasonable, since action a can constitute non-trivial learning. But suppose that there are infinitely many states in the equivalence class of s. In principle, the systems we study allow for all a successors to be distinct, which amounts to the test having infinitary discerning ability. It would be interesting to consider tests that have only finitary learning capability. We mention this issue only as a sample of the kind of non-trivial philosophical and technical questions that arise in modelling local epistemic actions.

Similarly, analogous to the way we have used test actions which do not change truth values; we can also consider external actions in the system which can only change truth values but not the knowledge of any agent in the system.

Regarding the negative result in the case of systems with many agents, there can be two important questions: (a) are these modal frames realistic? and (b) does this mean that the kind of dynamic logics envisaged here are not 'right' for epistemic dynamics among many agents?

To answer the first question, recall that the coding of RCP in the last section used two agents 1 and 2 with local propositions p and q which keep changing. Such a situation can be easily realised by two programs each of which cyclically reads one bit from a local source, "forgets" that value (by returning to the original state) and reads the next one. Note that such actions need never disturb truth values. For example, if the input is a stream of 1's, the proposition "the next value is 1" would remain true for ever, but knowledge requires reading the bit each time. Clearly, such local actions do change the knowledge of these agents and cannot affect the other's knowledge. Note that no interaction between the agents is assumed for the coding.

While the frames do make a strong asynchrony assumption (actions local to individual agents), we can easily code up using synchronisations as well. Independent synchronizations (one between 1 and 3 and another between 2 and 4, say) will again give rise to the commuting behaviour, and the negative result would go through. Thus, whatever be the realistic model of transition system with global states, expressive power stems mainly from the insistence that some actions in the system cause no epistemic change elsewhere in the system—which is merely the principle of locality.

That brings us to the second question. To answer this, we observe that when we generalised from the one agent case to systems with many agents, we readily moved to the product transition system. This was essentially a reduction of the new problem to the old one, by postulating a 'large' agent who behaves like all the agents in the system put together. Knowledge assertions are made at global states of this product system, and this has critical implications. The product space expands exponentially as the number of agents increases, and checking whether a knowledge property holds may be computationally expensive. Realistically, no agent in the system may have any way of computing its own knowledge or knowledge change due to an action! Also, the kind of commuting used for the negative result was very much a property of the global transition system.

We believe that when we reason at the level of global states, due to concurrency (dictated by independent knowledge change), the kind of undecidability results reported here are inescapable, as the tiling problems are easily encoded. The alternative that needs to be considered is to define local notions of knowledge, where the quantification ranges over 'small' neighbourhoods of states (rather than potentially 'large' equivalence classes), in such a way that each agent can compute its knowledge change. For this, it is also perhaps necessary to have 'local' propositions which are private to agents [4] (Observe that for the undecidability result we *necessarily* used global propositions, namely, the colours, and the one which coded the Y-axis).

Several attempts have been made on these lines [4, 6, 20, 24], but a satisfactory *logical* theory of epistemic locality and concurrency is still a challenge.

Postscript:
This paper owes its origin to a talk I gave in 1994 at the (Indian) National Seminar in Theoretical Computer Science in IIT-Kanpur [19] swhich led to [20]. One of the questions raised then was to identify and delineate a logical theory of epistemic locality. While this paper does not provide any definitive theory, it hopefully delineates some of the issues involved.

References

1. G. Aucher. Supervisory control theory in epistemic temporal logic. In A. L. C. Bazzan, M. N. Huhns, A. Lomuscio, and P. Scerri, editors, *International conference on Autonomous Agents and Multi-Agent Systems, AAMAS'14, Paris, France, May 5–9, 2014*, pages 333–340. IFAAMAS/ACM, 2014.
2. J. Czelakowski. Elements of formal action theory. In *Logic, Action, and Information*, pages 3–62, 1996.
3. H. v. Ditmarsch, W. van der Hoek, and B. Kooi. *Dynamic Epistemic Logic*. Springer Publishing Company, Incorporated, 1st edition, 2007.
4. K. Engelhardt, R. van der Meyden, and Y. Moses. Knowledge and the logic of local propositions. In *TARK*, pages 29–41, 1998.
5. R. Fagin, J. Y. Halpern, Y. Moses, and M. Y. Vardi. *Reasoning About Knowledge*. MIT Press, 1995.
6. R. Goldblatt. Parallel action: Concurrent dynamic logic with independent modalities. *Studia Logica*, 51(3/4):551–578, 1992.
7. J. Y. Halpern and R. Fagin. Modelling knowledge and action in distributed systems. *Distributed Computing*, 3(4):159–179, 1989. A preliminary version appeared in *Proc. 4th ACM Symposium on Principles of Distributed Computing*, 1985, with the title "A formal model of knowledge, action, and communication in distributed systems: Preliminary report".
8. J. Y. Halpern and M. Y. Vardi. The Complexity of Reasoning about Knowledge and Time. I Lower Bounds. *J. Comput. Syst. Sci.*, 38:195–237, 1989.
9. D. Harel. Recurring dominoes: Making the highly undecidable highly understandable (preliminary report). In *Fundamentals of Computation Theory, Proceedings of the 1983 International FCT-Conference, Borgholm, Sweden, August 21–27, 1983*, pages 177–194, 1983.
10. D. Harel, D. Kozen, and J. Tiuryn. *Dynamic Logic*. The MIT Press, October 2000.
11. P. J. Krasucki and R. Ramanujam. Knowledge and the ordering of events in distributed systems. In R. Fagin, editor, *Proceedings of the 5th Conference on Theoretical Aspects of Reasoning about Knowledge, Pacific Grove, CA, USA, March 1994*, pages 267–283. Morgan Kaufmann, 1994.
12. K. Lodaya, R. Parikh, R. Ramanujam, and P. S. Thiagarajan. A logical study of distributed transition systems. *Inf. Comput.*, 119(1):91–118, 1995.
13. R. Milner. *Communication and concurrency*. PHI Series in computer science. Prentice Hall, 1989.
14. S. Mohalik and R. Ramanujam. Automata for epistemic temporal logic with synchronous communication. *Journal of Logic, Language and Information*, 19(4):451–484, 2010.
15. S. Mohalik and I. Walukiewicz. Distributed games. In *Proceedings of the Conference on Foundation of Software Technology and Theoretical Computer Science, FSTTCS*, volume 2914 of *LNCS*, pages 338–351. Springer, 2003.
16. R. Parikh. Decidability and undecidability in distributed transition systems. In R. Narasimhan, editor, *A perspective in theoretical computer science — commemorative volume for Gift Siromoney*, pages 199–209. World Scientific, 1988.

17. R. Parikh and R. Ramanujam. Distributed processes and the logic of knowledge. In R. Parikh, editor, *Logic of Programs*, volume 193 of *Lecture Notes in Computer Science*, pages 256–268. Springer, 1985.
18. R. Parikh and R. Ramanujam. A knowledge based semantics of messages. *Journal of Logic, Language and Information*, 12(4):453–467, 2003.
19. R. Ramanujam. Knowledge and the next state modality. In P. Gupta, editor, *Proceedings of the Fourth National Seminar in Theoretical Computer Science, IIT, Kanpur*, pages 62–80, 1994.
20. R. Ramanujam. Local knowledge assertions in a changing world. In Y. Shoham, editor, *Proceedings of the Sixth Conference on Theoretical Aspects of Rationality and Knowledge, De Zeeuwse Stromen, The Netherlands, March 17–20 1996*, pages 1–14. Morgan Kaufmann, 1996.
21. R. Ramanujam and S. Simon. A communication based model for games of imperfect information. In *CONCUR 2010 - Concurrency Theory, 21th International Conference, CONCUR 2010, Paris, France, August 31–September 3, 2010. Proceedings*, pages 509–523, 2010.
22. B. K. Uday Khedker, Amitabha Sanyal. *Data Flow Analysis: Theory and Practice*. CRC Press, 2009.
23. J. van Benthem. *Exploring Logical Dynamics*. CSLI Publications, 1996.
24. J. van Benthem. Decisions, actions, and games: A logical perspective. In R. Ramanujam and S. Sarukkai, editors, *Logic and Its Applications, Third Indian Conference, ICLA 2009, Chennai, India, January 7–11, 2009. Proceedings*, volume 5378 of *Lecture Notes in Computer Science*, pages 1–22. Springer, 2009.
25. J. van Benthem and J. A. Bergstra. Logic of transition systems. *Journal of Logic, Language and Information*, 3(4):247–283, 1994.
26. J. van Benthem, J. Gerbrandy, T. Hoshi, and E. Pacuit. Merging frameworks for interaction. *J. Philosophical Logic*, 38(5):491–526, 2009.
27. J. van Benthem, J. van Eijck, and B. P. Kooi. Logics of communication and change. *Inf. Comput.*, 204(11):1620–1662, 2006.
28. H. P. van Ditmarsch, W. van der Hoek, and J. Ruan. Connecting dynamic epistemic and temporal epistemic logics. *Logic Journal of the IGPL*, 21(3):380–403, 2013.
29. Y. Wang and G. Aucher. An alternative axiomatization of DEL and its applications. In F. Rossi, editor, *IJCAI 2013, Proceedings of the 23rd International Joint Conference on Artificial Intelligence, Beijing, China, August 3–9, 2013*. IJCAI/AAAI, 2013.

Chapter 6
Avoiding Impossibility Theorems in Radical Inquisitive Semantics

Katsuhiko Sano

Abstract In nonradical inquisitive semantics, an intuitionistic Kripke model captures how group knowledge increases throughout a conversation and allows the inquisitive meaning of a sentence to be derived from its classical meaning. In radical inquisitive semantics, as proposed by Groenendijk and Roelofsen, positive and negative ways of reacting to a proposal are captured by the positive and negative inquisitive meanings of a sentence, respectively, which are inductively defined without employing any Kripke-type semantics. This paper demonstrates that, in principle, it is impossible to provide any natural Kripke-type semantics under radical inquisitive semantics. Moreover, an alternative way to establish the semantics is proposed that avoids this negative result.

6.1 Introduction

The aim of this paper is to examine the possible relationship between Kripke-type semantics for the syntax of intuitionistic logic expanded with strong negation (known as Nelson's constructive logics [11]) and radical inquisitive semantics, first proposed by Groenendijk and Roelofsen [10].

Nonradical inquisitive semantics [4, 5, 9] is a new formal framework for the semantics of both declarative and interrogative sentences. One of the main features of this semantics is the assumption of no type distinction between the declarative and interrogative, allowing both classical and inquisitive meanings to be associated with each sentence. For example, the declarative sentence "Pete will drink tea or coffee" proposes two alternatives: "Pete will drink tea" and "Pete will drink coffee." The notion of inquisitive meaning captures the information of these alternatives; that is, the inquisitive meaning of "Pete will drink tea or coffee" is defined as a *set* containing the classical meaning of "Pete will drink tea" and the classical meaning of "Pete will drink coffee." In conservative (nonradical) inquisitive semantics [4],

K. Sano (✉)
School of Information Science, Japan Advanced Institute of Science and Technology, Nomi, Japan
e-mail: v-sano@jaist.ac.jp

S. Ju et al. (eds.), *Modality, Semantics and Interpretations*,
Logic in Asia: Studia Logica Library, DOI 10.1007/978-3-662-47197-5_6

intuitionistic Kripke semantics captures how group knowledge increases through a conversation and allows the inquisitive meaning of a sentence to be derived from its classical meaning. Moreover, Ciardelli [2] has provided a direct inductive definition for the inquisitive meaning of a sentence.

In the example above, the negative reply "Pete will not drink tea or coffee" could be offered to the speaker. Conservative inquisitive semantics, however, cannot cover this negative reaction. Radical inquisitive semantics [10] is an extension of conservative semantics that provides the *positive* and *negative* inquisitive meanings, as well as the classical meaning, for a given sentence. However, radical inquisitive semantics does not employ Kripke-type semantics for deriving positive and negative inquisitive meanings but instead applies Ciardelli's [2] idea of inductive definition to directly define positive and negative inquisitive meanings. It is therefore natural to ask whether a Kripke-type semantics can be developed for radical inquisitive semantics that enables the derivation of negative inquisitive meaning from classical meaning. The main contribution of this paper is to establish that any Kripke-type semantics for intuitionistic logic expanded with strong negation fails to derive negative inquisitive meaning from classical meaning in the same sense as in conservative inquisitive semantics (Theorems 6.1 and 6.2).

This paper is organized as follows. Section 6.2 reviews nonradical inquisitive semantics, with a particular focus on the relationship between intuitionistic Kripke semantics and inquisitive meaning. Section 6.3 explains the semantic idea of radical inquisitive semantics. Section 6.4 provides the main results in the form of impossibility theorems (Theorems 6.1 and 6.2). Section 6.5 then proposes an alternative way to establish semantics that avoids this negative result, providing a version of Kripke-type semantics (similar to Nelson's constructive logics [11] with strong negation) that approximates radical inquisitive semantics. Section 6.6 concludes the paper.

6.2 Conservative Inquisitive Semantics

6.2.1 The Inquisitive Model

This section reviews the basic framework of inquisitive semantics, following previous work [4]. Let Prop be a finite set of propositional letters. The syntax $\mathcal{L}_I$ is the same syntax as in intuitionistic logic; i.e., it consists of the logical connectives $\{\vee, \wedge, \rightarrow, \bot\}$ as well as Prop. The negation $\neg$ is defined as the following ordinary abbreviation: $\neg\varphi := \varphi \rightarrow \bot$. The set of formulas of $\mathcal{L}_I$ is constructed as usual. $\omega := \{0, 1\}^{\mathsf{Prop}}$ is defined as the set of all (classical) valuation functions $v : \mathsf{Prop} \rightarrow \{0, 1\}$. Given a formula φ of $\mathcal{L}_I$, the classical meaning $|\varphi|$ is defined by

$$|\varphi| := \{v \in \omega \mid v(\varphi) = 1\},$$

i.e., $|\varphi|$ is the set of all classical valuations making φ true.

Definition 6.1 A subset $s \subseteq \omega$ is called a *state*. The set of all the states is denoted by S; i.e., $S := \{ s \mid s \subseteq \omega \} = \mathcal{P}(\omega)$.

Note that S is finite, since Prop is finite. Let $s = \emptyset$ be called the *inconsistent* state. It is clear that $\langle S, \supseteq \rangle$ forms a partial order.

Definition 6.2 (*Support*) Given a state s and a formula φ of $\mathcal{L}_I$, the notion of support $s \models^+ \varphi$ is defined by induction on φ as follows:

$$\begin{array}{ll} s \models^+ p & \text{iff } s \subseteq |p|, \\ s \models^+ \bot & \text{iff } s = \emptyset, \\ s \models^+ \varphi \vee \psi & \text{iff } s \models^+ \varphi \text{ or } s \models^+ \psi, \\ s \models^+ \varphi \wedge \psi & \text{iff } s \models^+ \varphi \text{ and } s \models^+ \psi, \\ s \models^+ \varphi \to \psi & \text{iff } \forall t \subseteq s. (t \models^+ \varphi \text{ implies } t \models^+ \psi). \end{array}$$

Define $[\![\varphi]\!]^+ = \{ s \in S \mid s \models^+ \varphi \}$.

Note that the following support clause can be derived for $\neg\varphi$.

$$s \models^+ \neg\varphi \text{ iff } \forall t \subseteq s. (t \neq \emptyset \text{ implies } t \not\models^+ \varphi).$$

The *persistency* of $\models^+$ may then be easily verified, i.e., $s \models^+ \varphi$ and $s \supseteq t$ jointly implies that $t \models^+ \varphi$, for all $s, t \in S$ and all formulas φ of $\mathcal{L}_I$. $\langle S, \supseteq, \models^+ \rangle$ is called *the* inquisitive model.

The above semantics may initially appear identical to Kripke semantics for intuitionistic logic. However, care must be taken in the treatment of $\bot$: the inconsistent state $s = \emptyset$ is the only state supporting $\bot$, while any possible world of any Kripke model for intuitionistic logic does not force $\bot$. Therefore, to reformulate the above semantics into a Kripke model for intuitionistic logic, the inconsistent state $\emptyset$ must be disregarded. Define $W_I := S \setminus \{ \emptyset \} = \{ s \subseteq \omega \mid s \neq \emptyset \}$. Then, $\mathfrak{M}_I := \langle W_I, \supseteq, \models^+ \rangle$ can be regarded as an intuitionistic Kripke model. Let $\mathfrak{M}_I, s \Vdash \varphi$ denote the satisfaction relation in the Kripke semantics of intuitionistic logic. Then, the following may then be shown (cf. [2, Proposition 2.1.10]).

Proposition 6.1 *For any formula φ of $\mathcal{L}_I$ and any state $s \in W_I$,*

$$s \models^+ \varphi \text{ iff } \mathfrak{M}_I, s \Vdash \varphi.$$

The root state $\omega = \{ 0, 1 \}^{\mathsf{Prop}}$ of $\langle S, \supseteq \rangle$ may be regarded as an *ignorant* state; i.e., all speech participants are ignorant of the classical truth values of Prop. Conversely, a singleton state $\{ v \}$ (where $v : \mathsf{Prop} \to \{ 0, 1 \}$) is the state where all speech participants completely specify the truth values of Prop given by the truth function v. How can the participants change their first ignorant state into a singleton state? The notion of *inquisitive meaning* becomes involved in this situation. Inquisitive semantics views inquisitive meanings as proposals to change the conversational participants' shared information, i.e., the common ground [4] (Note that Ciardelli and Roelofsen [4] used the term "proposition" instead of "inquisitive meaning.") Suppose that all participants in a conversation are in the ignorant state ω (regarded as the common ground of the participants) and one of the participants says the declarative "Pete will drink tea or coffee" to the other participants. Let p denote "Pete will drink tea" and q denote "Pete will drink coffee." The above declarative sentence is thus formalized as $p \vee q$ and its inquisitive meaning is $\{\,|p|, |q|\,\}$ (formal definition below). In this sense, the speaker raises an issue, and the participants must resolve the issue, i.e., choose one from the two alternatives $\{\,|p|, |q|\,\}$. If all of the participants agree to choose the alternative $|p|$, then they can update their ignorant state ω into $\omega \cap |p|$, i.e., $|p|$. Conversely, if all participants agree to choose the alternative $|q|$, their common ground ω will be updated into $|q|$. In this way, inquisitive semantics captures how a conversation proceeds among the participants.

The notion of inquisitive meaning is formally introduced below.

Definition 6.3 Let $X \subseteq S$. $s \in X$ is a *maximal element* in X if $s \subseteq t$ and $t \in X$ jointly imply $s = t$, for all $t \in S$. MAX(X) is the set of all the maximal elements in X (if $X = \emptyset$, we define MAX$(X) := \emptyset$).

Note that the finiteness of S assures the existence of a maximal element in X for any nonempty X, i.e., MAX$(X) \neq \emptyset$ when $X \neq \emptyset$. When no confusion arises, the parentheses (,) will be dropped from the notation "MAX(X)."

Definition 6.4 A possibility for φ in $\langle\, S, \supseteq, \models^{+} \rangle$ is a maximal supporting state of φ, i.e., an element of MAX $[\![\varphi]\!]^{+}$.

Each possibility for φ embodies a possible way to change the common ground.

Definition 6.5 The *inquisitive meaning* expressed by φ, denoted by $[\![\varphi]\!]$, is the set of all the possibilities for φ, i.e., MAX $[\![\varphi]\!]^{+}$.

In other words, the inquisitive meaning $[\![\varphi]\!]$ collects all the "*first*" states in which all participants agree to accept φ in the conversation. For example, $[\![p]\!] = \{\,|p|\,\}$, $[\![p \vee q]\!] = \{\,|p|, |q|\,\}$ and $[\![p \vee \neg p]\!] = \{\,|p|, |\neg p|\,\}$ (these may easily be calculated by the inductive definition of $\lceil\varphi\rceil$ introduced below). When $[\![\varphi]\!]$ contains at least two possibilities such as $[\![p \vee q]\!]$, the inquisitive meaning $[\![\varphi]\!]$ really raises an important issue that must be resolved by the other participants, as in the intuitive explanation above.

6.2.2 Inductive Definition of Inquisitive Meaning

A calculation of the inquisitive meaning $[\![\varphi]\!]$ is occasionally involved, as *all* supporting states of φ must be known in advance. Moreover, if $[\![\varphi]\!]$ is regarded as a "meaning" capturing the proposal by φ, it is desirable to possess a compositional or inductive way of calculating $[\![\varphi]\!]$. Ciardelli [2] proposed an inductive definition of inquisitive meanings. For technical purposes, this section focuses on an *alternative* notion of inquisitive meaning $\lceil\varphi\rceil$ (called *positive inquisitive meaning*) defined inductively as follows (see [2, Definition 6.2.1], although a different notation is used here):

Definition 6.6 (Positive Inquisitive Meaning $\lceil\varphi\rceil$)

$$\begin{aligned}
\lceil p\rceil &:= \{\,|p|\,\}\\
\lceil\bot\rceil &:= \{\,\emptyset\,\}\\
\lceil\varphi\vee\psi\rceil &:= \lceil\varphi\rceil\cup\lceil\psi\rceil\\
\lceil\varphi\wedge\psi\rceil &:= \{\,s\cap t\mid s\in\lceil\varphi\rceil \text{ and } t\in\lceil\psi\rceil\,\}\\
\lceil\varphi\to\psi\rceil &:= \big\{\,\gamma_f\mid f:\lceil\varphi\rceil\to\lceil\psi\rceil\,\big\}
\end{aligned}$$

where $\gamma_f := \bigcap_{s\in\lceil\varphi\rceil}(s\Rightarrow f(s))$ and $s\Rightarrow t := \overline{s}\cup t$.[1]

The inquisitive meaning of $\neg\varphi$ can be calculated as follows:

$$\lceil\neg\varphi\rceil := \{\,\textstyle\bigcap_{s\in\lceil\varphi\rceil}\overline{s}\,\},$$

where $\overline{s}=\omega\setminus s$. But, what is the relationship between the notion of positive inquisitive meaning $\lceil\varphi\rceil$ and the notion of support $[\![\varphi]\!]$? The following proposition [2, Proposition 6.2.2] explains a crucial link between the notions of support and positive inquisitive meaning.

Proposition 6.2 (Ciardelli [2], Fundamental Link) *For all states s and all formulas φ, $s\models^{+}\varphi$ iff $s\subseteq t$ for some $t\in\lceil\varphi\rceil$.*

This proposition says that φ is supported in a current state s iff an alternative t for φ is found such that the current state s "entails" the alternative t. For example, suppose that $s=\omega$ and $\varphi\equiv p\vee q$. Since $\lceil p\vee q\rceil=\{\,|p|,|q|\,\}$ and $\omega\not\subseteq|p|$ and $\omega\not\subseteq|q|$, $\omega\not\models^{+}p\vee q$. However, if $s=|p\wedge q|\subseteq\omega$, $|p\wedge q|\models^{+}p\vee q$. This situation occurs because $p\wedge q$ entails p (q is also fine), i.e., $|p\wedge q|\subseteq|p|$. According to this proposition, all maximal φ-supporting states coincide with all maximal states in $\lceil\varphi\rceil$ (cf. [2, Proposition 6.2.3]) as follows:

Proposition 6.3 (Ciardelli [2]) $\lceil\!\lceil\varphi\rceil\!\rceil=\mathrm{MAX}\,[\![\varphi]\!]^{+}=\mathrm{MAX}\,\lceil\varphi\rceil$.

Proof It suffices to show $\mathrm{MAX}\,[\![\varphi]\!]^{+}=\mathrm{MAX}\,\lceil\varphi\rceil$. First, the left-to-right direction is verified as follows. Fix any maximal φ-supporting state s. By Proposition 6.2 and $s\models^{+}\varphi$, an element $t\in\lceil\varphi\rceil$ exists such that $s\subseteq t$. The maximality of t in $\lceil\varphi\rceil$ can be shown as follows. Fix any $u\in\lceil\varphi\rceil$ such that $t\subseteq u$. Again by Proposition 6.2, $u\models^{+}\varphi$, which implies $s=u$ because s is a maximal φ-supporting state and $s\subseteq t\subseteq u$. This also implies that $t=u$, as desired.

[1]To obtain a *direct* inductive definition of $\lceil\!\lceil\varphi\rceil\!\rceil$, the operation "MAX" should be placed in front of the right-hand sides of all defining equations of $\lceil\varphi\rceil$ except atomic cases. It is then easily seen that $\lceil\!\lceil p\rceil\!\rceil=\{\,|p|\,\}$, $\lceil\!\lceil p\vee q\rceil\!\rceil=\{\,|p|,|q|\,\}$ and $\lceil\!\lceil p\vee\neg p\rceil\!\rceil=\{\,|p|,|\neg p|\,\}$.

Second, the right-to-left direction is demonstrated as follows. Fix any maximal element s in $\lceil\varphi\rceil$. By Proposition 6.2, $s \models^{+} \varphi$. It suffices to establish the maximality of s in $[\![\varphi]\!]^{+}$. Fix any $t \supseteq s$ with $t \models^{+} \varphi$. Again by Proposition 6.2, an element $u \in \lceil\varphi\rceil$ exists such that $t \subseteq u$. By $s, u \in \lceil\varphi\rceil$ and $s \subseteq t \subseteq u$, $s = t$ by the maximality of s in $\lceil\varphi\rceil$. □

In this sense, Proposition 6.2 serves as a *fundamental link* between the notions of support $[\![\varphi]\!]$ and positive inquisitive meaning $\lceil\varphi\rceil$ in this paper.

Remark 6.1 Ciardelli [3] studied a first-order extension of inquisitive semantics and showed that, in the first-order extension, the idea of inquisitive meaning $[\![\varphi]\!]$ as all *maximal* supporting states cannot be employed; however, he also provided an appropriate *inductive* definition of the notion of inquisitive meaning in the first-order extension. Moreover, Ciardelli demonstrated that his inductively defined notion of inquisitive meaning never becomes the *derived* notion from the notion of support in the first-order extension (cf. [3]). However, the corresponding result to Proposition 6.2 may still be shown in Ciardelli's first-order extension.

6.3 Radical Inquisitive Semantics

Suppose that a participant makes the proposal $p \vee q$ (say "Pete will drink tea or coffee") to the conversation. Since $[\![p \vee q]\!] = \{\,|p|, |q|\,\}$ ($= \lceil p \vee q\rceil$) contains more than one possibilities, he or she raise an issue that must be resolved by the other participants. In nonradical inquisitive semantics, this issue may only be resolved in a positive manner, i.e., choosing one from $\{\,|p|, |q|\,\}$. However, a negative way of resolving the issue may be considered by rejecting the proposal $p \vee q$, for example, by replying that "Pete will not drink tea nor coffee." This situation is captured by *radical* inquisitive semantics [10].

The syntax $\mathcal{L}_R$ here consists of the following logical connectives: $\wedge$, $\vee$, $\rightarrow$, and $\sim$ (different from $\neg$) as well as a finite set Prop of propositional letters. Following previous work [10], $\bot$ and $\neg$ are not considered in $\mathcal{L}_R$. When the classical meaning $|\varphi|$ of a formula φ of $\mathcal{L}_R$ is considered, $\sim$ is regarded as the classical negation. Radical inquisitive semantics differs from nonradical inquisitive semantics in that it directly extends the inductive definition of positive inquisitive meaning in $\mathcal{L}_I$ to cover the rejection of proposals [10] but it does not employ any extended version of Kripke-type semantics $s \models^{+} \varphi$.

Consider the following data from previous work [10] for rejecting proposals. Let p denote "Pete will play the piano" and q denote "Sue sings," and r denote "Mary dances."

(1) Pete will play the piano. (p)

(a) No, he will not play the piano. ($\sim p$)

(2) If Sue sings, then Pete will play the piano. ($q \to p$)

(a) No, if Sue sings Pete will not play. ($q \to \sim p$)

(3) If Sue sings or Mary dances, then Pete will play the piano. ($(q \vee r) \to p$)

(a) No, if Sue sings Pete will not play. ($q \to \sim p$)
(b) No, if Mary dances Pete will not play. ($r \to \sim p$)

Then, Groenendijk and Roelofsen [10] have inductively defined the notions of positive and negative inquisitive meaning as follows[2]:

Definition 6.7 (*Positive and Negative Inquisitive Meanings*) The following are added to the previous clauses for $\lceil\varphi\rceil$ except $\lceil\bot\rceil$ in Definition 6.6,

$$\begin{aligned} \lfloor p \rfloor &:= \{\, |\sim p|\,\} \\ \lceil\sim\varphi\rceil &:= \lfloor\varphi\rfloor \\ \lfloor\sim\varphi\rfloor &:= \lceil\varphi\rceil \\ \lfloor\varphi\wedge\psi\rfloor &:= \lfloor\varphi\rfloor \cup \lfloor\psi\rfloor \\ \lfloor\varphi\vee\psi\rfloor &:= \{\, s\cap t \mid s\in\lfloor\varphi\rfloor \text{ and } t\in\lfloor\psi\rfloor\,\} \\ \lfloor\varphi\to\psi\rfloor &:= \{\, s\Rightarrow t \mid s\in\lceil\varphi\rceil \text{ and } t\in\lfloor\psi\rfloor\,\}, \end{aligned}$$

where recall $s \Rightarrow t := \overline{s} \cup t$.

The rejecting proposals can then be calculated as follows:

(1) $\lfloor p\rfloor = \{\, |\sim p|\,\}$.
(2) $\lfloor q \to p\rfloor = \{\, |q \to\sim p|\,\}$.
(3) $\lfloor (q\vee r) \to p\rfloor = \{\, |q \to\sim p|, |r \to\sim p|\,\}$.

Further English examples and their formalization can be found in previous work [10]. Although some readers might wonder if Groenendijk and Roelofsen's definition of $\lfloor\varphi\to\psi\rfloor$ fits the intuition, this paper accepts the definition as it is to show that an appropriate Kripke-type semantics cannot be derived to satisfy an extended version of the fundamental link between the notions of support and (positive) inquisitive meaning (recall Proposition 6.2). Finally, the following proposition, which reflects the intuition underlying the example (3) above, can be obtained through an easy calculation:

Proposition 6.4 $\lfloor(\varphi\vee\psi)\to\theta\rfloor = \lfloor(\varphi\to\theta)\wedge(\psi\to\theta)\rfloor$.

---

[2]The definition of Groenendijk and Roelofsen [10] is not necessarily the only way to define these notions. However, the present paper accepts these definitions to demonstrate that *any* Kripke semantics for intuitionistic logic with the strong negation $\sim$ cannot *derive* the negative inquisitive meaning of this definition from , as can be accomplished in conservative inquisitive semantics.

6.4 Impossibility Theorems in Radical Inquisitive Semantics

In conservative inquisitive semantics, the inquisitive model $\langle S, \supseteq, \models^+ \rangle$ (recall $S = \mathcal{P}(\omega)$ and $\omega = \{0, 1\}^{\mathsf{Prop}}$) captures how the conversation proceeds starting from the ignorant state of $\langle S, \supseteq, \models^+ \rangle$. Because the behavior of $\sim$ in positive and negative inquisitive meanings given by Groenendijk and Roelofsen [10] is very similar to the strong negation in Nelson's constructive logics (an expansion of intuitionistic logic with strong negation $\sim$; see previous works [11, 12] for further details)[3], it is natural to consider the notion of rejection $\models^-$ as well as the notion of support $\models^+$. The guiding principle of the present work is to find a correct rejection clause and that the rejection clause allows the fundamental link between the notions of support and inquisitive meaning (Proposition 6.2) to be generalized such that

$$s \models^- \varphi \text{ iff } \exists t \in \lfloor \varphi \rfloor . s \subseteq t,$$

for all $s, t \in S$ and all formulas φ of $\mathcal{L}_R$. This clause would assure that all maximal rejecting states of φ coincide with MAX $\lfloor \varphi \rfloor$. The main difficulty consists in providing an appropriate rejection clause to the implication $\varphi \to \psi$, as the other support and rejection clauses can be naturally determined. A stand-in for the rejection clause of $\varphi \to \psi$ may be defined using a binary function $\mathbb{F} : \mathcal{P}(S) \times \mathcal{P}(S) \to \mathcal{P}(S)$.

Definition 6.8 Let $\mathbb{F}$ be a function $\mathcal{P}(S) \times \mathcal{P}(S) \to \mathcal{P}(S)$. The pair of $\models^+$ (*support*) and $\models^-$ (*rejection*) is defined as follows. The following clauses are added to the previous clauses of $\models^+$ except $\neg\varphi$:

$$\begin{array}{ll} s \models^- p & \text{iff } s \cap |p| = \emptyset \\ s \models^+ \sim\varphi & \text{iff } s \models^- \varphi \\ s \models^- \sim\varphi & \text{iff } s \models^+ \varphi \\ s \models^- \varphi \wedge \psi & \text{iff } s \models^- \varphi \text{ or } s \models^- \psi \\ s \models^- \varphi \vee \psi & \text{iff } s \models^- \varphi \text{ and } s \models^- \psi \\ s \models^- \varphi \to \psi & \text{iff } s \in \mathbb{F}([\![\varphi]\!]^+, [\![\psi]\!]^-). \end{array}$$

where $[\![\theta]\!]^+ := \{ t \in S \mid t \models^+ \theta \}$ and $[\![\theta]\!]^- := \{ t \in S \mid t \models^- \theta \}$.

Because $\lfloor \varphi \to \psi \rfloor$ depends on $\lceil \varphi \rceil$ and $\lfloor \psi \rfloor$, it may be assumed that the rejection clause $s \models^- \varphi \to \psi$ depends on $[\![\varphi]\!]^+$ and $[\![\psi]\!]^-$. An alternative method of providing a rejection clause for the implication may exist; for example, a possible rejection clause for the implication might depend on all of $[\![\varphi]\!]^+$, $[\![\varphi]\!]^-$, $[\![\psi]\!]^+$ and $[\![\psi]\!]^-$. This issue will be considered later.

Similarly to the notion of possibility, the notion of counter-possibility is defined as follows:

Definition 6.9 A *counter-possibility* for φ in $\langle S, \supseteq, \models^+, \models^- \rangle$ is a maximal rejecting state of φ, i.e., an element of MAX $[\![\varphi]\!]^-$.

---

[3]Reference [10], did not refer to the strong negation in Nelson's constructive logics.

By induction on φ, the following may be shown:

Proposition 6.5 *For all implication-free formulas φ of $\mathcal{L}_R$ and for all $s, t \in S$,*

$$s \models^+ \varphi \text{ iff } \exists t \in \lceil\varphi\rceil . s \subseteq t, \text{ and } s \models^- \varphi \text{ iff } \exists t \in \lfloor\varphi\rfloor . s \subseteq t.$$

For the negative inquisitive meaning, this proposition states that an implication-free formula φ is rejected in the current state s iff a counter-possibility t exists for φ such that the current state s "entails" the counter-possibility t. However, if the implication is considered, the situation changes drastically.

Theorem 6.1 (Impossibility Theorem) *There is no $\mathbb{F} : \mathcal{P}(S) \times \mathcal{P}(S) \to \mathcal{P}(S)$ such that*

$$s \models^- \varphi \text{ iff } \exists t \in \lfloor\varphi\rfloor . s \subseteq t,$$

for all states $s \in S$ and all formulas φ of $\mathcal{L}_R$.

Proof Suppose for the sake of contradiction that there is some $\mathbb{F} : \mathcal{P}(S) \times \mathcal{P}(S) \to \mathcal{P}(S)$ such that the desired equivalences above can be obtained. By assumption, the following equivalence is obtained:

$$\text{MAX}\, [\![\varphi]\!]^- = \text{MAX}\, \lfloor\varphi\rfloor. \tag{A}$$

By the rejection clause for the implication, the following may be demonstrated (note that this is the only place to use $\mathbb{F}$).

$$[\![p \to r]\!]^- = [\![(p \vee (p \wedge q)) \to r]\!]^-, \tag{B}$$

because $s \models^- p \to r$ iff $s \in \mathbb{F}([\![p]\!]^+, [\![r]\!]^-)$ iff $s \in \mathbb{F}([\![p \vee (p \wedge q)]\!]^+, [\![r]\!]^-)$ iff $s \models^- (p \vee (p \wedge q)) \to r$; note that $[\![p]\!]^+ = [\![p \vee (p \wedge q)]\!]^+$. The desired contradiction may be demonstrated as follows:

$$\begin{aligned}
\{\, |p \to {\sim} r| \,\} &= \text{MAX}\, \lfloor p \to r \rfloor \\
&= \text{MAX}\, [\![p \to r]\!]^- && \text{by (A)} \\
&= \text{MAX}\, [\![(p \vee (p \wedge q)) \to r]\!]^- && \text{by (B)} \\
&= \text{MAX}\, \lfloor (p \vee (p \wedge q)) \to r \rfloor^- && \text{by (A)} \\
&= \text{MAX}\, \lfloor ((p \to r) \wedge ((p \wedge q) \to r) \rfloor && \text{by Proposition 4} \\
&= \text{MAX}\, \{\, |p \to {\sim} r|, |(p \wedge q) \to {\sim} r| \,\} && \text{by Definition 6} \\
&= \{\, |(p \wedge q) \to {\sim} r| \,\},
\end{aligned}$$

which implies a contradiction. (It is clear that $|p \to {\sim} r| \neq |(p \wedge q) \to {\sim} r|$). □

Remark 6.2 An insight of the proof of Theorem 6.1 is to mimic the argument [6] of conditional logic that the axiom (**SDA**) of simplification of disjunctive antecedents:

$$((\varphi \vee \psi) > \theta) \to ((\varphi > \theta) \wedge (\psi > \theta))$$

implies the axiom (**SA**) of strengthening antecedents:

$$(\varphi > \theta) \rightarrow ((\varphi \wedge \psi) > \theta).$$

where $>$ is the conditional connective (which differs from the material or intuitionistic implications). If replacement of logically equivalent formulas for antecedents of $>$ holds, **SA** can be derived from **SDA** as follows. Because φ and $\varphi \vee (\varphi \wedge \psi)$ are logically equivalent,

$$(\varphi > \theta) \dashv\vdash (\varphi \vee (\varphi \wedge \psi)) > \theta.$$

By **SDA**,

$$(\varphi \vee (\varphi \wedge \psi)) > \theta \vdash (\varphi \wedge \psi) > \theta.$$

Therefore,

$$(\varphi > \theta) \vdash (\varphi \wedge \psi) > \theta.$$

The original derivation of **SA** from **SDA** by Ellis et al. [6] contains the negation symbol and uses the law of excluded middle. However, the above argument does not contain any negation symbol. This argument without the negation symbol was constructed by Greg Restall (p.c. with Greg Restall).[4]

Instead of the two place function $\mathbb{F}$ in $s \models^- \varphi \rightarrow \psi$, consider a four-place function $\mathbb{G}$ on $\mathcal{P}(S)$ and the following rejection clause for the implication[5]:

$$s \models^- \varphi \rightarrow \psi \text{ iff } s \in \mathbb{G}([\![\varphi]\!]^+, [\![\varphi]\!]^-, [\![\psi]\!]^+, [\![\psi]\!]^-).$$

In the proof of Theorem 6.1, the only necessary use of $\mathbb{F}$ is in the proof of the Eq. (B). Even when using the four-place function $\mathbb{G}$, the equation $[\![p \rightarrow r]\!]^- = [\![(p \vee (p \wedge q)) \rightarrow r]\!]^-$ is obtained, because $[\![p]\!]^- = [\![p \vee (p \wedge q)]\!]^-$, hence

$$\mathbb{G}([\![p]\!]^+, [\![p]\!]^-, [\![r]\!]^+, [\![r]\!]^-) = \mathbb{G}([\![p \vee (p \wedge q)]\!]^+, [\![p \vee (p \wedge q)]\!]^-, [\![r]\!]^+, [\![r]\!]^-).$$

Therefore, the following theorem may be obtained:

Theorem 6.2 (Generalized Impossibility Theorem) *There is no four-place function $\mathbb{G}$ on $\mathcal{P}(S)$ such that*

$$s \models^- \varphi \text{ iff } \exists t \in \lfloor \varphi \rfloor . s \subseteq t,$$

for all $s \in S$ and all formulas φ of $\mathcal{L}_R$.

---

[4]The author would like to thank Daisuke Bekki for sharing Greg Restall's argument.

[5]The author owes this suggestion to Floris Roelofsen.

6.5 Approximating Negative Inquisitive Meaning of Implication

Once negative results are obtained as Theorems 6.1 and 6.2, it is only possible to "approximate" the negative inquisitive meaning of $\varphi \to \psi$ in [10].[6] Throughout this section, the following rejection clause for implication is considered:

$$s \models^- \varphi \to \psi \text{ iff } \exists t.\ \big(t \models^+ \varphi \text{ and } \forall t' \supseteq t.\,(t' \models^+ \varphi \text{ implies } s \cap t' \models^- \psi)\big),$$

and the other support and rejection clauses are the same as those previously presented. This rejection clause was originally proposed by the current author. Notably, this rejection clause for the implication has not been previously studied in the context of Nelson's constructive logic with the strong negation. However, the clause has been used by Aher [1] to solve the free choice puzzle and (in a slightly adapted form) in recent work by Groenendijk and Roelofsen [8] on suppositional inquisitive semantics.

Proposition 6.6 (Persistence) *$[\![\theta]\!]^+$ and $[\![\theta]\!]^-$ are closed under $\supseteq$, i.e., downward closed, for all formulas θ of $\mathcal{L}_R$.*

The following proposition provides an intuition of rejection clauses for implication (notably, the finiteness of Prop must be used).

Proposition 6.7 *$s \models^- \varphi \to \psi$ iff $s \cap t \models^- \psi$ for some maximal φ-supporting state t, i.e., $t \in \mathrm{MAX}\,[\![\varphi]\!]^+$.*

Proof The right-to-left direction may easily be obtained, the left-to-right direction must be established. Assume that $s \models^- \varphi \to \psi$. By assumption, there exists $t \subseteq \omega$ such that $t \models^+ \varphi$ and $\forall t' \supseteq t.\,(t' \models^+ \varphi$ implies $s \cap t' \models^- \psi)$. A maximal φ-supporting state $t_{\max} \supseteq t$ exists (because our Prop is finite). By assumption, it may be deduced that $s \cap t_{\max} \models^- \psi$, as required. □

$\varphi \to \psi$ is therefore rejected at the current state s iff some *first* φ-supporting state t exists, and ψ is rejected at the updated current state $s \cap t$ by t. In a similar manner to Proposition 6.7, the support clause for implication may be reformulated as follows:

Proposition 6.8 (Groenendijk) *$s \models^+ \varphi \to \psi$ iff $s \cap t \models^+ \psi$ for all maximal φ-supporting states t, i.e., $t \in \mathrm{MAX}\,[\![\varphi]\!]^+$.*

Proof First, the left-to-right direction is demonstrated as follows. Assume that $s \models^+ \varphi \to \psi$ and fix any maximal φ-supporting state t. Thus, $t \models^+ \varphi$ holds. $s \cap t \models^+ \psi$ is shown as follows. Because $s \cap t \subseteq t$ and $t \models^+ \varphi$, $s \cap t \models^+ \varphi$ by Proposition 6.6. It therefore follows from the assumption of $s \models^+ \varphi \to \psi$ and $s \cap t \subseteq s$ that $s \cap t \models^+ \psi$, as desired.

---

[6] Wansing's *connexive logic* [13] provides a very similar idea to the underling idea of Groenendijk and Roelofsen [10] that the negation of $p \to q$ is equivalent to $p \to \sim q$.

Second, the right-to-left direction is established as follows. Assume $s \cap u \models^{+} \psi$ for all maximal φ-supporting states u and fix any $t \subseteq s$ with $t \models^{+} \varphi$. Because Prop is finite, a maximal φ-supporting state $t_{\max} \supseteq t$ exists. By assumption, $s \cap t_{\max} \models^{+} \psi$. Because $s \cap t \subseteq s \cap t_{\max}$, it is deduced from Proposition 6.6 that $s \cap t \models^{+} \psi$, hence $t \models^{+} \psi$ by $t \subseteq s$. (Note that $t \subseteq s$ iff $s \cap t = t$.) □

The remaining main concern is now the following question: can an inductive definition be provided for both all maximal φ-supporting states and all maximal φ-rejecting states? The answer is positive. Let the notions of positive inquisitive meaning $\lceil \varphi \rceil$ and *quasi*-negative inquisitive meaning $\lfloor \varphi \rfloor'$ be defined using the same atomic and inductive clauses for $\{\sim, \wedge, \vee\}$ as the notion of positive and negative inquisitive meanings (replacing all occurrences of $\lfloor \varphi \rfloor$ with $\lfloor \varphi \rfloor'$), as well as the clause for $\lceil \varphi \rightarrow \psi \rceil$ and the following clause:

$$\lfloor \varphi \rightarrow \psi \rfloor' := \left\{ s \Rightarrow t \mid s \in \mathrm{MAX}\lceil \varphi \rceil \text{ and } t \in \lfloor \psi \rfloor' \right\}.$$

The same calculation results may then be obtained for the English examples from (1) to (3). Moreover, the following generalization of Proposition 6.2 may also be obtained.

Theorem 6.3 *For all formulas φ of $\mathcal{L}_R$ and for all $s \in S$,*

$$s \models^{+} \varphi \text{ iff } \exists t \in \lceil \varphi \rceil . s \subseteq t, \textit{ and } s \models^{-} \varphi \text{ iff } \exists t \in \lfloor \varphi \rfloor' . s \subseteq t.$$

Therefore, $\mathrm{MAX}\,[\![\varphi]\!]^{+} = \mathrm{MAX}\lceil \varphi \rceil$ *and* $\mathrm{MAX}\,[\![\varphi]\!]^{-} = \mathrm{MAX}\lfloor \varphi \rfloor'$ *for all formulas φ of $\mathcal{L}_R$.*

Proof By induction on φ. The most crucial case is the rejection clause for $\varphi \rightarrow \psi$. Only checking this clause, it suffices to show that

$$s \models^{-} \varphi \rightarrow \psi \text{ iff } s \cap t \models^{-} \psi \text{ for some } t \in \mathrm{MAX}\lceil \varphi \rceil. \qquad (*)$$

Why is this equivalence sufficient? This situation can be demonstrated as:

$$\begin{aligned} \exists t \in \lfloor \varphi \rightarrow \psi \rfloor . s \subseteq t \text{ iff } & \exists t_1 \in \mathrm{MAX}\lceil \varphi \rceil .\ \exists t_2 \in \lfloor \psi \rfloor' . s \subseteq t_1 \Rightarrow t_2 \\ \text{iff } & \exists t_1 \in \mathrm{MAX}\lceil \varphi \rceil .\ \exists t_2 \in \lfloor \psi \rfloor' . s \cap t_1 \subseteq t_2 \\ \text{iff } & \exists t_1 \in \mathrm{MAX}\lceil \varphi \rceil . s \cap t_1 \models^{-} \psi \quad \text{(by the induction hypothesis).} \end{aligned}$$

So, it suffices to show that the last line is equivalent with $s \models^{-} \varphi \rightarrow \psi$, i.e., $(*)$.

Return to the proof of (*). By the induction hypothesis and the same argument as in Proposition 6.3, $\mathrm{MAX}\lceil \varphi \rceil = \mathrm{MAX}\,[\![\varphi]\!]^{+}$. To show (*), it suffices to show the following:

$$s \models^{-} \varphi \rightarrow \psi \text{ iff } s \cap t \models^{-} \psi \text{ for some } t \in \mathrm{MAX}\,[\![\varphi]\!]^{+}.$$

However, this is exactly the same as Proposition 6.7. □

6.6 Concluding Remark

While the direct inductive definition of inquisitive meaning represents a significant technical contribution, the impossibility theorems (Theorems 6.1 and 6.2) also indicate that, to incorporate the notion of rejecting a proposal into nonradical inquisitive semantics, a Kripke-type semantics with the strong negation $\sim$ must be constructed. Even if Groenendijk and Roelofsen's treatment of the English examples from (1) to (3) is not accepted, their definition of positive and negative inquisitive meanings [10] may be replaced by different Kripke-type semantics [12, 13].

If Groenendijk and Roelofsen's treatment of the English examples is accepted, together with the proposed rejection clause for the implication, this research direction fits well with the current development of *suppositional inquisitive semantics* [8], i.e., an updated version of radical inquisitive semantics. Moreover, the proposed rejection clause may be imported into logics that define both verification (support) and falsification (rejection), such as Nelson's constructive logic with strong negation [11, 12], Wansing's connexive logic [13], and/or the truthmaker semantics [7] proposed by Kit Fine. This applicability arises because no common agreement exists regarding how to define the rejection clause for the implication. In this sense, the present paper not only contributes to the inquisitive semantics research program but may also have broader relevance.[7]

References

1. M. Aher. Free choice in deontic inquisitive semantics (DIS). In M. Aloni, et al. editor, *Amsterdam Colloquium 2011*, volume 7218 of *LNCS*, pages 22–31. Springer-Verlag, 2012.
2. I. Ciardelli. Inquisitive semantics and intermediate logics. Master's thesis, Institute for Logic, Language and Computation, University of Amsterdam, 2009.
3. I. Ciardelli. A first-order inquisitive semantics. In M. Aloni, H. Bastiaanse, T. de Jager, and K. Schulz, editors, *Logic, Language, and Meaning: Selected Papers from the Seventeenth Amsterdam Colloquium.* volume 6042 of *LNCS*, pages 234–243. Springer-Verlag, 2010.
4. I. Ciardelli and F. Roelofsen. Generalized Inquisitive Logic: Completeness via Intuitionistic Kripke Models. In *TARK '09 Proceedings of the 12th Conference on Theoretical Aspects of Rationality and Knowledge*, pages 71–80, ACM New York, 2009.
5. I. Ciardelli and F. Roelofsen. Inquisitive logic. *Journal of Philosophical Logic*, 40(1):55–94, 2011.

[7]The author has presented material related to this paper at several occasions in the past three years and would like to thank the audiences of these events, including the second PhilLog-Math Workshop in Tokyo, the Relating Particles to Evidence and Inference Workshop in Goettingen, the Taiwan Philosophical Logic Colloquium 2012 in Taiwan, and the Second Asian Workshop on Philosophical Logic in Guangzhou. The author especially thanks Jeroen Groenendijk for his discussion during the author's stay at Amsterdam in 2009 and 2010; Floris Roelofsen for his comments on earlier drafts of the manuscript; and Daisuke Bekki for sharing Greg Restall's argument on the disjunctive antecedent of conditionals. The author is also grateful to the anonymous referee for their helpful comments. The work of the author was partially supported by a KAKENHI Grant-in-Aid for Young Scientists (B) No. 24700146.

6. B. Ellis, F. Jackson, and R. Pargetter. An objection to possible worlds semantics for counterfactual logics. *Journal of Philosophical Logic*, 6:355–357, 1977.
7. K. Fine. Truth-maker semantics for intuitionistic logic. *Journal of Philosophical Logic*, 43:549–577, 2014.
8. J. Groenendijk and F. Roelofsen. Toward a suppositional inquisitive semantics. To appear in M. Aher, D. Hole, E. Jerabek, and C. Kupke, editors, *Logic, Language, and Computation: revised selected papers from the 10th International Tbilisi Symposium on Language, Logic, and Computation*. Springer, 2014. Available from www.illc.uva.nl/inquisitive-semantics.
9. J. Groenendijk and F. Roelofsen. Inquisitive semantics and pragmatics. In J. M. Larrazabal and L. Zubeldia, editors, *Meaning, Content, and Argument: Proceedings of the ILCLI International Workshop on Semantics, Pragmatics, and Rhetoric*, pages 41–72, University of the Basque Country Publication Service, 2009. www.illc.uva.nl/inquisitive-semantics.
10. J. Groenendijk and F. Roelofsen. Radical inquisitive semantics. Presented at the Sixth International Symposium on Logic, Cognition, and Communication at the University of Latvia. Latest version available via www.illc.uva.nl/inquisitive-semantics, 2010.
11. D. Nelson. Constructible falsity. *Journal of Symbolic Logic*, 14:16–26, 1949.
12. S. Odintsov. *Constructive Negations and Paraconsistency*. Springer-Verlag, Dordrecht, 2008.
13. H. Wansing. Connexive logic. In Edward N. Zalta, editor, *The Stanford Encyclopedia of Philosophy*. Spring 2014 edition, 2014.

Chapter 7
Epistemic Informativeness

Yanjing Wang and Jie Fan

Abstract In this paper, we introduce and formalize the concept of *epistemic informativeness* (EI) of statements: the set of new propositions that an agent comes to know from the truthful announcement of the statements. We formalize EI in multi-agent Public Announcement Logic and characterize it by proving that two basic statements are the same in EI iff the logical equivalence of the two is common knowledge after a certain announcement. As a corollary applied to identity statements, $a = b$ and $a = a$ are different in EI iff $a = b$ is not common knowledge. This may shed new light on the differences in cognitive value of $a = a$ and $a = b$, even when they are both *known* to be true, as long as $a = b$ is not commonly known to all.

Keywords Cognitive value · Epistemic informativeness · Public announcement logic · Common knowledge · Frege's puzzle

7.1 Introduction

Frege's puzzle of identity statements, in its simplest form, can be stated as the following question:

> How do we explain the difference between $a = a$ and $a = b$ in cognitive value to a linguistically competent speaker when a and b are co-referential?

To our view, there are at least three subproblems to be answered:

- What is the concept of 'cognitive value'?
- What is the concept of 'linguistic competence'?
- What is the proposition expressed by $a = b$ exactly?

Y. Wang (✉) · J. Fan
Department of Philosophy, Peking University, Beijing, China
e-mail: y.wang@pku.edu.cn

J. Fan
e-mail: fanjie@pku.edu.cn

S. Ju et al. (eds.), *Modality, Semantics and Interpretations*,
Logic in Asia: Studia Logica Library, DOI 10.1007/978-3-662-47197-5_7

Any solution to the puzzle should first sharpen the concept of cognitive value of statements. Instead of defining the cognitive value directly, many approaches in the literature attribute the *differences* in cognitive value to the differences in their *informativeness* (cf. e.g., [8, 11, 17]). Intuitively, $a = a$ and $a = b$ are indeed not equally informative, but what exactly is this concept of informativeness? How to compare the informativeness of two arbitrary statements? In this paper, we present a formal epistemic treatment of informativeness of propositional statements, which is not restricted to identity statements only, and prove technical results which may shed new light on the epistemic aspects of Frege's puzzle. Our discussion lies at the propositional level, and thus cannot fully account for Frege's puzzle, but we do hope to convince the readers that at this abstraction level, interesting things can be already said about phenomena related to the puzzle, when the knowledge of *multiple agents* is discussed formally. The rest of this section is devoted to informal ideas. Formal definitions and proofs will be given in the next section.

Our journey starts with the initial observation by Frege in [4]: '$a = a$ holds *a priori*... while statements of the form $a = b$ often contain very valuable extensions of our knowledge...'. Intuitively, a statement is informative if it brings an extension to our knowledge. Thus it is crucial to understand what exactly is this extension. Note that the word 'extension' clearly suggests a *comparison* between the knowledge before and after the statement is made. Here, two questions arise naturally:

- Whose knowledge are we talking about in the comparison?
- How does the statement change knowledge?

In the previous work on Frege's puzzle, it is often implicitly assumed that there is a generic linguistically competent agent who is responsible for the informativeness of the statements. However, it is clear that a true statement ϕ may cause different knowledge extensions to different agents i and j, given that i knows ϕ already but j does not know it. Based on this observation, we should acknowledge the diversity of agents and their knowledge prior to the statement. Therefore, a reasonable definition of informativeness of a statement should be relative to a particular agent and also a concrete situation prior to the statement where the knowledge of the agent concerned is determined. The comparison is only possible if we fix these two factors.

To approach the second question, we first need to clarify how the agent concerned receives the statement. Our bottom-line assumption is that the statement is communicated to the agent (from some source). In this paper, we fix the arguably simplest communication method: public announcement of the statement, i.e., the statement is announced publicly to all.[1] Now how does an announcement change the knowledge of the agents? Clearly, it is not as simple as adding the statement into the 'knowledge database'. For example, if you know $p \to q$ but not p nor q, then an announcement of p may let you know both p and q. On the other hand, the announced statement can

[1] It is definitely possible to consider other communication methods which have different effects on the knowledge states of agents. The choice here is simple enough to make our points clear.

even be false after the announcement, e.g., the announcement of a Moore sentence 'p and you do not know that p' will make itself false by letting the listener know p.[2]

Here we will follow the dynamic semantics tradition which dates back to the early works of [6, 12, 15], where the semantics of a statement is attributed to its *potential* in changing the common ground of the participants of the dialogue. The modern logical development of this idea is the framework of Dynamic Epistemic Logic (**DEL**) initiated by [5, 9], where the communicative actions of statements are interpreted as transformers of knowledge states. We will make use of the simplest kind of **DEL**, the Public Announcement Logic (**PAL**) to formalize our concepts in the next section.

Now we are ready to state the informal definition of the central concept of this paper: *epistemic informativeness*.[3]

> The epistemic informativeness (EI) of a true statement to an agent given a concrete situation is the set of new propositions that the agent comes to know from the public announcement of the statement.

The adjective 'epistemic' suggests that this concept is a particular kind of informativeness: it is about knowledge but not belief which can be false,[4] nor the pragmatics-induced information which comes along with the statements as discussed by [8]. We claim that a difference in epistemic informativeness implies a difference in informativeness thus implies differences in cognitive value of statements, but the other way around may not hold, since the latter two concepts should be more general. Modest as it may look, epistemic informativeness can help us to explain non-trivial phenomena due to the fact that the knowledge in the definition is not only about basic facts but also about others' knowledge. As an example, let us consider the following strengthened version of Frege's puzzle:

> How do we explain the difference between $a = a$ and $a = b$ in cognitive value when they are both true and the agent already **knows** that $a = b$.

Here the multi-agent perspective is important. A public announcement of $a = b$ may not advance your knowledge about *basic facts* if $a = b$ is already known to you, but it may extend others' knowledge and this will in turn extend your knowledge about others' knowledge about $a = b$. Thus $a = b$ is still possibly informative even when the agent in concern knows it already. Actually, the situation is more subtle, for example, suppose that $a = b$ is known to *all* the agents, can it still be possibly different to $a = a$ in epistemic informativeness? More generally, when are two statements equally informative? Now we hit the boundary of the informal discussion and such issues will only be made clear using the formal tools in the next section.

---

[2]Cf. [7] for a detailed technical discussion of the Moore sentences in this setting.

[3]In the context of Frege's puzzle, a similar informal 'dynamic' conception of informativeness was briefly mentioned by [3], but not formalized precisely.

[4]False statements can also be informative in general if we are talking about belief.

In the formal part of the paper, we will do the following:

- We formalize the notion of epistemic informativeness of propositional statements and its conditional variant in Public Announcement Logic.
- We show that two basic statements are equally epistemically informative iff the logical equivalence of the two is commonly known after the announcement that one of them is true.
- As a consequence of the above result, (under two intuitive assumptions) if the proposition expressed by $a = b$ is not commonly known (no matter how close to common knowledge) then $a = b$ and $a = a$ are different in their epistemic informativeness.

At the end of the paper, we will come back to Frege's puzzle, and compare our approach to epistemic two-dimensionalism proposed by [1, 2].

7.2 Formalization and Proofs

We first review some basics about **PAL** (cf. e.g., [14]). Given a set of agent names **I** and a set of proposition letters **P**, the language of **PAL** is defined as follows:

$$\phi ::= p \mid \neg\phi \mid (\phi \wedge \phi) \mid K_i\phi \mid C\phi \mid \langle\phi\rangle\phi$$

where $p \in \mathbf{P}$, and $i \in \mathbf{I}$. $K_i\phi$ expresses that 'agent i knows that ϕ' and $C\phi$ reads 'ϕ is common knowledge among all the agents'.[5] $\langle\psi\rangle\phi$ says that 'ψ can be truthfully announced, and after its announcement, ϕ holds.' As usual, we define $\phi \vee \psi$, $\phi \to \psi$, $\hat{K}_i\phi$, and $[\psi]\phi$ as the abbreviations of $\neg(\neg\phi \wedge \neg\psi)$, $\neg\phi \vee \psi$, $\neg K_i\neg\phi$, and $\neg\langle\psi\rangle\neg\phi$ respectively. In particular, $[\psi]\phi$ says that *if* ψ can be announced, then after its announcement ϕ holds.

The semantics of **PAL** is defined on S5 Kripke structures $\mathcal{M} = \langle W, \{\sim_i \mid i \in \mathbf{I}\}, V_{\mathbf{P}}\rangle$, where W is a non-empty set of possible states (epistemic possibilities), $\sim_i$ is an equivalence relation over W, $V_{\mathbf{P}} : W \to 2^{\mathbf{P}}$ is a valuation assigning each world a set of basic propositions which are true on it. An S5 model with a designated world w in it is called a pointed model (notation: $\mathcal{M}_w$). The semantics of **PAL** formulas is defined as follows:

$$\begin{array}{rcl}
\mathcal{M}_w \vDash p & \Leftrightarrow & p \in V_{\mathbf{P}}(w) \\
\mathcal{M}_w \vDash \neg\phi & \Leftrightarrow & \mathcal{M}_w \nvDash \phi \\
\mathcal{M}_w \vDash \phi \wedge \psi & \Leftrightarrow & \mathcal{M}_w \vDash \phi \text{ and } \mathcal{M}_w \vDash \psi \\
\mathcal{M}_w \vDash K_i\psi & \Leftrightarrow & \text{for all } v \text{ such that } w \sim_i v : \mathcal{M}_v \vDash \psi \\
\mathcal{M}_w \vDash C\psi & \Leftrightarrow & \text{for all } v \text{ such that } w \sim^* v : \mathcal{M}_v \vDash \psi \\
\mathcal{M}_w \vDash \langle\psi\rangle\phi & \Leftrightarrow & \mathcal{M}_w \vDash \psi \text{ and } (\mathcal{M}|_\psi)_w \vDash \phi
\end{array}$$

[5]See [14] for a discussion on common knowledge. Here common knowledge of ϕ means all the agents know ϕ and all the agents know that all the agents know ϕ, and so on, *ad infinitum*.

where $\sim^*$ is the transitive closure of $\bigcup_{i \in \mathbf{I}} \sim_i$ and $\mathcal{M}|_\psi = (W', \{\sim'_i \mid i \in \mathbf{I}\}, V'_\mathbf{P})$ where:

$$W' = \langle v \mid \mathcal{M}_v \vDash \psi \rangle, \sim'_i = \sim_i |_{W' \times W'}, V'_\mathbf{P} = V_\mathbf{P}|_{W'}$$

Intuitively, agents commonly know ϕ at w if ϕ holds in all the reachable states from w via $\sim^*$. An announcement $\langle \psi \rangle$ is interpreted as a *model transformer* which deletes the states that do not satisfy ψ. As usual, we write $\Delta \vDash \phi$ if ϕ semantically follows from the set of formulas Δ, i.e., for any $\mathcal{M}_w$ that satisfies all the formulas in Δ, $\mathcal{M}_w \vDash \phi$. The set of validities of **PAL** can be axiomatized by an extension of the proof system of S5 (see [14] for details).

Clearly, $\mathcal{M}_w$ can be viewed as a concrete scenario where each agent's knowledge is determined. Now, to formalize EI, we just need to collect the new knowledge χ that the agent learns after the announcement, i.e. $\mathcal{M}_w \vDash \neg K_i \chi \wedge \langle \phi \rangle K_i \chi$. Moreover, besides a single concrete scenario, it is also natural to discuss EI given a class of concrete scenarios given by some assumptions, e.g., we may want to compare EI of $a = b$ and $a = a$ given that $a = b$ and $K_i(a = b)$ are both true. This leads us to the concept of conditional EI formalized below with respect to a set Δ of **PAL** formulas. EI can be lifted naturally to a conditional notion by collecting all the pairs of a concrete scenario and the corresponding set of new knowledge.[6]

Definition 7.1 Given a pointed model $\mathcal{M}_w$ which satisfies ϕ, the epistemic informativeness (EI) of ϕ to agent i at $\mathcal{M}_w$ is the set (denoted as $ei(\phi, i, \mathcal{M}_w)$):

$$\{\chi \mid \mathcal{M}_w \vDash \neg K_i \chi \wedge \langle \phi \rangle K_i \chi\}$$

Based on this, we can define the conditional epistemic informativeness of ϕ to agent i given the assumption set Δ (denoted as $ei(\phi, i, \Delta)$) as the following set:

$$\{\langle \mathcal{M}_w, \Gamma \rangle \mid \mathcal{M}_w \vDash \Delta \cup \{\phi\} \text{ and } \Gamma = ei(\phi, i, \mathcal{M}_w)\}$$

Under this definition, we can naturally compare the EI of different statements by their corresponding knowledge sets. In the rest of this paper, we will focus on the equivalence of EI. We call a **PAL**-formula ϕ a *basic formula* if it does not contain modalities (neither K_i nor C nor any $[\psi]$). It is not hard to see that the truth value of a basic formula is preserved under announcements, since the truth value of a basic formula only depends on the valuation $V_\mathbf{P}$ which essentially stays the same after the announcement.

Now we are ready to prove our main result: the characterization of EI-equivalence given the assumption set Δ. At first glance, the readers may think that we can simply use common knowledge of $\phi \leftrightarrow \psi$ to characterize the equality of ϕ and ψ in their

[6]Rendsvig [10] also used the update mechanism to define the *equality* of informativeness of identity statements, but in a very strict way: ϕ and ψ are equally informative if the corresponding announcements can delete the same states in the given model. Here we give a natural definition of informativeness itself, which induces a weaker notion of informational equivalence.

informativeness. However, this does not work even when we restrict ourselves to very simple propositional formulas. As an example, consider the following pointed model $\mathcal{M}, w$ (reflexive arrows omitted):

$$w : p, q \leftarrow 1 \rightarrow \neg p \neg q \leftarrow 2 \rightarrow p, \neg q$$

Clearly, updating p or q cause the same effect, i.e., $ei(p, 1, \mathcal{M}_w) = ei(q, 1, \mathcal{M}_w)$, but $\mathcal{M}_w \nvDash C(p \leftrightarrow q)$. Actually, the characterization result is more subtle, and that is why we need a proper technical treatment:

Theorem 7.1 *For any set* Δ *of* ***PAL*** *formulas and any basic* ***PAL*** *formulas* ϕ, ψ*:*

$$ei(\phi, i, \Delta) = ei(\psi, i, \Delta) \iff \Delta \vDash [\phi \vee \psi]C(\phi \leftrightarrow \psi).$$

Proof $\Leftarrow$: Suppose that $\Delta \vDash [\phi \vee \psi]C(\phi \leftrightarrow \psi)$. Now take an arbitrary $\mathcal{M}_w$ such that $\mathcal{M}_w \vDash \Delta$. Suppose that $\mathcal{M}_w \vDash \neg K_i \chi \wedge \langle \phi \rangle K_i \chi$ for some χ, we need to show $\mathcal{M}_w \vDash \neg K_i \chi \wedge \langle \psi \rangle K_i \chi$ which amounts to show $\mathcal{M}_w \vDash \psi$ and $(\mathcal{M}|_\psi)_w \vDash K_i \chi$. Now since $\mathcal{M}_w \vDash \Delta$ and $\mathcal{M}_w \vDash \phi$ (due to $\mathcal{M}_w \vDash \langle \phi \rangle K_i \chi$), we have $\mathcal{M}_w \vDash \phi \wedge [\phi \vee \psi]C(\phi \leftrightarrow \psi)$ which means $\phi \leftrightarrow \psi$ holds on all the w-reachable states in $\mathcal{M}|_{\phi \vee \psi}$. Now since w is reachable from w itself in $\mathcal{M}|_{\phi \vee \psi}$ (due to the fact that $\mathcal{M}$ and $\mathcal{M}|_{\phi \vee \psi}$ are S5 models), $(\mathcal{M}|_{\phi \vee \psi})_w \vDash \phi \leftrightarrow \psi$. Since $\mathcal{M}_w \vDash \phi$ and ϕ is basic, we have $(\mathcal{M}|_{\phi \vee \psi})_w \vDash \phi$, thus $(\mathcal{M}|_{\phi \vee \psi})_w \vDash \psi$ and $\mathcal{M}_w \vDash \psi$ for ψ is basic too. Now we show the w-reachable states in $\mathcal{M}|_\phi$ and $\mathcal{M}|_\psi$ are exactly the same. Suppose that v is reachable from w in $\mathcal{M}|_\phi$ via a path pa then pa should consist of ϕ-states only. Clearly, pa should also be in $\mathcal{M}_{\phi \vee \psi}$. Now since $\mathcal{M}_w \vDash \phi \wedge [\phi \vee \psi]C(\phi \leftrightarrow \psi)$, all the states in pa should also satisfy ψ which means pa is also in $\mathcal{M}|_\psi$. Therefore v is reachable from w in $\mathcal{M}|_\psi$. Similarly we can show that all the w-reachable states in $\mathcal{M}|_\psi$ are those reachable in $\mathcal{M}|_\phi$ which means the w-reachable parts in the $\mathcal{M}|_\phi$ and $\mathcal{M}|_\psi$ are isomorphic. Now it is clear that $(\mathcal{M}|_\psi)_w \vDash K_i \chi$. Till now we have shown $\chi \in ei(\phi, i, \mathcal{M}_w) \implies \chi \in ei(\psi, i, \mathcal{M}_w)$. The other implication is symmetric. Due to the arbitrariness of $\mathcal{M}_w$, we have $ei(\phi, i, \Delta) = ei(\psi, i, \Delta)$.

$\Rightarrow$: Towards contradiction, suppose that $ei(\phi, i, \Delta) = ei(\psi, i, \Delta)$ but $\Delta \nvDash [\phi \vee \psi]C(\phi \leftrightarrow \psi)$. Then there is a pointed model $\mathcal{M}_w$ such that $\mathcal{M}_w \vDash \Delta \cup \{\phi \vee \psi\}$, but $(\mathcal{M}|_{\phi \vee \psi})_w \nvDash C(\phi \leftrightarrow \psi)$. Thus by the semantics of the common knowledge operator C, there is a finite path from w to a state v in $\mathcal{M}|_{\phi \vee \psi}$ such that $(\mathcal{M}|_{\phi \vee \psi})_v \nvDash \phi \leftrightarrow \psi$. Suppose that pa is (one of) the shortest such paths then all the states preceding v in pa satisfy $\phi \leftrightarrow \psi$. Since pa is in $\mathcal{M}|_{\phi \vee \psi}$ and it is the shortest, all the states preceding v in pa satisfy $\phi \wedge \psi$ ($\star$). Now W.L.O.G. we assume $(\mathcal{M}|_{\phi \vee \psi})_v \vDash \phi \wedge \neg \psi$ thus $\mathcal{M}_v \vDash \phi \wedge \neg \psi$ since ϕ and ψ are basic. Since $ei(\phi, i, \Delta) = ei(\psi, i, \Delta)$, it is not hard to see that $\mathcal{M}_w \vDash \phi \leftrightarrow \psi$. Since $\mathcal{M}_w \vDash \Delta \cup \{\phi \vee \psi\}$, we know $\mathcal{M}_w \vDash \phi \wedge \psi$. Now let χ be $C\psi$, it is clear that $\mathcal{M}_w \vDash \neg K_i \chi$ and $\mathcal{M}_w \vDash \langle \psi \rangle K_i \chi$. However, $\mathcal{M}_w \nvDash \langle \phi \rangle K_i \chi$ since $\mathcal{M}_v \nvDash \phi \leftrightarrow \psi$ and the path pa from w to v is preserved in $\mathcal{M}|_\phi$ due to the fact ($\star$).

In words, the above theorem says that given an assumption, two basic formulas ϕ and ψ have the same EI if and only if the logical equivalence of the two is common knowledge after it is announced that one of them is true. Note that $\phi \leftrightarrow \psi$ does not need to be common knowledge to equate the EI of ϕ and ψ.[7] Also note that agent i disappeared at the right-hand side of the equivalence stated in the above theorem, which suggests that without mentioning the agent in question, we can also meaningfully talk about the EI-equivalence of two statements given the same assumption. In fact, since $C\chi \leftrightarrow K_i C\chi$ is valid for any $i \in \mathbf{I}$ and $\chi \in \mathbf{PAL}$, the agent i is implicitly there.

Let $\Delta_n^\psi = \{K_{i_1} K_{i_2} \cdots K_{i_k} \psi \mid k \leq n, i_h \in \mathbf{I}\}$, in particular $\Delta_0^\psi = \{\psi\}$ then the following corollary is immediate, based on the observation that if ϕ is valid then $\phi \vee \psi$ is valid and $\phi \leftrightarrow \psi$ is equivalent to ψ.

Corollary 7.1 *For any basic **PAL** formulas ϕ and ψ, any set of **PAL** formulas Δ, if ϕ is valid then:*

1. $ei(\phi, i, \Delta) = ei(\psi, i, \Delta) \iff \Delta \vDash C\psi$
2. $ei(\phi, i, \Delta_n^\psi) \neq ei(\psi, i, \Delta_n^\psi)$ *for all* $n \in \mathbb{N}$.

Note that (2) follows from (1) since $\Delta_n^\psi \nvDash C\psi$ for any $n \in \mathbb{N}$. This shows that unless ψ is common knowledge under the current assumption, it is different to a tautology in EI.

Finally, let us get back to the strengthened version of Frege's puzzle mentioned before, where we are supposed to explain the differences in cognitive value of $a = a$ and $a = b$ even when $a = b$ is known to the agents. To apply the above corollary, let us first make two 'innocent' assumptions:

A $a = b$ and $a = a$ express some propositions, no matter what they are.
B the proposition expressed by $a = a$ is valid.

Under (A) and (B), Corollary 7.1 tells us that given any Δ, $a = a$ and $a = b$ have different EI unless the proposition expressed by $a = b$ is common knowledge. Note that, under non-trivial a and b, such as Hesperus and Phosphorus, the common knowledge of the proposition expressed by $a = b$ seems to be very hard to obtain, given the set of agents including *all* the people in the world. Therefore $a = b$ is almost always different from $a = a$ in EI of their corresponding propositions, which may help to explain our intuition of the differences in cognitive value between two statements.

7.3 Conclusion

We introduced the formal concept of epistemic informativeness based on a multi-agent dynamic epistemic perspective, and characterized its equivalence by using common knowledge after an announcement. We suggest that the lack of common

[7] Actually, $[\phi \vee \psi]C(\phi \leftrightarrow \psi)$ can be formulated as a weaker version of common knowledge of $\phi \leftrightarrow \psi$, which is called relativized common knowledge (cf. [13]).

knowledge of the logical equivalence of two statements is (partly) responsible for the difference in cognitive value of the two. Clearly, similar analysis can be done with respect to belief and communication methods other than public announcements.

Coming back to Frege's puzzle, as we claimed, epistemic informativeness can be used to explain the differences in cognitive value. This epistemic account for cognitive value can be compared to the theory of epistemic two-dimensional semantics (ETDS) proposed by [1], where *epistemic intension* plays a similar role as EI and the *scenarios* are like the possible states in our epistemic models. According to ETDS, two sentences that share the same subjunctive intension (secondary intension) may still differ in cognitive value due to differences in epistemic intension (primary intension). However, there is a fundamental difference between epistemic intension and EI: epistemic intension of a sentence is a function mapping scenarios to extensions (simply `ture` or `false`) while EI of a sentence can be viewed as a function mapping multi-agent epistemic pointed models to collections of new knowledge. It seems that EI is a more refined candidate for the Fregean 'sense', although in the current formal rendering it also shares some of the drawbacks that epistemic intension suffers, e.g., the current formal account of EI cannot explain the differences in cognitive value of different tautologies, since tautologies are taken to be common knowledge due to logical omniscience of the underlying epistemic framework.[8] To obtain a more reasonable formal account, we may select the appropriate epistemic framework modelling bounded reasoning power.

As the readers must have noticed, our formal discussion is purely propositional, thus we cannot formalize the exact proposition expressed by equalities such as Phosphorus = Hesperus. Moreover, this propositional abstraction level does not facilitate us to formally talk about the linguistic competence of the agents, for which we do need extra epistemic operators expressing 'I know what Hesperus is/means', as discussed in [16]. To really compare with ETDS which reconciles apriority and necessity, we also need to talk about necessity and interpret it with respect to metaphysically possible worlds. Nevertheless, separating different issues relevant in Frege's puzzle may give us a clearer picture of the merit of the puzzle and its solutions. We leave an in-depth formal study to Frege's puzzle based on EI to a further occasion.

Acknowledgments We are grateful to Wen-fang Wang for his insightful comments on an earlier version of this paper. Yanjing Wang acknowledges support of the key project 12&ZD119 of the National Social Science Foundation of China.

[8]For example, '$2^{57885161} - 1$ is a prime number' may have the same EI as '2 is a prime number', although intuitively these two sentences should induce different knowledge updates if not all the tautologies are common knowledge.

References

1. Chalmers DJ (2004) Epistemic two-dimensional semantics. Philosophical Studies 118:153–226
2. Chalmers DJ (2011) The nature of epistemic space. In: Egan A, Weatherson B (eds) Epistemic Modality, Oxford University Press, pp 1–54
3. Fiengo R, May R (2002) Identity statements. In: Logical Form and Language, Clarendon Press, pp 169–203
4. Frege G (1892) Über Sinn und Bedeutung. Zeitschrift für Philosophie und philosophische Kritik 100:25–50
5. Gerbrandy J, Groeneveld W (1997) Reasoning about information change. Journal of Logic, Language and Information 6(2):147–169
6. Groenendijk J, Stokhof M (1991) Dynamic predicate logic. Linguistics and Philosophy 14(1):39–100
7. Holliday WH, Icard TF (2010) Moorean phenomena in epistemic logic. In: Advances in Modal Logic, pp 178–199
8. Perry J (1988) Cognitive significance and new theories of reference. Noûs 22(1):1–18
9. Plaza JA (1989) Logics of public communications. In: Emrich ML, Pfeifer MS, Hadzikadic M, Ras ZW (eds) Proceedings of the 4th International Symposium on Methodologies for Intelligent Systems, pp 201–216
10. Rendsvig RK (2012) Modeling semantic competence: a critical review of freges puzzle about identity. New Directions in Logic, Language, and Computation pp 152–162
11. Salmon N (1986) Frege's Puzzle. The MIT Press
12. Stalnaker R (1978) Assertion. In: Cole P (ed) Syntax and Semantics, vol 9, New York Academic Press
13. van Benthem J, van Eijck J, Kooi B (2006) Logics of communication and change. Information and Computation 204(11):1620–1662
14. van Ditmarsch H, van der Hoek W, Kooi B (2007) Dynamic Epistemic Logic. Springer
15. Veltman F (1996) Defaults in update semantics. Journal of Philosophical Logic 25(3):221–261
16. Wang Y, Fan J (2013) Knowing that, knowing what, and public communication: Public announcement logic with Kv operators. In: Proceedings of IJCAI, pp 1139–1146
17. Yagisawa T (1993) A semantic solution to frege's puzzle. Philosophical Perspectives 7:135–154

Chapter 8
Formalizing the IMA Language: Toward the Minimalist Program for Compositional Semantics

Xuefeng Wen

Abstract Computational semantics via logical approach mainly focuses on the composition of meanings. Traditional approaches to it are based on typed logic via categorial grammar, which are not so successful when applied to very different languages than English. Recently, some alternative approaches with flatter types and underspecified semantics have been proposed. This paper is in the same line of these alternatives, but goes further and thoroughly. To avoid the presumed grammatical and semantic rules which are not universal across languages, we give a logic for a hypothetical language called the Isolating-Monocategorial-Associational (IMA) language, which can be assumed to be a prototype of natural languages with minimal grammar and semantics. We also give several extensions of the logic, motivated by different specifications. By formalizing the IMA language, we intend to reveal the universal mechanism of semantic composition in natural languages and to propose a general framework for compositional semantics.

8.1 Introduction

Since Montague's seminal work [14] on the formalism of natural language, typed logic via categorial grammar has been one of the main logical approaches to computational semantics [2, 16, 17]. This approach has been quite successful when applied to English and other similar languages. When applied to languages which are very different from English, however, it is less successful, which motivates several alternative approaches, such as Glue by linear logic via lexical functional grammar [7, 11], the minimal recursion semantics [6], two-sorted predicate logic via pregroup grammars [19], and type free logic without functors and operands [8], among others. The common features of the semantic representation in these alternatives are as follows:

X. Wen (✉)
Institute of Logic and Cognition, Department of Philosophy,
Sun Yat-sen University, Guangzhou 510275, China
e-mail: wxflogic@gmail.com

S. Ju et al. (eds.), *Modality, Semantics and Interpretations*,
Logic in Asia: Studia Logica Library, DOI 10.1007/978-3-662-47197-5_8

- more independent of the grammar: the semantic representation can be applied to different grammars.
- flatter types and lower order: instead of generalizing to the worst in Montague's style (which often yields higher types), higher types are used as little as possible.
- underspecified semantics: the semantic representation is rather flexible, leaving the semantic ambiguity unresolved.

This paper is in the same line of the above direction, but goes further and thoroughly. We will not give semantic representation for any specific natural language. Instead, we give a formalism of a hypothetical language called the Isolating-Monocategorial-Associational (IMA) language, proposed by Gil with the following properties [10]:

- *morphologically isolating*: there is no word-internal morphological structure;
- *syntactically monocategorial*: there are no distinct syntactic categories;
- *semantically associational*: there are no distinct construction-specific rules of semantic interpretation, i.e. the meaning of a composite expression is associated with the meanings of its constituents in an underspecified way.

Thus, the IMA language can be regarded as a prototype of natural language with the minimal constraints on grammars and semantics. By formalizing it, we intend to reveal the universal mechanism of semantic composition in natural languages and to propose a most general framework for compositional semantics, so that the formal semantics for any specific natural language can be obtained from the framework by adding constraints on it. We call it the minimalist program for semantics, analogous to Chomsky's minimalist program for grammars [5].

The rest of this paper is organized as follows. Section 8.2 challenges the English-based approach to compositional semantics. Section 8.3 introduces the IMA language, showing its features and significance. In Sect. 8.4, we present a minimal logic with formal syntax, semantics, and a proof system for the IMA language, where soundness and completeness of the logic are proved. In Sect. 8.5, we give several possible extensions to the minimal logic, motivated by different specifications. We conclude our paper by emphasizing the significance of the minimalist program for compositional semantics.

8.2 English as a Formal Language Revisited

The following are two basic hypotheses that prevail in the current logical approach to semantics.

(H1) *Transparent mapping*. Contrary to Frege and Russell's view that the form of natural language is misleading, Montague contended that no important theoretical difference exists between formal and natural languages. As a consequence, the translation from natural languages to formal languages could be transparent and automatic without much human intervention [15].

(H2) *Semantic universals*. There are semantic universals across languages, such as the NP-Quantifier Universal and the Determiner Universal. The former says that every natural language has syntactic constituents (called noun-phrases) whose semantic function is to express generalized quantifiers over the domain of discourse. The latter says that every natural language contains basic expressions (called determiners) whose semantic function is to assign to common count noun denotations (i.e., sets) A a quantifier that lives on A [1].

Both hypotheses are challenged in the cross-linguistic studies. For example, it is now consensus in the literature that neither the NP-Quantifier Universal nor the Determiner Universal is correct [9]. Actually, there is great diversity across natural languages, both in grammar and in semantics. Some languages use prepositions (e.g., English and French), whereas others use postpositions (e.g., Quechua); in some languages (e.g., Mandarin), the distinction between verbs and adjectives is not as clear as it is in others (such as English); some languages use many bound morphemes for function items (e.g., the Bantu languages and the Amerindian languages), whereas others use only free-standing morphemes (e.g., most West African languages and many Asian languages) [20]. Moreover, expressions in different languages with the same surface structure may have different semantics. If (H1) is adopted, then we have to propose for each natural language a formal language.

Even for logical constants like conjunction and disjunction, there is great diversity across languages. As noted in [18, 21], in some languages (such as Samoyed languages and Pacoh) there is no word or morpheme for conjunction. The only way to express conjunction is by juxtaposition of the conjuncts. However, no language was found to have such a zero strategy for disjunction. This shows some asymmetry between conjunction and disjunction. The asymmetry, however, is disguised by the particularity of English. Indeed, even if English can be regarded as a formal language, it is far from being a good or typical one, though it is the most prevailing one. Consider the following example introduced in [4].

(1) Unicycles have wheels.
(2) Jim's unicycle has wheels.

On one hand, (1) entails (2) logically. On the other hand, the grammar of English makes (1) true and (2) false. Nevertheless, if we translate the two sentences into Chinese, there would be no problem at all, since Chinese do not have plurals in morphology. Many problems studied in semantics are like this. They are just problems of English itself. Devoting too much energy to such problems will disguise truly universal problems. Here is another example [13] that illustrates the defects of English as a formal language. Consider the following two sentences.

(3) The dog ran into the house.
(4) The dog entered the house.

Intuitively, (3) entails (4). But this semantic intuition cannot be characterized by standard logic, unless we add some meaning postulates for "run into". This problem, however, does not exist for French, since (3) would be expressed by "Le chien est entrédans la maison en courant', whose direct translation in English is "The dog entered the house by running". Now the entailment of (4) from (3) is straightforward, without any meaning postulates.

We do not mean here to replace English by French (or any other natural language) as our base for formalization. Actually, every extant natural language has its own advantages and disadvantages as a formal language. Instead of formalizing any real natural language, we propose to study the simplest and ideal language first, and then approach real languages step by step. This methodology is analogous to that in physics, where mass points instead of real physical objects are chosen to be the starting point of research. Here, our starting point is the IMA language, a hypothetical language proposed by linguists in [10].

8.3 The IMA Language as a Prototype

The first property of the IMA language, morphological isolation, indicates that the lexical structure of the language is reduced to the minimum. It is the most familiar property for natural languages compared to the other two. As is well known, isolating languages such as Vietnamese and Chinese have much less word-internal morphological structure than synthetic languages (such as Russian) and polysynthetic languages (such as Mohawk). Although no natural language is found purely isolating, it is quite easy to conceive such a language with adequate expressive power.

The second property of the IMA language, syntactical monocategoriality, indicates that the sentential structure of the language is reduced to the minimum. Syntactic categories have generally been presumed to be universal in natural languages. In particular, no natural language has ever been found to be purely monocategorial. But the inventories of syntactic categories do vary across languages. Moreover, some languages have much less clear distinction between categories than others. For example, many presumed adjectives in Chinese can also be used as nouns without any morphological change. It is also observed that languages such as Munda and Austronesian seem to lack the distinction even between nouns and verbs, at least prima facei [12]. This suggests that semantics via syntactic categories may not be universal enough.

The third property of the IMA language, semantical associationality, indicates that the specification of the semantic composition is reduced to the minimum. Since semantic roles and features are indicated very differently in different languages, the best one can guess when hearing a foreign expression is that the meaning of the whole expression is associated with the meanings of its parts. We assume it to be a general rule, based on which further specifications could be made.

According to [10], the IMA language is significant in the following five domains: (a) phylogeny: in view of the evolutionary history, early human language was the IMA language; (b) ontogeny: in view of individual development, early child language is the IMA language; (c) semiotics: some artificial languages are the IMA language; (d) typology: some languages, such as Riau Indonesian are very close to the IMA language; and (e) cognition: the IMA language is a prototype of general human cognition. We will not argue for these points but only assume them to be the case. Since the least particular semantic rules are presumed in the IMA language, it is a good starting point for a minimalist program for compositional semantics for natural languages.

8.4 A Logic for the IMA Language

We formalize the IMA language in this section, both its syntax and semantics. We also give a proof system for inference in this language. Soundness and completeness of the proof system are proved.

8.4.1 Syntax

Definition 8.1 Given a set $\mathscr{A}$ of atomic terms, the *syntax* of $\mathscr{L}_{\text{IMA}}$ is given by the following BNF:

$$t ::= a \mid (t_1 \ldots t_n),$$

where $a \in \mathscr{A}$ and $n \geq 2$.

We denote by $\mathscr{T}$ the set of all terms t. Terms which are not atomic are called *complex*. Atomic terms are used to represent words of the IMA Language, while complex terms can be constructed from any finite terms by concatenation, which is an approximation to the isolating and monocategorial property of the IMA language. This reduces the grammar of the language to a minimal level.

Note that n is not a constant but a variable in the syntax. If we use an operator to construct complex terms in $\mathscr{T}$, then the arity of the operator is not fixed, but flexible. This is quite different from the usual syntax of a formal language, where the operators for constructing complex expressions are usually with fixed arities. To make our syntax more orthodox, we need an n-ary operator for every $n \geq 2$.

According to our syntax, $(ab)c$, $a(bc)$, and abc are different terms. An alternative to the syntax which appears simpler may be as follows:

$$t ::= a \mid (t_1 t_2),$$

i.e. all complex terms are constructed by binary concatenations. But we think this syntax is too rigid for the IMA language, since there could be terms like abc which is a juxtaposition of the three words a, b, c rather than a juxtaposition of ab and c, or a and bc. Though it is possible to identify $(ab)c$ with $a(bc)$ in the semantics so that any of the two can be used for representing abc, it will often reduce the three constructions to the same in general, which is not desired. For this reason, we prefer our original syntax with variable arity of concatenation.

8.4.2 Semantics

The syntactical monocategoriality of the IMA language induces that it is better to assume only one semantic type for it. Thus a model consisting of objects and relations on the objects for predicate logic is no longer suitable for the IMA language. To interpret $\mathscr{L}_{\text{IMA}}$, we assume that the universe of the models consisting of meanings. Instead of various relations for interpreting predicates, we have only one relation (with variable arity) in the model. The relation is interpreted as the decomposition relation of meanings, i.e. $Rxx_1 \dots x_n$ means that the meaning x can be decomposed into the meanings $x_1, \dots, x_n$ (in this order). The interpretation of an atomic term is a set of meanings which are all possible meanings of the term. The interpretation of a complex term is the set of all meanings which can be decomposed by the relation R such that each component meaning is in the interpretation of the corresponding component of the term.

Definition 8.2 A *model* for $\mathscr{L}_{\text{IMA}}$ is a triple $\mathfrak{M} = \langle M, R, I \rangle$, where

- $M \neq \emptyset$, consisting of *meanings*,
- $R \subseteq \bigcup\limits_{n \geq 3} M^n$, is called a *decomposition relation* on meanings,
- $I : \mathscr{A} \to \wp(M)$, is called an *assignment*, mapping each atomic term to a subset of M.

Definition 8.3 Given a model $\mathfrak{M} = \langle M, R, I \rangle$ for $\mathscr{L}_{\text{IMA}}$, the *interpretation* of a term t under $\mathfrak{M}$, denoted $|t|^{\mathfrak{M}}$, is defined as follows:

$$|a|^{\mathfrak{M}} = I(a), \text{ for } a \in \mathscr{A},$$

$$|t_1 \dots t_n|^{\mathfrak{M}} = \left\{ x \in M \mid \exists x_1 \dots x_n \left(Rxx_1 \dots x_n \wedge \bigwedge_{i=1}^{n} x_i \in |t_i|^{\mathfrak{M}} \right) \right\}.$$

The semantic entailment is defined by the meaning inclusion instead of truth preservation.

Definition 8.4 Given a pair (t, s) of terms, we say that s *is semantically entailed from* t, denoted $t \vDash s$, if for every model $\mathfrak{M}$ for $\mathscr{L}_{\text{IMA}}$, $|s|^{\mathfrak{M}} \subseteq |t|^{\mathfrak{M}}$.

Intuitively, $t \vDash s$ means that the meaning of s is contained in t.

8.4.3 Proof System

Definition 8.5 We give a Gentzen-style calculus for $\mathscr{L}_{\text{IMA}}$ as follows:

Axiom: (id) $\dfrac{}{t \vdash t}$

Inference rules: (R1) $\dfrac{t_i \vdash s_i, \text{ for } 1 \leq i \leq n}{t_1 \dots t_n \vdash s_1 \dots s_n}$ (R2) $\dfrac{t \vdash u \quad u \vdash s}{t \vdash s}$

The following lemma will be used for the proof of completeness.

Lemma 8.1 $\exists s_1 \ldots s_n (s_1 \ldots s_n \vdash s \wedge \bigwedge_{i=1}^{n} t_i \vdash s_i)$ *iff* $t_1 \ldots t_n \vdash s$.

Proof The direction from left to right is straightforward, using the two inference rules in sequence. For the other direction, let $s_i = t_i$. □

Lemma 8.2 *The cut rule* $\dfrac{t \vdash u \quad u \vdash s}{t \vdash s}$ *is eliminable.*

Proof The proof is by the standard induction on the cut degree. We leave the details to the reader. □

Since cut is eliminable and (R1) has the sub-formula property, the following theorem is straightforward.

Theorem 8.1 $\mathscr{L}_{\text{IMA}}$ *is decidable.*

Actually, it is not difficult to see that all valid inferences in $\mathscr{L}_{\text{IMA}}$ are instances of $t \vdash t$.

8.4.4 Soundness and Completeness

The proof of completeness is by constructing canonical models as usual. The universe of the canonical model, however, does not consists of maximal consistent sets as before, but the set of all terms, which is similar to the construction of Lindenbaum–Tarski algebra.

Definition 8.6 The *canonical model* $\mathfrak{M}^c = \langle M^c, R^c, I^c \rangle$ for $\mathscr{L}_{\text{IMA}}$ is defined as follows:

- $M^c = \mathscr{T}$,
- $R^c t t_1 \ldots t_n$ iff $t_1 \ldots t_n \vdash t$, for $n \geq 2$,
- $I^c(a) = \{t \in \mathscr{T} \mid a \vdash t\}$, for $a \in \mathscr{A}$.

Lemma 8.3 *For every pair* (t, s) *of terms,* $s \in |t|^{\mathfrak{M}^c}$ *iff* $t \vdash s$.

Proof The proof is by induction on the complexity of t.

Case 1: $t = a \in \mathscr{A}$. Then $s \in |t|^{\mathfrak{M}^c}$ iff $s \in I^c(a) = \{x \mid a \vdash x\}$ iff $a \vdash s$ iff $t \vdash s$.

Case 2: $t = t_1 \ldots t_n$. Then $s \in |t|^{\mathfrak{M}^c}$ iff $s \in |t_1 \ldots t_n|^{\mathfrak{M}^c}$ iff $s \in \{x \mid \exists s_1 \ldots s_n (R^c x s_1 \ldots s_n \wedge \bigwedge_{i=1}^{n} s_i \in |t_i|^{\mathfrak{M}^c})\}$ iff $\exists s_1 \ldots s_n (R^c s s_1 \ldots s_n \wedge \bigwedge_{i=1}^{n} s_i \in |t_i|^{\mathfrak{M}^c})$ iff $\exists s_1 \ldots s_n (s_1 \ldots s_n \vdash s \wedge \bigwedge_{i=1}^{n} t_i \vdash s_i)$ iff $t_1 \ldots t_n \vdash s$ iff $t \vdash s$, where the fourth "iff" is by the induction hypothesis, and the fifth "iff"s is by Lemma 8.1. □

Theorem 8.2 *The proof system for* $\mathscr{L}_{\text{IMA}}$ *is sound and complete with respect to its semantics, i.e. for every pair* (t, s) *of terms,* $t \vdash s$ *iff* $t \models s$.

Proof Soundness can be easily verified. For completeness, suppose $t \nvdash s$. Then by Lemma 8.3, $s \notin |t|^{\mathfrak{M}^c}$. Since $s \vdash s$, we have $s \in |s|^{\mathfrak{M}^c}$ by Lemma 8.3. It follows that $|s|^{\mathfrak{M}^c} \nsubseteq |t|^{\mathfrak{M}^c}$. Hence, $t \nvDash s$. □

8.5 Possible Extensions

The logic given in Sect. 8.4 is a minimal logic, which is quite naive. We give some possible extensions of the logic under various specifications to characterize more complex languages.

8.5.1 Adding Constraints on R

The following are possible constraints on R and their corresponding axioms:

Constraints		Axioms	
(C1)	$Rxyz \wedge Ryuv \rightarrow Rxuvz$	(A1)	$t_1t_2t_3 \vdash (t_1t_2)t_3$
(C2)	$Rxyz \wedge Rzuv \rightarrow Rxyuv$	(A2)	$t_1t_2t_3 \vdash t_1(t_2t_3)$
(C3)	$Rxyz \rightarrow Rxzy$	(A3)	$t_1t_2 \vdash t_2t_1$

We leave the proofs of their correspondences to the reader.

8.5.2 Adding Function Words

Though syntactic categories vary across languages, the distinction between content words and function words seem universal, which is supported by neurological evidence [3]. Function words can be represented by functions on terms in syntax and by functions on meanings in semantics. Different function words may have different constraints. Here we only give a formalism without any constraints on them.

Definition 8.7 Given a set $\mathscr{A}$ of atomic terms and a set $\mathscr{F}$ of functional symbols with $\mathscr{A} \cap \mathscr{F} = \emptyset$, we define the *language* $\mathscr{L}_{\text{IMAF}}$ for the IMA language with functional symbols as follows:

$$t ::= a \mid (t_1 \ldots t_n) \mid ft_1 \ldots t_{r(f)},$$

where $a \in \mathscr{A}$ and $f \in \mathscr{F}$ with arity $r(f)$.

Definition 8.8 A *model* for $\mathscr{L}_{\text{IMAF}}$ is a triple $\mathfrak{M} = \langle M, R, I \rangle$, where

- $M \neq \emptyset$, consisting of meanings,
- $R \subseteq \bigcup_{n \geq 3} M^n$, is called a decomposition relation on meanings,
- $I : \mathscr{A} \cup \mathscr{F} \rightarrow \wp(M)$, is called an assignment, mapping each atomic term to a subset of M, and each functional symbol f to a function

$$f^{\mathfrak{M}} : M^{r(f)} \rightarrow \wp(M).$$

Definition 8.9 Given a model $\mathfrak{M} = \langle M, R, I \rangle$ for $\mathscr{L}_{\text{IMAF}}$, the *interpretation* of a term t under $\mathfrak{M}$, denoted $|t|^{\mathfrak{M}}$, is defined as follows:

$$|a|^{\mathfrak{M}} = I(a), \text{ for } a \in \mathscr{A},$$

$$|t_1 \dots t_n|^{\mathfrak{M}} = \left\{ x \in M \mid \exists x_1 \dots x_n \left(Rxx_1 \dots x_n \wedge \bigwedge_{i=1}^{n} x_i \in |t_i|^{\mathfrak{M}} \right) \right\},$$

$$|ft_1 \dots t_{r(f)}|^{\mathfrak{M}} = \bigcup_{x_i \in |t_i|} f^{\mathfrak{M}}(x_1, \dots, x_{r(f)}).$$

Definition 8.10 The proof system for $\mathscr{L}_{\text{IMAF}}$ is obtained from that for $\mathscr{L}_{\text{IMA}}$ by adding the following inference rule:

$$\text{(R3)}\ \frac{t_i \vdash s_i, \text{ for } 1 \leq i \leq r(f)}{ft_1 \dots t_{r(f)} \vdash fs_1 \dots s_{r(f)}}$$

Definition 8.11 The *canonical model* $\mathfrak{M}^c = \langle M^c, R^c, I^c \rangle$ for $\mathscr{L}_{\text{IMAF}}$ is obtained from that for $\mathscr{L}_{\text{IMA}}$ by adding the following clause:

- $I^c(f) = f^{\mathfrak{M}^c} : s_1, \dots, s_{r(f)} \mapsto \{s \mid fs_1 \dots s_{r(f)} \vdash s\}$.

Lemma 8.4 *For every pair* (t, s) *of terms,* $s \in |t|^{\mathfrak{M}^c}$ *iff* $t \vdash s$.

Proof The proof is by induction on the complexity of t. The first two cases are as before.

Case 3: $t = ft_1 \dots t_{r(f)}$. Then $s \in |t|^{\mathfrak{M}^c}$ iff $s \in |ft_1 \dots t_{r(f)}|^{\mathfrak{M}^c}$ iff

$$\exists s_1 \dots s_{r(f)} \left(s \in f^{\mathfrak{M}^c}(s_1, \dots, s_{r(f)}) \wedge \bigwedge_{i=1}^{r(f)} s_i \in |t_i| \right)$$

iff

$$\exists s_1 \dots s_{r(f)} \left(fs_1 \dots s_{r(f)} \vdash s \wedge \bigwedge_{i=1}^{r(f)} t_i \vdash s_i \right)$$

iff $t \vdash s$, where the third "iff" is by the induction hypothesis, the direction from left to right of the last "iff" is by (R3) and (R2), and the other direction is by letting $s_i = t_i$. □

Using the above lemma, we can easily prove the following theorem.

Theorem 8.3 *The proof system for* $\mathscr{L}_{\text{IMAF}}$ *is sound and complete with respect to its semantics, i.e. for every pair* (t, s) *of terms,* $t \vdash s$ *iff* $t \vDash s$.

8.5.3 Adding More Grammars

Though languages like Chinese do not have clear syntactic categories, there are three basic syntactic structures which are assumed to be prevailing: juxtaposition, modification from left to right, and supplement from right to left. Thus the concatenation splits into three operators, which correspond to three decomposition relations on meanings.

Definition 8.12 Given a set $\mathscr{A}$ of atomic terms, we define the *language* $\mathscr{L}_{\text{IMAG}}$ for the IMA language with basic grammars as follows:

$$t ::= a \mid (t \circ t) \mid (t \rhd t) \mid (t \lhd t),$$

where $a \in \mathscr{A}$.

The operator $\circ$ is used for juxtaposition, $\rhd$ for modification from left to right, and $\lhd$ for supplement from right to left. The presumed semantic constraints on juxtaposition is easy to give, while the constraints for the other two are not so obvious. We leave them underspecified.

Definition 8.13 A *model* for $\mathscr{L}_{\text{IMAG}}$ is a tuple $\mathfrak{M} = \langle M, R_\circ, R_\rhd, R_\lhd, I\rangle$, where

- $M \neq \emptyset$ is a non-empty set, consisting of meanings,
- For $* \in \{\circ, \rhd, \lhd\}$, $R_* \subseteq M^3$ is a ternary relation on M such that
  - $R_\circ xyz \wedge R_\circ yuv \to \exists w(R_\circ xuw \wedge R_\circ wvz)$
  - $R_\circ xyz \wedge R_\circ zuv \to \exists w(R_\circ xwv \wedge R_\circ wyu)$
  - $R_\circ xyz \to R_\circ xzy$
- $I : \mathscr{A} \to \wp(M)$, is called an assignment, mapping each atomic term to a subset of M.

Definition 8.14 Given a model $\mathfrak{M} = \langle M, R_\circ, R_\rhd, R_\lhd, I\rangle$ for $\mathscr{L}_{\text{IMAG}}$, the *interpretation* of a term t under $\mathfrak{M}$, denoted $|t|^{\mathfrak{M}}$, is defined as follows:

$$|a|^{\mathfrak{M}} = I(a), \quad \text{for } a \in \mathscr{A},$$
$$|(t_1 * t_2)|^{\mathfrak{M}} = \{x \in M \mid \exists y \in |t_1|^{\mathfrak{M}} \exists z \in |t_2|^{\mathfrak{M}} R_* xyz\}, * \in \{\circ, \rhd, \lhd\}.$$

8.5.4 Adding Contexts

Contexts can be introduced to reduce ambiguities. By introducing contexts, terms are interpreted locally in contexts. The interpretation of a complex term in a context is defined by the interpretations of its components in accessible contexts. Like the decomposition relation, the accessibility relation is also with variable ariy. Besides the accessibility relation, there is a relation ordering the frequency of meanings for each context. Interpretations in a context are the most frequent meanings ordered by the context.

Definition 8.15 A *model* for $\mathscr{L}_{\mathrm{IMAC}}$ is a tuple $\mathfrak{M} = \langle M, W, R, r, \{\leq_w\}_{w\in W}, I\rangle$, where

- $M \neq \emptyset$, consisting of meanings,
- $W \neq \emptyset$, consisting of contexts,
- $R \subseteq \bigcup\limits_{n\geq 3} M^n$, is called a decomposition relation on meanings,
- $r \subseteq \bigcup\limits_{n\geq 3} W^n$, is called an *accessibility relation on contexts*,
- for each $w \in W$, $\leq_w \subseteq M \times M$ is a partial order on meanings, called *frequency relation*,
- $I : \mathscr{A} \to \wp(M)$, is called an assignment, mapping each atomic term to a set of meanings in M.

Definition 8.16 Given a model $\mathfrak{M} = \langle M, W, R, r, \{\leq_w\}_{w\in W}, I\rangle$ for $\mathscr{L}_{\mathrm{IMAC}}$, the *interpretation* of a term t under $\mathfrak{M}$ in context $w \in W$, denoted $|t|^{\mathfrak{M},w}$, is defined as follows:

$$\begin{aligned} |a|^{\mathfrak{M},w} &= \min_w I(a), \\ |t_1 \ldots t_n|^{\mathfrak{M},w} &= \min_w \Bigg\{ x \in M \mid \exists w_1 \ldots w_n \in W \exists x_1 \ldots x_n \\ &\qquad \Bigg(rww_1 \ldots w_n \wedge Rxx_1 \ldots x_n \wedge \bigwedge_{i=1}^{n} x_i \in |t_i|^{\mathfrak{M},w_i} \Bigg) \Bigg\} \end{aligned}$$

where

$$\min_w X = \{x \in X \mid \forall x' \in X(x' \leq_w x \to x = x')\}.$$

Definition 8.17 The *canonical model* $\mathfrak{M}^c = \langle M^c, W^c, R^c, r^c, \{\leq^c_w\}_{w\in W}, I^c\rangle$ for $\mathscr{L}_{\mathrm{IMAC}}$ is defined as follows:

- $M^c = W^c = \mathscr{T}$,
- $R^c tt_1 \ldots t_n$ iff $r^c tt_1 \ldots t_n$ iff $t_1 \ldots t_n \vdash t$, for $n \geq 2$,
- for each $w \in W$, $\leq^c_w = \emptyset$,
- $I^c(a) = \{t \in \mathscr{T} \mid a \vdash t\}$, for $a \in \mathscr{A}$.

The proof system for $\mathscr{L}_{\mathrm{IMAC}}$ is the same as that for $\mathscr{L}_{\mathrm{IMA}}$.

Lemma 8.5 *For every pair* (t, s) *of terms,*

1. $s \in |t|^{\mathfrak{M}^c,w} \Longrightarrow t \vdash s$, *for all* $w \in \mathfrak{M}^c$.
2. $t \vdash s \Longrightarrow s \in |t|^{\mathfrak{M}^c,s}$.

Proof 1. By induction on t.

Case 1: $t = a \in \mathscr{A}$. Then $s \in |t|^{\mathfrak{M}^c,w} \Longrightarrow s \in \min_w I^c(a) \Longrightarrow s \in I^c(a) \Longrightarrow a \vdash s \Longrightarrow t \vdash s$.

Case 2: $t = t_1 \dots t_n$. Then $s \in |t|^{\mathfrak{M}^c,w}$

$\Longrightarrow s \in \min_w\{x \in M \mid \exists w_1 \dots w_n \in W^c \exists s_1 \dots s_n(r^c ww_1 \dots w_n \wedge R^c xs_1 \dots s_n \wedge \bigwedge_{i=1}^n s_i \in |t_i|^{\mathfrak{M}^c,w_i})\}$

$\Longrightarrow s \in \{x \in M \mid \exists w_1 \dots w_n \in W^c \exists s_1 \dots s_n(r^c ww_1 \dots w_n \wedge R^c xs_1 \dots s_n \wedge \bigwedge_{i=1}^n s_i \in |t_i|^{\mathfrak{M}^c,w_i})\}$

$\Longrightarrow \exists w_1 \dots w_n \in W^c \exists s_1 \dots s_n(r^c ww_1 \dots w_n \wedge R^c ss_1 \dots s_n \wedge \bigwedge_{i=1}^n s_i \in |t_i|^{\mathfrak{M}^c,w_i}))$

$\Longrightarrow \exists s_1 \dots s_n(R^c ss_1 \dots s_n \wedge \bigwedge_{i=1}^n s_i \in |t_i|^{\mathfrak{M}^c,w_i})$

$\Longrightarrow \exists s_1 \dots s_n(s_1 \dots s_n \vdash s \wedge \bigwedge_{i=1}^n t_i \vdash s_i)$ (by the induction hypothesis)

$\Longrightarrow t_1 \dots t_n \vdash s \Longrightarrow t \vdash s$.

2. By induction on t.

Case 1: $t = a \in \mathscr{A}$. Then $t \vdash s \Longrightarrow a \vdash s \Longrightarrow s \in I^c(a) \Longrightarrow s \in \min_s I^c(a) \Longrightarrow s \in |t|^{\mathfrak{M}^c,s}$.

Case 2: $t = t_1 \dots t_n$. Then $t \vdash s \Longrightarrow t_1 \dots t_n \vdash s$

$\Longrightarrow \exists s_1 \dots s_n(s_1 \dots s_n \vdash s \wedge \bigwedge_{i=1}^n t_i \vdash s_i)$ (by letting $s_i = t_i$)

$\Longrightarrow \exists s_1 \dots s_n(s_1 \dots s_n \vdash s \wedge \bigwedge_{i=1}^n s_i \in |t_i|^{\mathfrak{M}^c,s_i})$ (by the induction hypothesis)

$\Longrightarrow \exists w_1 \dots w_n \in W^c \exists s_1 \dots s_n(r^c sw_1 \dots w_n \wedge R^c ss_1 \dots s_n \wedge \bigwedge_{i=1}^n s_i \in |t_i|^{\mathfrak{M}^c,w_i}))$ (by letting $w_i = s_i$)

$\Longrightarrow s \in \{x \in M \mid \exists w_1 \dots w_n \in W^c \exists s_1 \dots s_n(r^c sw_1 \dots w_n \wedge R^c xs_1 \dots s_n \wedge \bigwedge_{i=1}^n s_i \in |t_i|^{\mathfrak{M}^c,w_i})\}$

$\Longrightarrow s \in \min_s\{x \in M \mid \exists w_1 \dots w_n \in W^c \exists s_1 \dots s_n(r^c sw_1 \dots w_n \wedge R^c xs_1 \dots s_n \wedge \bigwedge_{i=1}^n s_i \in |t_i|^{\mathfrak{M}^c,w_i})\}$

$\Longrightarrow s \in |t|^{\mathfrak{M}^c,s}$.

□

Using the above lemma, we can easily prove the following theorem.

Theorem 8.4 *The proof system for $\mathscr{L}_{\text{IMAC}}$ is sound and complete with respect to its semantics, i.e. for every pair (t, s) of terms, $t \vdash s$ iff $t \models s$.*

8.6 Concluding Remarks

As the starting point of the minimalist program for compositional semantics, we give a logic for the IMA language. Despite its naivety, formalizing such a minimal language can be taken as a common foundation of all natural languages. We also give several extensions for our logic, illustrating how to extend the formalization to approach real natural languages gradually, each step the formal system coming closer to natural language. We contend that this minimalist program will help us to find out what is common and what is really different in semantics and inference behind the superficial diversity of natural languages during the formalization. Future work includes applying the formal systems to natural languages (such as Chinese) to explain some particular semantic and inferential phenomena.

Acknowledgments This research was supported by the National Fund of Social Science (No. 13BZX066) and the Fundamental Research Funds for the Central Universities (No. 13wkpy71).

References

1. Barwise, J., Cooper, R.: Generalized quantifiers and natural language. Linguistics and Philosophy **4**(2), 159–219 (1981). doi:10.1007/BF00350139
2. Carpenter, B.: Type-Logical Semantics. The MIT Press (1997)
3. Carroll, D.W.: Psychology of Language, 5th edn. Wadsworth Publishing (2007)
4. Chomsky, N.: Essays on Form and Interpretation. North-Holland (1977)
5. Chomsky, N.: The Minimalist Program. The MIT Press, Cambridge, Mass. (1995)
6. Copestake, A., Flickinger, D., Pollard, C., Sag, I.: Minimal Recursion Semantics: An Introduction. Research on Language & Computation **3**(4), 281–332 (2005). doi:10.1007/s11168-006-6327-9
7. Dalrymple, M., Lamping, J., Saraswat, V.: LFG semantics via constraints. In: Proceedings of the 6th meeting of the European ACL, pp. 97–105. University of Utrecht (1993)
8. Erdélyi-Szabó, M., Kálmán, L., Kurucz, A.: Towards a natural language semantics without functors and operands. Journal of Logic, Language and Information **17**(1), 1–17 (2008)
9. von Fintel, K., Matthewson, L.: Universals in semantics. The Linguistic Review **25**(12), 139–201 (2008). doi:10.1515/TLIR.2008.004
10. Gil, D.: Isolating-monocategorial-associational language. In: H. Cohen, C. Lefebvre (eds.) Handbook of Categorization in Cognitive Science, pp. 348–379. Elsevier (2005)
11. Kokkonidis, M.: First-Order Glue. Journal of Logic, Language and Information **17**(1), 43–68 (2007). doi:10.1007/s10849-006-9031-0
12. Labelle, M.: The acquisition of grammatical categories: the state of the art. In: H.C. Lefebvre, Claire (eds.) Handbook of Categorization in Cognitive Science, pp. 433–457. Elsevier (2005)
13. Levinson, S.C.: Language and Mind: Let's Get the Issues Straight! In: D. Gentner, S. Goldin-Meadow (eds.) Language in Mind: Advances in the Study of Language and Cognition, pp. 25–46. The MIT Press (2003)

14. Montague, R.: The proper treatment of quantification in ordinary English. In: Jaako Hintikka, Julius Moravcsik, Patrick Suppes (eds.) Approaches to Natural Language, pp. 221–242. Reidel, Dordrecht (1973)
15. Montague, R.: English as a formal language. In: R. Thomason (ed.) Formal Philosophy, Selected Papers of Richard Montague. Yale University Press (1974)
16. Moortgat, M.: Categorial type logics. In: J. van Benthem, A.T. Meulen (eds.) Handbook of Logic and Language, pp. 93–177. Elsevier. (1997)
17. Morril, G.V.: Type logical grammar: categorial logic of signs. Kluwer, Dordrecht (1994)
18. Payne, J.: Complex phrases and complex sentences. In: T. Shopen (ed.) Language Typology and Syntactic Description: Complex Constructions, Vol.2, pp. 3–41. Cambridge University Press, Cambridge (1985)
19. Preller, A.: Toward discourse representation via pregroup grammars. Journal of Logic, Language and Information **16**(2), 173–194 (2007). doi:10.1007/s10849-006-9033-y
20. Shi, R.: Early syntactic categories in infants' language. In: H.C. Lefebvre, Claire (eds.) Handbook of Categorization in Cognitive Science, pp. 481–495. Elsevier (2005)
21. Winter, Y.: Syncategorematic conjunction and structured meanings. In: Proceedings of SALT 5, pp. 387–404 (1995)

Chapter 9
Similarity of States in Modal Logic

Fei Zha

Abstract The similarity between states is an important issue in modal logic. There are many formalisms that have been introduced to express different kinds of similarities in conditional logic, probabilistic logic, and dynamic logic and so on. However, in these cases similarities between states are directly given by the models. In this paper, we introduce two kinds of models and provide two different judgment standards of the similarity between states, while the accessibility of relations on our models are generated by similarities instead of giving this in the definitions of frames or models. In our first type of models, we compare the propositional assignments at states to measure the degree of similarity among states. We give the axiomatizations of the formula sets of this class of models and prove the completeness and soundness. The second type of model is about conditionals, in which we assign to each proposition a group of sets of propositions called the context of the proposition and extend this assignment to all the formulas. Finally, we assign two formulas ϕ and a world w, a collection of sets of worlds by the contexts of ϕ.

9.1 Motivation

In virtue of possible world semantics, logicians have developed many formalisms which are used to describe or analyze the rules of important phenomenon in many research areas, such as philosophy, linguistic, cognitive science, computer science, and so on. The basic structures of those formalisms are a series of transitions among states. In these semantics, a state (or node, possible world) which represents certain situation is described by propositions that are true at the state and this is determined by the assignment of the model. Here, Let us call the characters described by propositional assignment the inner characters of a state. On the other hand, formulas with modal operators describe the accessibility relation among these states. As opposed to the inner characters of a state, the formulas with modal operators that are true at a state describe the outer characters of the state. In most kinds of possible world

F. Zha (✉)
Faculty of Philosophy, Nankai University, No. 94 Weijin Road, Nankai Dist, Tianjin, China
e-mail: zhafei1@gmail.com

S. Ju et al. (eds.), *Modality, Semantics and Interpretations*,
Logic in Asia: Studia Logica Library, DOI 10.1007/978-3-662-47197-5_9

semantics, the accessibility relations are just given directly in a frame, independent of any assignments which are given arbitrarily in models.

However, in applications, sometimes when we describe a phenomenon, a state may determine which states are its accessible states. For example, in epistemic logic, a possible world can be seen from our real world, because possible world should never be beyond our imagination which is based on the real world. In such cases, we could build some relevance between the inner characters of states and the accessibility relation among them. The feature of this relevance leans on what we want to capture by a modal logic, and what we want to retain in Kripke models.

A basic idea is that a state can influence or determine which states are its adjacent states, or rather, the inner characters of states could have a significant effect on whether they are adjacent. In a more complicated case, for example, in a linear irreversible process, such kinds of relationship could not only exist between one state and the next, but also the one after next, and so on. In such two kinds of cases, our processes are similar to Markov processes or non-Markov processes in probability theory and statistics. The last case will not be explored in detail in this paper and for the first case, it is easy to associate with the similarities between states which is an important issue in modal logic: two states are adjacent if and only if they are similar.

We discuss similarity in this paper in the sense that two states are adjacent if and only if they are similar. There are two kinds of models that we introduce in which the accessible relations are generated according to the similarity among states. We provide two different judgment standards of the similarity between states corresponding to these two kinds of models.

9.2 Models of Restricted Flux Generated by Assignments

We name our first kind of models 'Models of Restricted Flux generated by assignments' [1]. As we know, we can interpret the assignment of a model as a class of propositional assignments, each of which assign each proposition a value on one state. In a model of restricted flux generated by assignments, we assume all the inner characters have been expressed by the propositional assignment on each state. On such a background, we can regard a sole state just as a propositional assignment. Then whether two states can be accessible to each other determined by the mechanism which we use to compare their assignments to measure their similarity.

When we build a model, we are provided by a set of states first. After this, we are given the assignment of this set. Or you can regard these two steps as just only step: you are given a group of propositional assignments. Then by the comparability mechanisms, we generate the accessibility relations with these assignments.

9.2.1 The Change Between Adjacent States

How do we measure the similarity between two assignments? An easy answer is to count the changes between two assignments. When a group of assignments be put in front of us, we could count out different numbers of changes among them, some numbers look very small, and some numbers could be very large. A next logical step is to define a series of degrees of similarity according to the set of natural numbers:

1. Every natural number will correspond to an accessibility relation which expresses a degree of similarity.
2. When a state connect with current state by a relation, the degree of this relation is determined by the degree of similarity between two states.
3. However, a larger window would always bring you a broader view, so if a relation have a degree of natural number n, a state will be linked with those states which are not only similar with the state on degree n, but also degrees less than n.

9.2.2 The Models

Definition 1 The language $\mathcal{L}^{FX}$ consists of a countable set of propositions $Pr = \{p_1, p_2, \ldots\}$, Boolean connectives $\neg$ and $\vee$, and a series of universal modal operator $\Box_1, \Box_2, \Box_3, \ldots$. Formulas of $\mathcal{L}^{FX}$ is constructed as follows:

$$\varphi =:: p \mid \bot \mid \neg\varphi \mid \varphi_1 \vee \varphi_2 \mid \Box_1\varphi \mid \Box_2\varphi \mid \Box_3\varphi \mid \ldots.$$

Definition 2 A model generated by an assignment is a triple $\mathbf{M}^{FR} = (W, V, R)$. W is a set of possible worlds which is not empty. V is a mapping: $Pr \to \rho(W)$, which is called an assignment of W. R is a set of numerable binary relations $\{R_h \mid h \neq 0, h \in \mathbb{N}\}$ on W, and each R_h is a binary relation generated by (W, V, h) on W which is defined as follows

(1) $Dm : W \times W \times Pr \to \{0, 1\}$ is a function, which is given by

$$Dm(w, v, p) = \begin{cases} 1 & w \notin V(p) \text{ and } v \in V(p) \\ 1 & w \in V(p) \text{ and } v \notin V(p) \\ 0 & \text{otherwise} \end{cases}$$

(2) $Sm(w, v)$ is a summation function: $Sm(w, v) = \sum_{j=1}^{\infty} Dm(w, v, p_j)$
(3) $R_h = \{(w, v) | w \in W, v \in W \;\&\; Sm(w, v) \leq h\}$

$Dm(w, v, p)$ is a character function that indicates whether or not the value of p has been changed between w and v. $Sm(w, v)$ shows how many propositions have changed between w and v. When $Sm(w, v) \leq h$, w will be connected to v by the binary relation R_h.

Definition 3 Given a model $\mathbf{M}^{FR} = (W, V, R)$, $\mathbf{M}^{FR}, w \models \varphi$ is read as that φ is true at w in $\mathbf{M}^{FR}$, and is defined as follows:

$\mathbf{M}^{FR}, w \models p$ iff $w \in V(p)$
$\mathbf{M}^{FR}, w \models \neg\varphi$ iff $\mathbf{M}^{FR}, w \not\models \varphi$
$\mathbf{M}^{FR}, w \models \varphi \vee \psi$ iff $\mathbf{M}^{FR}, w \models \varphi$ or $\mathbf{M}^{FR}, w \models \psi$
$\mathbf{M}^{FR}, w \models \Box_h\varphi$ iff for any $v \in W$ and $(w, v) \in R_h$, we have $\mathbf{M}^{FR}, v \models \varphi$

By the standard convention, we extend the assignment V for the proposition symbols to arbitrary formulas. That is, $V(\varphi)$ denote the set $V(\varphi) := \{w \mid \mathbf{M}^{FR}, w \models \varphi\}$ on which φ will be true.

Definition 4 $\mathfrak{M}^{FR}$ is the class of models generated by assignments.

Remark 1 As we see, the generation of a $\mathbf{M}^{FR}$ is a global process, in which we calculate every $Sm(w, v)$, $(w, v) \in W \times W$, and identify the degree of similarity of (w, v). In our model a node w will not accessible to another node v only if the pairs (w, v) have a infinite degree of similarity. However, this does not mean we have to introduce some language including global modal operators to characterize our models and indeed our language does no't include any global modal operators.

On the other hand, we can generate our relations just according to a equivalence relation R^E on a given model, i.e., we only judge the similarity degree between the pairs which belong to the equivalence relation. In such case, the relations generated is no longer global, because they are confined to the connected component of the given equivalence relation. As we do not introduce any global modal operators, the former two kinds of models can't be distinguished by our language.

9.2.3 The Properties of Models

Theorem 1 *In any model generated by assignment, for any R_i, R_j and $i \le j$, there will be $R_i \subset R_j$. We call this property the nestedness of restricted relations, and write as: $\forall wu.(w, u) \in R_i \rightarrow (w, u) \in R_j$.*

Proof For any pair $(w, v) \in R_i$, we have $Sm(w, v) \le i$. Because of $i < j$, $Sm(w, v) \le j$. Then according to the definition of R_j, we have $(w, v) \in R_j$. □

Theorem 2 *All of the models in $\mathfrak{M}^{FR}$ are reflexive and symmetrical.*

Because of the building process of the model, it is obvious that any $R_h \in R$ is reflexive and symmetrical. If $(w, v) \in R_h$, then the number of changes of propositions between w and v will be no more than natural number h. We call this property

Neighborhood Similarity:

$\forall wv.R_h wv \rightarrow Sm(w, v) \le h$

As long as the number of changes of propositions between two states is a natural number h, there will be a relation R_h by which from one state we can arrive at another. We call this property **Restricted Connectivity**:

$\forall wv.Sm(w, v) \leq h \rightarrow R_h wv$

9.2.4 Axioms

The system $\mathbf{K}^{FR}$ is composed by the following axioms and rules, where h stands for any nature number

Prop: Propositional tautologies
K: $\Box_h(\varphi \rightarrow \psi) \rightarrow (\Box_h\varphi \rightarrow \Box_h\psi)$
T: $\varphi \rightarrow \Diamond_h\varphi$ *(reflexive)*
B: $\varphi \rightarrow \Box_h\Diamond_h\varphi$ *(symmetrical)*
SSR: $\Diamond_i\varphi \rightarrow \Diamond_j\varphi$, here, $j \geq i$
MP: $\varphi_1, \varphi_1 \rightarrow \varphi_2/\varphi_2$
RN: $\varphi/\Box_h\varphi$

Theorem 3 *For any model generated by an assignment, the axioms* SSR *correspond to Nestedness:* $\forall wu.(w, u) \in R_i \rightarrow (w, u) \in R_j$.

Proof Suppose, $\mathfrak{M}^{FR} \not\models \Diamond_i\varphi \rightarrow \Diamond_j\varphi$, here, $j \geq i$, iff
there is a model $\mathbf{M}^{FR}$ and a node w, formula ϕ and relations $R_i, R_j, i \leq j$, $\mathbf{M}^{FR}, w \not\models \Diamond_i\varphi \rightarrow \Diamond_j\varphi$, iff
$w \models \Diamond_i\phi$, and $w \not\models \Diamond_j\phi$, iff, $\exists u \in W, R_iwu$, this let $u \models \phi$ and $(w, u) \notin R_j$, iff $\mathbf{M}^{FR} \models \exists wu.R_iwv \wedge \neg R_jwv, i \leq j$, iff, $\mathbf{M}^{FR} \not\models \forall wu.(w, u) \in R_i \rightarrow (w, u) \in R_j$, iff $\mathfrak{M}^{FR} \not\models \forall wu.(w, u) \in R_i \rightarrow (w, u) \in R_j$. □

Except the above axioms and rules, we need more axioms to describe featured properties such as Neighborhood similarity and Restricted connectivity.

Cc(h, n): $\Diamond_{h-1}(l(p_1) \wedge l(p_2) \wedge \ldots \wedge l(p_n)) \rightarrow \pi(h, (l(p_1), l(p_2), \ldots, l(p_n)))$ (Neighborhood similarity)

Formula with the form $l(p)$ means either p or $\neg p$; $n \geq h$; for any $p_i, p_j, i, j \leq n$; if $i \neq j$, we have $p_i \neq p_j$. And $\pi(h, (l(p_1), l(p_2), \ldots, l(p_n))) = \bigvee\{\bigwedge \Sigma \mid \Sigma \subseteq \{l(p_1), l(p_2), \ldots, l(p_n)\}, |\Sigma| = n - h + 1\}$

And when $n = h$, the formula will be more intuitive as follow:

Cc(h) $(l(p_1) \wedge l(p_2) \wedge \ldots \wedge l(p_h)) \rightarrow \Box_{h-1}(l(p_1) \vee l(p_2) \vee \ldots \vee \wedge l(p_h))$

The formula can be read as: when $l(p_1), l(p_2), \ldots, l(p_h)$ are true on current point, on no matter which accessible points by relation R_{h-1}, they could not be false together. By these formulas, we characterize the Neighborhood similarity on the model.

In fact, *Cc(h)* and *Cc(h, n)* is equivalent in K^{FR} when they are used to expressed neighborhood similarity. *Cc(h, n)* can be used only some extreme cases, for example, we introduce a series of new axioms *Cs(h, m)*:

$$(l(p_1) \wedge l(p_2) \wedge \ldots \wedge l(p_h) \wedge l(q_1) \wedge l(q_2) \cdots \wedge l(q_m)) \rightarrow (\bigwedge_{i=1}^{2^h} \Diamond_h (\bigwedge_{j=1}^{h} Q_{ij} \wedge (l(q_1) \wedge l(q_2) \wedge \ldots \wedge l(q_m))))$$

Here, $h > 0, m \geq 0$, Q_{ij} is any one or its negation from $p_1, p_2 \ldots, p_h$. The axioms *Cs(h, m)* can describe such a property: From current node w, you can arrive any node v such that $Sm(w, v) \in \mathbb{N}$, namely the number of propositions which change value from w to v is finite.

Cs(h, m) together with *Cc(h, n)* and *K, T, B* and all the propositional tautologies constitute a system which characterize a special kind of models [1, 2]: for any propositional assignment, there is always a node in this kind of models on which the assignment can be satisfied.

In this system, all the modal operators can be eliminated. *Cc(h, n)* is used in the proof of this conclusion.

To avoid unnecessary burden on intelligence, in this article we just adopt *Cc(h)*.

Theorem 4 *For any model generated by an assignment, the axioms* Cc(h) *correspond to Neighborhood Similarity:* $\forall wv.R_h wv \rightarrow Sm(w, v) \leq h$.

Proof 1. Suppose $\mathfrak{M}^{FR} \not\models Cc$, then there is a model $\mathbf{M}^{FR} \in \mathfrak{M}^{FR}$, $\mathbf{M}^{FR} \not\models Cc$. So it exists $h \in \mathbb{N}$,and $l(p_1), l(p_2), \ldots, l(p_h)$, which let $\mathbf{M}^{FR} \not\models (l(p_1) \wedge l(p_2) \wedge \ldots \wedge l(p_h)) \rightarrow \Box_{h-1}(l(p_1) \vee l(p_2) \vee \ldots \vee l(p_h))$. So there must be a $w \in W$, $\mathbf{M}^{FR}, w \models (l(p_1) \wedge l(p_2) \wedge \ldots \wedge l(p_h))$ and $\mathbf{M}^{FR}, w \not\models \Box_{h-1}(l(p_1) \vee l(p_2) \vee \ldots \vee l(p_h))$, i.e., $\mathbf{M}^{FR}, w \models \Diamond_{h-1} \neg (l(p_1) \vee l(p_2) \vee \ldots \vee l(p_h))$. So it exists $v \in W$, $R_{h-1} wv$, which let $\mathbf{M}^{FR}, v \models \neg l(p_1) \wedge \neg l(l_2) \wedge \ldots \wedge \neg l(p_h)$, so $Sm(w, v) \geq h$, conflict $\forall wv.R_h wv \rightarrow Sm(w, v) \leq h$.

2. For any model $\mathbf{M}^{FR} \in \mathfrak{M}^{FR}$, if $\mathbf{M}^{FR} \not\models \forall wv.R_h wv \rightarrow Sm(w, v) \leq h$, then there are $w, v \in W$, $R_h wv$ and $Sm(w, v) > h$. So it exists $l(p_1), l(p_2), \ldots, l(p_h)$, that $\mathbf{M}^{FR}, w \models (l(p_1) \wedge l(p_2) \wedge \ldots \wedge l(p_h))$, and $\mathbf{M}^{FR}, v \models \neg l(p_1) \wedge \neg l(l_2) \wedge \ldots \wedge \neg l(p_h)$. Then $\mathbf{M}^{FR} \not\models (l(p_1) \wedge l(p_2) \wedge \ldots \wedge l(p_h)) \rightarrow \Box_{h-1}(l(p_1) \vee l(p_2) \vee \ldots \vee l(p_h))$. Because $(l(p_1) \wedge l(p_2) \wedge \ldots \wedge l(p_h)) \rightarrow \Box_{h-1}(l(p_1) \vee l(p_2) \vee \ldots \vee l(p_h)) \in Cc(h)$, so $\mathbf{M}^{FR}, w \not\models Cc(h)$. Then $\mathfrak{M}^{FR} \not\models Cc$. □

Now we need to find some formulas to characterize the Restricted Connectivity, however, there are no formulas could characterize any kinds of connectivity in modal logic. So we have to find some properties, which can bring the canonical model (at least a part of the canonical model) the **Restricted Connectivity**, and at the same time, could be described by some modal formulas.

We provide two properties: **Restricted transitivity** and **Restricted Euclidicity**

Restricted transitivity $\forall wuv.(((Sm(w,u)=d)\wedge(R_d wu))\wedge((Sm(u,v)=e)\wedge(R_e uv))\wedge(Sm(w,v)=f))\rightarrow R_f wv$

Restricted Euclidicity $\forall wuv.(((Sm(w,u)=d)\wedge(R_d wu))\wedge((Sm(w,v)=f)\wedge(R_f wv))\wedge(Sm(u,v)=e))\rightarrow R_e uv$

Restricted transitivity means if w, u are adjacent in a relationship, u, v are adjacent in another relationship, then there must be a relationship in which w, v are adjacent. We use formulas *STR* describe this property.

Restricted Euclidicity means if w, u are adjacent in a relationship, w, v are adjacent in another relationship, then there must be a relationship in which u, v are adjacent. We use formulas *SER* describe this property.

STR: $(((\bigwedge\pi_{a_i})\wedge(\bigwedge\pi_{b_j})\wedge(\bigwedge\pi_{c_k}))\wedge\Diamond_{i+j}((\neg(\bigvee\pi_{a_i})\wedge\neg(\bigvee\pi_{b_j})\wedge(\bigwedge\pi_{c_k}))\wedge\Diamond_{i+k}((\bigwedge\pi_{a_i})\wedge\neg(\bigvee\pi_{b_j})\wedge\neg(\bigvee\pi_{c_k})\wedge\varphi)))\rightarrow\Diamond_{j+k}((\bigwedge\pi_{a_i})\wedge\neg(\bigvee\pi_{b_j})\wedge\neg(\bigvee\pi_{c_k})\wedge\varphi)$

SER: $(((\bigwedge\pi_{a_i})\wedge(\bigwedge\pi_{b_j})\wedge(\bigwedge\pi_{c_k}))\wedge\Diamond_{i+j}(((\neg(\bigvee\pi_{a_i})\wedge\neg(\bigvee\pi_{b_j})\wedge(\bigwedge\pi_{c_k}))\wedge\varphi)))\rightarrow\Box_{j+k}(((\bigwedge\pi_{a_i})\wedge\neg(\bigvee\pi_{b_j})\wedge\neg(\bigvee\pi_{c_k}))\rightarrow\Diamond_{i+k}(((\neg(\bigvee\pi_{a_i})\wedge\neg(\bigvee\pi_{b_j})\wedge(\bigwedge\pi_{c_k}))\wedge\varphi)))$

in the above two formulas, a, b, c are letters, i, j, k denote natural numbers, which are greater or equal to 0; $\pi_{a_i}=\{l(p_{a_1}), l(p_{a_2}), l(p_{a_3})\ldots l(p_{a_i})\}$, and for any $l(p_n)$, if $l(p_n)\in\pi_{a_i}$, then $l(p_n)\notin\pi_{b_j}$, & $l(p_n)\notin\pi_{c_k}$, and if $l(p_n)\in\pi_{b_j}$ or $l(p_n)\in\pi_{c_k}$, it is just like the case of $l(p_n)\in\pi_{a_i}$; when $i=0$, we have $\pi_{a_i}=\emptyset$

let $A=((\bigwedge\pi_{a_i})\wedge(\bigwedge\pi_{b_j})\wedge(\bigwedge\pi_{c_k}))$

let $B=((\neg(\bigvee\pi_{a_i})\wedge\neg(\bigvee\pi_{b_j})\wedge(\bigwedge\pi_{c_k}))$

let $C=((\bigwedge\pi_{a_i})\wedge\neg(\bigvee\pi_{b_j})\wedge\neg(\bigvee\pi_{c_k}))$

then the axioms *STR* can be denoted by $STR(\pi_{a_i},\pi_{b_j},\pi_{c_k})=(A\wedge\Diamond_{i+j}(B\wedge\Diamond_{i+k}(C\wedge\varphi)))\rightarrow\Diamond_{j+k}(C\wedge\varphi)$

and the axioms *SER* can be denoted by $SER(\pi_{a_i},\pi_{b_j},\pi_{c_k})=(A\wedge\Diamond_{i+j}(B\wedge\varphi))\rightarrow\Box_{j+k}(C\rightarrow\Diamond_{i+k}(B\wedge\varphi))$

STR describe such a situation: On the current point w, all the formulas (propositions or negative propositions) in set $\pi_{a_i}, \pi_{b_j}, \pi_{c_e}$ are true, and on the point u which is accessible from w by R_{i+j}, all the values of the formulas in set π_{a_i}, π_{b_j} have changed, but the formulas in set π_{c_k} still hold. According to Axiom *Cc(h, n)*, because of $R_{i+j}wu$, there are up to $i+j$ propositions can change between w and u. So except the propositions in π_{a_i} and π_{b_j}, there are not more propositions have changed the truth values.

When we arrive at point v from u by R_{i+k}, comparing with u, the propositions in π_{a_i}, π_{c_k} change, and the propositions in π_{b_j} remain, then because of the relationship R_{i+k}, the propositions in π_{a_i}, π_{c_k} are all the propositions which have changed from u to v.

Now we can check that between w and v, only the propositions in π_{b_j} and π_{c_k} have different truth values, and our axiom *STR* predict that $R_{i+k}wv$.

SER describe Restricted Euclidicity by the same way.

By *STR* and *SER*, we can generate a submodel of the canonical model from any maximal $\mathbf{K}^{FR}$-consistent set by the step-by-step method, on which all the $R_h \in R$ is reflexive, symmetrical, Neighborhood similar and Restricted connective.

Theorem 5 *For any model generated by an assignment, the axioms* STR *correspond to Restricted transitivity:* $\forall wuv.(((Sm(w, u) = d) \wedge (R_d wu)) \wedge ((Sm(u, v) = e) \wedge (R_e uv)) \wedge (Sm(w, v) = f)) \rightarrow R_f wv$.

Proof (1) Suppose $\mathfrak{M}^{FR} \not\models STR$, then there is a model $\mathbf{M}^{FR} \in \mathfrak{M}^{FR}$, a node $w \in W$ and set of propositions $\pi_{a_i}, \pi_{b_j}, \pi_{c_k}$, $\mathbf{M}^{FR}, w \not\models STR(\pi_{a_i}, \pi_{b_j}, \pi_{c_k})$, $STR(\pi_{a_i}, \pi_{b_j}, \pi_{c_k}) \in STR$. let $A = ((\bigwedge \pi_{a_i}) \wedge (\bigwedge \pi_{b_j}) \wedge (\bigwedge \pi_{c_k}))$, $B = ((\neg(\bigvee \pi_{a_i}) \wedge \neg(\bigvee \pi_{b_j}) \wedge (\bigwedge \pi_{c_k}))$, $C = ((\bigwedge \pi_{a_i}) \wedge \neg(\bigvee \pi_{b_j}) \wedge \neg(\bigvee \pi_{c_k}))$, then $\mathbf{M}^{FR}, w \not\models A \wedge \Diamond_{i+j}(B \wedge \Diamond_{i+k}(C \wedge \varphi))) \rightarrow \Diamond_{j+k}(C \wedge \varphi)$. So we have $\mathbf{M}^{FR}, w \models A \wedge \Diamond_{i+j}(B \wedge \Diamond_{i+k}(C \wedge \varphi)))$ and $\mathbf{M}^{FR}, w \not\models \Diamond_{j+k}(C \wedge \varphi)$. According to the former, $w \models A, \exists u, R_{i+j}wv$, and $u \models B$ and $u \models \Diamond_{i+k}(C \wedge \varphi)$. So $\exists v, R_{i+k}uv, v \models (C \wedge \varphi)$. By axioms *Cc(i+j)*, (*Cc(i+k)*), we get $(wu) \notin R_{i+j-1}, (uv) \notin R_{i+k-1}$, then $Sm(w, u) = i + j, Sm(u, v) = i + k$. According to the constitutions of A, B, C, we can see $Sm(w, v) = j + k$.

But $\mathbf{M}^{FR}, w \not\models \Diamond_{j+k}(C \wedge \varphi)$, i.e., $\mathbf{M}^{FR}, w \models \Box_{j+k}\neg(C \wedge \varphi)$, and $\mathbf{M}^{FR}, v \models (C \wedge \varphi)$. So, $(w, v) \notin R_{j+k}$. $\mathbf{M}^{FR} \not\models \forall wuv.(((Sm(w, u) = i + j) \wedge (R_{i+j}wu)) \wedge ((Sm(u, v) = i + k) \wedge (R_{i+k}uv)) \wedge (Sm(w, v) = j + k)) \rightarrow R_{j+k}wv$.

So $\mathfrak{M}^{FR}$ is not restricted transitive.

(2) This process is reversible. □

Theorem 6 *For any model generated by an assignment, the axioms* SER *correspond to Restricted Euclidicity:* $\forall wuv.(((Sm(w, u) = d) \wedge (R_d wu)) \wedge ((Sm(w, v) = f) \wedge (R_f wv)) \wedge (Sm(u, v) = e)) \rightarrow R_e uv$.

Proof This proof is similar as the previous one. □

9.2.5 Soundness

According to the corresponding relations we have proved, it is easy to check the soundness of $\mathbf{K}^{FR}$ with respect to $\mathfrak{M}^{FR}$.

Theorem 7 *For any* $\mathbf{K}^{FR}$ *formula* ϕ, *if* $\vdash_{\mathbf{K}^{FR}} \phi$, *then* $\mathfrak{M}^{FR} \models \phi$.

9.2.6 Canonical Model

Definition 5 The canonical model $\mathbf{M}^C$ for $\mathbf{K}^{FR}$ is the triple (W^C, R^C, V^C) where:

1. W^C is the set of all $\mathbf{K}^{FR}$-maximal consistent sets.
2. R^C is the sets of binary relations on all level on W^C, i.e., $R^C = \{R^C_h | h \in \mathbb{N}\}$, and $R^C_h wv$ if for all formulas ϕ, $\phi \in u$ implies $\Diamond_h \in w$. R^C is called the canonical relation.
3. V^C is the valuation defined by $V^C(p) = \{w \in W^C | p \in w\}$. V^C is called the canonical valuation.

Lemma 1 ***Existence Lemma****: For* $\mathbf{K}^{FR}$*, any node* $w \in W^C$ *and any natural number* h*, if* $\Diamond_h \phi \in w$*, then there is a node* $v \in W^C$ *such that* $R^C_h wv$ *and* $\phi \in v$.

Lemma 2 ***Truth Lemma****: For* $\mathbf{K}^{FR}$ *and any formula* ϕ, $\mathbf{M}^C, w \models \phi$*, iff,* $\phi \in w$.

Theorem 8 *The canonical model satisfies the property of nestedness of restricted relations:* $\forall wu.(w, u) \in R_i \rightarrow (w, u) \in R_j, i \leq j$.

Proof $\forall (w, u) \in R^C_i, \forall \phi \in u$ implies $\Diamond_i \phi \in v$. As $\Diamond_i \varphi \rightarrow \Diamond_j \varphi \in v$, we have $\Diamond_j \phi \in v$. So $(w, u) \in R^C_j$. □

Theorem 9 *The canonical model satisfies Neighborhood Similarity* $\forall wv.R_h wv \rightarrow Sm(w, v) \leq h$.

Proof Take any $w, v \in W^C$, suppose $R^C_h wv$, and assume we do not have $Sm(w, v) \leq h$, then $Sm(w, v) > h$. So there are $l(p_1), l(p_2), \ldots, l(p_h), l(p_{h+1}) \in w$ and $\neg l(p_1), \neq l(p_2), \ldots, \neg l(p_h), \neg l(p_{h+1}) \notin u$. So $(l(p_1) \wedge l(p_2) \wedge \ldots \wedge l(p_h) \wedge l(p_{h+1})) \in w$, and $(\neg l(p_1) \wedge \neg l(p_2) \wedge \ldots \wedge \neg l(p_h) \wedge \neg l(p_{h+1})) \in u$, and because $Cc(h) \subset w$, so $(l(p_1) \wedge l(p_2) \wedge \ldots \wedge l(p_{h+1})) \rightarrow \Box_h(l(p_1) \vee l(p_2) \vee \ldots \vee \wedge l(p_{h+1})) \in w$, then $\Box_h(l(p_1) \vee l(p_2) \vee \ldots \vee \wedge l(p_{h+1})) \in w$, $(l(p_1) \vee l(p_2) \vee \ldots \vee \wedge l(p_{h+1})) \in u$, which is conflict with $(\neg l(p_1) \wedge \neg l(p_2) \wedge \ldots \wedge \neg l(p_h) \wedge \neg l(p_{h+1})) \in u$. So we have $Sm(w, v) \leq h$. □

Theorem 10 *The canonical model is Restricted transitive:* $\forall wuv.(((Sm(w, u) = d) \wedge (R_d wu)) \wedge ((Sm(u, v) = e) \wedge (R_e uv)) \wedge (Sm(w, v) = f)) \rightarrow R_f wv$.

Proof Pick any w, u, v in canonical model. Let $(Sm(w, u) = d)$, $(R^C_d wu))$, $((Sm(u, v) = e)$, $(R^C_e uv))$, $(Sm(w, v) = f)$. Then because the canonical model is neighborhood similar, there are just d propositions which change values between w and u, e propositions which change values between u and v, and f propositions which change values between w and v. And some propositions which have changed from w to u may change again from u to v. So we let $d = i+j, e = i+k, f = j+k$, i propositions change from w to u, but do not change from u to v, k propositions change from w to u, and change again from u to v, and k propositions do not change from w to *to*, but change from u to v. Then there are three sets $\pi_{a_i}, \pi_{b_j}, \pi_{c_e}$, whose elements are propositions and negative propositions, such that $\pi_{a_i}, \pi_{b_j}, \pi_{c_e} \in w$; $(w, u) \in R^C_{i+j}$,

$\pi_{c_k} \in u, \pi_{a_i} \cap u = \emptyset, \pi_{b_j} \cap u = \emptyset; (u, v) \in R^C_{i+k}, \pi_{a_i} \in v, \pi_{b_j} \cap v = \emptyset, \pi_{c_k} \cap v = \emptyset$. Let $A = ((\bigwedge \pi_{a_i}) \wedge (\bigwedge \pi_{b_j}) \wedge (\bigwedge \pi_{c_k}))$; $B = ((\neg(\bigvee \pi_{a_i}) \wedge \neg(\bigvee \pi_{b_j}) \wedge (\bigwedge \pi_{c_k}))$; $C = ((\bigwedge \pi_{a_i}) \wedge \neg(\bigvee \pi_{b_j}) \wedge \neg(\bigvee \pi_{c_k}))$.

Then we need to show $R^C_f wv$, and it means that for any formula $\phi \in v$, we have $\Diamond_{j+k}\phi\ w$.

So for any formula ϕ, suppose $\phi \in v$. Then we have $C \wedge \phi \in v$, and because $R^C_{i+k}uv$, $\Diamond_{i+k}(C \wedge \phi) \in u$. As $B \in u$, it is the case that $(B \wedge \Diamond_{i+k}(C \wedge \phi) \in u$. Finally, because $A \in w$ and R^C_{i+j}, we have $A \wedge \Diamond_{i+j}(B \wedge \Diamond_{i+k}(C \wedge \phi)) \in w$. $(A \wedge \Diamond_{i+j}(B \wedge \Diamond_{i+k}(C \wedge \phi))) \rightarrow \Diamond_{j+k}(C \wedge \phi)$ is a axiom(*STR*), so it is in w, then we have $\Diamond_{j+k}(C \wedge \phi) \in w$, by boolean modal formula $\Diamond(p \wedge q) \rightarrow (\Diamond p \wedge \Diamond q)$, we have $\Diamond_{j+k}\phi \in w$. □

Theorem 11 *The canonical model is Restricted Euclidean:* $\forall wuv.(((Sm(w, u) = d) \wedge (R_d wu)) \wedge ((Sm(u, v) = e) \wedge (R_e uv)) \wedge (Sm(w, v) = f)) \rightarrow R_f wv$.

Proof This proof is similar as the previous one. □

9.2.7 Step-by-Step

Definition 6 A network $\mathbf{N} = (N, R, v)$, such that R is a set of numerable binary relations $\{R_h \mid h \neq 0, h \in \mathbb{N}\}$ on N, and v is a labeling function mapping each point in N to a maximal consistent set [3].

Definition 7 A network $\mathbf{N} = (N, R, v)$ is coherent if it satisfies:

C1 $\forall st \in N.R_i st \rightarrow R_j st$, such that $i < j$.
C2 $\forall st \in N.R_h st \rightarrow Sm(v(s), v(t)) \leq h$.
C3 $\forall st \in N.Sm(v(s), v(t)) \leq h \rightarrow R_h st$.
C4 $\forall st \in R_h st \rightarrow R^c_h v(s)v(t)$.

R^c_h is canonical relation. And from C1 and C2,

Definition 8 A network $\mathbf{N} = (N, R, v)$ is modally saturated if it satisfies: if $\Diamond_h\phi \in v(s)$ for some $s \in N$, then there is some $t \in N$ such that $R_h st$ and $\phi \in v(t)$. A network is perfect if it is both coherent and modally saturated.

Definition 9 Let $\mathbf{N} = (N, R, v)$ be a network. The model $\mathfrak{J}_\mathbf{N} = (N, R, V_\mathbf{N})$ is the underlying model of $\mathbf{N}$. The induced valuation $V_\mathbf{N}$ is defined by $V_\mathbf{N}(p) = \{s \in N | p \in v(s)\}$.

Lemma 3 ***Truth Lemma***: *Let* **N** *be a perfect network. Then for all formulas* ϕ, *and all nodes* s *in* N,

$$\mathfrak{J}_\mathbf{N}, s \models \phi \textbf{ iff } \phi \in v(s)$$

Proof By induction on the degree of ϕ.

Case 1: $\phi = p$, by definition.
Case 2: The steps of the booleans are straightforward.
Case 3: $\phi = \Diamond_h \psi$.

- From left to right: $\mathfrak{J}_{\mathbf{N}}, s \models \Diamond_h \psi$, then $\exists t \in N, R_h st$, and $\mathfrak{J}_{\mathbf{N}}, t \models \psi$. So $R_h^C v(s)v(t)$ (by Definition 7), and $\psi \in v(t)$ (by inductive assumption) then we have $\Diamond_h \psi \in v(s)$ (By the definition of canonical model).
- From right to left: $\Diamond_h \psi \in v(s)$, then there is some $t \in N$ such that $R_h st$ and $\psi \in v(t)$ (By Definition 8). By inductive assumption, $\mathfrak{J}_{\mathbf{N}}, t \models \psi$, and $R_h^C v(s)v(t)$(by Definition 7). By the truth lemma of canonical model, we get the left. □

Definition 10 Let $\mathbf{N} = (N, R, v)$ be a network. An defect of $\mathbf{N}$ consists of a node s and a formula $\Diamond_h \phi \in v(s)$ for which there is no t in N such that $R_h st$ and $\phi \in v(t)$.

Definition 11 Let $\mathbf{N}_0$ and $\mathbf{N}_1$ be two networks. We say that $\mathbf{N}_1$ extends $\mathbf{N}_0$ (notation: $\mathbf{N}_1 \rhd \mathbf{N}_0$).

Lemma 4 ***Repair Lemma*** *For any defect of a finite, coherent network* $\mathbf{N}$, *there is a finite, coherent* $\mathbf{N}' \rhd \mathbf{N}$ *lacking this defect.*

Proof Let $\mathbf{N} = (N, R, v)$ be a finite, coherent network and assume that $\mathbf{N}$ has some defect. We prove the Lemma by showing that any defect can be removed.

If $(s, \Diamond_i \phi)$ is a defect of $\mathbf{N}$, it is possible that $(s, \Diamond_{i-1} \phi)$ and $(s, \Diamond_{i+1} \phi)$, and it is also possible for $(s, \Diamond_{i-2} \phi)$, and $(s, \Diamond_{i+2} \phi)$ and so on. In the extended network, if the defect $(s, \Diamond_i \phi)$ has been eliminated, if $(s, \Diamond_{i+1} \phi), (s, \Diamond_{i+2} \phi), \ldots$ are also the defects of $\mathbf{N}$, they will be eliminated together. It is because for any $(s, \Diamond_j \phi), j > i$, in $\mathbf{N}'$, $(s, t) \in R_j$(By Definition 7C1), so $R_j^C v(s)v(t)$. But $(s, \Diamond_{i-1} \phi), (s, \Diamond_{i-2} \phi), \ldots$ can't be eliminated together.

Let $(s, \Diamond_i \phi)$ is a defect of $\mathbf{N}$, check whether $(s, \Diamond_{i-1} \phi)$ is a defect of $\mathbf{N}$. If it is, then check $(s, \Diamond_{i-2} \phi)$, and so on, until $(s, \Diamond_{i-n} \phi)$ isn't a defect of $\mathbf{N}$. Then if we eliminate $(s, \Diamond_{i-n} \phi)$ in new network, all of these defects would be eliminated together.

Choose some new point t (that is $t \notin N$) and let Ψ be an MCS containing $\phi, R_{i-n+1}^C v(s)\Psi$ and $(v(s), \Psi) \notin R_{i-n}^C$. There is necessarily such a Ψ: According to the Existence Lemma of canonical model, Ψ which contain $\phi, R_{i-n+1}^C v(s)\Psi$ must exist.

Because $(s, \Diamond_{i-n} \phi)$ isn't a defect of $\mathbf{N}$, then either $\Box_{i-n} \neg \phi \in v(s)$ or $\exists m \in N, R_{i-n} smand\phi \in v(m)$. If $\exists m \in N, R_{i-n} smand\phi \in v(m)$, then $(s, \Diamond_{i-n+1} \phi)$ will no longer be a defect. So it must be $\Box_{i-n} \neg \phi \in v(s)$, then we get $(v(s), \Psi) \notin R_{i-n}^C$.

Define $\mathbf{N}' = (N', R', v')$ as follow:

$$N' := N \cup \{t\}$$
$$R' := \{R_h \cup \{(x, t) | x \in N, R_h^C v(x)\Phi\} \cup \{(t, x) | x \in N, R_h^C \Phi v(x)\} | R_h \in R\}$$
$$v' := f \cup \{(t, \Phi)\}$$

Now we check whether $\mathbf{N}'$ is coherent:

C1, C2, C4 can get directly by the properties of canonical model. Which we need check is C3: $\forall st \in N.Sm(v(s), v(t)) \leq h \rightarrow R_h st$, which is not characterized by the canonical model. But as we know, the canonical model has characterized **Restricted transitivity**, and **Restricted Euclidicity**:

$\forall wuv.(((Sm(w, u) = d) \wedge (R_d wu)) \wedge ((Sm(u, v) = e) \wedge (R_e uv)) \wedge (Sm(w, v) = f)) \rightarrow R_f wv$
$\forall wuv.(((Sm(w, u) = d) \wedge (R_d wu)) \wedge ((Sm(w, v) = f) \wedge (R_f wv)) \wedge (Sm(u, v) = e)) \rightarrow R_e uv$

Now consider two nodes $x, y \in N'$ such that $Sm(v(x), v(y)) \leq h$. The only cases worth checking are when either x or y is the new point t. If we have $y = t$, let $Sm(v(x), v(s)) = m$, then $R_m xs$ (By C3 in **N**). Because we have $Sm(v(s), \Phi) = i - n + 1, R_i - n + 1st$, by C4 $R_m^C v(x)v(s)$ and $R_{i-n+1}^C v(s)\Phi$, then because the canonical model characterizes **Restricted transitivity**, let $Sm(v(x), \Phi) = e$, then $R_e xt$.

In the case of $x = t$, the process is similar. □

Theorem 12 *K^{FR} is strongly complete with respect to the class of models generated by assignments.*

Proof Given a consistent set of formulas, expand it to a maximal consistent set Φ of $\mathbf{K}^{FR}$. We build a coherent network $\mathbf{N_0} = (N_0, R_0, v_0)$, $N_0 = w$, $R_0 = \emptyset$, $v_0(w) = \Phi$. We eliminate the defects on the network step-by-step. On each step $n + 1$, we get a new coherent network $\mathbf{N_{n+1}}$ lacking some defects of $\mathbf{N_n}$. This process have countable infinite steps. Combine all of these network on all the steps, we get our perfect network **N**. Finally, by the perfection of **N** it follows from Lemma 3 that the induced model $\mathfrak{J}_\mathbf{N}$ satisfies Φ at w. □

9.2.8 Applications

In system $\mathbf{K}^{FR}$, we assume that the things represented by each propositions have the same utility.

In applications, this feather means $\mathbf{K}^{FR}$ can only be used to describe specific type of phenomena, a scenario of which we represent by a state may show certain kinds of uniformity. It means that we can find a perspective from which different propositions could be judged to have equal weight.

For example, in an enclosed space, there is a group of factors which have equal status on their environmental influences. Each factor can be activated or inactivated, which can be expressed by a proposition or its negation. Then different assignment of propositions can represent different states of the enclosed space. If numbers of propositions which need to be assigned by different values are very little, two states could be considered similar.

For another example, we have not fully understood functions of the most human genes. Instead, we can only use the amount of different genes of two persons to measure the genetic difference. In this sense, every gene has the equal weight.

In fact, such a condition is a weakness of $\mathbf{K}^{FR}$ which limits its scope of application. In next section, based on $\mathbf{K}^{FR}$, we develop a new system $\mathbf{K}^{FXE}$ which will overcome is weakness.

9.3 Many Dimensions Model Generated by an Assignment

9.3.1 Language and Model

The models generated by assignments could be used to analyze the correlation between many groups of properties or parameters.

As mentioned earlier, we have given the model which is generated by assignments. Sometimes, we might just be interested on some aspects of properties at a node or state, and want to compare different nodes on these aspects, i.e., only consider some fragments of each propositional assignment. Let an aspect means a subset of Pr. A comparison on a certain aspect $asp_i = \{q_1, q_2, \ldots\}$ means when we measure the degree of similarity between two nodes, we just consider the changes of propositions which are elements of asp_i.

On the other hand, in the previous model, the degree of similarity is determined equally by each changing propositions. However, in general, different propositions should have different weights and their changes would bring different effect when we measure the degree of similarity. So we can give a mapping $Pr \rightarrow \mathbb{N}$ to assign each proposition a weight of change. Accordingly, the degree of similarity would be the result of the operation on the weights of changing propositions.

Furthermore, processes of state transition are usually irreversible, which means if we can go to point b from point a by a step, maybe we need several steps from point b to point a. In a model generated by an assignment, it means the model will lose the symmetry, while a proposition and its negation will not always be assigned to the same weight.

To accommodate such demands, we will extend our language, and adjust our set of axioms.

Definition 12 Some concepts

1. For any set of propositions A, $A^{cp} = \{\neg q | q \in A\} \cup A$
2. An aspect is a subset of Pr, and some aspects constitute a set $ASP = \{asp_1, asp_2, \ldots, \} \subseteq \rho(Pr)$
3. For each asp_n there is a weight function $\tau_{asp_n} : asp_n^{cp} \rightarrow \mathbb{N}$

4. $\star$ is a binary operator on $\mathbb{N}$ which satisfies commutative law and associative law, have an identity element '0' and for any $n, m \in \mathbb{N}$, we always have $n \star m \geq m$, and $n \star m \geq n$
5. For any $asp_n \in ASP$, there is a series of universal modal operators $[asp_n]_1$, $[asp_n]_2$, $[asp_n]_3 \ldots$

The language $\mathcal{L}^{FXE}$ consists of a countable set of propositions $Pr = \{p_1, p_2 \ldots\}$, a set of aspects $ASP = \{asp_1, asp_2, \ldots, \} \subseteq \rho(Pr)$, a weighting function τ, Boolean connectives $\neg$ and $\vee$, a binary operator $\star$ and a series of universal modal operator $[asp_n]_1$, $[asp_n]_2$, $[asp_n]_3 \ldots$ for each $asp_n \in ASP$. Formula with the form $l(p)$ means either p or $\neg p$. Formulas of $\mathcal{L}^{FXE}$ is constructed as follows:

$$\varphi = p \mid \bot \mid \neg\varphi \mid \varphi_1 \vee \varphi_2 \mid [asp_n]_1\varphi \mid [asp_n]_2\varphi \mid [asp_n]_3\varphi \mid \ldots$$
$$\mid [asp_n]_{(\tau_{asp_n}(l(p_1))\star\tau_{asp_n}(l(p_2))\star\ldots\star\tau_{asp_n}(l(p_m)))}\varphi \mid \ldots.$$

where $l(p_1), l(p_2), \ldots, l(p_m) \in asp_n$. A dual operator $\langle asp_n\rangle_h$ is defined as $\langle asp_n\rangle_h\varphi = \neg[asp_n]_h\neg\varphi$

Definition 13 A many dimensions model generated by an assignment is a sextuple $\mathbf{M}^{MD} = (W, V, ASP, \tau, \star, \mathbf{R})$. $W$is a set of possible worlds which is not empty. V is a mapping: $Pr \to \rho(W)$, which is called an assignment of W. τ is the collection of all the weighting functions $\tau = \{\tau_{asp_n} | asp_n \in ASP\}$ $\mathbf{R}$ is a collection for the all the accessibility relation of groups, where for each $asp_n \in ASP$,

- there is a set of numerable binary relations $R^{asp_n} = \{R_h^{asp_n} \mid h \neq 0, h \in \mathbb{N}\}$ on W,
- $\mathbf{R} = \{R^{asp_n} | asp_n \in ASP\}$,

and each $R_h^{asp_n}$ is a binary relation generated by (W, V, h) on W which is defined as follows:

(1) $Dm : W \times W \times asp_n^{cp} \to \mathbb{N}$ is a function, which is given by

$$Dm(w, v, asp_n, l(p)) = \begin{cases} \tau_{asp_n}(l(p)) & w \in V(l(p)) \text{ and } v \notin V(l(p)) \\ 0 & \text{otherwise} \end{cases}$$

(2) $Sm(w, v, asp_n)$ is a function: $Sm(w, v, asp_n) = Dm(w, v, asp_n, p_1) \star Dm(w, v, asp_n, \neg p_1) \star Dm(w, v, asp_n, p_2) \star Dm(w, v, asp_n, \neg p_2) \star \ldots$, iff, $asp_n = \{p_1, p_2, \ldots\}$
(3) $R_h^{asp_n} = \{(w, v) | w \in W, v \in W \;\&\; Sm(w, v, asp_n) \leq h\}$

$Dm(w, v, asp_n, l(p))$ is a character function which calculates the change degree between w and v caused by $l(p)$ on the aspect of asp_n. $Sm(w, v, asp_n)$ calculate the total change degree, i.e., the similarity degree between w and v. When $Sm(w, v) \leq h$, w will be connected to v by the binary relation R_h.

Definition 14 Given a model $\mathbf{M}^{MD} = (W, V, ASP, \tau, \star, \mathbf{R})$, $\mathbf{M}^{MD}, w \models \varphi$ is read as that φ is true at w in $\mathbf{M}^{MD}$, and is defined as follows:

$\mathbf{M}^{MD}, w \models p$ iff $w \in V(p)$
$\mathbf{M}^{MD}, w \models \neg\varphi$ iff $\mathbf{M}^{MD}, w \not\models \varphi$
$\mathbf{M}^{MD}, w \models \varphi \vee \psi$ iff $\mathbf{M}^{MD}, w \models \varphi$ or $\mathbf{M}^{FR}, w \models \psi$
$\mathbf{M}^{MD}, w \models [asp_n]_h\varphi$ iff for any $v \in W$ and $(w, v) \in R_h^{asp_n}$, we have $\mathbf{M}^{MD}, v \models \varphi$

By the standard convention, we extend the assignment V for the proposition symbols to arbitrary formulas. That is, $V(\varphi)$ denote the set $V(\varphi) := \{w | \mathbf{M}^{MD}, w \models \varphi\}$ on which φ will be true.

In this new model, if for a asp_n, $\neg(\forall p \in asp_n.\tau_{asp_n}(p) = \tau_{asp_n}(\neg p))$, then obviously, any $R_h^{asp_n} \in R^{asp_n}$ will lose symmetry and preserve reflexivity. And the Neighborhood similarity and restricted connectivity will be rephrased as:

- $\forall wv.R_h^{asp_n}wv \rightarrow Sm(w, v, asp_n) \leq h$
- $\forall wv.Sm(w, v, asp_n) \leq h \rightarrow R_h^{asp_n}wv$

9.3.2 Axioms

The system $\mathbf{K}^{FXE}$ is composed by the following axioms and rules, where h stands for any nature number

Prop: Propositional tautologies
K: $[asp_n]_h(\varphi \rightarrow \psi) \rightarrow ([asp_n]_h\varphi \rightarrow [asp_n]_h\psi)$
T: $[asp_n]_h\varphi \rightarrow \varphi$(reflexive)
MP: $\varphi_1, \varphi_1 \rightarrow \varphi_2/\varphi_2$
RN: $\varphi/[asp_n]_h\varphi$
SSR: $\langle asp_n\rangle_i\varphi \rightarrow \langle asp_n\rangle_j\varphi, i \leq j$
Cc(asp_n): $(l(p_1) \wedge l(p_2) \wedge \ldots \wedge l(p_h)) \rightarrow$
$[asp_n]_{\tau_{asp_n}(l(p_1))\star\tau_{asp_n}(l(p_2))\star\ldots\star\tau_{asp_h}(l(p_h))}(l(p_1) \vee l(p_2) \vee \ldots \vee l(p_h))$
STR: $(A \wedge \langle asp_n\rangle_{\mu^{aspn}(\pi_{a_i})\star\mu^{aspn}(\pi_{a_j})}(B \wedge \langle asp_n\rangle_{\mu^{aspn}(\pi_{a_i})\star\mu^{aspn}(\pi_{a_k})}(C \wedge \varphi))) \rightarrow$
$\langle asp_n\rangle_{\mu^{aspn}(\pi_{a_j})\star\mu^{aspn}(\pi_{a_k})}(C \wedge \varphi)$
SER: $(A \wedge \langle asp_n\rangle_{\mu^{aspn}(\pi_{a_i})\star\mu^{aspn}(\pi_{a_j})}(B \wedge \varphi)) \rightarrow$
$[asp_n]_{\mu^{aspn}(\pi_{a_j})\star\mu^{aspn}(\pi_{a_k})}(C \rightarrow \langle asp_n\rangle_{\mu^{aspn}(\pi_{a_i})\star\mu^{aspn}(\pi_{a_k})}(B \wedge \varphi))$

a, b, c are letters, i, j, k denote natural numbers, which are greater or equal to 0; $\pi_{a_i} = \{l(p_{a_1}), l(p_{a_2}), l(p_{a_3}) \ldots l(p_{a_i})\}$, $\mu^{asp_n}(\pi_{a_i}) = \tau_{asp_n}(l(p_{a_1})) \star \tau_{asp_n}(l(p_{a_2})) \star \ldots \star \tau_{asp_n}(l(p_{a_i}))$, then $l(p_n) \notin \pi_{b_j}$, & $l(p_n) \notin \pi_{c_k}$, and if $l(p_n) \in \pi_{b_j}$ or $l(p_n) \in \pi_{c_k}$, it is just like the case of $l(p_n) \in \pi_{a_i}$; when $i = 0$, we have $\pi_{a_i} = \emptyset$

let $A = ((\bigwedge \pi_{a_i}) \wedge (\bigwedge \pi_{b_j}) \wedge (\bigwedge \pi_{c_k}))$
let $B = ((\neg(\bigvee \pi_{a_i}) \wedge \neg(\bigvee \pi_{b_j}) \wedge (\bigwedge \pi_{c_k}))$
let $C = ((\bigwedge \pi_{a_i}) \wedge \neg(\bigvee \pi_{b_j}) \wedge \neg(\bigvee \pi_{c_k}))$

9.3.3 Soundness and Completeness

According to the soundness and completeness of K^{FR}, it is easy to check the soundness and completeness of K^{FXE}.

9.3.4 Some Strategies of Data Analysis Based on $\mathbf{M}^{FXE}$

When we describe a process of state transition with a Kripke model, an accessibility relation consists of a series of paths from states to states, where a path represents a process of transition. In dynamic logic, such processes are determined by initial states and programs. However, outside of theoretic computer science, phenomena often do not occur in such a way. It would be not only a sole process but several processes that determine a state simultaneously, and accordingly this state can be regarded as a crossing of different precesses. The best example of such phenomena are the cases that each individual of humanity is treated as a carrier of states. Individuals of humanity are nodes of various natural processes or social and historical processes. In genetics, everybody is a node in the total genetic process of human being, while there are several subprocesses underlie this total process, such as maternal inheritance, paternal inheritance.

If they are just underlying concurrent processes, it will be hard to obverse and confirm these processes. But sometimes a process leaves traces. Still, take inheritance as an example, genetic processes are presented by genetic traits on macroscale. From the observation on these genetic traits in several generations, we can grasp the continuity of the changes from generation to generation, and the DNA is the traces of the process in the microscale. More importantly, the process of genetic variations are highly consistent with some Mathematical laws [4] which are the research content of coalescent theory.

The Y-chromosome is easy to study since it can only be carried by males, and a man can carry not a pair but only one Y-chromosome, so there is no Y-chromosome recombination. The same thing happen on females: the mitochondrial DNA of fertilized eggs completely come from the mother's eggs. There are mainly three kinds of genetic variation: genetic recombination, chromosomal variation and genetic mutation. Genetic recombination and genetic mutation cause genetic polymorphism. Single Nucleotide Polymorphisms (SNPs) is a kind of genetic polymorphism, which is the most common type of genetic variant in human genome. Though extensive investigation to single Nucleotide Polymorphisms in human population, we have shown that the variations of Y-chromosome and the variations of mitochondrial DNA can be regarded as Markov processes. The accuracy of these processes make the mutations of Y-chromosome or mitochondrial DNA can be used to measure the rhythm of variations, predicate the variations of apparent characteristic of human body, and find out the family history of an individual, although we may not fully understand the specific processes of gene expression. In this sense, we can regard the Y-chromosome SNPs or mitochondrial SNPs as the traces of human populations genetic processes.

The many dimension models generated by assignments provide us a kind of structures to deal with big data [5], with which we can organize all of individual information of a specific group on various aspects and generate a series of concurrent processes taking different individuals as nodes. By comparing these processes, we can discover the correlation between the information on different aspects. The comparisons will bring us two kinds of correlations in general, asynchronous or synchronous. If two concurrent processes are asynchronous, such as the relevance of maternal inheritance and paternal inheritance, we will study how do they impact or disturb each other, such as the coefficient of inbreeding and genetic disease. And if two they are approximately synchronized, such as the relevance of DNA and Apparent characters, we can verify this correlation by confirming some probabilistic relation between two generating relations with an appropriate variance. Based on such correlation we can predicate one by another one.

9.4 The Similarity of the Structures of Assignments

The issue of similarity is central to logic of ontological conditionals. There are so many systems of ontological conditionals, to deal with subjunctive conditionals or counterfactuals. Most of them are in term of Kripke semantics. A common practice is to assign to a world and formula or a world and a pair of formulas a subset of W or a collection of subset of W. This assignment will be denoted by a selection function such as $F(A, w)$. Although there are always some restrictions which will be given on these selection functions, the assignments are rarely given to the atomic formulas and be extended to all the formulas. There are two barriers which prevent us to do this:

What is the value of $(A > B) > C$? One barrier is that when a subjunctive conditional is the antecedent of another subjunctive conditional, how could we determine the value of the latter. As long as we interpret conditionals by possible world semantics, it will be hard to understand the situation such sentences bring us. So we just kick this trouble to the selection function.

Another barrier to give an inductive definition of the selection function, is the expression of the similarity between the current world and other worlds. The worlds which be assigned to sentences and current world should be similar to current world on a certain extent. Different systems appeal to different extent, but none of them have provided a criterion to judge whether a world is similar to the current world, and on what extent. If we have a clear criterion, we can define the set of the worlds which are closer to the current world for each atomic sentence, and extend this definition to most sentences (except those subjunctive conditionals with a antecedent of subjunctive conditional).

A criterion It seems our system based on "Models generated by assignments" provide such an alternative, but could we just judge two possible worlds are similar by a number? It seems that a structural modeling of similarity would be more appropriate.

Compared with the previously introduced model, a structural modelling of similarity should be easier to accept intuitively in a formalism about ontological conditionals. But except counting changes of truth values, how could we find another way to express the similarity of possible world?

First, the assignments of sentences could not show any structural features by themselves, unless we give them such features. Second, atomic sentences should be logically independent, so we can assign them values freely. However, their connotations are often relative. Here I am not going to limit the freedom of assigning, but provide a kind of internal structure to the set of propositions (Pr) for a model which is a bit like a frame: a set of possible worlds with an accessibility relation. This structure will be compatible with any sets of possible worlds and any assignments. Third, together with these structures, we can generate the accessibility relations for any assignment.

When we imagine a possible world to understand a subjunctive conditionals or counterfactuals, we may add some changes to the factual world, this is the thought of "minimal change theories and small change theories," to use the terminology employed in Cross and Nute; or we could just consider the things related to the antecedent and consequent of our conditional, do not care about other things, so such possible worlds would just resemble the factual world in certain very minimal respects, this is the thought of "Maximal Change Theories," to use the terminology employed in Cross and Nute. Both of the two kinds of theories have an implicit consideration about the thing which we named "context." The thing we called "context" here, loosely speaking, is a set of propositions which each have interrelated connotations. In the first case, we adjust the truth values of the propositions in some contexts of the antecedent of a conditional when we try to build a possible world. In the second case, we just remain the values of propositions in some contexts of the antecedent and do not care about other propositions which are outside of these contexts. Our models will be closer to the second case where we borrow the thought of "Maximal Change Theories."

Now we introduce the notion "a context of a sentence or proposition." As we know, the selection functions of formalisms of ontological conditionals were always not concrete, so we do not know exactly how they choose worlds or classes of worlds. They look as black boxes which are used to satisfy logician's some kinds of ambiguous intuition. Our formalism try to build some structural relation between current world and possible worlds we select. Context is the device we use to build this relation.

Contexts in linguistics are basic phenomena. Frege told us "never ...ask for the meaning of a word in isolation, but only in the context of a proposition." No doubt, in nature language, this principle also applies to sentences or propositions.

When we state a proposition, there will be always some kinds of contexts. We have been told any two things or events in our world could be linked by no more than 3 or 4 sentences. But could these 3 or 4 sentences be used to justify a collective topic? In the process of finding links, we use 3 or 4 sentences, but every time we introduce a new sentence, we have changed a context.

We describe the world by describing facts or states of affairs with propositions. It seems that all the things in our world are related. But most of them are not related directly: When we talk about a subject, event A could be linked to event B, and under another topic, event B could be linked to event C. So a event could appear in different discussions, every of them we named a context of the event.

Here "what is a context?" seems a sophisticated question in language philosophy: it could be an argument, a debate or discussion, a description, and a situation or scenario, and so on. Maybe we could consider it as a constant, consistent and comprehensible language activity, or the content of such activity. However, such a kind of vague, broad things involve some underlying laws. For example, a context often bears a center named topic or theme (usually expressed by a word, phase, or propositions or questions and so on). This center often implies the motivation of the language activity. Another law is that the center cannot be extended infinitely, speaker or speaker must keep restrained and prevent themselves from wandering off the topic.

Every proposition or sentence could lead us to contexts in which it is the center. In fact, according to the motivation of speakers, a proposition could induce different context. Every context can be summarized by a group of propositions or sentences with a tree relation between central proposition as its root and the propositions which summarize the context as its branches. In fact, these propositions will become subtopics where we try to expand our discussion. When the space for discussion is enlarged, some of these propositions induce new contexts and combine them into original context, so the original context is extended to a larger context just as the growth of tree.

When we estimate a counterfactual, the context of the counterfactual determines what kinds of possible worlds we choose. In the possible worlds we choose, the antecedent of the counterfactual should be true, but propositions in the context should retain truth values in current world, otherwise, the discussion around the counterfactual will become pointless.

For example, when we debate on Napoleon's invasion of Russia, you may say "If I was Napoleon, I would win the war." But later, when you tell us in great interesting how you lead an army which is consisted by planes and tanks to attack the Russian army 200 years ago, we group of audiences would have nothing to say. We could accept your counterfactual only if you assume that your army is just Napoleon's army which consisted by French peasants in nineteenth century, no planes, no tanks and no penicillin, meanwhile you and your army are suffering from typhus. Because these elements are the component of our context.

Obviously, our context is not the whole argument or debate. It is the common frame of different language activities which resemble each other. It can be summarized by a group of propositions and set some boundaries for our language activities. However, there are so many kinds of language activities: in some ones, context are clear and sensible, such as an argument or a debate. Sometimes, the context would be very broad and inexact. For example, a conversation between two strangers should conform to social convention, besides there is no other restriction. In such cases, it is hard to say whether there is a context, or what is the context in such occasions.

Now the setting about context in our formalism is a little tricky. A pragmatic approach is to resort to corpus. As machine translation use probabilistic relations between words, we can construct contexts based on conditional probabilities between propositions in the whole corpus. We will discuss this attempt in our further work, but in the paper, we just grudgingly accept the undefined set of "context" as mentioned above.

Definition 15 The language $\mathcal{L}^{ss}$ consists of a countable set of propositions $Pr = \{p_1, p_2 \ldots\}$, Boolean connectives $\neg$ and $\wedge$, and two binary modal operator $\succ_{\Diamond}, \succ_{\Box}$. Formulas of $\mathcal{L}^{FX}$ is constructed as follows:

$\varphi =:: p \mid \bot \mid \neg\varphi \mid \varphi_1 \wedge \varphi_2 \mid \varphi_1 \succ_{\Box} \varphi_2 \mid \varphi_1 \succ_{\Diamond} \varphi_2.$
For any formula φ

- If φ include any modal operator, it can't appear on the first argument of any modal operator. This means only the formulas of propositional calculus could appear on the first argument of any modal operator.
- Any formulas which appear on the first argument of a modal operator will be treat as its main disjunctive normal form.

Definition 16 We express the internal structure of the set of propositions by a function Fs as follows:

1. $Ps = \{p_1, \neg p_1, p_2, \neg p_2, p_3, \neg p_3 \ldots\} = Pr \cup \{p_i | p_i \in Pr, i \in \mathbb{N}\}$
2. $Fs : Ps \rightarrow \rho(\rho(Ps))$

Here assign to one each of propositions and negations a set of the subsets of Ps. We name these subsets the contexts of a proposition or a negative proposition.

In the function $Fs : Ps \rightarrow \rho(\rho(Ps))$, we assign every atomic proposition or negative proposition a group of set of atomic propositions and negative propositions), because a proposition and its negation would be related to different context. A group of set of propositions and negation is a group of contexts. A proposition will correspond to several different context.

Now we introduce a new connective $\wedge^R$ which is called *right conjunctive symbol*, which is just same as $\wedge$ in common sense. But this conjunction does not satisfy commutative law when it is being a variable of function *Fs*. That because when we try to find out the contexts of a conjunction of propositions, conjuncts are usually not equally important. We will talk about an issue, we will add some restrictions or conditions on this discussion. You can connect the issue and the restrictions or conditions together by $\wedge$, but the issue itself have different status from the restrictions or conditions, although all of them are represented by propositions.

So we have $p \wedge q \leftrightarrow p \wedge^C q$, and $Fs(p \wedge q) \neq Fs(p \wedge^R q) \neq Fs(q \wedge^R p)$, but $Fs(\neg(p \wedge^R q)) = Fs(\neg(q \wedge^R p)) = Fs(\neg p \vee \neg q)$. So the formulas as the argument of function *Fs* is constructed as follows:

$$\varphi =:: p \mid \bot \mid \neg\varphi \mid \varphi_1 \wedge \varphi_2 \mid \varphi_1 \wedge^R \varphi_2$$

Definition 17 An context of a right conjunction $l(p) \wedge^R l(q)$ is a cluster of context $cluster = (context_1, context_2, context_3, \ldots, context_n) \in Fs(l(p) \wedge^R l(q))$, such that

1. If $n = 1$, we have $cluster = context_1$, $context_1 \in Fs(l(p))$, and $l(q) \in context_1$,
2. $\forall 1 \leq i < n$, $context_i \ll context_{i+1}$,
3. $\forall 1 \leq i \leq i+m \leq n$, $(context_i \lll context_m) = (context_i \ll context_{i+1} \ll \ldots \ll context_{i+m})$
4. $context_1 \in Fs(l(p))$, $l(q) \in context_n)$,
5. $\forall context_i \ll context_{i+1} \in cluster, \exists l(r) \in context_i \& context_{i+1} \in Fs(l(r))$,
6. $\forall j, j \neq n,\ context_j \notin Fs(l(p))$
7. $\forall j, j \neq n,\ l(q) \notin context_j$

$Fs(l(p) \wedge^R l(q))$ is the collection of all the contexts of $l(p) \wedge^R l(q)$.

Definition 18 Let $cluster_a = (context_{a_1}, context_{a_2}, \ldots, context_{a_n}) \in Fs(p \wedge^R q)$, $cluster_b = (context_{b_1}, context_{b_2}, \ldots, context_{b_m}) \in Fs(q \wedge^R r)$, then $cluster_{a+b} = (context_{a_1}, context_{a_2}, \ldots, context_{a_n}, context_{b_1}, context_{b_2}, \ldots, context_{b_m}) \in Fs(p \wedge^R q \wedge^R r)$

Definition 19 1. $Fs(\phi \vee \psi) ::= Fs(\phi) \cup Fs(\psi)$

2. $Fs(\phi \wedge^R \psi \wedge^R \varphi) ::= \{cluster_{a+b} | cluster_a \in Fs(\phi \wedge^R \psi), cluster_b \in Fs(\psi \wedge^R \varphi)\}$
3. $Fs(\phi \wedge \psi) ::= Fs((\phi \wedge^R \psi) \vee (\psi \wedge^R \phi)) = Fs(\phi \wedge^R \psi) \cup Fs(\psi \wedge^R \phi)$

We extend the assignment of *Fs* for the proposition symbols to arbitrary any formulas without modal operators.

Definition 20 A model structurally generated by an assignment is a quadruple $\mathbf{M}^{ps} = (W, Fs, V, F_\star)$. W is a set of possible worlds which is not empty. *Fs* is defined as before. V is a mapping: $Pr \to \rho(W)$, which is called an assignment of

W. $F_\star$ is a function which is defined as follows Let $|cluster| = \bigcup_{i=1}^{n}(\bigcup context_i)$, when $cluster = (context_1, \ldots, context_n)$. $F_\star$ assigns to each ϕ and each world a collection of the subsets of W. $F_\star(\phi, w) = \{\{u|u \in V(\phi)\ \&\forall l(p) \in |cluster_i|, w \in V(l(p))\ \textit{iff}\ u \in V(l(p))\}|cluster_i \in Fs(\phi)\}$. ϕ could be any formula without modal operators.

Definition 21 Given a model $\mathbf{M}^{ps} = (W, Fs, V, F_\star)$, $\mathbf{M}^{ps}, w \models \varphi$ is read as that φ is true at w in $\mathbf{M}^{FR}$, and is defined as follows:

$\mathbf{M}^{ps}, w \models p$ iff $w \in V(p)$
$\mathbf{M}^{ps}, w \models \neg\varphi$ iff $\mathbf{M}^{FR}, w \not\models \varphi$
$\mathbf{M}^{ps}, w \models \varphi \wedge \psi$ iff $\mathbf{M}^{FR}, w \models \varphi$ and $\mathbf{M}^{FR}, w \models \psi$
$\mathbf{M}^{ps}, w \models \phi \succ_\Box \psi$ iff $\forall X \in F_\star(\phi, w), \forall x \in X, \mathbf{M}^{ps}, x \models \psi$
$\mathbf{M}^{ps}, w \models \phi \succ_\Diamond \psi$ iff $\exists X \in F_\star(\phi, w), \forall x \in X, \mathbf{M}^{ps}, x \models \psi$

ϕ could be any formulas without modal operators, and φ, ψ could be any formulas in our language. By the standard convention, we extend the assignment V for the proposition symbols to arbitrary formulas. That is, $V(\varphi)$ denote the set $V(\varphi) :=\{w|\ \mathbf{M}^{ps}, w \models \varphi\}$ on which φ will be true.

Obviously, our language is not complete, which lacks symbols to express situations about contexts and clusters. And in our model, the function Fs is a temporary mechanism, which should be replaced by something that can be expressed in Kripke structure. Solving these two problems are premises of axiomatization of our models which will be further worked.

Acknowledgments This research is supported by "The Fundamental Research Funds for the Central Universities" (NKZXB1257).

References

1. Fei Zha, Hu Liu. 2011. Similarity of States and Models of Restricted Flux. *Studies in Logic*, 13:1–19.
2. Wiebe van der Hoek, Michael Worldridge. 2005. On the logic of cooperation and propositional control. *Artificial Intelligence*, 164: 81–119.
3. Patrick Blackburn, Maarten de Rijke, Yde Venema. 2001. *Modal Logic*, New York: Cambridge University Press.
4. Jotun Hein, Mikkel H. Schierup, Carsten Wiuf. 2005. *Gene Genealogies, Variation and Evolution: A Primer in Coalescent Theory*, Oxford: Oxford University Press.
5. Viktor Mayer-Schönberger, Denneth Cukier. 2013, *Big Data-a revolution that will transform how we live, work, and think*, New York: John Murray Publishers Ltd.
6. Donald Nute, Charles B. Cross. 2002. Conditional Logic. in *Handbook of Philosophical Logic*, 2nd Edn Vol 4, ed. D.M.Gabbay, 1–99. Dordrecht: Kluwer Academic Publishers.

Chapter 10
An Explanation for the Ternary Relation R in the Relational Semantics of Relevance Logic

Beihai Zhou and Qing Jia

Abstract Relational semantics is one of the most popular forms of semantics for relevance logic. However, this semantics, especially the ternary relation R lacks intuition, and that is why there are various interpretations for R. The original motivation for creating relevance logic is to give a better description of inference, thus if an interpretation for R could match this motivation better, then it will be more intuitive than the relational semantics and other interpretations. Therefore, this paper focuses on inference semantics, which could be viewed as a relational semantics with a ternary relation R, and R represents a relation among rules, premises and conclusions. These two forms of semantics are equivalent with respect to the relevance logic system $\mathbf{R}_{+}$. Actually, relational semantics could be regarded as a characterization of the formal structure of inference, and relevance logic may be defined as the logic of some kind of inference.

Keywords Inference semantics · Relational semantics · Relevance logic

10.1 Introduction

Relevance logic was castigated for 'having no semantics' at its early stage. (Dunn and Restall [5]). This problem was solved by Routly and Meyer [13–15], Urquhart [16], etc. Among these solutions, Routly and Meyer's semantic approach, namely the so-called relational semantics is one of the most acknowledged forms of semantics. In relational semantics, a model $\mathcal{M}$ is a tuple $\langle$K, R, 0, $*$, $\vDash\rangle$, in which R is a ternary relation on K. For any formula A, B and a $\in$ K, $\mathcal{M}$, a $\vDash A \rightarrow B$ iff for any b, c in K, if

This research is supported by the National Social Science Fund of China (12&ZD119).

B. Zhou (✉)
Department of Philosophy, Peking University, Beijing, China
e-mail: zhoubh@phil.pku.edu.cn

Q. Jia
Institute of Philosophy, Chinese Academy of Social Sciences, Beijing, China
e-mail: v100jq@163.com

S. Ju et al. (eds.), *Modality, Semantics and Interpretations*,
Logic in Asia: Studia Logica Library, DOI 10.1007/978-3-662-47197-5_10

Rabc and $\mathcal{M}, b \models A$, then $\mathcal{M}, c \models B$. By relational semantics, the soundness theorem and completeness theorem of many important relevance logical systems could be proved. Therefore, from the technical point of view, it is a desirable semantics for relevance logic. However, this semantics, especially the ternary relation R, is not as intuitive as the standard relational semantics for modal logic, and that is why there are so many interpretations for R.

The original motivation of creating relevance logic is to give a better description of inference. So if we could give an interpretation for R based on this motivation, then it will be much more intuitive than relational semantics and other interpretations.

There are three components in an inference: rule(s), premise(s) and conclusion(s), i.e. for an inferential rule $A \rightarrow B$, if A is a premise, then B could be obtained as a conclusion by applying the rule $A \rightarrow B$ to A. More generally, if r is a set of rules, a is a set of premises, then a set of conclusions denoted by b could be obtained by using some rules in r to some premises in a. Therefore, there is a triple $\langle r, a, b\rangle$ with respect to r, a and b. Of course, r could be applied to some other set of premises a', then there will be other set of conclusions b', and the triple could be represented as $\langle r, a', b'\rangle$ instead. Therefore, by applying r to different sets of premises, we could get different sets of conclusions and even a set of triples, namely a ternary relation $R = \{\langle r, a, b\rangle, \langle r, a', b'\rangle, \langle r, a'', b''\rangle, \langle r, a''', b'''\rangle \ldots\ldots\}$.

Based on the composition of inference, a ternary relation as above could be formed. Furthermore, the formal structure of any inference could be represented by some sets of formulas, because the rule(s), premise(s) and conclusion(s) of an inference are all sets of formulas.

Let Z be a set of sets of formulas, a be a set of premises, b be a set of conclusions and r be a set of rules such that $a, b, r \in Z$, and r is a special element in Z that includes all rules of inference, by which conclusions in b could be obtained from premises in a. In general, for any a, b and c in Z, $Rabc$ means that c could be obtained via applying a to b.

According to the analysis above, the triple $\langle Z, R, r\rangle$ could be used as a frame to describe the formal structure of inference. Suppose that $\mathfrak{S}$ is a collection of this kind of triples, and $L_{\mathfrak{S}} = \cap\{r \mid \langle r, Z, R\rangle \in \mathfrak{S}\}$. Then $L_{\mathfrak{S}}$ is a set of rules, and a subset of every r in $\langle Z, R, r\rangle$.

Suppose that there are some restrictions on $\mathfrak{S}$. Then $L_{\mathfrak{S}}$ is a set of inferential rules under these restrictions. So $L_{\mathfrak{S}}$ presents a form of logic viewed from the aspect of semantics. This semantics could be named as *inference semantics*. Zhou [18] proved the soundness theorem and completeness theorem of $\mathbf{E_{fde}}$ by inference semantics. That paper proposes a new interpretation for the ternary relation R in relational semantics. Zhou [19] discussed the application of inference semantics to the ternary relation R. However, the most influential form of semantics for $\mathbf{E_{fde}}$ is the set-theoretical semantics, which does not involve the ternary relation R, and Zhou [19] only gave us some intuition instead of concrete theorems. Therefore, in this paper, inference semantics will be applied to another important relevance logical system $\mathbf{R_+}$. $\mathbf{R_+}$ is an extension of $\mathbf{R_\rightarrow}$, and $\mathbf{R_\rightarrow}$ is a system of relevance implication. Anderson and Belnap [1] gave an axiomatic presentation of R_+. For the proofs of metatheorems, $\mathbf{R_+}$ is not harder than $\mathbf{R_\rightarrow}$; instead, it is easier than the whole $\mathbf{R}$

(Anderson and Belnap [2]). Therefore, we choose $\mathbf{R}_+$ as our first step to show that inference semantics could be applied to relevance logic.

In the following sections, we will use IS and RS to denote inference semantics and relational semantics respectively.

10.2 The System $\mathbf{R}_+$ and Its Relational Semantics

In Anderson and Belnap [1], to illustrate a system of "relevance implication", they gave a system $\mathbf{R}_\to$, which is a typical system of relevance logic. $\mathbf{R}_\to$ is complete with respect to a class of models (Anderson and Belnap [2]). However, $\mathbf{R}_+$, which is an extension of $\mathbf{R}_\to$, has the strong completeness result with respect to the canonically defined frame (Anderson and Belnap [2]). Because of this distinction, we will use $\mathbf{R}_+$ as an example of illustrating the relation between IS and RS in the following sections.

The language $\mathscr{L}$ of $\mathbf{R}_+$ contains enumerable variables, $p, q, \ldots$, connectives, $\to, \wedge, \vee$ and left-bracket "(", right-bracket ")".

Formulas of $\mathbf{R}_+$ $A ::= p|A \wedge A|A \vee A|A \to A$

Let $V_{\mathscr{L}}$ be the set of variables in the language $\mathscr{L}$ and $F(\mathscr{L})$ be the set of formulas in the language $\mathscr{L}$.

Axioms and Rules of $\mathbf{R}_+$

A1 $A \to A$
A2 $(A \to B) \to ((C \to A) \to (C \to B))$
A3 $(A \to (A \to B)) \to (A \to B)$
A4 $(A \to (B \to C)) \to (B \to (A \to C))$
A5 $((A \to B) \to (A \to C)) \to (A \to (B \wedge C))$
A6 $A \wedge B \to A, A \wedge B \to B$
A7 $A \to A \vee B, B \to A \vee B$
A8 $((A \to C) \wedge (B \to C)) \to (A \vee B \to C)$
A9 $A \wedge (B \vee C) \to (A \wedge B) \vee C$

R1 From A and B to infer B.
R2 From A and B to infer $A \wedge B$.

Definition 10.2.1 A triple $\langle \mathrm{K, R, 0} \rangle$ is a frame of $\mathbf{R}_+$, iff

(1) K is a set of set-ups;
(2) $0 \in \mathrm{K}$, and 0 is a logical set-up;
(3) R is a ternary relation on K, which satisfies the following conditions[1]:

For any a, a′, b, c in K,

(i) Identity: R0aa

[1] For these clauses in Definition 10.2.1(3), their order has been changed from the order in Anderson and Belnap [2] for the convenience of the following propositions.

(ii) Idempotence: Raaa.
(iii) Commutativity: Rabc $\Rightarrow$ Rbac.
(iv) Associativity: R^2(ab)cd $\Rightarrow$ R^2a(bc)d^2.[2]
(v) Monotony: Rabc and R0a′a $\Rightarrow$ Ra′bc.

Definition 10.2.2 A quadruple $\mathcal{M} = \langle \text{K, R, 0}, \models \rangle$ is a model of $\mathbf{R}_+$ iff

(1) $\langle$K, R, 0$\rangle$ is a frame of $\mathbf{R}_+$;
(2) $\models$ is a valuation relation from K to $F(\mathscr{L})$, which satisfies the following conditions:

For any a, b, c in K,

(i) For any $p \in V(\mathscr{L})$, if $\mathcal{M}$, a $\models p$ and R0ab, then $\mathcal{M}$, b $\models p$;
(ii) $\mathcal{M}$, a $\models A \wedge B$ iff $\mathcal{M}, a \models A$ and $\mathcal{M}, a \models B$;
(iii) $\mathcal{M}$, a $\models A \vee B$ iff $\mathcal{M}, a \models A$ or $\mathcal{M}, a \models B$;
(iv) $\mathcal{M}$, a $\models A \to B$ iff if Rabc and $\mathcal{M}$, b $\models A$, then $\mathcal{M}$, c $\models B$.

Definition 10.2.3 For any formula A and a model $\mathcal{M}$ of $\mathbf{R}_+$, A is verified on $\mathcal{M}$ if $\mathcal{M}, 0 \models A$. A is valid if A is verified on all models.

Under these definitions, the soundness theorem and completeness theorem of $\mathbf{R}_+$ could be proved (Anderson and Belnap [2], Dunn and Restall [5]).

10.3 The Inference Semantics for the System $\mathbf{R}_+$

The aim of IS is to describe the formal structure of inference, which could represent a ternary relation among the set of rules, the set of premises and the set of conclusions, because every inference includes premise(s), rule(s) and conclusion(s). As for different kinds of inference, there will be different requirements on the set of rules, the set of premises or the set of conclusions, and the corresponding semantic structure should have some properties or conditions to reflect these requirements. In the following paragraphs, $\mathbf{R}_+$ will be used as an example to show the inferences that $\mathbf{R}_+$ depicts via IS.

Notation: Let a, b be any set of formulas. Then $[ab] =_{df} \{B | A \to B \in a \wedge A \in b\}$.

Definition 10.3.1 A triple $\langle \text{Z}, R, r \rangle$ is an IS-frame, iff

(1) $Z \subseteq \wp(F(\mathscr{L}))$;
(2) $r \in Z$ and r is a set of logical rules;
(3) R is a ternary relation on Z. For any $a, b, c \in Z$, $Rabc$ iff $[ab] \subseteq c$.

Definition 10.3.2 A quadruple $\mathfrak{M}' = \langle Z, R, r \Vdash \rangle$ is an IS-model, iff

(1) $\langle Z, R, r \rangle$ is an IS-frame;

---

[2]For any a, b, c, d in K, R^2(ab)cd $=_{df} \exists x$(Rab$x$ $\wedge$ R$x$cd), R^2a(bc)d $=_{df} \exists x$(Raxd $\wedge$ $Rbcx$).

(2) $\Vdash$ is a valuation relation from Z to $F(\mathscr{L})$, which satisfies the following conditions:

For any a, b, c in Z,

(i) $\mathfrak{M}', a \Vdash p$ iff $p \in a$;
(ii) $\mathfrak{M}', a \Vdash A \wedge B$ iff $\mathfrak{M}', a \Vdash A$ and $\mathfrak{M}', a \Vdash B$;
(iii) $\mathfrak{M}', a \Vdash A \vee B$ iff $\mathfrak{M}', a \Vdash A$ or $\mathfrak{M}', a \Vdash B$;
(iv) $\mathfrak{M}', a \Vdash A \rightarrow B$ iff if $Rabc$ and $\mathfrak{M}', b \Vdash A$, then $\mathfrak{M}', c \Vdash B$.

Definition 10.3.3 A triple $\langle Z, R, r\rangle$ is an IS-frame of $\mathbf{R}_+$, iff

(1) $\langle Z, R, r\rangle$ is an IS-frame;
(2) $\mathrm{Th}(\mathbf{R}_+) \subseteq r$
(3) For any $a, b, c \in Z$ and any $A, B \in F(\mathscr{L})$, the following conditions are satisfied:

(i) Identity: $[ra] \subseteq a$;
(ii) Idempotence: $[aa] \subseteq a$;
(iii) Commutativity: $[ba] \subseteq [ab]$;
(iv) Associativity: $[a[bc]] \subseteq [[ab]c]$;
(v) Monotony: $[ra'] \subseteq a \Rightarrow [a'b] \subseteq [ab]$.

Definition 10.3.4 A quadruple $\langle Z, R, r, \Vdash\rangle$ is an IS-model $\mathfrak{M}$ of $\mathbf{R}_+$, iff

(1) $\langle Z, R, r\rangle$ is an IS-frame of $\mathbf{R}_+$;
(2) $\Vdash$ is a valuation relation from Z to $F(\mathscr{L})$.

Definition 10.3.5 For any formula A and any class of IS-models $\mathscr{M}$ of $\mathbf{R}_+$, A is valid on $\mathscr{M}$ iff for any IS-model $\mathfrak{M} = \langle Z, R, r, \Vdash\rangle$, if $\mathfrak{M} \in \mathscr{M}$, then $A \in r$. This could be called the $\mathbf{R}_+$-validity.

Let $\mathrm{L}_{\mathrm{R}+}$ be a set that includes all $\mathbf{R}_+$-valid formulas. In IS, $\mathrm{L}_{\mathrm{R}+}$ is a set of logical rules, which satisfies those conditions in Definition 10.3.3. If $\mathbf{R}_+$ is sound and complete with respect to IS, then $\mathbf{R}_+$ could be viewed as a form of logic of inference. This will be proved in the next section by the equivalence relation between RS and IS with respect to $\mathbf{R}_+$. In addition, by IS, we will see clearly what kind of inference $\mathbf{R}_+$ describes.

Proposition 10.3.1 *The model of* $\mathbf{R}_+$ *exists.*

Proof We will construct a model which satisfies all these conditions in Definition 10.3.3.

Let $Z' = \{\boldsymbol{r}, \boldsymbol{a}, \boldsymbol{b}, \boldsymbol{c}, \boldsymbol{d}, \boldsymbol{e}\}$ In this set,
$\boldsymbol{r} = \mathrm{Th}\mathbf{R}{+} \cup \{p, q, r, s, p \rightarrow q\}$
$\boldsymbol{a} = \{p, q, r, p \wedge q \rightarrow q, p \rightarrow q\}$
$\boldsymbol{b} = \{r, s, r \rightarrow r \vee p\}$
$\boldsymbol{c} = \{p, q, p \rightarrow q, q \rightarrow q\}$
$\boldsymbol{d} = \{q, s, q \rightarrow q\}$
$\boldsymbol{e} = \{q, q \rightarrow q\}$

If $\boldsymbol{x}$ is a set of formulas, then x could be used to denote the smallest set which includes $\boldsymbol{x}$ and is closed under R1 (from A and $A \rightarrow B$ to infer B), R2 (from A and B to infer $A \wedge B$) and the introduction of disjunction (from A or B to infer $A \vee B$. So if $Z = \{r, a, b, c, d, e\}$, then the model based on it will be a model of $\mathbf{R}_{+}$.

First $\langle Z, R, r\rangle$ is an IS-frame, by Definition 10.3.1.

Second $\langle Z, R, r\rangle$ satisfies those conditions in Definition 10.3.3. It is obvious that $\text{Th}(\mathbf{R}_{+}) \subseteq r$. By an induction on the construction of every element of Z, conditions in Definition 10.3.3(3) could be satisfied by $\langle Z, R, r\rangle$. □

10.4 The Equivalence Between RS and IS

From the technical aspect, the equivalence between RS and IS still needs to be proved. Using $\mathbf{R}_{+}$ as an example, we will show that RS is equivalent to IS with respect to $\mathbf{R}_{+}$.

Definition 10.4.1 For any two models M, M', M and M' are equivalent, if for any formula A, A is valid on M iff A is valid on M'.

Definition 10.4.2 For any relevance logical system **S**, if both RS and IS are semantics of **S**, then RS and IS are equivalent with respect to **S** iff

(1) for any IS-model $\mathfrak{M}$ of **S**, there is a RS-model $\mathcal{M}$ of **S**, such that $\mathfrak{M}$ and $\mathcal{M}$ are equivalent;
(2) for any RS-model $\mathcal{M}$ of **S**, there is an IS-model $\mathfrak{M}$ of **S**, such that $\mathcal{M}$ and $\mathfrak{M}$ are equivalent.

Proposition 10.4.1 *If* $\mathfrak{M} = \langle Z, R, r, \Vdash\rangle$ *is an IS-model of* $\mathbf{R}_{+}$, *then* $\mathfrak{M}$ *is a RS-model of* $\mathbf{R}_{+}$.

Proof Let $\mathfrak{M} = \langle Z, R, r, \Vdash\rangle$ be an IS-model of $\mathbf{R}_{+}$. Then by Definition 10.2.2, we have to prove that:

(1) $\langle Z, R, r\rangle$ is a RS-frame of $\mathbf{R}_{+}$
(2) $\Vdash$ is a valuation relation from K to $F(\mathscr{L})$.

For (1)

By Definitions 10.3.2 and 10.3.3, $Z \neq \emptyset$ and $r \in Z$. So we still have to show that $\langle Z, R, r\rangle$ satisfies those conditions in Definition 10.2.1(3)(i)–(v).

By Definition 10.3.3(3)(i) and (ii), we have $Rraa$ and $Raaa$.

By Definition 10.3.3(3)(iii), we have that for any set of formulas c, $[ab] \subseteq c \Rightarrow [ba] \subseteq c$, namely $Rabc \Rightarrow Rbac$.

By Definition 10.3.3(3), we have that for any set of formulas d, $[[ab]c] \subseteq d \Rightarrow [[ab]c] \subseteq d$, namely $R[ab]cd \Rightarrow Ra[bc]d$. Therefore, $(Rab[ab] \wedge R[ab]cd) \Rightarrow (Ra[bc]d \wedge Rbc[bc])$, namely (1) $(Rab[ab] \wedge R[ab]cd) \Rightarrow \exists x(Raxd \wedge Rbcx)$. By Definition 10.3.3(3), we have (2) $\exists \text{x}(Rabx \wedge Rxcd) \Rightarrow (Rab[ab] \wedge R[ab]cd)$. By (1) and (2), $\exists \text{x}(Rabx \wedge Rxcd) \Rightarrow \exists \text{x}(Raxd \wedge Rbcx)$.

By Definition 10.3.3(3)(v), we have that for any set of formulas c, $[ra'] \subseteq a \Rightarrow ([ab] \subseteq c \Rightarrow [a'b] \subseteq c)$, therefore, $[r'a] \subseteq a \wedge [ab] \subseteq c \Rightarrow [a'b] \subseteq c$, namely $Rabc \wedge Rra'a \Rightarrow Ra'bc$.

For (2)

By Definition 10.2.2, we have to show that for any $p \in V(\mathscr{L})$, if $\mathfrak{M}, a \models p$ and $Rrab$, then $\mathfrak{M}, b \models p$. Let $\mathfrak{M}, a \models p$. By Definition 10.3.2, $p \in a$. By Definition 10.3.3(2), $p \to p \in r$. By $p \to p \in r$ and $Rrab$ and $p \in a$, we have $b \in p$, namely $\mathfrak{M}, b \models p$. □

Definition 10.4.3 For any RS-model $\mathcal{M} = \langle \mathrm{K}, \mathrm{R}, 0, \models \rangle$, $\mathcal{S}(\mathcal{M}) = \langle \mathcal{S}(\mathrm{K}), \mathcal{S}(\mathrm{R}), \mathcal{S}(0), \mathcal{S}(\models) \rangle$ is a formulistic model of $\mathcal{M}$, iff

(1) for any $\mathrm{a} \in \mathrm{K}$, $\mathcal{S}(\mathrm{a}) = \{A | \mathcal{M}, \mathrm{a} \models A\}$;
(2) $\mathcal{S}(\mathrm{K}) = \{\mathcal{S}(\mathrm{a}) | \mathrm{a} \in \mathrm{K}\}$;
(3) for any $a, b, c \in \mathcal{S}(\mathrm{K})$, $\mathcal{S}(\mathrm{R})abc$ iff $[ab] \subseteq c$;
(4) $\mathcal{S}(\models)$ is the valuation relation $\Vdash$ in IS-model.

For any RS-frame $\mathcal{F} = \langle \mathrm{K}, \mathrm{R}, 0 \rangle$, $\mathcal{S}(\mathcal{F}) = \langle \mathcal{S}(\mathrm{K}), \mathcal{S}(\mathrm{R}), \mathcal{S}(0) \rangle$ is a formulistic frame of $\mathcal{F}$ iff (1)–(3) are satisfied.

Proposition 10.4.2 *Suppose that $\mathcal{F} = \langle K, R, 0 \rangle$ is a RS-frame and $\mathcal{S}(\mathcal{F}) = \langle \mathcal{S}(K), \mathcal{S}(R), \mathcal{S}(0) \rangle$ is a formulistic frame of $\mathcal{F}$. If $\mathcal{F}$ is a RS-frame of* $\mathbf{R}_+$, *then $\mathcal{S}(\mathcal{F})$ is an IS-frame of* $\mathbf{R}_+$.

Proof $\langle \mathrm{K}, \mathrm{R}, 0 \rangle$ is a RS-frame, so $\mathrm{K} \neq \emptyset$ and $0 \in \mathrm{K}$. Therefore, $\mathcal{S}(\mathrm{K}) \neq \emptyset$ and $\mathcal{S}(0) \in \mathcal{S}(\mathrm{K})$. By Definition 10.3.3, we still need to show that $\mathcal{S}(\mathrm{R})$ satisfies all those conditions in Definition 10.3.3(3)(i)–(v).

For clause (i)

We have to prove that for any $a \in \mathcal{S}(\mathrm{K})$, $[\mathcal{S}(0)a] \subseteq a$. Let $a \in \mathcal{S}(\mathrm{K})$. By Definition 10.4.3, there is an $\mathrm{a} \in \mathrm{K}$ such that $a = \mathcal{S}(\mathrm{a})$. $\mathcal{F} = \langle \mathrm{K}, \mathrm{R}, 0 \rangle$ is a RS-frame, so R0aa holds, that is, for any formulas A and B, if $\mathcal{M}, 0 \models A \to B$ and $\mathcal{M}, \mathrm{a} \models A$, then $\mathcal{M}, \mathrm{a} \models B$, by Definition 10.2.2(2)(iv).

Therefore, we have that if $A \to B \in \mathcal{S}(0)$ and $A \in \mathcal{S}(\mathrm{a})$, then $B \in \mathcal{S}(\mathrm{a})$, namely, $[\mathcal{S}(0)a] \subseteq a$.

For clause (ii)

We have to show that $[aa] \subseteq a$. By Definition 10.4.3, there is an $\mathrm{a} \in \mathrm{K}$ such that $a = \mathcal{S}(\mathrm{a})$. $\mathcal{F} = \langle \mathrm{K}, \mathrm{R}, 0 \rangle$ is an RS-frame, so Raaa holds. By Definitions 10.2.2 and 10.4.3, we have that if $A \to B \in \mathcal{S}(\mathrm{a})$ and $A \in \mathcal{S}(texta)$, then $B \in \mathcal{S}(texta)$, namely $[aa] \subseteq a$.

For clause (iii)

We have to show that for any $a, b \in \mathcal{S}(\mathrm{K})$, $[ba] \subseteq [ab]$, namely for any $c \in \mathcal{S}(\mathrm{K})$, $[ab] \subseteq c \Rightarrow [ba] \subseteq c$. For any formulas A and B, suppose that $A \to B \in b$ and $A \in a$. Because $A \to ((A \to B) \to B)$ is a theorem of $\mathbf{R}_+$, $A \to ((A \to B) \to B) \in \mathcal{S}(0)$. By $\mathcal{S}(\mathrm{R})\mathcal{S}(0)aa$ and $A \in a$ and $A \to ((A \to B) \to B) \in \mathcal{S}(0)$, we have $(A \to B) \to B \in a$. By $(A \to B) \to B \in a$ and $A \to B \in b$, we have $B \in [ab]$. By $[ab] \subseteq c$, we have $B \in c$.

For clause (iv)

We have to show that for any $a, b, c \in \mathcal{S}(\mathrm{K})$, $[a[bc]] \subseteq [[ab]c]$, namely for any $d \in \mathcal{S}(\mathrm{K})$, $[[ab]c] \subseteq d \Rightarrow [a[bc]] \subseteq d$. Therefore, we need to prove that for any formulas A and B, if (1) $A \to B \in a$ and (2) $A \in [bc]$, then $B \in d$ could be proved from (3) $[[ab]c] \subseteq d$.

By (2), there is a formula C, (4)$C \to A \in b$ and (5) $C \in c$. Because $(C \to A) \to ((A \to B) \to (C \to B))$ is a theorem of $\mathbf{R}_{+}$, $(C \to A) \to ((A \to B) \to (C \to B)) \in \mathcal{S}(0)$. By (4) and $\mathcal{S}(\mathrm{R})\mathcal{S}(0)bb$, we have $(A \to B) \to (C \to B) \in b$. By (1), we have (6) $C \to B \in [ba]$. By (6) and (7) $[ba] \subseteq [ab]$, $C \to B \in [ab]$. By (5) and (7), $B \in [[ab]c]$. Therefore, $B \in d$.

For clause (v)

We have to show that for any $a, b \in \mathcal{S}(\mathrm{K})$, $[ra'] \subseteq a \Rightarrow [a'b] \subseteq [ab]$. Suppose that $B \in [a'b]$. If there is a formula A such that $A \to B \in a'$ and $A \in b$, then $A \to B \in a'$ because $(A \to B) \to (A \to B) \in r$. By $A \in b$, we have $B \in [ab]$. □

Proposition 10.4.3 *Suppose that $\mathcal{M} = \langle K, R, 0, \vDash\rangle$ is a RS-model and $\mathcal{S}(\mathcal{M}) = \langle \mathcal{S}(K), \mathcal{S}(R), \mathcal{S}(0), \mathcal{S}(\vDash)\rangle$ is a formulistic model of $\mathcal{M}$. If $\mathcal{M}$ is an RS-model of $\mathbf{R}_{+}$, then $\mathcal{S}(\mathcal{M})$ is an IS-model of $\mathbf{R}_{+}$.*

Proof By Proposition 10.4.2, $\langle \mathcal{S}(\mathrm{K}), \mathcal{S}(\mathrm{R}), \mathcal{S}(0)$ is an IS-frame of $\mathbf{R}_{+}$. By Definition 10.4.3, $\mathcal{S}(\vDash)$ is a valuation relation in IS-model. Therefore, $\mathcal{S}(\mathcal{M})$ is an IS-model of $\mathbf{R}_{+}$. □

Proposition 10.4.4 *Suppose that $\mathcal{M} = \langle K, R, 0, \vDash\rangle$ is an RS-model, $\mathcal{S}(\mathcal{M}) = \langle \mathcal{S}(K), \mathcal{S}(R), \mathcal{S}(0), \mathcal{S}(\vDash)\rangle$ is a formulistic model of $\mathcal{M}$ and A is an arbitrary formula. For any $a \in \mathcal{S}(K)$, $\mathcal{S}(\mathcal{M}), a \Vdash A$ iff $A \in a$.*

Proof If A is a variable, then the conclusion holds by Definition 10.3.2(2)(i).

If $A = B \wedge C$, then we could suppose that for an $a \in \mathcal{S}(\mathrm{K})$, $B \wedge C \in \mathcal{S}(\mathrm{K})$. So there is an a $\in$ K such that $\mathcal{M}$, a $\vDash B \wedge C$. By Definition 10.2.2, we have $\mathcal{M}$, a $\vDash B$ and $\mathcal{M}$, a $\vDash C$. Therefore, $B \in a$ and $C \in a$. By the induction hypothesis, $\mathcal{S}(\mathcal{M}), a \Vdash B$ and $\mathcal{S}(\mathcal{M}), a \Vdash C$. By Definition 10.3.2, $\mathcal{S}(\mathcal{M}), a \Vdash B \wedge C$.

Let $B \wedge C \notin$. By the same proof method as above, we could get $\mathcal{S}(\mathcal{M}), a \nvDash B \wedge C$.

It is obvious that if $A = B \vee C$, then the conclusion holds.

If $A = B \to C$, then we could suppose that for any $b, c \in Z$, if $Rabc$ and $B \in b$, then $C \in c$. By induction hypothesis, we have that for any $b, c \in Z$, if $Rabc$ and $\mathcal{S}(\mathcal{M}), b \Vdash B$, then $\mathcal{S}(\mathcal{M}), C \Vdash c$. By Definition 10.3.2, $\mathcal{S}(\mathcal{M}), a \Vdash A \to B$.

Let $B \to C \notin a$. By $a \in \mathcal{S}(\mathcal{M})$, there is an a $\in$ K such that $a = \mathcal{S}(a)$ and $\mathcal{M}$, a $\nvDash B \to C$. By Definition 10.2.2, there are b, c $\in$ K such that Rabc and $\mathcal{M}, b \vDash B$ and $\mathcal{M}, c \nvDash C$. Therefore, there are $b, c \in \mathcal{S}(\mathcal{M})$ such that $b = \mathcal{S}(\mathrm{b})$, $c = \mathcal{S}(\mathrm{c})$, $B \in b$ and $C \notin b$. By Rabc, we have that for any formula B and C, if $\mathcal{M}$, a $\vDash B \to C$ and $\mathcal{M}$, b $\vDash B$,then $\mathcal{M}$, c $\vDash C$. Therefore, for any formula B and C, if $B \to C \in a$ and $B \in b$, then $C \in c$. By Definition 10.3.1, we have $Rabc$.

If $B \to C \notin a$, then there are $b, c \in \mathcal{S}(\mathcal{M})$ such that $Rabc$ and $B \in b$ and $C \notin c$. By induction hypothesis, there are $b, c \in \mathcal{S}(\mathcal{M})$ such that $Rabc$ and $\mathcal{S}(\mathcal{M}), b \Vdash B$ and $\mathcal{S}(\mathcal{M}), c \Vdash C$. By Definition 10.3.2, $\mathcal{S}(\mathcal{M}), a \nVdash B \to C$. □

Proposition 10.4.5 *Suppose that* $\mathcal{M} = \langle K, R, 0, \models \rangle$ *is a RS-model of* $\mathbf{R}_+$, $\mathcal{S}(\mathcal{M}) = \langle \mathcal{S}(K), \mathcal{S}(R), \mathcal{S}(0), \mathcal{S}(\models) \rangle$ *is a formulistic model of* $\mathcal{M}$. $\mathcal{M}$ *is equivalent with* $\mathcal{S}(\mathcal{M})$.

Proof Let A be an arbitrary formula. By Proposition 10.4.4, we could get that $\mathcal{S}(\mathcal{M})$, $\mathcal{S}(0) \Vdash A$ iff $A \in \mathcal{S}(0)$. Because $A \in \mathcal{S}(0)$ iff $\mathcal{M}, 0 \models A$, we have that $\mathcal{S}(\mathcal{M}), \mathcal{S}(0) \models A$ iff $\mathcal{M}, 0 \models A$. □

Proposition 10.4.6 *For* $\mathbf{R}_+$, *RS and IS are equivalent.*

Proof This is a corollary of Propositions 10.4.1, 10.4.3 and 10.4.5. □

10.5 What Does Relational Semantics Describe?

What do RS-models (models in RS) and RS-frames (frames in RS) describe? Logicians have already strived for finding out the answer to this question. So far there are many (philosophical) interpretations for RS, especially for the ternary relation R. In Dunn [4], K is treated as a set of pieces of information. On his reading, Rabc means that "the combination of the information states a and b is contained in the information state c". Other interpretations are suggested by Barwise [3], Retall [12], Mares [7], Israel and Perry [6], Mares [8], etc. A common feature of these interpretations is that they use information theory or different branches in information theory as their foundation to give an interpretation for RS, especially for the ternary relation R.

Although these interpretations mentioned above seem reasonable, none of them are coincident with the history of relevance logic. From C.I. Lewis' analysis of these "paradoxes of material implication", logicians have been searching for a description of ordinary inference. Unsatisfied with the description that was supplied by material implication, Lewis proposed strict implication. Shortly afterwards, "paradoxes of strict implication" occurred, so relevance logic became a hope for solving the problem of "paradoxes of material implication" and gained increasing importance. All these works embroidered on the theme of describing ordinary inference. Although the historical reason may not be the decisive factor to say that relevance logic is of ordinary inference, there is indeed a background of inference behind those axioms and rules in relevance logic.

RS is an almost perfect form of formal semantics for relevance logic. If these interpretations from information theory are also perfect, then relevance logic could be viewed as a form of logic for the fusion of information. However, with the development of relevance logic, it becomes a topical issue that involves the intuition behind itself. This situation shows that these interpretations are not satisfactory.[3]

[3]In the period of this writing, we contacted N. Belnap about his idea of the semantics of relevance logic, especially about RS. He said "I spent many years thinking about the 3-termed relation for relevance logic. At the end, all I came away with as far as intuition goes was the three VERY short quotes in vol. II of Entailment that I found by Robert Meyer, Alistair Urquhart, and Kit Fine. The

The presentation of IS aims at giving an explanation of RS, especially of the ternary relation R. From the aspect of intuition, IS is based on the intuition of inference. It could be viewed as a form of semantics with the ternary relation, which is built on the basis of the relation among the set of rules, the set of premises and the set of conclusions. Obviously, IS has given a formal description of inference. Technically, there is a corresponding relation between IS and RS. By this relation, RS could own an intuition, which is supplied by IS. Although the technical result we have is only about the system $\mathbf{R}_+$, namely RS and IS are equivalent to each other with respect to $\mathbf{R}_+$, some essential components have already existed in the proof. For the interpretation of the ternary relation R, IS says that any inference must include rule(s), premise(s) and conclusion(s), and the relation among these three parts could be abstracted as the ternary relation R. Therefore, for interpretation of the ternary relation R, IS is better than those interpretations based on information theory.

Taking $\mathbf{R}_+$ as an example, all these clauses in Definition 10.3.3(3) could be interpreted as follows. If there is a category of inference that is described by $\mathbf{R}_+$, then it should satisfy the following conditions:

(i) Identity: For any set of formulas a, a could be deduced from itself, if logical rules are applied to it;
(ii) Idempotence: For any set of formulas a, a is a set of conclusions that is deduced from itself, if a is a set of rules simultaneously;
(iii) Commutativity: The set of rules and the set of premises could be interchanged with each other.
(iv) Associativity: In the proof of clause (ii) of Proposition 10.4.2, two prime theorems that we used are $(C \to A) \to ((A \to B) \to (C \to B))$ and $(A \to (B \to C) \to (B \to (A \to C))$. Therefore, we could say that this clause corresponds to syllogistic inference and the interchange relation between the set of rules and the set of premises;
(v) Monotony: In IS, this clause is corresponding to the relation $[ra'] \subseteq a \Rightarrow [a'b] \subseteq [ab]$. If the set of logical rules and $[ra']$ are subset of a, respectively, then the set of conclusions which you get by using a as a set of rules will include the set of conclusions you will get by using a' as a set of rules. This property could be viewed as the monotony of inference.

Of course, RS-models are not the same as IS-models, because IS-models require that all elements in the domain of IS models should be the set of formulas in order to describe semantic models of inference by IS models, whereas there is no such restriction in RS-models. From this point of view, RS is more abstract than IS. In addition, there are some other reasons to view RS as an abstract IS. This situation is analogous with what happened in possible world semantics. In possible world semantics, $\langle W, R\rangle$ is a frame, in which W is a set of possible worlds, and R is an accessible relation on possible worlds. In a more abstract manner, W is a non-empty

(Footnote 3 continued)
theory is formally very beautiful, but I have NO IDEA what it means. Since those three quotes are so short, I concluded that none of them was able to say anything further. "His evaluation of the issue that RS is short of intuition is that "But to my mind, it amounts to just 'sand in the eyes"'.

set, and R is a binary relation on W. This form of semantics could be constructed or applied to mathematics, computer science, linguistics and other fields without the intuition about possible worlds. Therefore, we can safely say that RS could be regarded as an abstraction of IS, because IS is an intuitive interpretation of RS.

The occurrence of relevance logic is meant for describing inference. Based on the intuition of inference, logicians constructed proof systems of relevance logic. Through the process of the research of these systems, RS occurred. This form of semantics provides a description of the formal structure of inference. This interpretation gives an intuitive interpretation for the ternary relation R, and what is more, this interpretation is coincident with the history of relevance logics.

10.6 Conclusion

For relevance logic, RS is technically beautiful but not very intuitive. The interpretation of the ternary relation R in RS relies on what kind of logic that relevance logic is.

IS-models could represent the formal construction of inference and have its own (philosophical) interpretation, which is clear and intuitive. By the equivalence between IS-models and RS-models, RS could be transformed into IS. More importantly, this equivalence shows that relevance logic is a kind of logic of inference. This conclusion is coincident with the historical development of relevance logic.

From the technical point of view, we only use $\mathbf{R}_+$ as an example to show the equivalence between RS and IS. So in order to get a more general result, it is worthwhile for the future work to prove that this equivalence relation also holds for other relevance logical systems.

Acknowledgments We are grateful to N. Belnap for his help and advice during the writing of this paper.

References

1. Anderson, A. R. and Belnap, N. (1975): *Entailment: The Logic of Relevance and Necessity*, volume I. Princeton: Princeton University Press.
2. Anderson, A. R. and Belnap, N. (1992): *Entailment: The Logic of Relevance and Necessity*, volume II. Princeton: Princeton University Press.
3. Barwise, J. (1993): Constraint, Channels and the Flow of Information, in P. Aczel ed., *Situation Theory and Its Application*, volume 3. Stanford: CSLI Publication.
4. Dunn, J. (1986): Relevance Logic and Entailment, in D. Gabbay and F. Guenthner ed., *Handbook of Philosophical Logic*, volume 3. Dordrecht: Riedel Publishing Company.
5. Dunn, J. and Restall, G. (2002): Relevance Logic, in D. Gabbay and F. Guenthner ed., *Handbook of Philosophical Logic* 2nd, volume 6. Netherlands: Kluwer Academic Publishers.
6. Israel, D. and Perry, J. (1990): What is Information?, in P. Hanson ed., *Information, Language and Cognition*. Vancouver: University of British Columbia Press.

7. Mares, E. (1997): Relevant Logic and the Theory of Information. *Synthese*, 109: 354–360.
8. Mares, E. (2004): *Relevant Logic: A Philosophical Interpretation*. Cambridge: Cambridge University Press.
9. Mares, E. and Meyer, R. (2001): Relevant Logics, in L. Goble ed., the Blackwell Guide to Philosophical Logic. Massachusetts: Blackwell Publishers Ltd.
10. Meyer, K. (1966): *Topics in Modal and Many-valued Logic*. PhD thesis, University of Pittsburgh.
11. Priest, G. (2008): *An Introduction to Non-classical Logic: From If to Is*. Cambridge: Cambridge University Press.
12. Retall, G. (1996): Information Flow and Relevant Logics, in J. Seligman and D. Westerstahl eds., *Logic, Language and Computation*, volume 1. Stanford: CSLI Publication.
13. Routley, R. and Meyer, R. (1972): The Semantics of Entailment: II. *Journal of Philosophical Logic*d, 1:53–73.
14. Routley, R. and Meyer, R. (1972): The Semantics of Entailment: III. *Journal of Philosophical Logic*, 1: 192–208.
15. Routley, R. and Meyer, R. (1973): The Semantics of Entailment, in H. Leblanc, ed., *Truth, Syntax and Modality*. Proceedings of the Temple University Conference on Alternative Semantics. Amsterdam: North Holland.
16. Urquhart, A. (1972): *The Semantics of Entailment*. PhD thesis, University of Pittsburgh.
17. Yang, E. (2014) Algebraic Kripke-Style Semantics for Relevance Logics. *Journal of Philosophical Logic*, 43: 803–826.
18. Zhou, Beihai. (1996): A Model for System E_{fde} from Inference Semantics. *Studies in Dialectics of Nature*, 12: 10–12 (Chinese).
19. Zhou, Beihai. (1996): Inference, Models of Inference Semantics and Inference Semantics. in the Chinese Association of Logic ed., *Proceedings of the* 5th *symposium of Chinese Association of Logic*. Beijing: Social Sciences Academy Press (Chinese).

Chapter 11
The Minimal System of Justification Logic with Names

Rui Zhu and Xinwen Liu

Abstract In the paper *Justification logics and hybrid logics*, Melvin Fitting initiated the idea of combining justification logics and hybrid logics into a single system. However, for some technical reason, he presented a basic-hybrid justification logic JT instead of J with proving completeness theorem and realization theorem. The task of weakening this logic to J was left as an open problem in conclusion. This paper aims at solving this problem to further facilitate the proof of the properties of this logic as well as the derivation of other members of this logic family.

11.1 Introduction

Justification logic originates from the logic LP, shortened for Logic of Proofs which was introduced by S. Artemov [2]. It provides the modal logic S4 with an arithmetical semantics. Justification logic, as the family of the logic LP, takes a new element called justification term in their language as an abstraction of explicit provability. Likewise, hybrid logics have a new element as an abstraction of satisfaction. An interesting work done by Melvin Fitting mixed these two logics' machineries into so-called basic-hybrid JT. Because the axiom of factivity $u : X \rightarrow X$ which corresponds to the axiom $\Box X \rightarrow X$ is included, Fitting's logic is not the minimal system for the hybrid version of justification logics. In Fitting's 2010 paper *Justification logics and hybrid logics* [9], Fitting thinks of his work as just a beginning, and he lists some open problems of which the first one is to weaken this logic to analog of K so that other family members like K4 and S4 can be constructed one after another. This paper is an answer to the question left by Fitting as well as an extension of his work.

R. Zhu (✉)
Philosophy Department of Graduate School, Chinese Academy of Social Sciences, Beijing, People's Republic of China
e-mail: raycaesar@126.com

X. Liu
Institute of Philosophy, Chinese Academy of Social Sciences, Beijing, People's Republic of China
e-mail: liuxw-zxs@cass.org.cn

S. Ju et al. (eds.), *Modality, Semantics and Interpretations*,
Logic in Asia: Studia Logica Library, DOI 10.1007/978-3-662-47197-5_11

In Fitting's paper, factivity axioms is added to prove an essential property of justification logic called *Internalization*. In general, only with this property, the central part of justification logics called *realization* that connects modal logic with justification logic will hold. To facilitate the proof of internalization, Fitting adds the axiom of factivity but he also knows that this addition is to some extent unnecessary. He claims that replacing factivity axioms with these two axiom schemas $t : @_i X \rightarrow @_i X$ and $t : \neg @_i X \rightarrow \neg @_i X$ can also lead to the theorem of internalization. As a matter of fact, if we eliminate factivity axioms directly, the rest of the basic-hybrid logic JT is sufficient with desired property. This logic is the analog of K.

11.2 The Basic-Hybrid Justification Logic

The basic-hybrid justification logic is the combination of justification logics with a part of hybrid logic. We keep the same setting as Fitting, assuming that no named world is assumed. The only difference is that Fitting's system including factivity axiom because of some technical reason. We will solve this technical problem in this section.

11.2.1 Language and Axioms

The language of basic-hybrid justification logic is a mixture of hybrid language and justification language with some new symbols. This new language brings nominal i that denotes a certain possible world in the model and prefix operator $@_i$, known as satisfaction operation, from hybrid language. For each i, there is a $@_i$ and for any formula X, $@_i X$ is true at any world, which means X is satisfiable in the world that i refers to. From justification logic, justification term t : is taken, regarded as a relative evidence. The justification terms are made of justification constants and justification variables, together with two binary operations: *application* $\cdot$ and *sum* $+$. The constants are usually denoted by $c_1, c_2, c_3, \ldots$ that represents atomic justifications with no further analysis required, while the variables are usually denoted by $x_1, x_2, x_3, \ldots$ representing uncertain justifications. As for the *application* operation, it indicates that if t is a justification of $X \rightarrow Y$ and u is a justification of X, then $t \cdot u$ is a justification of Y. The *sum* operation unites justifications, e.g., $t + u$ justifies no matter what t justifies and u justifies.

There is an additional rule, saying that if t is a justification term and X is a formula, then $t : X$ is a formula as well. Informally, $t : X$ predicates that X is the case justified by t's reference. We assume more powerful association for the colon operator and omit parentheses as much as possible. For instance, $t : X \rightarrow X$ should be regarded as $(t : X) \rightarrow X$.

The new symbols are variants of justification terms and justification operators. To be specific, for any nominal i, there is a justification constant f_i and two operators $!_i$ and $?_i$. They are *remote fact checker*, *remote positive justification checker*, and *remote negative justification checker*, respectively. Their intuition will be given when referring to their corresponding axioms. For the formation rules of justification terms, if t is a justification term, so are $!_i t$ and $?_i t$. Now let $\mathscr{J}\mathscr{H}(@)$ denote the minimal version of this new language. Justification terms and $\mathscr{J}\mathscr{H}(@)$ are defined, respectively, as below:

$$t ::= x \mid c \mid (t \cdot t) \mid (t + t) \mid f_i \mid !_i t \mid ?_i t$$

$$X ::= i \mid p \mid \bot \mid \neg X \mid X \wedge Y \mid t : X \mid @_i X$$

The axiom system of basic-hybrid justification logic is also a combination of the logics mentioned earlier, but with some new axioms for each new symbols. We refer to this axiom system as the **basic-hybrid** J which contains axioms:

1. All tautologies
2. $K_@$ $@_i (X \to Y) \to (@_i X \to @_i Y)$
3. Self-dual $@_i X \leftrightarrow \neg @_i \neg X$
4. Introduction $(i \wedge X) \to @_i X$
5. Ref $@_i i$
6. Sym $@_i j \leftrightarrow @_j i$
7. Nom $\left(@_i j \wedge @_j X\right) \to @_i X$
8. Agree $@_j @_i X \leftrightarrow @_i X$
9. + axioms $t : X \to (t + u) : X$ and $u : X \to (t + u) : X$
10. $\cdot$ axiom $t : (X \to Y) \to (u : X \to (t \cdot u) : X)$
11. Remote fact checker for each nominal i and propositional letter p, $@_i p \to f_i : @_i p$ and $@_i \neg p \to f_i : @_i \neg p$ (not schemes)
12. Remote positive justification checker $@_i t : X \to (!_i t) : @_i t : X$
13. Remote negative justification checker $@_i \neg t : X \to (?_i t) : @_i \neg t : X$

and rules:

Modus Ponens If $\vdash X$ and $\vdash X \to Y$, then $\vdash Y$
@-Necessitation If $\vdash X$, then $\vdash @_i X$
Iterated Axiom Necessitation If X is an axiom and $c_1, c_2, c_3, \ldots, c_n$ are justification constants, then $\vdash c_1 : c_2 : c_3 : \ldots : c_n : X$
Iterated Remote Axiom Necessitation Let i be any nominal. If X is an axiom and $c_1, c_2, c_3, \ldots, c_n$ are justification constants, then $\vdash c_1 : c_2 : c_3 : \ldots : c_n : @_i X$

Axioms 1–8, rules of Modus Ponens and @-Necessitation come from normal hybrid logic, while axioms 9–10 and Iterated Axiom Necessitation rule from standard justification logics. The axioms 11, 12, 13, and Iterated Remote Axiom Necessitation here correspond to the three new symbols. Their setting will work in the proof of theorem of internalization. For the ground of their setting, Fitting here cited the viewpoint from Wittgenstein in [15] "[t]he facts in logical space are the world." Following this thought, the axiom 11 contains unique non-axiom schemes where p denotes any propositional variable and cannot be replaced by any formula. Next, if t justifies some X in the world i as claimed, then we need a further evidence to justify the truth of the claim and the truth should be checkable in every possible world in the model. This idea gives rise to the axiom 12 and axiom 13, where $!_i$ and $?_i$ equal to the evidence of existing of the formula in form of $t : X$. Because an axiom is still an axiom no matter where it is, we expect the fact that an axiom belonging to some named world can be justified. Thus, the rule of Iterated Remote Axiom Necessitation is introduced.

The rule of Iterated Axiom Necessitation can be regarded as an analog of $\Box$-necessitation, but only at the axiomatic level. By this rule, our axiom and usage of constant symbols do not need further analysis. Assume X is an axiom, by the rule, we can obtain the provability of $c_1 : c_2 : X$. We take c_2 as a justification of X and c_1 a justification of the case that c_2 justifies X. By this rule, we may obtain a formula with a large number of justification term ahead. If we can keep track of indices of terms, it will be helpful in manipulation, so we bring along the *Constant Specification*, distributing constants to axioms.

Definition 11.1 For a given logic $\mathscr{L}$, a *Constant Specification CS* is a set of formulas of the form $c_1 : c_2 : c_3 : \ldots : c_n : A$, where each c_i is a constant and A is an axiom of $\mathscr{L}$. *CS* meets the following closed condition:

$$\text{If } c_1 : c_2 : c_3 : \ldots : c_n : A \in CS, \text{ then } c_2 : c_3 : \ldots : c_n : A \in CS.$$

There are different types of Constants Specification, for example, when $CS = \varnothing$, it implies that nothing should be justified. What we will use later is called *axiomatically appropriate*. It is provided if X is an instance of an axiom, then for any $n \in \mathbb{N}$, there are $c_1, c_2, c_3, \ldots, c_n$ such that $c_1 : c_2 : c_3 : \ldots : c_n : X \in CS$.

11.2.2 Internalization

Fitting gives the proof of internalization of basic-hybrid JT in his paper, but he makes use of the axiom of factivity and he further claims that proving this theorem needs the following two axiom schemes:

$$t : @_i X \to @_i X$$
$$t : \neg @_i X \to \neg @_i X$$

In fact, it is sufficient to prove internalization only by the basic-hybrid J only. Most parts of the new proof are similar to Fitting's original one. But in an important procedure, we use another method instead of factivity axiom.

Lemma 11.2 *For every atomic formula X, and for every nominal i, there are closed justification terms t and u such that both $@_i X \to t : @_i X$ and $@_i \neg X \to t : @_i \neg X$ are provable in basic-hybrid* J.

Situation of atomic formula can either be a propositional letter or $\bot$. The proof of the lemma is not difficult either.

The next item plays an essential role in the proof of Internalization. Using induction on the complexity degree of formulae. The foundation of this induction is Lemma 11.2. The proof comprises six cases.

Proposition 11.3 *For every formula X, not necessarily atomic, and for every nominal i, there are closed justification term t and u such that both $@_i X \rightarrow t : @_i X$ and $@_i \neg X \rightarrow t : @_i \neg X$ are provable in basic-hybrid* J.

Proof We prove this proposition by induction on the degree of X, which is defined as the number of connectives, @ symbols, and t : occurrences in X. The atomic case is covered by Lemma 11.2. Beyond the atomic level, we have another three cases, each of which has positive and negative subcases. For case: X is $Y \rightarrow Z$, Fitting has already given its proof. The case: X is $w : Y$ can be obtained by using Remote positive justification checker and Remote negative justification checker. What plays a central part of this paper is the proof of the case: X is $@_j Y$, shown as follows.

Case: X is $@_j Y$**, positive subcase.**

Using the induction hypothesis, for some closed justification term u, we have the provability of $@_j Y \rightarrow u : @_j Y$. By Agree axiom, we have $@_j Y \leftrightarrow @_i @_j Y$. By Iterated Axiom Necessitation, there is some t such that $t : (@_j Y \leftrightarrow @_i @_j Y)$ is provable. For $(@_j Y \leftrightarrow @_i @_j Y) \rightarrow (@_j Y \rightarrow @_i @_j Y)$ is a tautology, by Iterated Axiom Necessitation, there is some constant d such that $d : ((@_j Y \leftrightarrow @_i @_j Y) \rightarrow (@_j Y \rightarrow @_i @_j Y))$ is provable. By $\cdot$ axiom, We have $d : ((@_j Y \leftrightarrow @_i @_j Y) \rightarrow (@_j Y \rightarrow @_i @_j Y)) \rightarrow (t : (@_j Y \leftrightarrow @_i @_j Y) \rightarrow (d \cdot t) : (@_j Y \rightarrow @_i @_j Y))$. By making use of Modus Ponens twice, we have the provability of $(d \cdot t) : (@_j Y \rightarrow @_i @_j Y)$.

By $\cdot$ axiom, we have $(d \cdot t) : (@_j Y \rightarrow @_i @_j Y) \rightarrow (u : @_j Y \rightarrow ((d \cdot t) \cdot u) : @_i @_j Y)$. By Modus Ponens, we can get $u : @_j Y \rightarrow (((d \cdot t) \cdot u) : @_i @_j Y$. The following is obvious, for all tautologies are axioms, so is $(u : @_j Y \rightarrow ((d \cdot t) \cdot u) : @_i @_j Y) \rightarrow ((@_j Y \rightarrow u : @_j Y) \rightarrow (@_j Y \rightarrow ((d \cdot t) \cdot u) : @_i @_j Y))$. By Modus Ponens, we can get $@_j Y \rightarrow ((d \cdot t) \cdot u) : @_i @_j Y$, next, just as before, we have the axiom $(@_i @_j Y \rightarrow @_j Y) \rightarrow ((@_j Y \rightarrow ((d \cdot t) \cdot u)) : @_i @_j Y) \rightarrow (@_i @_j Y \rightarrow ((d \cdot t) \cdot u) : @_i @_j Y))$. By Modus Ponens again, $(@_i @_j Y \rightarrow ((d \cdot t) \cdot u) : @_i @_j Y)$ is achieved as desired.

Case: X is $@_j Y$**, negative subcase.**

It seems that this subcase is similar to the preceding one and the only extension in the proof should be the usage of self-dual axiom. In fact, it is not easy like that, this subcase needs more complex calculus.

We need an important condition first, for $@_i @_j Y \leftrightarrow \neg @_i \neg @_j Y$ is the Self-dual axiom, there is some constant e_1 such that $e_1 : @_i @_j Y \leftrightarrow \neg @_i \neg @_j Y$.

For $(@_i @_j Y \leftrightarrow \neg @_i \neg @_j Y) \rightarrow (\neg @_i @_j Y \rightarrow \neg\neg @_i \neg @_j Y)$ is a tautology, there is some constant e_2 such that $(e_1 \cdot e_2) : (\neg @_i @_j Y \rightarrow \neg\neg @_i \neg @_j Y)$. For $\neg\neg @_i \neg @_j Y \rightarrow @_i \neg @_j Y$ is a tautology as well, there is some e_3 such that $e_3 : \neg\neg @_i \neg @_j Y \rightarrow @_i \neg @_j Y$. In addition, $(\neg\neg @_i \neg @_j Y \rightarrow @_i \neg @_j Y) \rightarrow ((\neg @_i @_j Y \rightarrow \neg\neg @_i \neg @_j Y) \rightarrow (\neg @_i @_j Y \rightarrow @_i \neg @_j Y))$ is a tautology, there is some constant e_4 such that $e_4 : ((\neg\neg @_i \neg @_j Y \rightarrow @_i \neg @_j Y) \rightarrow ((\neg @_i @_j Y \rightarrow \neg\neg @_i \neg @_j Y) \rightarrow (\neg @_i @_j Y \rightarrow @_i \neg @_j Y))$. Using $\cdot$ axiom and Modus Ponens, we can get $(e_3 \cdot e_4) : ((\neg @_i @_j Y \rightarrow \neg\neg @_i \neg @_j Y) \rightarrow (\neg @_i @_j Y \rightarrow @_i \neg @_j Y))$, using them again, we have $((e_1 \cdot e_2) \cdot (e_3 \cdot e_4)) : (\neg @_i @_j Y \rightarrow @_i \neg @_j Y)$.

By induction hypothesis, for some closed justification term u, we have the provability of $@_j \neg Y \rightarrow u : @_j \neg Y$. Because $@_j Y \leftrightarrow \neg @_j \neg Y$ is an instance of Self-dual axiom, there is a constant w_1 such that $w_1 : (@_j Y \leftrightarrow \neg @_j \neg Y)$. For $(@_j Y \leftrightarrow \neg @_j \neg Y) \rightarrow (@_j \neg Y \rightarrow \neg @_j Y)$ is a tautology, there is a constant w_2 as its justification term. So by $\cdot$ axiom and Modus Ponens, we can obtain $(w_1 \cdot w_2) : (@_j \neg Y \rightarrow \neg @_j Y)$. For $u : @_j \neg Y \rightarrow ((w_1 \cdot w_2) : (@_j \neg Y \rightarrow \neg @_j Y) \rightarrow (u \cdot (w_1 \cdot w_2)) : \neg @_j Y)$ is a $\cdot$ axiom and $(u : @_j \neg Y \rightarrow ((w_1 \cdot w_2) : (@_j \neg Y \rightarrow \neg @_j Y) \rightarrow (u \cdot (w_1 \cdot w_2)) : \neg @_j Y)) \leftrightarrow ((w_1 \cdot w_2) : (@_j \neg Y \rightarrow \neg @_j Y) \rightarrow ((u : @_j \neg Y) \rightarrow (u \cdot (w_1 \cdot w_2)) : \neg @_j Y))$ is a tautology. By Modus Ponens, we can obtain $(w_1 \cdot w_2) : (@_j \neg Y \rightarrow \neg @_j Y) \rightarrow (u : @_j \neg Y \rightarrow (u \cdot (w_1 \cdot w_2)) : \neg @_j Y)$, then $u : @_j \neg Y \rightarrow (u \cdot (w_1 \cdot w_2)) : \neg @_j Y$ will be proved by using Modus Ponens again. For $(u : @_j \neg Y \rightarrow (u \cdot (w_1 \cdot w_2)) : \neg @_j Y) \rightarrow ((@_j \neg Y \rightarrow u : @_j \neg Y) \rightarrow (@_j \neg Y \rightarrow (u \cdot (w_1 \cdot w_2)) : \neg @_j Y))$ is a tautology, we can obtain $@_j \neg Y \rightarrow (u \cdot (w_1 \cdot w_2)) : \neg @_j Y$ by applying Modus Ponens twice.

By Agree axiom, we have $@_j Y \leftrightarrow @_i @_j Y$, and by Iterated Axiom Necessitation, there is some constant t such that $t : (@_j Y \leftrightarrow @_i @_j Y)$ is provable. For $(@_j Y \leftrightarrow @_i @_j Y) \rightarrow (\neg @_j Y \rightarrow \neg @_i @_j Y)$ is a tautology, by Iterated Axiom Necessitation, there is some constant d such that $d : ((@_j Y \leftrightarrow @_i @_j Y) \rightarrow (\neg @_j Y \rightarrow \neg @_i @_j Y))$ is provable. By $\cdot$ axiom, we have $d : ((@_j Y \leftrightarrow @_i @_j Y) \rightarrow (\neg @_j Y \rightarrow \neg @_i @_j Y)) \rightarrow (t : (@_j Y \leftrightarrow @_i @_j Y) \rightarrow (d \cdot t) : (\neg @_j Y \rightarrow \neg @_i @_j Y))$. By Modus Ponens, we have $(d \cdot t) : (\neg @_j Y \rightarrow \neg @_i @_j Y)$. For $(\neg @_i @_j Y \rightarrow @_i \neg @_j Y) \rightarrow ((\neg @_j Y \rightarrow \neg @_i @_j Y) \rightarrow (\neg @_j Y \rightarrow @_i \neg @_j Y))$ is a tautology, there is some constant v such that $v : (\neg @_i @_j Y \rightarrow @_i \neg @_j Y) \rightarrow ((\neg @_j Y \rightarrow \neg @_i @_j Y) \rightarrow (\neg @_j Y \rightarrow @_i \neg @_j Y))$, then by $\cdot$ axiom and Modus Ponens, we have $((v \cdot ((e_1 \cdot e_2) \cdot (e_3 \cdot e_4))) \cdot (d \cdot t)) : (\neg @_j Y \rightarrow @_i \neg @_j Y)$.

According to $\cdot$ axiom, we have $((v \cdot ((e_1 \cdot e_2) \cdot (e_3 \cdot e_4))) \cdot (d \cdot t)) : (\neg @_j Y \rightarrow @_i \neg @_j Y) \rightarrow ((u \cdot (w_1 \cdot w_2)) : \neg @_j Y \rightarrow (((v \cdot ((e_1 \cdot e_2) \cdot (e_3 \cdot e_4))) \cdot (d \cdot t)) \cdot (u \cdot (w_1 \cdot w_2))) : @_i \neg @_j Y)$. By Modus Ponens, we can get $(u \cdot (w_1 \cdot w_2)) : \neg @_j Y \rightarrow (((v \cdot ((e_1 \cdot e_2) \cdot (e_3 \cdot e_4))) \cdot (d \cdot t)) \cdot (u \cdot (w_1 \cdot w_2))) : @_i \neg @_j Y$. The remains are similar to the preceding subcase. By induction hypothesis, tautology and Self-dual axiom, it's easy to get the provability of $@_i \neg @_j Y \rightarrow (((v \cdot ((e_1 \cdot e_2) \cdot (e_3 \cdot e_4))) \cdot (d \cdot t)) \cdot (u \cdot (w_1 \cdot w_2))) : @_i \neg @_j Y)$ as it is desired. □

With Proposition 11.3, we can prove the following internalization theorem without any difficulty and this have been done by Fitting in his paper.

Theorem 11.4 (Internalization). *If X is a theorem of basic-hybrid* J*, then there is a closed justification term t such that $t : X$ is also a theorem.*

11.2.3 Semantics

Following Fitting's setting in his paper, we can obtain the semantics of basic-hybrid J by a modification of semantics for justification logic.

A basic-hybrid J model is a quadruple $\mathcal{M} =< \mathcal{G}, \mathcal{R}, \varepsilon, \mathcal{V} >$, where $\mathcal{G}$ and $\mathcal{R}$ are a universe and an accessibility relation, respectively. The $\mathcal{V}$ is a valuation assigning to a set of states each propositional letter. ε as the new item is called *admissible justification* function or *evidence* function. It designates to each formula X and each term t a set of states where t is taken as relative evidence of formula X and $\varepsilon\ (t, X)$ stands for the set. $\varepsilon(c, X)$ is true at some state u if $u \in \varepsilon(c, X)$, and ε meets *Constant Specification CS* provided, if $c : X \in CS$, then $\varepsilon(c, X) = \mathcal{G}$.

Since many new elements and their axioms are added to the system, the model for the logic must be modified to validate these axioms. For the $\cdot$ operation and the $+$ operation, admissible justification function ε must meet two conditions:

Weaking: $\varepsilon(s, X) \cup \varepsilon(t, X) \subseteq \varepsilon(s + t, X)$
Application: $\varepsilon(t, X \to Y) \cap \varepsilon(u, X) \subseteq \varepsilon(t \cdot u, Y)$

Second, we must make sure that the valuation of $\mathcal{V}(i)$ is a singleton. This is the condition required by hybrid logic model. For we do not assume existence of named world, $\mathcal{V}$ is not required to map the set of nominals onto the set of worlds.

Third, Because three operations on justification term are added, the definition of admissible justification function must be extended as follow.

f_i **remote fact checker**: For a propositional letter p and a nominal i, if $\mathcal{V}(i) \in \mathcal{V}(p)$, then $\varepsilon(f_i, @_i p) = \mathcal{G}$; and if $\mathcal{V}(i) \notin \mathcal{V}(p)$, then $\varepsilon(f_i, \neg @_i p) = \mathcal{G}$.
$!_i$ **remote positive justification checker**: If $\mathcal{V}(i) \in \varepsilon(t, X)$, then $\varepsilon(!_i t, @_i t : X) = \mathcal{G}$.
$?_i$ **remote negative justification checker**: If $\mathcal{V}(i) \notin \varepsilon(t, X)$, then $\varepsilon(?_i t, @_i \neg t : X) = \mathcal{G}$.

Next, we define the relation of satisfaction by the forcing relation symbol $\Vdash$. According to the tradition, let Γ, Δ represent elements of $\mathcal{G}$.

$$\mathcal{M}, \Gamma \Vdash p \iff \Gamma \in V(p), \text{ for } p \text{ a proposition letter}$$
$$\mathcal{M}, \Gamma \nVdash \bot$$
$$\mathcal{M}, \Gamma \Vdash X \to Y \iff \mathcal{M}, \Gamma \nVdash X \text{ or } \mathcal{M}, \Gamma \Vdash Y$$
$$\mathcal{M}, \Gamma \Vdash t : X \iff \mathcal{M}, \Delta \Vdash X \text{ for all } \Delta \in \mathcal{G} \text{ with } \Gamma \mathcal{R} \Delta \text{ and } \Gamma \in \varepsilon(t, X)$$
$$\mathcal{M}, \Gamma \Vdash @_i X \iff \mathcal{M}, \mathcal{V}(i) \Vdash X$$

The first three clauses are as usual, the last one comes from hybrid side since @ is in the language. The fourth condition says that $t : X$ is true at Γ if and only if both X is true at every accessible world of Γ and t is an evidence of X in Γ. There is another stronger version of semantics which demands the model $\mathcal{M}$ with the following condition: for all $\Delta \in \mathcal{G}$ with $\Gamma \mathcal{R} \Delta$, if $\mathcal{M}, \Delta \Vdash X$, then $\mathcal{M}, \Gamma \Vdash t : X$. This semantics implies that everything necessarily has its reason so that it is known as property of *fully explanatory*.

This completes the specification of models for basic-hybrid J. Next we will define an important notion to be used soon.

Definition 11.5 A model $\mathcal{M} =< \mathcal{G}, \mathcal{R}, \varepsilon, \mathcal{V} >$ meets a *Constant Specification CS* in the $\Gamma \in \mathcal{G}$ if for all formulas $t : X$ from *CS*, $\Gamma \in \varepsilon(t, X)$. A model $\mathcal{M} =< \mathcal{G}, \mathcal{R}, \varepsilon, \mathcal{V} >$ meets *CS* if it satisfies *CS* in each $\Gamma \in \mathcal{G}$.

11.2.4 Completeness and Realization

In this section, we fix an axiomatically appropriate Constant Specification *CS* and give the proof of soundness and completeness below.

Theorem 11.6 (Completeness and Soundness). A formula X is provable in the basic-hybrid J using *CS* if and only if X is true at all states of all basic-hybrid J models that meet *CS* if and only if X is true at all states of all models that meet Specification *CS* and are fully explanatory.

The soundness is trivial, so we omit it here. For completeness, our proof is divided into three steps. Let S be a consistent set of formulas of $\mathcal{JH}(@)$. First, we construct a standard justification model in hybrid version $\mathcal{M}_1 =< \mathcal{G}_1, \mathcal{R}_1, \varepsilon_1, \mathcal{V}_1 >$:

Let $\mathcal{G}_1$ be the class of all K_h-maximal consistent set
$\Gamma \mathcal{R}_1 \Delta \iff \Gamma^{\#} \subseteq \Delta$, where $\Gamma^{\#} = \{X \mid t : X \in \Gamma \textit{ for some } t\}$
$\varepsilon_1(t, X) = \{\Gamma \in \mathcal{G}_1 \mid t : X \in \Gamma\}$
$\mathcal{V}_1(p) = \{\Gamma \in \mathcal{G}_1 \mid p \in \Gamma\}$

Then, we extend S to a K_h-maximal consistent set Σ and obviously $\Sigma \in \mathcal{G}_1$. For a nominal i, let $\Delta_i = \{Z \mid @_i Z \in \Sigma\}$ and $\Delta_i \in \mathcal{G}_1$ due to [5]. We construct a generated submodel $\mathcal{M}_2$ of $\mathcal{M}_1$ based on the Σ and various Δ_i to ensure each nominal assigned by a single state of the model.

Finally, we check whether $\mathcal{M}_2$ meets those restrictions given in Sect. 11.2.3. Details are left to readers. If $\mathcal{M}_2$ is really a basic-hybrid J model, we call it the *S-canonical model*.

Completeness now can be obtained in the standard way. In the paper [9], Fitting already gave a proof of the realization theorem by semantic method. Because we does not modify the language given by Fitting, we can introduce it directly here.

Theorem 11.7 (Realization). If X is a theorem of basic-hybrid logic, there is some replacement of all $\Box$ and $@_i$ occurrences, with the result being a theorem of basic-hybrid J, using some axiomatically appropriate Constant Specification.

11.3 Conclusion

By the above work, we have achieved the goal of weakening logic JT by giving a basic-hybrid J and proving its necessary theorems without factivity axiom $u : X \rightarrow X$. However, some open problems remain to be worked out.

The first one is the possibility of weakening the basic-hybrid J further. We here just eliminate the factivity axiom from the logic given by Fitting. But it is possible to go on weakening it in the setting of axioms 12, 13, and the rule of Iterated Remote Axiom Necessitation for these three parts are obviously set for proving Internalization. By solving this problem, the name of this logic can also be firmed up. In Fitting's original work, he called this logic basic-hybrid justification logic at first, but during the construction, he just refers to it as basic-hybrid J , even hybrid/justification logic. In our opinion, it is not suitable to name it hybrid justification logic directly, because besides those taken from justification logic and hybrid logic, some axioms and rule are added according to Wittgenstein's philosophy, and there may be other ways to combine these two logics.

The second problem is to consider the situation of named model. This is also a problem left by Fitting. For the logic with named model is more powerful, there will be a big adjustment in our axiom system.

The third problem is to provide a constructive proof for realization theorem of which the key point is the machinery of replacement of satisfaction operation.

For the relatives of the basic-hybrid J, if we can solve their internalization theorems and completeness theorems, other things will fall into place soon. Therefore, by our current work, it would not be of any difficulty to build analogs of K4, S4 and S5.

Acknowledgments This work is supported by The National Social Science Funds of China (12BZX061, Names of Possible Worlds). We would like to express our gratitude to all those who helped us during the writing of this paper. First, we are deeply indebted to the host of the second Asian Workshop on Philosophical Logic who are very hospitable to us in Sun Yat-sen University and the anonymous referee who gave us a significant review about our paper. Second, sincere thanks should go to Melvin Fitting and Patrick Blackburn who considered this paper in the M&M 2014, and provided us with valuable advice. Last not the least, we should extent our gratitude to Dr. Haixia Man whose revising is of help and importance for the final version the the paper.

References

1. C. Areces, B. ten Cate, in: *Hybrid Logics*, ed. by P. Blackburn, J. van Benthem and F. Wolter, Handbook of Modal Logic. Elsevier, Amsterdam, 2007, 821–868.
2. S. N. Artemov, Logic of Proofs, *Annals of Pure and Applied Logic*. Volume 67, 1994, 29–59.
3. S. N. Artemov, Explicit Provability and Constructive Semantics, *The Bulletin of Symbolic Logic*. Volume 7, Number 1, March 2001, 1–36.
4. S. N. Artemov, The Logic of Justification, *The Review of Symbolic Logic*. Volume 1, Number 4, December 2008, 477–513.

5. P. Blackburn, M. de. Rijke, Y. Venema, *Modal Logic*, "Tracts in Theoretical Computer Science". Cambridge University Press, 2001.
6. P. Blackburn, B. ten. Cate, Pure Extensions, Proof Rules, and Hybrid Axiomatics, *Studia Logica*. Volume 84, 2006, 277–322.
7. M. Fitting, The Logic of Proofs, Semantically, *Annals of Pure and Applied Logic*. Volume 132, February 2005, 1–25.
8. M. Fitting, Justification Logics, Logics of Knowledge, and Conservativity, *Annals of Mathematics and Artificial Intelligence*, Volume 53, August 2008, 153–167.
9. M. Fitting, Justification Logics and Hybrid Logics, *Journal of Applied Logic*, volume 8, issue 4, December 2010, 356–370.
10. K. Gödel, Eine Interpretation des intuistionistischen Aussagenkalkuls, Ergebnisse eines mathematischen kolloquiums 4 (1933), 39–40, translated as An interpretation of the intuitionistic propositional calculus, in: S. Feferman (ed.), *Kurt Gödel Cellected Works, vol. I*. Oxford University Press, 1986, 296–301.
11. K. Gödel, Vortrag bei Zilsel, 1938, translated as Lecture at Zilesls, in: S. Feferman et al (eds.), *Kurt Gödel Collected Works, vol. III*. Oxford University Press, 2002.
12. R. Goetschi, R. Kuznetz, Realization for Justification Logics via Nested Sequents: Modularity through Embedding, *Annals of Pure and Applied Logic*, Volume 163, Issue 9, September 2012, 1271–1298.
13. A. Mkrtychev, Models for the Logic of Proofs, in: S. Adian, A. Nerode (eds.), *Logical Foundations of Computer Science Proceedings of the 4th International Symposium, LFCS'97*. Yaroslavl, Russia, July 6–12, 1997, in: LNCS 1234, Springer, 1997, 266–275.
14. L. Schröder, D. Pattinson, Named Models in Coalgebraic Hybrid Logic, *27th International Symposium on Theoretical Aspects of Computer Science*, Volume 5, January 2010, 1–12.
15. L. Wittgenstein, *Tractatus Logico-Philosophicus*, Routledge & Kegan Paul, 1961, English translation by D.F. Pears and B.F. McGuinness, Original German publication, 1921.

MIX
Papier aus verantwortungsvollen Quellen
Paper from responsible sources
FSC® C105338

If you have any concerns about our products,
you can contact us on
ProductSafety@springernature.com

In case Publisher is established outside the EU,
the EU authorized representative is:
Springer Nature Customer Service Center GmbH
Europaplatz 3, 69115 Heidelberg, Germany

Printed by Libri Plureos GmbH
in Hamburg, Germany